The Bible

in the Literary
Imagination of the

Spanish Golden Age

Images and Texts from
Columbus to Velázquez

EARLY MODERN CATHOLICISM AND THE VISUAL ARTS SERIES, VOL. 3

The Bible

IN THE LITERARY
IMAGINATION OF THE

Spanish Golden Age

IMAGES AND TEXTS FROM
COLUMBUS TO VELÁZQUEZ

Terence O'Reilly

SAINT JOSEPH'S UNIVERSITY PRESS
PHILADELPHIA, PENNSYLVANIA

Publication of this book was assisted by a subvention from the
Program for Cultural Cooperation between Spain's Ministry of Culture and United States Universities

ISBN 978-0-916101-63-3

Library of Congress Cataloging-in-Publication Data

O'Reilly, Terence.
  The Bible in the literary imagination of the Spanish golden age :
images and texts from Columbus to Velazquez / Terence O'Reilly.
      p. cm. — (Early Catholicism and the visual arts series; v. 3)
  Includes bibliographical references and index.
  ISBN 978-0-916101-63-3 (alk. paper)
  1. Spanish literature—Classical period, 1500-1700—History and
criticism. 2. Bible—In literature. 3. Religion and literature—
Spain. 4. Bible—In art. I. Title.
  PQ6066.O73 2010
  860.9'3822—dc22
                              2009047767

Published by Saint Joseph's University Press
5600 City Avenue
Philadelphia, PA 19131
www.sjupress.com

Book design by Carol McLaughlin
Cover design by Ian Riley

Saint Joseph's University Press is a member of the Association of Jesuit University Presses

In memory of

L. J. Woodward
Teacher   Scholar   Friend

Contents

Illustrations ix

A Note on Biblical References xiv

Preface xv

Introduction 2

CHAPTER ONE
DISTANT ISLES: THE LITERARY IMPACT OF THE DISCOVERIES 10
    Columbus
    Amadís de Gaula
    San Juan de la Cruz
    Luis de Góngora
    Baltasar Gracián
    Conclusion

CHAPTER TWO
DEVOTIONAL WRITING: THE *SPIRITUAL EXERCISES* OF IGNATIUS LOYOLA 60
    The Grades of Fear
    Imagery
    Other Schemata
    Conclusion

CHAPTER THREE
PROSE FICTION: *LAZARILLO DE TORMES* 88

    Tratado primero
    Tratado segundo
    Tratado tercero
    Tratado quinto
    Tratado séptimo
    Conclusion

CHAPTER FOUR
POETRY: LUIS DE LEÓN AND THE ASCENSION OF CHRIST 114

    The Distress of the Disciples
    The Shorter Version
    Witnesses of the Ascension
    Santo Tomás de Villanueva
    The Longer Version
    Meditation

CHAPTER FIVE
DRAMA: *EL CONDENADO POR DESCONFIADO* 148

    The Fear of God
    Despair
    Wisdom

CHAPTER SIX
PAINTING: THE BIBLICAL *bodegones* OF VELÁZQUEZ 176

    Christ in the House of Martha and Mary
    The Foreground Figures
    The Still-Life
    The Frame
    Coherence
    The Supper at Emmaus
    Emmaus
    The *Paterfamilias*
    Exegesis
    Conclusion

Epilogue 217

Notes 221

Works Cited 263

Biblical Index 291

Index 295

Illustrations

INTRODUCTION

Fig. 1.   Attributed to El Greco (1541-1614). *St. Jerome as a Cardinal*. 1590-1600. Oil on canvas. 59 x 48 cm. National Gallery, London. Bought 1882. © The National Gallery, London. The book that Jerome is reading and his Cardinal's robes underline the authority of the *Biblia Vulgata*, the standard text of Scripture in Golden Age Spain.

CHAPTER ONE

Fig. 1.1.   Sebastiano del Piombo (Sebastiano Luciani) (c.1485-1547). *Portrait of a Man, said to be Christopher Columbus*. 1519. Oil on canvas. 106.7 x 88.3 cm. The Metropolitan Museum of Art. Gift of J. Pierpont Morgan, 1900. © The Metropolitan Museum of Art.

Fig. 1.2.   *King Ferdinand Directing Columbus on His Travels*. An illustration in Christopher Columbus, *La lettera dellisole che ha trouato nuouamente il Re dispagna*, translated by Giuliano Dati (Florence: Lorenzo Morgiani and Johannes Petri, 1493). © British Library Board. All Rights Reserved. IA.27798. From the Italian translation in *octava rima* of Columbus's letter to Luis de Santangel (15 February 1493), announcing his discovery of the islands in the East.

Fig. 1.3.   *Christopher Columbus Exploring and Naming an Archipelago of Islands*. An illustration in Christopher Columbus, *De insulis nuper in mari Indico repertis* (Basle: Johannes Bermann de Olpe, 1494). From the Latin translation of Columbus's letter to Luis de Santangel, first published in 1493 in Barcelona, Antwerp, Paris, and Basle.

Fig. 1.4.   *The Transitional Type of Mappamundi*, dating from the fourteenth and fifteenth centuries, showing the islands believed to lie in the Far East. Reproduced from J.B. Harley and David Woodward, ed., *Cartography in Prehistoric, Ancient and Medieval Europe and the Mediterranean* (Chicago: University of Chicago Press, 1987), 297, fig.18.7. © University of Chicago.

Fig. 1.5.   *World Map by Henricus Martellus*. From *Insularium illustratum Henrici Martelli Germani*, a manuscript produced in Florence c. 1489. © British Library Board. All Rights Reserved. Add. MS. 15, 760, folios 68v-69.

Fig. 1.6.   *Amadís de Gaula*. An illustration at the beginning of Book 2, Chapter 44, which tells of the adventures of Amadís and his companions in the *Insola Firme*. From *Amadís de Gaula* (Seville: Cromberger, 1526), folio 82r.

Fig. 1.7.   *Amadís de Gaula*. The opening of Book Three in the edition of *Amadís* published in Venice in 1533 by Juan Antonio de Sabia, folio 160r.

Fig. 1.8. *Maris Pacifici.* A map showing the Pacific Ocean and parts of North and South America, including California, the islands of the Carribean, and Peru. From Abraham Ortelius, *Theatrum Orbis Terrarum* (Antwerp: Plantin, 1595). © British Library Board. All Rights Reserved. Maps, C.2.d.6,6.

Fig. 1.9. *San Juan de la Cruz Writing.* An engraving by Matías de Arteaga in an edition of the saint's *Obras espirituales* published in 1703 in Seville by Francisco Leefdael (p. 3). San Juan is shown at a desk with a pen in his hand and before an open book in which he has written the words, *Subida del Monte Carmelo* (The Ascent of Mount Carmel). He has paused and is gazing in ecstasy at a vision of Christ crucified who is uttering the words, "Ego sum via" (I am the way) (John 14:6), while the Holy Spirit, in the form of a dove, whispers in his ear, "Beati immaculati in via" (Blessed are the undefiled in the way) (Psalm 118:1).

Fig. 1.10. Diego Rodríguez de Silva y Velázquez (1599-1660). *Luis de Góngora y Argote.* 1622. Oil on canvas. 50.2 x 40.6 cm. Museum of Fine Arts, Boston. Maria Antoinette Evans Fund, 32.79. Photograph © 2009 Museum of Fine Arts, Boston.

Fig. 1.11. *Baltasar Gracián* (1601-58). A detail from a portrait formerly in the Jesuit College of Catalayud and now in the Sala de Juntas of La Universidad Nacional de Educación a Distancia in Catalayud (Zaragoza). c. 1700. Oil on canvas.

Fig. 1.12. *El Criticón.* The title page of the First Part of *El Criticón* (Zaragoza: Juan Nogues, 1651), which was published under a pseudonym, *García de Marlones*, an anagram of the author's surnames, *Gracián* and *Morales*.

Fig. 1.13. Thomas More, *Utopia.* A woodcut illustration from the edition published by Froben in Basle in March 1518. © British Library Board. All Rights Reserved. G.23981,12.

CHAPTER TWO

Fig. 2.1. Jacopino del Conte (1510-98). *Ignatius of Loyola.* 1556. Oil on panel. 17.9 x 13.7 inches. Rome, General Curia of the Society of Jesus. One of the earliest portraits of Ignatius. It was executed shortly after his demise, using the death mask as a model.

Fig. 2.2. *The Spiritual Exercises.* The first printed edition of the work (Rome: apud Antonium Bladum, 1548) was a Latin version of the Spanish text prepared by the French Jesuit, André des Freux.

Fig. 2.3. Attributed to Peter Paul Rubens (1577-1640). *Ignatius at Manresa.* From the *Vita beati P. Ignatii Loiolae Societatis Iesu fundatoris* (Rome, 1609), folio 12, a collection of eighty-one images of the life of Ignatius engraved by Jean-Baptiste Barbe, who asked the young Rubens to contribute drawings.

Fig. 2.4. Attributed to Peter Paul Rubens (1577-1640). *Ignatius in Ecstasy.* From the *Vita beati P. Ignatii Loiolae Societatis Iesu fundatoris* (Rome, 1609), folio 68.

Fig. 2.5. *The Appearance of the Risen Christ to His Mother.* An engraving in Jerome Nadal, S.J., *Adnotationes et meditationes in Evangelia* (Annotations and Meditations on the Gospels) (first published in Antwerp in 1595). Nadal (1507-80), a close collaborator of Ignatius, produced this influential collection of engravings and meditations, based on the Sunday Gospels of the liturgical year, to assist the training of young Jesuit seminarians. From the third edition (Antwerp: Plantin, 1607).

CHAPTER THREE

Fig. 3.1. Title page of *La vida de Lazarillo de Tormes y de sus fortunas: y adversidades* (Alcalá de Henares: Salzedo, 1554). © British Library Board. All Rights Reserved. C.57.aa.21. This edition of the work and three others of 1554 (Antwerp, Burgos, Medina del Campo) indicate the existence of earlier editions, now lost.

Fig. 3.2. Table 1. Biblical Allusions in *Lazarillo de Tormes*.

Fig. 3.3. The description of the initiation of Lázaro on Salamanca bridge in *La vida de Lazarillo de Tormes, y de sus fortunas y aduersidades* (Antwerp: Martín Nucio, 1554), folios 6v-7r. © British Library Board. All Rights Reserved. G.10133. In this passage of the work the biblical allusions are particularly dense.

Fig. 3.4. Table 2. Biblical Allusions in *Lazarillo de Tormes*.

CHAPTER FOUR

Fig. 4.1. *Fray Luis de León*. A portrait by Francisco Pacheco (1564-1644), from the *Libro de descripción de verdaderos retratos de ilustres y memorables varones*. The biblical passage cited is an adaptation of Ecclesiasticus 15:5: "The Lord filled him with the spirit of wisdom and understanding."

Fig. 4.2. Juan de Flandes (active from 1496; died 1519). *The Ascension of Christ*. c.1500. Tempera on wood. 110 x 84 cm. Museo del Prado, Madrid.

Fig. 4.3. Albrecht Dürer (1471-1528). *The Ascension of Christ*. c.1510. Woodcut print on paper. 126 x 97 mm. © Trustees of The British Museum.

Fig. 4.4. Juan de Juanes (Vicente Juan Masip) (c.1523-79). *Santo Tomás de Villanueva* (1486-1555). In the collection of the Stirlings of Keir. Photo: Warburg Institute. © National Galleries of Scotland.

Fig. 4.5. *Santo Tomás de Villanueva*. The reverse of a medal struck for Pope Alexander VII (1655-67), during whose reign the Augustinian friar was canonised (in 1658). © Warburg Institute.

CHAPTER FIVE

Fig. 5.1. The view from the balcony in the *Corral del Príncipe* in Madrid [Carlos Dorremochea]. An artist's impression of the interior of a Spanish playhouse of the seventeenth century. From John J. Allen, *The Reconstruction of a Spanish Golden Age Playhouse: El Corral del Príncipe, 1583-1744* (Gainesville: University Presses of Florida, 1983), 68-69. Reprinted with permission of the University Press of Florida.

Fig. 5.2. Italian School. *The Council of Trent, 4 December 1563*. 16th century. Oil on canvas. 117 x 176 cm. Louvre, Paris, France. Lauros, Giraudon. The Bridgeman Art Library. The Council was convened by Pope Paul III in December 1545, and met on three separate occasions before closing in December 1563.

Fig. 5.3. *Catechism of the Council of Trent*. The title page of the first edition (Rome: Manutius, 1566). The *Catechism* had a formative influence on the devotional and catechetical literature by which the teachings of the Council were disseminated in Spain and the New World.

Fig. 5.4.   The title page of the *Guía del Cielo* by Pablo de León, O.P. (Alcalá de Henares: Juan de Brocar, 1553). The book, probably written c.1520, was published two decades after the author's death (1531).

Fig. 5.5.   *Christ on the Cross, with The Virgin Mary and St John the Evangelist.* An illustration in a popular collection of writings by San Alonso de Orozco (1500-1591), *Recopilación de las obras [...] Agora nueuamente emendadas por el mismo auctor* (Alcalá de Henares: Andrés de Angulo, 1570), opposite folio 1r.

Fig. 5.6.   The title page of the *Audi, filia* of San Juan de Ávila (1500-1569) in *Primera parte de las obras del padre maestro Iuan de Ávila* (Madrid: Luis Sánchez, 1595). The first edition of the *Audi, filia* (Alcalá de Henares, 1556) was included in the Inquisition Index of 1559. The revised edition, published in 1574, became a bestseller.

Fig. 5.7.   Fray Luis de Granada, O.P. An eighteenth-century print by Jerónimo Andrade. The writings of Luis de Granada (1504-88) were popular throughout Europe in the late sixteenth and early seventeenth centuries.

CHAPTER SIX

Fig. 6.1.   Diego Rodríguez de Silva y Velázquez (1599-1660). *Kitchen Scene with Christ in the House of Martha and Mary.* 1618. Oil on canvas. 60 x 103.5 cm. Bequeathed by Sir William H. Gregory, 1892. © The National Gallery, London.

Fig. 6.2.   Pieter Aertsen (Lange Pier) (1507/8-1575). *Christ in the House of Martha and Mary.* 1553. Oil on canvas. © Museum Boijmans Van Beuningen, Rotterdam.

Fig. 6.3.   Joachim Beuckelaer (active 1560-74). *Kitchen Scene with Christ in the House of Martha and Mary.* 1568. Oil on canvas. Museo del Prado, Madrid.

Fig. 6.4.   Vincenzo Campi (1536-91). *Martha Preparing the Meal for Jesus* or *Jesus at the House of Martha and Mary.* Oil on canvas. Galleria e Museo Estense, Modena, Italy. Alinari. The Bridgeman Art Library.

Fig. 6.5.   *Mary of Burgundy Praying from Her Book of Hours.* An illustration in *The Hours of Mary of Burgundy*, folio 14v. Codex Vindobonensis 1857. Österreichische Nationalbibliothek, Vienna. © Austrian National Library Vienna, Picture Archive.

Fig. 6.6.   School of Fra Angelico (c.1387-1455). *Christ Mocked in the Presence of the Virgin and St. Dominic.* Fresco. Church of San Marco, Florence, Italy. Alinari. The Bridgeman Art Library.

Fig. 6.7.   Petrus Christus (d. 1475/1476). *Portrait of a Young Man.* 1450-60. Oil on oak. 35.4 x 26 cm. Salting Bequest, 1910. © The National Gallery London.

Fig. 6.8.   Jean Colombe (c.1430-c.1493). *Boethius and Philosophy.* British Library Harley MS. 4335, folio 1. © The British Library Board.

Fig. 6.9.   Lorenzo Lotto (c.1480-1556). *Brother Gregorio Belo of Vicenza.* 1547. Oil on canvas. 87.3 x 7.1 cm. The Metropoilitan Museum of Art, Rogers Fund, 1965 (65.117). © The Metropolitan Museum of Art.

Fig. 6.10. Juan de Juanes (Vicente Juan Masip) (c.1523-79). *St. Stephen in the Temple.* c. 1565. Oil on canvas. 160 x 125 cm. Museo del Prado, Madrid.

Fig. 6.11. Francisco Pacheco (1564-1644). *St. Sebastian in Bed, Attended by St. Irene*. Formerly in Alcalá de Guadaira: Hospital of St. Sebastian. Destroyed in 1936.

Fig. 6.12. Pieter Aertsen (Lange Pier) (1507/8-75). *Christ with Mary and Martha*. 1552. Oil on panel. 60 x 101.5 cm. Kunsthistorisches Museum, Vienna, Austria. The Bridgeman Art Library.

Fig. 6.13. Albrecht Dürer (1471-1528). *Melancholia*. 1514. Print from an engraving, on paper. 241 x 189 mm. © Trustees of the British Museum.

Fig. 6.14. Diego Rodríguez de Silva y Velázquez (1599-1660). *The Supper at Emmaus*. 1622-23. Oil on canvas. 123.2 x 132.7 cm. The Metropolitan Museum of Art. Bequest of Benjamin Altman, 1913. © The Metropolitan Museum of Art.

Fig. 6.15. Francisco de Zurbarán (1598-1664). *The Saviour Blessing*. 1638. Oil on canvas. 99 x 71 cm. Museo del Prado, Madrid.

Fig. 6.16. Diego Rodríguez de Silva y Velázquez (1599-1660). *Kitchen Maid with the Supper at Emmaus*. Oil on canvas. 55 x 118 cm. National Gallery of Ireland, Beit bequest, 1987. Photograph courtesy of the National Gallery of Ireland.

Fig. 6.17. Michelangelo Merisi da Caravaggio (1571-1610). *The Supper at Emmaus*. 1601. Oil and tempera on canvas. 141 x 196.2 cm. Presented by Hon. George Vernon, 1839. © The National Gallery, London.

Fig. 6.18. Titian (Tiziano Vecellio) (c.1488-1576). *The Supper at Emmaus*. c.1535. Oil on canvas. 169 x 244 cm. Louvre, Paris, France. Giraudon. The Bridgeman Art Library.

Fig. 6.19. Michelangelo Merisi da Caravaggio (1571-1610). *The Supper at Emmaus*. 1606. Oil on canvas. 141 x 175 cm. Pinacoteca di Brera, Milan, Italy. The Bridgeman Art Library.

Fig. 6.20. Albrecht Dürer (1471-1528). *The Supper at Emmaus*. 1510. Woodcut print on paper. 126 x 96 mm. © Trustees of the British Museum.

A Note on Biblical References

During the sixteenth and seventeenth centuries, the version of the Bible permitted for general use within the realms of the Catholic Monarchy was the Vulgate, the Latin translation associated with St Jerome (c. 341-420). References to Scripture are therefore to this version,[1] and quotations from it in English are normally drawn from the Douay-Rheims Bible (New Testament: Rheims, 1582; Old Testament: Douay, 1609-10), revised by Richard Challoner in 1749-50.[2]

Preface

This book has been written in the conviction that in order to understand and appreciate the literary culture of the Spanish Golden Age, we need to refine and extend our awareness of how the Christian Bible was read, interpreted, and transmitted in the society of the time. It is not, however, a study of the reception of the Bible in the Catholic Monarchy, nor does it consider in detail the biblical scholarship in which the Golden Age excelled. Its focus is instead the literature and art of the age, which it approaches by examining closely a selection of remarkable texts and paintings produced in Spain between the times of Columbus and Velázquez.

Much of the research that informs the book began in my classes in University College Cork, and I am grateful for the support and friendship of my colleagues in the Department of Hispanic Studies: David Mackenzie, Stephen Boyd, Nuala Finnegan, Anne Walsh, and Martín Veiga. Individual chapters carry with them particular debts. The Introduction reproduces, with the permission of the publisher, some passages from my chapter on Golden Age Studies in *The Companion to Hispanic Studies*, edited by Catherine Davies (London: Arnold, 2002).[1] The argument developed in Chapter One was formulated initially in a public lecture at the University of Victoria, British Columbia, where I was invited as the Landsdowne Lecturer in January 2002, and I am grateful to Dr. Elena Rossi and her colleagues in the Department of Hispanic and Italian Studies for their hospitality on that occasion. Chapter Two, on the *Spiritual Exercises*, is a revised and extended version in English of a paper I gave in Spanish in Loyola at the invitation of the late Juan Plazaola, S.J.[2] Chapter Five, on *El condenado por desconfiado*, benefitted from the advice of two experts on the play, the late Daniel Rogers and Bob Oakley. Chapter Six grew out of discussions about Velázquez with David Davies, who kindly guided my reading in the specialist literature, and the late Elisabeth Stopp. Throughout the process of writing, the Editorial Director of Saint Joseph's University Press, Fr. Joseph Chorpenning, O.S.F.S., was unfailing in his support, and the completion of the project was made possible by a Government of Ireland Senior Research Fellowship, awarded by the Irish Research Council for the Humanities and Social Sciences. For practical help of various kinds, I am grateful to many friends and colleagues, including Barry Ife, Colin Thompson, Barry Taylor,

Don Cruickshank, Jeremy Roe, Joseph Munitiz, S.J., Elena Rossi, Diarmuid Scully, Claire O'Reilly, Brian O'Leary, S.J., Alejandro Coroleu, Tyler Fisher, Rodrigo Cañete, Ronan Madden, Charlie Ruxton, Kay Doyle, and Sinéad Watkins. My greatest debt is to my wife, for her encouragement at every stage, and for her studies of medieval iconography and exegesis, which have helped me to understand the subtle interplay of these traditions in *siglo de oro* Spain.

Terence O'Reilly

The Bible

in the Literary Imagination of the

Spanish Golden Age

Images and Texts from
Columbus to Velázquez

1   Attributed to El Greco (1541-1614). *St. Jerome as a Cardinal*. 1590-1600. Oil on canvas.
     59 x 48 cm. National Gallery, London. Bought 1882.
     © The National Gallery, London.
     The book that Jerome is reading and his Cardinal's robes underline the authority of the *Biblia
     Vulgata*, the standard text of Scripture in Golden Age Spain.

Introduction

The study of the literary impact of the Bible in the Spanish Golden Age is a relatively neglected field. This is partly because of the received view that in early modern Spain the text of Scripture was not generally known, a view which may be traced back to the period of the Reformation, and specifically to the Inquisition's decision in 1559 to ban vernacular versions of the Bible, both partial and complete.[1] The reservations about this development that some Catholics of the time expressed were echoed vociferously by their Protestant contemporaries in exile, and they were voiced again in the early nineteenth century by anti-clerical liberals, eager to bring the Inquisition to an end.[2] It is true that in the Golden Age access to the vernacular Scriptures was restricted: the only complete version in Castilian, by a Protestant, Casiodoro de Reina, was not known in Spain itself,[3] and the Inquisition did not lift its ban until 1790, when a translation of the Bible by a Catholic, Felipe Scío de San Miguel, appeared in print for the first time.[4] None the less, the impact of such measures was less consistent and extensive than has often been supposed. Just as certain parts of the Bible were available before 1559 in translation, notably the Psalms and the Epistles and Gospels of the liturgical year, so in the seventeenth century Spanish poets "were as free to versify the Psalms, Job and the Lamentations of Jeremiah as were Donne, Milton and Nahum Tate."[5] Devotional and catechetical writings, which were popular throughout society, and read by women as well as men, cited biblical texts and drew on biblical themes, and biblical stories and motifs were disseminated, too, through sermons, poems, drama, paintings, and other works of art.[6] The lay spirituality fostered by such means was not biblical in the Protestant sense of "a personal formation based primarily on direct reading of Scripture,"[7] but it was centered, like its Protestant counterparts, on the person of Jesus and His saving death, foreshadowed in the Old Testament and proclaimed in the New.

The Latin Bible, meanwhile, was the focus of intense scholarly interest. In the sixteenth century Spanish philologists took the lead in preparing editions of the original text of the Bible and its ancient translations into Latin and Greek. In the process they produced two polyglot bibles, each in its own way a masterpiece of printing, the first in Alcalá de Henares (1514-17), the second in Antwerp (1569-

72).[8] Later, in the seventeenth century, most of the important biblical commentaries that circulated in Catholic Europe were written by Spanish theologians.[9] The fruits of such scholarship, moreover, were accessible to the significant number of male readers (lay as well as clerical and religious) who had a working knowledge of Latin. Such readers could consult, if they wished to, the Latin version of the Bible ascribed to St. Jerome (the Vulgate text), which was available in convenient editions, printed for private use. The importance attached to Latin was to some extent a result of its role in the universities, whose male students (women were not admitted) included two social groups: members of the religious orders whose members required advanced studies, and laymen who wished to serve the Crown, in the peninsula or overseas, as *letrados* (civil servants with a training in law). To meet the demand for places, over twenty new universities were created in Castile before 1600, and since, in principle, the instruction and course books were in Latin, it became necessary to expand Latin teaching at the pre-university level as well. Grammar schools for boys were accordingly founded, including a substantial number run by the Society of Jesus.[10] The degree of latinity acquired by educated men in Spain no doubt varied enormously, but the fact that for most of them Latin was their second language had its effect on literature and art. Writers and artists could take for granted at least a certain familiarity with biblical allusions, and, at best, a sensitive response to the biblical texts that informed their works.

The present book considers, in a sequence of studies, some of the ways in which the biblical culture of Spain left its impress on the literature and art of the time. It does so by tracing the presence of biblical images in a selection of works composed between the reigns of Ferdinand and Isabella (1474-1516) and Philip IV (1621-65). Together these works represent some of the major genres, literary and artistic, that flourished in the Golden Age, including travelogues, works of devotion, narrative fiction, biblical exegesis, poetry, popular drama, and religious painting. They also illustrate the role played by ancestral images in a period of cultural change. It used to be believed that Golden Age Spain was a closed society, hostile to enquiry and dissent, and that, after the *Index* and other repressive measures of 1559, Spaniards became increasingly cut off from intellectual developments beyond the Pyrenees. Modern historians and hispanists, however, have questioned this view, and its underlying assumption that the Spanish Crown had a coherent ideology that it used the Inquisition to impose. They have argued instead that Spain never ceased to respond, in its own distinctive way, to the changes in sensibility that were taking place in early modern Europe, and they have sought evidence of this in the literature of the time, whose vitality continued unabated into the late seventeenth century.[11] Each of the works studied here may be read as a response to cultural change, a response reflected specifically in the use made of biblical images. Rarely are these images mere ornaments of thought, attached, as it were, to ideas in order to make a point. Normally they function as part of the matrix of symbols and myths by which Golden Age Spaniards interpreted the world in which they lived. In times of rapid change, as the philosopher Mary Midgley has observed, "imaginative patterns" of this sort need to be "reshaped or balanced" in order to accommodate the new: "instead of dying, they transform themselves gradually into something different, something that is often hard to recognise and understand."[12]

Chapter One tackles an issue that has given rise to much discussion in recent years: the literary impact in Spain of the New World. The Atlantic voyage of Christopher Columbus in 1492, and the conquest and colonisation of the Americas that followed, gave Spain vast territories overseas, and made Castilian, in the long run, a world language. They also inspired a body of writing, the *Crónicas de Indias* [Chronicles of the Indies], which includes eye-witness accounts by conquistadors, ethnographic studies by missionaries, and general histories penned in Spain.[13] The significance of the events they were recording was not lost on the writers of such works, who were keen to incorporate them into their own world-views. None the less, it is not easy to detect the presence of the New World in the literary imagination of the Golden Age. In the fiction, poetry, and drama of the period it is rarely accorded a central role; often, indeed, it does not figure at all. Where, then, did the Discoveries leave their mark? Part of the answer, it is argued here, has to do with imagery. When Columbus and the first chroniclers wished to convey the wonder inspired by the marvels they had seen, they turned to ancestral images of Paradise in the Bible, the classics, and medieval legend. In the process, the images themselves became charged with new connotations, which, passing into the language, formed part of the cultural heritage on which later writers drew. The chapter takes as an example the ancient topos of islands at the end of the world, which was applied in Old Testament prophecies to the lands that the word of God was one day destined to reach. After showing that the topos influenced the expectations with which Columbus set sail, as well as his subsequent attempts to interpret the lands and peoples he had found, it traces the presence of the image and its New World associations in biblical commentaries, chivalric and Cervantine romance, the mystical writings of San Juan de la Cruz, the poetry of Luis de Góngora, and the allegorical fiction of Baltasar Gracián. It concludes by considering briefly how the image, in its transformed state, was taken up and developed in turn by writers outside Spain itself.

While Spain in the early Golden Age was expanding westwards, it was also opening up at home to movements of religious renewal. Their influence may be seen in the reform of the religious orders, which began in Castile and Aragon in the late fifteenth century, and in the popularity of religious literature in Spanish, which the printing press made available throughout the peninsula. A large part of this literature consisted of translations of spiritual classics, such as the *Imitation of Christ* and the *Vita Christi* [Life of Christ] of Ludolph of Saxony, but it included also original works in the vernacular, some of which became well known in the rest of Europe and in the Spanish colonies overseas.[14] Chapter Two concerns the most famous and influential of these, the *Exercicios espirituales* [Spiritual Exercises] of Ignatius Loyola. The text was composed, in its essentials, during the early 1520s in Spain, though it was not printed until 1548, by which time Ignatius and his companions had founded the Society of Jesus in Rome. Designed as a manual to be used by the person "giving" the exercises, rather than as a text to be read by the one "receiving" them, its contents could be adapted to a wide range of needs, and it informed the Society's many pastoral activities, not only in Spain and Europe, but in America and Asia too. Its origins, however, were more humble and obscure than its later celebrity might suggest. When Ignatius first drafted it, he was leading the secluded life of a poor penitent in Manresa, and, because his earlier education as a courtier had not extended to Latin, his reading was restricted to writings in Spanish. He possessed a Book of Hours, and probably a translation of the readings of the Mass, but otherwise he knew the Bible only indirectly. None the less, the exercises he composed were influenced profoundly by Scripture, as modern scholarship has shown. The presence of the Bible is immediately apparent in the meditations on the life of Christ, which fill three of the four parts (or Weeks) into which the text is divided, but it may be detected also in the organising principles on which the work as a whole is based. The most prominent of these is the "election of a state of life," which comes to a head in the Second Week, when the retreatant is meditating on the public ministery of Jesus and the decision of the disciples to follow Him. Less prominent is the movement from servile fear to filial fear (or love), which is expected to occur over the four Weeks as the retreatant ponders the Gospel story. Chapter Two begins by arguing that the theology of fear on which the *Exercicios* draw may be traced back, through medieval writers, to the biblical exegesis of the Fathers of the Church. It then goes on to show in detail that it underlies a sequence of key images, also rooted in Scripture, which the retreatant applies to his or her self as the *Exercicios* unfold. Finally, it suggests that the contrast between these two organising principles, whose relationship is not made explicit in the text, helps to explain the disagreements that have divided modern commentators about the purpose Ignatius intended his exercises to serve.

Chapter Three turns to the presence of the Bible in *Lazarillo de Tormes* (c.1554), one of the earliest and most popular examples of realist fiction in Europe, and evidence of the influence in Spain of the European Renaissance. The humanism of

Italy and the Low Countries had begun to make an impression in Castile and Aragon during the 1400s, but in the early decades of the sixteenth century its influence deepened, particularly after the accession to the throne in 1517 of Charles of Ghent, whose election two years later as Holy Roman Emperor gave Castile an important role in the Hapsburg Empire, and brought Spanish courtiers, students, and scholars into closer contact with their European contemporaries. From this point on the movements of religious renewal in the peninsula became caught up in the more general European call for Church reform, in which humanists everywhere played a leading part. The writings of Erasmus proved particularly popular, not only in the universities and in the imperial court, but among the reading public as well.[15] These events formed the context in which the *Lazarillo* was composed: its anonymous author shows an easy familiarity with humanist learning, and a sharp eye for the need for Church reform.[16] The interpretation of his work, however, has proved notoriously problematic, for reasons advanced forty years ago by José Caso González, and still true: "Todo en él es oscuro y arcano: el autor, la fecha de composición, la de la primera edición, el significado de la novela, las infinitas dificultades de la lengua, las fuentes, la transmisión textual" [Everything in it is obscure and arcane: the author, the date of its composition, the date of the first edition, the meaning of the novel, the endless difficulties of the language, the sources, the transmission of the text].[17] The biblical allusions it contains illustrate the point: modern editors have noted their presence in the text, but they have not agreed about their number, provenance, or function. The present chapter argues that they are more numerous than has been supposed, and it underlines the fact that many of them derive from proverbial sayings and jokes, a testimony to the transmission of biblical topics at a popular level. It argues also that they have a thematic role. R.W. Truman has shown that the story may be read as a comic parody of the *homo novus* tradition, the humanist convention of praising the man of humble birth who has risen in society by his own efforts and acquired "the true nobility that is based on virtue, rather than ancestry."[18] The biblical allusions in the work drive the parody home, by pointing discreetly, and at significant moments, to scriptural notions of true virtue or *honra*, notions of which the low-born narrator appears (disingenuously perhaps) unaware.

The early 1550s saw the emergence in Spain not only of realist prose fiction but of poetry informed by biblical themes and written in the Renaissance style. Two works signalled its arrival. A collection of religious verse by Jorge de Montemayor, published late in 1552 or early in 1553, included a long meditation on Psalm 50 composed in hendecasyllables, one of the poetic lines that Garcilaso and Boscán, imitating Italian models, had introduced into Spanish a decade before.[19] About the same time Benito Arias Montano used the new metres to compose a poetic paraphrase of the *Song of*

Songs, which circulated in manuscript among his friends.[20] Montano's interest in Scripture, which led him later in life to edit the polyglot bible of Antwerp, was inspired by the renewal of biblical studies at the university of Alcalá de Henares, where he attended the lectures of the great Cistercian exegete, Cipriano de la Huerga.[21] Chapter Four looks at the poetry of Fray Luis de León, his contemporary, who also studied under Huerga, and later held the chair of Biblical Studies at Salamanca. His poems, like his writings in prose, bear the mark of an intense and erudite interest in the Bible. Few of them, however, deal explicitly with scriptural subjects. One of the exceptions is his ode on the Ascension of Christ, which survives in two versions, the longer of which is generally considered spurious. Both are based on the accounts of the Ascension in the Gospels and the *Acts of the Apostles*. The chapter examines the influence on the shorter version of two exegetical traditions associated with the Ascension in patristic and medieval commentaries, and popularised during the Golden Age through paintings and sermons. It then reconsiders, in their light, the disputed authenticity of the longer version, and it concludes that there are cogent reasons for thinking it to be the work of Fray Luis himself.

The poems of Fray Luis were not published during his lifetime, and as a result they were confined to a relatively small circle of readers until 1631, when an edition, prepared by Francisco de Quevedo, appeared in print.[22] Chapter Five turns to the more public and popular genre of the *comedia*, which flourished after theatres began to be established in the towns of Castile during the 1580s. Its subject is *El condenado por desconfiado* [The Man Condemned for Lack of Trust], a play of the early 1620s attributed to Tirso de Molina, which dramatises a thorny problem of theology, much debated earlier in the century: the precise roles of grace and free will in the process of justification. Modern commentators have acknowledged the skill with which the playwright turned this technical and abstract question into powerful theatre: "even for us now the play succeeds in making this issue as dramatically real and immediate as any threat of physical death; its impact on an audience of seventeenth-century believers is not difficult to imagine."[23] They have disagreed, however, about the theological sources on which the work depends. For some it reflects ideas expressed in the *de auxiliis* controversy, when theologians from various religious orders, principally Jesuits and Dominicans, disputed the relation between grace and free will without reaching a consensus view. Others, by contrast, have argued, following Terence May, that "the play is pastoral, not scholastic, and the wisdom it aims at is practical, not speculative."[24] Chapter Five finds evidence for the latter approach in works of devotion and catechesis written in Spain after the Council of Trent, which had set out its teaching on free will and grace in the *Decree on Justification* of 1547. This pastoral literature, which the intended audience would have known, is permeated with biblical quotations, images and themes, many of which the play takes up and develops in order to focus attention on three concerns in particular: the fear of God, the temptation to despair, and the nature of wisdom.

The concluding chapter moves on from the drama of the early seventeenth century to consider the religious art of the period and the literary traditions that influenced it. It examines in detail the literary context of two *bodegones* (genre scenes combined with a still-life), both inspired by biblical subjects, that Diego Velázquez painted as a young man in Seville, before leaving for Madrid in 1623: *Cristo en la casa de Marta y María* [Christ in the House of Martha and Mary] (National Gallery, London) and *La cena de Emaús* [The Supper at Emmaus] (National Gallery, Dublin). The two paintings, despite many contrasting features, are similar in composition: both portray a kitchen interior of the artist's own period, with a biblical scene, framed, in the background. What is the relation, in each case, between the secular and sacred elements? The question has been debated extensively, but without agreement. Chapter Six suggests that part of the answer may lie in the cultivation of metaphysical wit that characterised the literary movement known as *conceptismo*. In both paintings Velázquez appears to have adapted iconographic conventions familiar to his contemporaries in order to create a *misterio*. The term, rooted in biblical exegesis, was used in secular and religious writings of the time to denote an enigma so compelling that the reader is led to seek a hidden sense. It then explores what the hidden sense of each painting might be, by examining them in the light of contemporary texts influenced by the Bible, notably meditation manuals, scriptural commentaries, and the liturgy of the Church, and it concludes that if the two are conceived as a pair, and viewed with *agudeza* [Wit], they may be said to explore distinct but complementary ways of reconciling contemplation and action, an ideal upheld consistently in religious writings of the Golden Age, both learned and popular.

1.1 Sebastiano del Piombo (Sebastiano Luciani) (c.1485-1547). *Portrait of a Man, said to be Christopher Columbus*. 1519. Oil on canvas. 106.7 x 88.3 cm. The Metropolitan Museum of Art. Gift of J. Pierpont Morgan, 1900.
© The Metropolitan Museum of Art.

Chapter One

Distant Isles: The Literary Impact of the Discoveries

The encounter between the Old World and the New which began in October 1492 eventually transformed both cultures, though in different ways. The impact of Castile on Spanish America was immediate, extensive and in many respects destructive, as Bartolomé de las Casas forcefully showed. The impact of the New World on Castile, however, was more muted.[1] In Spanish literature of the Golden Age, for instance, the New World is rarely given prominence. In some works, it is central, notably *La Araucana*, the epic poem by Alonso de Ercilla set in the Viceroyalty of Peru, and in many one encounters the figure of the *indiano* (a person who has travelled, or returned, to Spain from the New World),[2] but on the whole the literary imagination of Castile continued to be focused on, and shaped by, the culture of the Western Mediterranean. As Francisco Ruiz Ramón has observed:

> A la deslumbrante riqueza y variedad de las *Relaciones* y *Crónicas* de Indias corresponde inversamente la increíble pobreza, cuantativa y cualitativamente a la vez, del tema americano en el teatro clásico español. Pobreza igualmente visible en los otros géneros literarios; pues no hay ni un Romancero de América, ni una novela de América, ni un teatro de América de envergadura producidos por los autores españoles de los siglos XVI y XVII [The dazzling wealth and variety of the *Relations* and *Chronicles* of the Indies is matched in inverse proportion by the incredible poverty, both quantative and qualitative, of the theme of America in the classic drama of Spain. A poverty equally visible in the other genres of literature: for no anthology of ballads about America, no fiction to do with America, no drama concerning America of real importance exists, produced by Spanish writers of the sixteenth and seventeenth centuries].[3]

In recent years, some scholars have argued that the literary impact of the New World was profound but oblique, and therefore to some extent invisible. Barry Ife, for instance, has suggested that the experiments in fictional prose that culminated in the writings of Cervantes were provoked indirectly by the non-fictional narratives that the encounter with the New World inspired, while Diana de Armas Wilson has argued that the scattered allusions to America in *Don Quixote* are not incidental to Cervantes' purpose but imply a powerful critique of the imperial enterprise of Castile.[4] The present essay seeks to take the argument further by tackling the question from another point of view. Although it will touch on the history of the novel, its starting point is not fiction but a phenomenon that Ángel Rosenblat described in vivid terms: "Los descubridores y pobladores hicieron entrar la realidad americana en los moldes de las palabras, los nombres y las creencias de Europa" [The explorers and settlers made the reality of America enter into the moulds of the words, names and beliefs of Europe].[5] As the work of many scholars has revealed, the explorers, settlers and chroniclers who first came to terms with the Discoveries interpreted them in the light of their own European past, and in doing so they projected onto them certain ancestral images, literary, religious, and mythological. A good deal of attention has been directed to tracing the presence of such images and their origins,[6] but comparatively little to one consequence of their use in this way: a reshaping of the moulds into which the American reality had been poured.[7] The images themselves were modified and acquired new associations, which later writers were quick to note and exploit.

Among the many examples that might be cited to illustrate this process, one stands out: the image of distant and mysterious islands located at the ends of the Earth, which had strong roots in the Bible, the Classics, and medieval legend. It was associated with the Discoveries from the start, and its presence may be detected in a wide range of texts and genres, beginning with the travelogues and exegesis of Columbus himself.

COLUMBUS

In the course of the fifteenth century, four new groups of islands were discovered in the Eastern Atlantic (the Azores, Madeira, the Canaries, Cape Verde), and as the century drew to a close there seemed good reason to assume that further islands would one day be found.[8] The assumption is apparent in the commission Columbus received, in which Ferdinand and Isabella appointed him Viceroy and Governor in perpetuity of every island he should encounter in "the Ocean Sea," meaning by this phrase the one great Ocean which was held to surround the land mass of the world.[9] When Columbus, therefore, came across an archipelago of islands in 1492, he was not, in one sense, surprised. On the fourteenth of November, he recorded in his journal that he had encountered the numberless isles that appeared in the Far East on *mappaemundi* [medieval maps of the world],[10] and later, on the twenty-first of February, he wrote that he had reached the Earthly Paradise, which many medieval authorities placed in the Far East as well.[11]

However, the assurance with which Columbus named and labelled the new islands veiled a deep uncertainty, as modern scholars have shown, for the people and the landscapes he observed did not accord with what he had been led to expect by his earlier voyages and by the travel tales of medieval authors, such as Marco Polo.[12] The astonishment this caused may be seen in his descriptions of flora and fauna. On the sixteenth of October, for instance, he wrote of a remarkable tree that he had noted on the island of Fernandina:

> Y vide muchos árboles muy diformes de los nuestros, y dellos muchos que tenían los ramos de muchas maneras y todo en un pie, y un ramito es de una manera y otro de otra; y tan disforme, que es la mayor maravilla del mundo quánta es la diversidad de la una manera a la otra. Verbigracia: un ramo tenía las fojas de manera de cañas, y otro de manera de lantisco, y así en un solo árbol de çinco o seys destas maneras, y todos tan diversos [And I saw many trees of a very different kind from ours, many of which had several different kinds of branches on one trunk; one branch is of one kind and one of another and they are so unlike each other that it is the greatest wonder of the world, so great is the difference. For example, one branch had six leaves like a cane, one like a mastic tree, and so on, so that there were five or six kinds, all very diverse from each other].[13]

The following day he recorded his impressions of the island's landscape, formed during a walk of two hours:

> En este tiempo anduve así por aquellos árboles que eran la cosa más fermosa de ver que otra que se aya visto, veyendo tanta verdura en tanto grado como en el mes de mayo en el Andaluzía. Y los árboles todos están tan disformes de los nuestros como el día de la noche, y así las frutas y así las yervas y las piedras y todas las cosas. Verdad es que algunos árboles eran de la naturaleza de otros que ay en Castilla; por ende avía muy gran diferençia, y los árboles de otras maneras eran tantos que no ay persona que lo pueda dezir ni asemejar a otros de Castilla [During this time I wandered among those trees which were more beautiful to look at than anything else that has ever been seen; I saw as much greenery as in May in Andalusia, and the trees are as different from ours as the day from the night, and the fruits too and the grass and the stones and everything else. It is true that some

1.2 *King Ferdinand Directing Columbus on His Travels.* An illustration in Christopher Columbus, *La lettera dellisole che ha trouato nuouamente il Re dispagna*, translated by Giuliano Dati (Florence: Lorenzo Morgiani and Johannes Petri, 1493). © British Library Board. All Rights Reserved. IA.27798. From the Italian translation in *octava rima* of Columbus's letter to Luis de Santangel (15 February 1493), announcing his discovery of the islands in the East.

num copia falubritate admixta bominu : quæ nifi
quis viderit:credulitatem fuperat . Huius arbores
pafcua & fructus / multū ab illis Iohanę differūt .
Hæc præterea Hifpana diuerfo aromatis genere /
auro metallifcp abundat.cuius quidem & omnium
aliarum quas ego vidi : & quarum cognitionem
baheo incolę vtriufcp fexus :nudi femp incedunt :

1.3 *Christopher Columbus Exploring and Naming an Archipelago of Islands.* An illustration in
Christopher Columbus, *De insulis nuper in mari Indico repertis* (Basle: Johannes Bermann de Olpe,
1494). From the Latin translation of Columbus's letter to Luis de Santangel, first published in
1493 in Barcelona, Antwerp, Paris, and Basle.

of the trees were like some found in Castile, yet they were still very different and there were so many other types of trees that they could not be said to be comparable with those in Castile].[14]

On meeting the native indians, he had a similar experience. When he gave them "things of little value," such as red hats and glass beads, he was astonished by their disproportionate joy:

> [...] les di a algunos dellos unos bonetes colorados y unas cuentas de vidrio que se ponían al pescueço y otras cosas muchas de poco valor con que ovieron mucho plazer y quedaron tanto nuestros que era maravilla [I gave some of them red hats and glass beads that they put round their necks, and many other things of little value, with which they were very pleased and became so friendly that it was a wonder to see].[15]

In such descriptions he draws attention repeatedly to two things: on the one hand, to similarities with the Old World, on the other, to radical differences from it; and he indicates that the gap between these is vast, provoking a wonder impossible to express.[16]

The uncertainty Columbus felt helps to explain the fervour with which he combed ancient authorities to find an explanation of the new lands, a fervour that grew more intense after his third voyage in 1500, when he returned to Castile in chains and in disgrace, determined to restore his reputation. It was then that he began to compile (with the help of Gaspar Gorricio, a Carthusian) the *Libro de las profecías* [The Book of Prophecies], a collection of mainly biblical and patristic texts in which the Discoveries, as he saw it, had been foretold.[17] In this anthology, the image of distant isles has pride of place. The nucleus of the book, as Roberto Rusconi has shown, includes two passages that Columbus found in a collection of writings attributed to St. Augustine, published in Venice in 1491.[18] Two of the passages cite in Latin the Septuagint version of Zephaniah 2:11: "Prevalebit Dominus adversus eos, et exterminabit omnes deos gentium terre; et adorabunt eum, unusquisque de loco suo, omnes insule gentium" [The Lord will prevail against them, and He will destroy all the gods of the peoples of the earth; and they will worship Him, every one from his own place, all the islands of the nations]. On these words, the second passage comments, "Neque enim sole insule, sed ita omnes gentes, ut etiam omnes insule gentium, quandoquidem alibi non insulas nominat, sed universum orbem terrarum" [Not just the islands, but all the peoples and all the islands of the nations, seeing that elsewhere he does not refer to the islands, but to the whole earth]. It then goes on to explain:

His atque huiusmodi profeticis documentis predictum ostenditur, quod videmus impleri per Christum futurum fuisse, ut Deus Israel, quem unum verum Deum intelligimus, non in una ipsa gente, que appellata est Israel, sed in omnibus gentibus coleretur et omnes falsos deos gentium et a templis eorum et a cordibus cultorum suorum demoliretur. [These and similar prophetic writings demonstrate what we realise has been fulfilled in Christ: that the God of Israel, whom we know to be the one true God, will be worshipped not just by the one people that is called Israel but by all people, and that all the false gods of the peoples will be destroyed in the temples and in the hearts of those who worship them].

In the margin beside these extracts, Columbus noted: "Universum orbem et omnes insulas convertentur ad Dominum" [They will convert the whole earth and all the islands to the Lord].[19]

For the Fathers of the Church, the words of Zephaniah, and similar prophecies, were coming true in their own time, as the Christian Gospel spread through the known world. The Romans had claimed a god-given jurisdiction not only over the continental land mass, but also over the islands round its edge, inhabited by barbarians. Similarly, in the Old Testament the islands at the edge of the world, where idolatrous pagans dwelt, were seen by the prophets as one day being converted to Israel's God. Drawing on both traditions, the Fathers argued that the Christian faith, emanating from Rome, was divinely ordained to spread throughout the limits of the Empire to the islands beyond, and the image was applied by the early medieval popes to their missionary initiatives in Europe.[20] St. Augustine drew on it tellingly in his letter to Hesychius in order to make the point that "no part of the earth is excluded from having the Church":

nulla relinquitur insularum, quarum nonnullae etiam in Oceano sunt constitutae, et quasdam earum Evangelium iam suscepisse didicimus. Atque ita et in insulis singulis quibusque impletur quod dictum est, *Dominabitur a mari usque ad mare*, quo unaquaeque insula cingitur; sicut in universo orbe terrarum, quae tanquam omnium quodammodo maxima est insula, quia et ipsam cingit Oceanus, ad cuius littora in occidentalibus partibus Ecclesiam pervenisse iam novimus, et quocumque littorum nondum pervenit, perventura est utique fructificando atque crescendo [None of the islands is left out, some of which are found in the Ocean, and of these we have heard that some have already received the Gospel. Thus, in some single islands there is a fulfillment of what was said: "He shall rule from sea to sea" (Psalm 71:8): the sea by which every single island is surrounded, as is the case of the whole world, which is, in a sense, the greatest island of all because the Ocean girds it about. It is to some of its shores in the West that we know the Church has come, and whatever shores it has not yet reached it will eventually reach, bringing forth fruit and growing].[21]

For Augustine and his contemporaries, the islands to which the Gospel had spread were not only those within the Mediterranean, such as Cyprus and Sicily, but also those beyond it, notably Britain. For Columbus, however, reading the Scriptures in 1500, the islands mentioned seemed to be those on the edge of Asia that he believed he had travelled to and seen. The *Libro de las profecías*, accordingly, includes a selection of texts, drawn from both Testaments, about islands and their role in God's plans. It is placed, significantly, at the end of the book, in the section entitled "Concerning the future. On the last days."[22] Certain themes recur. The islands at the world's end are subject to the Lord and reflect His glory (Psalm 96:1; Isaiah 11:11, 24:15); they await His coming and His law (Isaiah 42:3-4, 51:5, 60:9); to them He will send a sign (Isaiah 66:19; Jeremiah 2:10, 25:17-18, 22); they will listen to His word (Ecclesiasticus 47:17; Isaiah 41:1, 5; 49:1; Jeremiah 31:10); and from them He will receive, in turn, due homage and gifts (Psalm 71:10). Gorricio, who compiled the texts using a concordance, concludes it with the words, "Multa alia omittimus conscribenda de insulis maris, credentes hec pauca sufficere ad propositum nostrum" [We have omitted writing many things about the islands of the sea, believing that these few things will be sufficient for our purpose].[23] It is clear, as Rusconi points out, that he had intended "to cite all biblical passages referring to islands because their identification with the lands discovered by Columbus had become a crucial factor in the explorer's thinking."[24]

In the writings of Columbus, in other words, biblical images come alive with relevance to his life and the events of his time. The novelty of this is apparent if we consider how the biblical islands were seen a generation or so before he set sail. Denis the Carthusian, for instance, writing in the mid 1400s, had dismissed the possibility that men and women might dwell beyond the Ocean's bounds: the distances, he held, were too great for navigation, as Augustine had shown.[25] He accepted that the distant isles in Scripture prefigured the preaching of the Gospel worldwide, but he believed that this preaching had taken place long before, in the early history of the Church. In his commentary on the words of Isaiah, "Listen, islands, and hearken, peoples from afar" (49:1), he wrote:

> [...] per insulas intelligi possunt vel Ecclesiae Christi ex gentibus congregatae, quae variis persecutionibus affliguntur, quemadmodum terrae mari conclusae, fluctibus maris contunduntur; vel ipsae terrae aquis maris circumdatae, quarum multae ad fidem conversae sunt, ut Cyprus, Sicilia, Anglia [By the islands may be understood the Churches of Christ that have been formed among the nations, which are harassed by various persecutions, like lands hemmed in by the sea which are pounded by the waves; or, alternatively, they may be the lands themselves that the waters of the sea surround, many of which were converted to the faith, among them Cyprus, Sicily and England].[26]

The islands for him, as for the Fathers, were those the Romans knew.

Columbus's reading of the Bible, moreover, not only expressed his interest in prophecy, but was itself prophetic. Although the *Libro de las profecías* was not published in the Golden Age, many Spaniards of the period came to read the Old Testament in a similar way. They included Luis de León, who found allusions to the New World in several parts of Scripture, including the Song of Songs.[27] Medieval commentators on the Song had generally followed St. Bede in supposing that the enigmatic words, "soror nostra parva et ubera non habet" (Song 8:8, "Our sister is little, and has no breasts") referred to the limited resources of the early Church as it embarked on preaching the Gospel worldwide,[28] and their reading was reaffirmed in the late sixteenth century in the influential commentary of Gilbert Génébrard, as well as in that of his Spanish contemporary, Cipriano de la Huerga, whose classes Fray Luis attended as a student.[29] In his own commentary, however, Fray Luis applied it to those peoples "remote from our world" whom Spanish seafarers had reached:

> Nam sub persona huius sororis natu minoris, et parum forma praestantis, cuius de collocatione sponsa sollicitari dicitur, multi significantur populi atque gentes longe a nostro orbe remotae ad Christum adducendae noua quadam Euangelii tradendi ratione: hoc est, significatur Hispanorum nauigationibus reperti orbis, euisque incolarum ad Christi fidem nuper facta conuersio [In the person of this younger sister, unusually small in stature, whose marriage is said to concern the bride, are signified the many peoples and nations very remote from our world who would be brought to Christ by a new preaching of the Gospel: it signifies, that is, the world discovered by the voyages of Spaniards, and its inhabitants, who in recent times have been converted to the faith of Christ].[30]

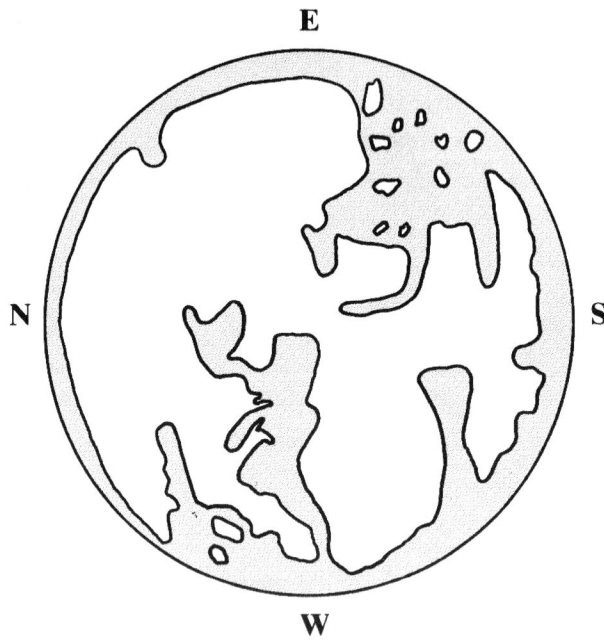

1.4 *The Transitional Type of Mappamundi*, dating from the fourteenth and fifteenth centuries, showing the islands believed to lie in the Far East. Reproduced from J. B. Harley and David Woodward, eds., *Cartography in Prehistoric, Ancient and Medieval Europe and the Mediterranean* (Chicago: University of Chicago Press, 1987), 297, fig.18.7.
© University of Chicago.

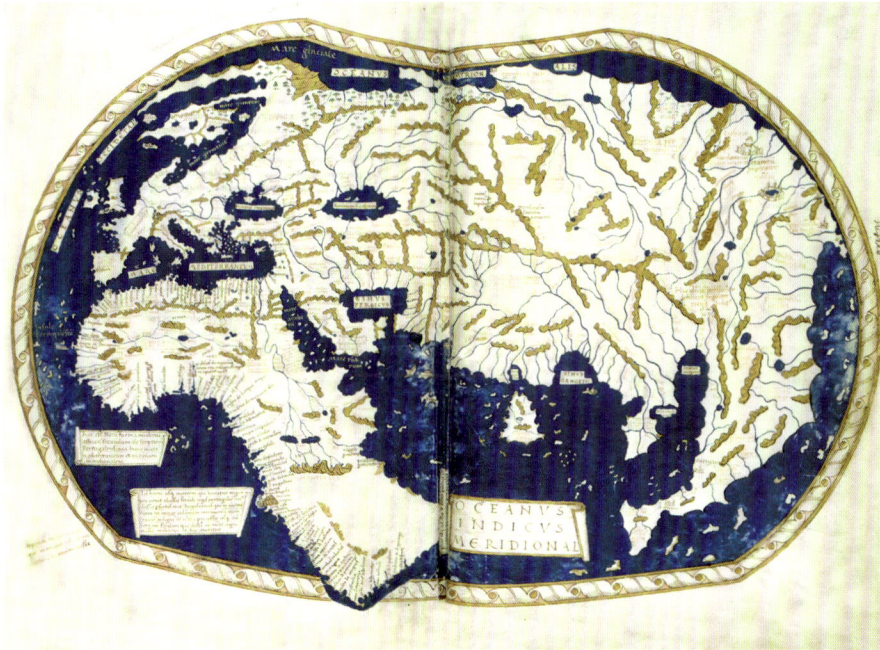

1.5 *World Map by Henricus Martellus*. From *Insularium illustratum Henrici Martelli Germani*, a manuscript produced in Florence c.1489.

One biblical passage that proved of particular interest to exegetes was the account in the Third Book of Kings of how King Solomon's ships crossed the seas to bring him gold from Ophir:

> King Solomon also built a fleet at Asion-Gaber, near Ailath on the shore of the Red Sea, in the territory of Edom. In this fleet Hiram sent men of his own, mariners that had long experience of the sea, to serve with King Solomon's men. They sailed as far as Ophir, and thence brought back to Solomon four hundred and twenty talents' weight of gold (3 Kings 9:26-28).[31]

The passage occurs twice in the last section of the *Libro de las profecías*, accompanied by an extract from the *Postillae* of Nicholas of Lyra, in which Ophir is described as "a province of India," rich in gold, and by marginal notes in Columbus's hand which indicate his belief that Ophir was an island, located off the Asian coast.[32] Writing earlier in the 1490s from the Spanish court, the humanist Peter Martyr de Anglería had recorded Columbus's conviction that in the Indies he had discovered the site of Solomon's goldmine in Ophir,[33] and in a letter of 1502 to Pope Alexander VI Columbus himself had declared that Ophir was the island of La Española that he had discovered ten years before.[34] The claim, from the beginning, was controversial. In 1503, there appeared in Seville a translation into Spanish of the *Travels* of Marco Polo which contained in its first prologue a sharp attack on someone (unnamed but undoubtedly Columbus) who had located Ophir in the western seas,[35] and similar reservations were expressed by Peter Martyr, who argued in the first *Decade* of the *De Orbe Novo Decades* [Decades of the New World] (Seville, 1511) that Columbus had found not Ophir but the legendary islands of Antilla, which some late medieval maps placed to the west of the Azores, in the remote Atlantic.[36] At a popular level, however, Columbus's belief caught on, a fact noted by Fray Toribio de Benavente, one of twelve Franciscan missionaries who sailed to the New World in 1524:

> cuando los españoles se embarcan para venir a esta tierra, a unos les dicen, a otros se les antoja, que van a la isla de Ofir, de donde el rey Salomón llevó el oro muy fino, y que allí se hacen ricos cuantos a ella van; otros piensan que van a las islas de Társis [...] [When Spaniards embark to travel to this land, some are told, and others fancy, that they are going to the island of Ophir, from where King Solomon took away gold of high quality, and that all those who make the journey to it become rich there; others think that they are going to the islands of Tarshish].[37]

As the sixteenth century unfolded, views continued to differ. Gonzalo Fernández de Oviedo affirmed in his *Historia general de las Indias* [General History of the Indies](Seville, 1535) that the islands in question were the Hesperides to which Pliny had referred,[38] but in 1545 Ophir was identified with La Española once again in the biblical annotations ascribed to the great French exegete, François Vatable.[39] Later still, in 1572, Benito Arias Montano argued that Ophir was sited further East, in Peru, implying that Solomon had crossed the Pacific to obtain its gold.[40] In 1590, the Jesuit José de Acosta dismissed such conjectures in his history of the Indies on the grounds that Solomon's sailors would have lacked the expertise to make so long a trip.[41] None the less, he accepted the general principle which Fray Luis had affirmed: that it was legitimate, indeed laudable, to suppose that the Discoveries had been foreseen in Old Testament times:

> es cierto que el Espíritu Sancto supo todos los secretos tanto antes: y parece cosa muy razonable que de un negocio tan grande, como es el descubrimiento y conversión a la Fe de Christo del Nuevo Mundo, aya alguna mención en las Sagradas Escrituras [It is certain that the Holy Spirit knew all hidden things so long in advance: and it seems most reasonable that so great a matter as the discovery and conversion to the faith of Christ of the New World should receive some mention in Sacred Scripture].[42]

For all these writers, and others, the encounter between the New World and the Old had made biblical prophecy truly prophetic once again.

Amadís de Gaula

Scholarly debate about the mutual impact of the Old World and the New has focused attention on the role of the romances of chivalry, particularly the earliest example of the genre, *Amadís de Gaula* [Amadis of Gaul], a reworking of traditional Arthurian material by Garci Rodríguez de Montalvo, which was imitated in numerous sequels throughout the sixteenth century, and eventually became the basis of Cervantes's parody in *Don Quixote*.[43] Some critics have argued that the romances shaped the imaginations and actions of the early explorers, and they have found evidence for their view in the account by Bernal Díaz del Castillo of the moment when Hernán Cortés and his men first beheld the Aztec capital.[44] As they looked on its size and extent, and its buildings rising mysteriously out of water, they were filled with wonder, and spoke with one another about the enchanted visions in *Amadís*:

℧Capitu . xliiij. Como
Amadis cō sus hermanos ɀ Agrajes su pɿi
mo se partieron a dōde el rey Lisuarte e sta⁊
ua:ɀ como les fue auētura de yɿ ala insola fir
me encantada a pɿouar las auēnturas: ɣ lo q̃
alli les acaescio.

1.6   *Amadís de Gaula*. An illustration at the beginning of Book 2, chapter 44, which tells of the
adventures of Amadís and his companions in the *Insola Firme*. From *Amadís de Gaula* (Seville:
Cromberger, 1526), folio 82r.

desde que vimos tantas ciudades y villas pobladas en el agua, y en tierra firme otras grandes poblaciones, y aquella calzada tan derecha por nivel cómo iba a México, nos quedamos admirados, y decíamos que parecía a las cosas de encantamiento que cuentan en el libro de Amadís [...] y aun algunos de nuestros soldados decían que si aquello que veían si era entre sueños. Y no es de maravillar que yo aquí lo escriba desta manera, porque hay que ponderar mucho en ello, que no sé cómo lo cuente, ver cosas nunca oídas ni vistas y aun soñadas, como vimos [When we saw so many inhabited towns and villages in the water, and other large towns on the dry land, and how that straight and level causeway led to Mexico, we were astounded, and we remarked that it was like the enchantments recounted in the book of Amadis [...] and some of our soldiers even asked if what they were seeing was in dreams. And it should cause no surprise that I am writing about it here in these terms, for it is something to be pondered deeply, and I do not know how to put it into words: the sight of the things we beheld, which had never been heard or seen or even dreamed before].[45]

Others, however, have been sceptical, among them Barry Ife, who has suggested that "we have here a case of two related phenomena arising quite independently from a single set of cicumstances":

> What I doubt the passage can sustain [...] is the view that the *conquistadores* in some way modelled themselves on the heroes of the chivalresque [...] this passage was written in the 1560s when reference to Amadís had become a commonplace way of signalling surprise and delight at the exotic, and it appears to be the only allusion of its kind in the first wave of writing about America.

He points out that before the publication in 1508 of the first known edition of *Amadís*, "Columbus had made four voyages to America, and died," and he concludes: "rather than the conquerors modelling themselves on Amadís, I wonder if the influence did not run the other way."[46]

The complexity of the question may be gauged by examining two of the various islands that the *Amadís* describes. The first of these, the *Insola Firme*, is mentioned initially at the start of the second book, where the reader is informed that in the remote past it was home to Apolidón, a prince of Greece, who found in it, "all the delights it is possible to have" (*todos los deleytes que hallarse podrían*).[47] Later, in the fourth book, it is described in more detail. On the island is a tower inside a beautiful garden, watered by four streams and enclosed within a wall. The trees in the garden bear fruit all year round, and it is paved with precious stones, some of them white as crystal, others ruby-red.[48] Behind these features of the Earthly Paradise may be detected a number of legends, especially two: the classical myth of the Fortunate Isles, places of felicity far off in the sea, inhabited by semi-divine beings; and the medieval belief that Eden was still present in the world on a distant island, a notion that Dante had developed in the *Purgatorio*.[49] The ancient images acquire fresh associations, however, when the narrator goes on to tell how the garden's precious stones were obtained. Apolidón, he writes, imported them from certain islands in the East, rich in gold, where many wondrous things (*cosas extrañas*) exist, quite different from those in "these lands":

> El suelo era losado de piedras blancas como el cristal y otras coloradas y claras como rubís, y otras de diversas maneras, las cuales Apolidón mandara traer de unas ínsolas que son a la parte de Oriente donde se crían las piedras preciosas y se fallan en ellas mucho oro y otras cosas extrañas y diversas de las que acá en las otras tierras parescen, las cuales cría el gran calor del sol que allí contino fiere [The ground was paved with stones, some white as glass, others as colourful and bright as rubies, and others again of various kinds, all of which Apolidón had ordered to be brought from some islands that lie towards the East, where precious stones are cultivated, and where one finds much gold and other things both wondrous and different from those to be seen in other lands over here, all of them caused by the great heat of the sun that shines there continuously].

Apolidón, furthermore, was the first to travel to the islands. People had previously feared to go there because they were inhabited by savage beasts, but he cleverly devised means (*artificios*) by which they could sail to them safely and back:

> no son pobladas salvo de bestias fieras, de guisa que fasta aquel tiempo deste gran sabidor Apolidón, que con su ingenio fizo tales artificios en que sus hombres sin temor de se perder pudieron a ellas passar [...] ninguno antes a ellas avía passado [They are inhabited only by wild animals, and as a result, until the time of this great wise man, Aploidón, who intelligently devised means for his men to

travel to them without fear of death [...] no one had ever been to them before].

The inhabitants of other realms, meanwhile, observed these events and learned from them; and the result was not only great wealth for Apolidón, but an influx of novelties:

> donde los otros comarcanos tomaron aviso [...]; assí que desde entonces se pobló el mundo de muchas cosas de las que fasta allí no se avían visto, y de allí ovo Apolidón grandes riquezas [Of this the neighbouring peoples took note [. . .]; so that after that time the world filled up with many things never seen before, and from this Apolidón acquired great wealth].

The many parallels between this account and the islands that Columbus found make it natural to ask if Montalvo wrote it with the New World in mind. The possibility that he did so certainly exists. The textual history of *Amadís* is complex, and in many respects still obscure, but it is generally accepted that Montalvo completed the fourth book in the mid-1490s, after news of Columbus's landfall first broke.[50] Other evidence points in the same direction. It has been argued persuasively that the episodes connected with the *Ínsola Firme* were not part of the material Montalvo edited but an invention of his own, and that the name itself was suggested to him by *Tierra Firme*, a term used commonly in geographical writings and maps of the late fifteenth century.[51] Moreover, in the first three books, whose substance derives chiefly from edited material, the islands mentioned are evoked briefly, and in vague, generic terms; in the fourth book, by contrast, they are described in relative detail, and there is an increase, too, in their numbers and narrative role. From this María Rosa Lida concluded: "todo apunta al influjo de los Descubrimientos coetáneos" [everything points to the influence of the contemporary Discoveries].[52]

Montalvo's precise intentions remain, inevitably, a matter for conjecture, but there is no doubt that for many readers in the sixteenth century the New World associations of his islands proved inescapable. This is clear from the second example to be considered, the island in the fifth book of *Amadís*, *Las Sergas de Esplandián* [The Exploits of Esplandián], from which modern California takes its name. The narrator introduces it in the following terms:

> Sabed que a la diestra mano de las Indias ovo una isla llamada California mucho llegada a la parte del Paraíso terrenal, la cual fue

Libzo tercero œl no ble ⁊ virtuofo Ca uallero Amadis œ Gaula.

1.7 *Amadís de Gaula.* The opening of Book Three in the edition of *Amadís* published in Venice in 1533 by Juan Antonio de Sabia, folio 160r.

poblada de mugeres negras, sin que algún varón entre ellas oviesse, que casi como las amazonas era su estilo de bivir [Know that to the right of the Indies there was an island called California, very close to the Earthly Paradise, which was populated by dark-skinned women, without there being any man among them, for their way of life was almost identical with that of the Amazons].[53]

The warlike women on the island, who have no truck with men except to conceive, resemble, as he indicates, the Amazons of classical and medieval myth, and he goes on to adapt a traditional tale, recounted in the thirteenth century by Guido de Columnis, in which the Amazons, led by their queen Penthesilea, travelled to Troy from the borders of the known world in order to help its besieged citizens, only to be defeated by the Greeks under Achilles and Pyrrhus, his son. In Montalvo's version, the king of the Persians calls on all pagan princes to help him besiege Christian Constantinople, and the Californians respond by sending a fleet, led by Calafia, their queen. When they reach Constantinople, however, they are defeated by the Christians under Amadís and his son, Esplandián.[54]

The Amazons are recalled as well in the description of California's location, which resembles many that we find in medieval texts of the realm where the women warriors lived. Marco Polo, for instance, believed that the Amazons inhabited an island not far from the Gulf of Aden in the Arabian Sea, and a similar notion informs the *Sumas de historia troyana*, a Spanish work of about 1350, in which the site of their homeland is described:

devedes saber que al diestro de Asia en la grant mar, allí donde Asia se ayunta a Europa, dentro en la grant mar que çerca toda la tierra ay una ysla muy grande [You should know that to the right of Asia in the great sea, at the point where Asia is joined to Europe, within the great sea that circles the whole earth, there is a very large island].[55]

This description does not differ greatly from the one we find in the *Amadís*, but when the fifth book was being completed, at some point, probably, between 1492 and 1497, the associations of the image were changing fast.[56] On several occasions during his first voyage, Columbus noted his conviction that a little further to the West lay an island inhabited exclusively by the Amazons of legend, a conviction it was reasonable of him to hold granted the premise: that he had reached the coastline of Asia.[57] By 1510, when the earliest known edition of *Sergas* appeared, the situation had altered once more.[58] It was becoming evident then that Columbus had landed not in Asia but on a new continent somewhere between Europe and the East, and this was confirmed three years later, in 1513, when Vasco Núñez de Balboa crossed the isthmus of Panama and reached the Pacific.[59] In these circumstances it was logical to suppose that the isle of the Amazons lay somewhere off the western coast of Mexico. Such was the belief of Hernán Cortés, who was instructed to find it by the Governor of Cuba in 1518. Six years later, in a report to the Emperor Charles V, he signalled that in his view the discovery of the island was imminent.[60]

The confidence that Cortés felt was shared by his Spanish contemporaries, including Juan Rodríguez Cabrillo, in whose writings of the early 1540s the name "California" was first applied to the peninsula off the Mexican coast.[61] Like other explorers of the time, Cabrillo believed that the peninsula in question was an island. It was natural, therefore, for him and his contemporaries to associate it with the island in Montalvo's work. The ease with which they did so, however, tells us something about how they read chivalric romance. In their view, the notion that the Amazons might have sailed across the Pacific to reach their goal did not lack verisimilitude, and although the credulity this implies may surprise us now, we should bear in mind that for the humanist Arias Montano the voyage to Peru of King Solomon's ships, the historicity of which he did not doubt, implied a similar feat. What altered after 1492, initially, was not belief in the literal truth of either Scripture or legend, but the imagined topographies in which both were placed.

In Spanish poetry and prose of the later Golden Age, islands abound, especially in romances of chivalry inspired by the *Amadís* and epic poems shaped by Ariosto and Camões.[62] Few of them are located in the Americas, but often they have New World associations.[63] *El Bernardo* (1624) of Bernardo de Balbuena, for instance, a literary epic composed in Mexico but set in the legendary world of Charlemagne's time, evokes a distant isle of fabulous wealth:

> En medio un claro mar que al alba bella
> del día le abre la primer ventana,
> debajo de la más feliz estrella
> que vida al mundo y resplandores mana,
> una isla tiene asiento y dentro della
> cuanto bien cabe en la codicia humana,
> tan florida y tan llena de tesoro
> que es, puesto a su riqueza, pobre el oro

> [In the midst of a bright sea which opens the first window to the
> day's lovely dawn, beneath the most happy of stars that pours life

1.8 *Maris Pacifici.* A map showing the Pacific Ocean and parts of North and South America, including California, the islands of the Carribean, and Peru. From Abraham Ortelius, *Theatrum Orbis Terrarum* (Antwerp: Plantin, 1595).

and light upon the world, there lies an island, and within it as many good things as human covetousness desires, so fertile and so full of treasure that compared with its wealth gold is impoverished].

Here, as José Lara Garrido has noted, allusions to the islands of classical and medieval myth are combined with the sense of wonder and the longing for treasure that the Discoveries had provoked. A few lines later, indeed, the New World is referred to directly in a passage that describes how the rapacity (*la codicia*) of outsiders has damaged the island's bliss:

La ambición es aquí feroz corsario;
los intereses grandes robadores;
la hambrienta codicia en mil derrotas
ha hecho a nuevas Indias grandes flotas

[Ambition here is a great corsair; vested interests are great thieves; hungry greed has turned the new Indies into great fleets scattered in a thousand directions].[64]

In the prose fiction of Cervantes, similarly, islands are common, among them the island in Part One of *Don Quixote* that the Knight promises to give Sancho in fealty, as well as the landlocked "ínsula de Barataria" in Part Two that Sancho actually governs. Both are parodies of a feudal motif found in *Amadís* and its successors, but they may be read too as a satire of corrupt practices in Spanish governance, not only at home but also in the New World.[65] There is, in addition, the mysterious North Sea island in *Los trabajos de Persiles y Sigismunda* [The Trials of Persiles and Sigismunda] which Periandro, the protagonist, claims to have visited with a group of companions.[66] The shore on which they landed, he says, was covered in grains of gold and small pearls; the meadows and streams beyond were composed of emeralds and liquid diamonds; and, in a wood whose beauty filled them with wonder, they beheld trees that bore fruit in every season, fruit that resembled yet surpassed what they had known before:

Descubrimos luego una selva de árboles de diferentes géneros, tan hermosos, que nos suspendieron las almas y alegraron los sentidos. De algunos pendían ramos de rubíes que parecían guindas, o guindas que parecían granos de rubíes; de otros pendían camuesas, cuyas mejillas la una era de rosa, la otra de finísimo topacio; en aquél se mostraban las peras, cuyo olor era de ámbar y cuyo color de los que forma el cielo cuando el sol se traspone. En resolución, todas las frutas de quien tenemos noticia estaban allí en su sazón, sin que las diferencias del año las estorbasen; todo allí era primavera, todo verano, todo estío sin pesadumbre y todo otoño agradable, con estremo increíble [We then discovered a forest of trees of various species, so beautiful that our souls were transfixed and our senses delighted. Some had branches with rubies that looked like cherries, or cherries that looked like grains of ruby; from others hung pippins, coloured rose on one side and the finest topaz on the other; on one tree could be seen pears that smelled of amber and whose colours were those of the sky at the setting of the sun. In short, all the fruits known to us were present there in season, unimpeded by the changes of the year: everything there was spring, everything was summer, everything was summertime undisturbed and everything was pleasant autumn, to a degree beyond belief].[67]

His description calls to mind the *Amadís* and the medieval fables that informed it, but now the New World associations are explicit, not implied. All five senses were ravished there, he affirms, and he concludes by noting that when they took the fruit into their hands they felt that they were holding not only Arabian gold but "pearls from the South and diamonds from the Indies."[68]

SAN JUAN DE LA CRUZ

The ancient image of life as a sea journey that ends in death, which may be traced back to the Greek writers of Antiquity, was taken up by the Fathers of the Church and developed on Christian lines: for them, the journey goes beyond death and ends in God, the soul's safe harbour.[69] During the Middle Ages, it became a *topos* in innumerable works of devotion, among them the influential *Soliloquia* attributed to St. Augustine, a text well known in sixteenth-century Spain, both in Latin and Castilian.[70] Its closing pages picture the vicissitudes of life in Time as a stormy sea, across which the soul travels homeward, its hope placed firmly in the Lord, who stands waiting on the further shore:

O patria nostra, patria secura, a longe te videmus. Ab hoc mari te salutamus [...] "Exaudi nos Deus salutaris noster, spes omnium finium terrae, et in mare longe." In mari turbulento versamur: tu in litore stans adspicis pericula nostra: salvos nos fac propter nomen tuum

1.9 *San Juan de la Cruz Writing.* An engraving by Matías de Arteaga in the edition of the saint's *Obras espirituales* published in 1703 in Seville by Francisco Leefdael (p. 3). San Juan is shown at a desk with a pen in his hand and before an open book in which he has written the words, *Subida del Monte Carmelo* (The Ascent of Mount Carmel). He has paused and is gazing in ecstasy at a vision of Christ crucified who is uttering the words, "Ego sum via" (I am the way) (John 14:6), while the Holy Spirit, in the form of a dove, whispers in his ear, "Beati immaculati in via" (Blessed are the undefiled in the way) (Psalm 118:1).

[Oh homeland of ours, safe homeland, from a great distance we look upon you. From this sea we greet you. [...] "Hear us, God our Saviour, the hope of all the ends of the Earth, and in the sea far off" (Psalm 64:6). We are tossed on a turbulent sea; you, standing on the shore, behold our danger: save us, for the sake of your name].[71]

When the image recurs in devotional writings of the Spanish Golden Age, it is often in a modified form, influenced by the Discoveries. Fray Luis de Granada drew upon it, like the Pseudo-Augustine before him, to illustrate the need for hope amid life's trials, but in his version the safe harbour of Heaven is associated with "great treasure," and identified as the Indies promised to God's sons:

dice el Apóstol: *Spe gaudentes, in tribulatione patientes*, aconseján-donos que nos alegremos con la esperanza y con ella tengamos en las tribulaciones paciencia, pues tan grande ayudador y galardonador de nuestros trabajos nos dice ella que tenemos en Dios. Este es uno de los grandes tesoros de la vida cristiana, éstas las Indias y patrimonios de los hijos de Dios y éste el común puerto y remedio de todas las miserias de esta vida [The Apostle says, *Rejoicing in hope, patient in tribulation* (Romans 12:12), advising us to rejoice in hope and to draw from it patience in tribulation, for it tells us that in God we have so great a helper and rewarder of our sufferings. This is one of the great treasures of the Christian life, these are the Indies and the inheri-tances of the sons of God, and this is the shared harbour and the remedy for all the misfortunes of the present life].[72]

Mystical writings of the time developed the image on similar lines. Writing in the early seventeenth century, Fray Agustín Antolínez affirmed in his prose treatise, *Amores de Dios y el alma* [The Love Affair between God and the Soul], that within the soul there is a New World, rich in precious metals and stones, where God is enthroned:

sepan que un alma es un Mundo abreviado, a do hay sus calles, sus casas, sus caminos, sus montes y sus ríos y su mar. Y allá al fin de él, hay otro Nuevo mundo. Parece de otro metal el alma; porque allí, en aquello tan apartado y de la otra parte de este mar—que es como el fin del alma—tiene Dios su asiento y trono, y alumbra con sus rayos de tal suerte, que lleva aquello del alma plata y oro y perlas preciosísimas [Know that a soul is a World reduced in scale, with its streets, its houses, its paths, its mountains and its rivers and its sea. And there, at its furthest end, there is another, New world. The condition of the soul seems different; for there, in that part which is so remote and on the far side of this sea—the furthest end of the soul, as it were—God has His seat and throne, and He shines with His light so brightly that in that part of the soul there are silver and gold and most precious pearls].

To find God, therefore, one must embark on a voyage, and traverse the inner sea:

> Pues es así, para encontrar a su Dios, ¿qué remedio? Hacer una embarcación y engolfarse en este mar ancho del alma, y dar las velas al viento, y caminar hasta que vengan a topar con el fin del alma, y allí encontrará a Dios [Since that is how things are, how can one find God? By setting sail and travelling deeply into this expansive sea of the soul, and spreading the sails before the wind, and continuing on until you encounter the furthest end of the soul, and there you will find God].[73]

The poet Francisco de Aldana had earlier made a similar point in his verse epistle to Arias Montano, where the contemplative life is compared to a sea journey within the soul directed towards a realm of hidden treasure, the "Indies of God":

> !Oh grandes, oh riquísimas conquistas
> de las Indias de Dios, de aquel gran mundo
> tan escondido a las mundanas vistas!
> [Oh great and most rich conquests
> of the Indies of God, of that great world
> so hidden from worldly eyes!].[74]

Aldana's contemporary, San Juan de la Cruz, used the metaphor too. According to the saint's early biographer, Alonso de la Madre de Dios, he wrote to several of his fellow friars shortly before his death to explain that he no longer intended to join them in a planned mission to Mexico.[75] Instead he wished to stay where he was, in the Carmelite house of La Peñuela, preparing for a journey he was soon to make to Indies of another kind:

> después de haberles agradecido su determinación y caridad que le hacían, añade haberse venido aquí a la Peñuela a preparar el

matalotaje para las Indias del cielo y que en esto pensaba acabar allí los pocos días que le faltaban de vida [After thanking them for their commitment and for the charity they were showing him, he added that he had come here to la Peñuela to prepare provisions for the Indies in Heaven, and that he intended to spend in this way the few days of his life that remained].

To one of his correspondents, Juan de Santa Ana, he wrote eloquently of the treasures to be found in the Indies above, and he urged him to desist from his efforts to reach the Indies below:

> hablándole de esta preparación o matalotaje para la tal embarcación, descúbrele cuán ricas Indias es el cielo y cuán grandes y ciertos sus tesoros. Aconséjale cese de tratar de pasar a otras Indias que éstas [speaking to him of this preparation and provisioning for the voyage in question, he reveals to him how rich an Indies Heaven is, and how great and certain are its treasures. He advises him to stop trying to reach any Indies other than these].[76]

In his poems, San Juan does not refer to the Indies directly. He does, however, use the motif of a journey, notably in the *Noche oscura* [The Dark Night] and the *Cántico espiritual* [The Spiritual Canticle], and in the latter work he also uses the image of distant isles, to which he gives a mystical sense. The journey that the *Cántico* describes takes place on land, in an imaginary terrain shaped largely by the Song of Songs.[77] Its two allusions to a seascape, therefore, are striking. In stanza 13 the Bride praises her beloved by evoking the beauty of the natural world, of which the islands are a part:

> Mi Amado, las montañas,
> los valles solitarios nemorosos,
> las ínsulas extrañas,
> los ríos sonorosos,
> el silbo de los aires amorosos
> [My Beloved, the mountains,
> the solitary, wooded valleys,
> the resounding rivers,
> the whistling of the loving breezes].

Later, in stanza 32, she beseeches him to turn his gaze towards the female companions who escort her as she travels through the islands:

> Escóndete, Carillo,
> y mira con tu haz a las montañas,
> y no quieras decillo;
> mas mira las compañas
> de la que va por ínsulas extrañas
> [Hide, my sweet darling,
> and look upon the mountains with your visage,
> and do not say it;
> but look at the companies
> of her who goes among strange islands].[78]

In his commentary, San Juan indicates that the islands to which the Bride refers are an image of God Himself. They are, he explains, remote: "Las ínsulas extrañas son ceñidas con la mar y allende de los mares, muy apartadas y ajenas de la comunicación de los hombres" [The strange islands are surrounded by the sea and far beyond the seas, very distant and cut off from communication with men]. They also inspire wonder: "En ellas se crían y nacen cosas muy diferentes de las de por acá, que hacen grande novedad y admiración a quien las ve" [On them are produced and brought forth things very different from things over here, and these cause great surprise and wonder in whoever sees them]. And in both respects they call to mind the divine: "Y así, por las grandes y admirables novedades y noticias extrañas, alejadas del conocimiento común, que el alma ve en Dios, le llama *ínsulas extrañas*" [And so, on account of the great and wondrous marvels and strange insights, far removed from everyday knowledge, which the soul sees in God, she calls him *strange islands*] (CA 13-14:8).

A number of scholars have detected in these words an allusion to the encounter between the Old World and the New.[79] The islands San Juan describes, which lie at the limits of the Ocean, are normally inaccessible, like those that Columbus found; and, like the islands of Columbus, they are astonishing, because they differ radically from what has hitherto been known. The stanzas in which they are mentioned, moreover, are linked by San Juan to images of discovered treasure. In stanza 13, the soul is said to behold and delight in riches beyond telling: "ve el alma y gusta en esta divina unión abundancia y riquezas inestimables" [The soul sees and tastes, in this divine union, abundance and riches beyond telling] (CA 13-14:4); and in stanza 32, she is compared to two characters in the parables who find unexpected wealth (Matthew 13:44-46): "es semejante al mercader de la margarita, o, por mejor decir, al hombre que, hallando el tesoro escondido en el campo, fue y escondióle con gozo y poseyóle" [She resembles the merchant who found the pearl, or, more exactly, the man who, on finding the treasure hidden in the field, went and hid it joyfully and possessed it] (CA 32:1). In the poem itself, the New World associations at which the commentary hints are carried by the adjective *extraño*. Its root meaning, derived from the Latin *extraneus*, is "alien, foreign, other,"[80] but, in the course of the sixteenth century, it acquired two additional senses: first, "remote, withdrawn, unseen," and second, "singular, awesome."[81] In addition, it was often associated with the Discoveries. Torres Naharro, for instance, described his collection of drama and verse, the *Propalladia* (1517), as a caravel sailing westwards to find "nueva noticia de *extraños* pueblos" [new knowledge of strange peoples].[82] Eleven years later, in 1528, the humanist Hernán Pérez de Oliva wrote that Columbus had made his second voyage in order to "mezclar el mundo y dar a aquellas tierras *extrañas* la forma de la nuestra" [mix the various parts of the world and give to those strange lands the form of our own].[83] Later still, in 1590, the Jesuit José de Acosta prefaced his natural history of the Indies with the words:

> Del Nuevo Mundo y Indias Occidentales han escripto muchos autores diversos libros y relaciones en que dan noticia de las cosas nuevas y *estrañas* que en aquellas partes se han descubierto [...]. Mas hasta agora no he visto autor que trate de declarar las causas y razón de tales novedades y *estrañezas* de naturaleza [The New World and the Indies of the West have been the subject of various books and accounts by numerous authors which have announced the new and strange things discovered in those parts [...]. But so far I have seen no author try to set out the causes and the reason for such wonders and strange things in Nature].[84]

San Juan's commentary picks up on the developing senses of the word, and applies them to the mystery of God:

> extraño le llaman a uno por una de dos cosas: o porque se anda retirado de la gente, o porque es excelente y particular entre los demás hombres en sus hechos y obras. Por estas dos cosas llama el alma aquí a Dios extraño, porque no solamente es toda la extrañez de las ínsulas nunca vistas, pero también sus vías, consejos y obras son muy extrañas y nuevas y admirables para los hombres [A person is called strange for one of two reasons: either because he lives apart from people, or

because he is excellent and noteworthy among others because of his deeds and works. For these two reasons the soul here calls God strange, for not only is he all the strangeness of the unseen islands, but also his ways, counsels and works are very strange and novel and wonderful to men] (CA 13-14:8).

Equally significant is San Juan's use of the noun *ínsula*. By the sixteenth century, it had become archaic, and the normal term for "island" was *isla*. It continued to be used, however, in the romances of chivalry, and, in many cases, the islands they depict are said to be *extrañas* because of the marvels they contain. From this, some scholars have concluded that in his poem and commentary the saint had the chivalric romances in mind.[85] Their argument is plausible: in the writings of other Spanish mystics, notably Ignatius Loyola and Teresa of Avila, chivalric images often occur, in a divinised form. Another context, however, is possible too. San Juan composed the first twenty-nine stanzas of the *Cántico* during the months he spent imprisoned in Toledo, between December 1577 and August 1578. Almost the only reading he was allowed at the time was a breviary containing the office of his order, which he normally recited every day.[86] Although we do not know precisely which edition of the Carmelite breviary he used,[87] we may be confident that in its pages he would have encountered allusions to the islands of the Bible, not only in the Psalms (*q.v.* Psalm 71:10; 96:1) but also in the liturgical texts accompanying them.[88] In the Carmelite breviary of Venice, 1504, for instance, there are several references in the antiphons and responses to God's presence at the ends of the Earth, and to the summons issued by Him there to the distant isles:[89]

> *In manu tua, Domine: Deus fines terrae* (cf. Psalm 94:4). Antiphon, folio 20v.
> *Dominus iudicabit fines terrae* (cf. 1 Kings 2:10). Antiphon, folio 24r.
> *Exaudi nos Deus, salutaris noster: spes omnium finium terrae et in mari longe* (cf. Psalm 64:6). Response, folio 48v; 50r.
> *Audite verbum Domini gentes: et annuntiate illud in finibus terrae: in insulis quae procul sunt dicite: Salvator noster veniet* (cf Jeremiah 31:10). Response, folio 84r; 86r; 87r.[90]

It is likely that these, or similar, passages left their mark on San Juan's poem, and that his choice of the word *ínsula* for "island" was dictated, at least in part, by its closeness to the Latin of the Vulgate.[91] Like other Spanish poets of his time, San Juan practised "mixed" *imitatio*: the imitation of several models simultaneously, with the intention of

1.10 Diego Rodríguez de Silva y Velázquez (1599-1660). *Luis de Góngora y Argote*. 1622. Oil on canvas. 50.2 x 40.6 cm. Museum of Fine Arts, Boston. Maria Antoinette Evans Fund, 32.79. Photograph © 2009 Museum of Fine Arts, Boston.

creating from them something new.[92] He was, however, less constrained than most of them by Renaissance norms of decorum.[93] It may be, therefore, that in the image of the *ínsulas extrañas* he sought to bring together two traditions, the chivalric and the biblical, that such norms usually kept apart. By the time he did so, however, both traditions had been touched and changed by the encounter between the Old World and the New, and it was the New World dimension that he developed in his commentary, extending in the process the language of mystical experience that he had inherited from the Christian past.

LUIS DE GÓNGORA

The Latinate poetry of the seventeenth century, though cultivated on both sides of the Atlantic, does not normally focus on the New World. An exception is the *Soledad Primera* [First Solitude] (1613) of Luis de Góngora, which includes a vivid evocation of the Discoveries.[94] The poem's narrative thread and many of its themes and images are drawn from the writers of Antiquity, but these precedents are renewed by being placed imaginatively in the world of Golden-Age Spain. The storyline, for instance, may be traced back to a Greek model, the *Euboean Discourse* of Dio Chrysostom (a.d. 40 - after 112), in which a traveller from the city who is critical of urban life is shipwrecked on an unknown coast, from where he wanders through a pastoral landscape.[95] In Góngora's version, the countryside through which he moves, and the people who inhabit it, are recognisably Spanish and contemporary.[96] There, at one point, he encounters an elderly man who in his youth sailed the seas of the world, until eventually he met disaster in the Pacific, losing both his fortune and his son, whereupon he withdrew to the country. It is this character, the *político serrano* [the urbane man from the hills] (line 364), who recounts in a lengthy speech the history of seafaring from its beginnings to modern times. In doing so, he recalls, among other events, the first voyage of Columbus, the crossing of the isthmus of Panama by Núñez de Balboa, Vasco da Gama's journey round the southern tip of Africa, and the circumnavigation of the globe by Magellan's ship and crew. All these incidents are related, however, without moving beyond classical terms: the Spanish and Portuguese explorers are alluded to impersonally, and the only places named are ones that the Romans would have known.[97] The result is a display of metaphysical wit in which ancient conceptions of the world are both called to mind and shown to have been surpassed.

The classical traditions that the poem invokes include a number to do with Ocean, which the ancient Greeks envisaged as a vast expanse of water flowing around the island of the inhabited Earth.[98] Its circular image may be found in the oldest surviving Greek maps, and also in early epic poems, among them the *Iliad* of Homer, where Ocean is depicted on the shield of Achilles as a river running continuously round the rim.[99] Long after Homer had ceased to be accepted as an authority on cosmographical lore, it continued to inform Greek poetry, and it was prolonged into Roman times by the Latin poets, as well as by the geographer Strabo.[100] In the early Middle Ages, it received the approval of St. Isidore of Seville,[101] and, with his authority behind it, it continued to shape medieval maps of the world up to the time of Columbus.[102] Góngora alludes to the image in his description of the isthmus of Panama, traversed by Balboa in 1513 (lines 425-29):

> el istmo que al Océano divide,
> y, sierpe de cristal, juntar le impide
> la cabeza, del Norte coronada,
> con la que ilustra el Sur cola escamada
> de antárticas estrellas
> [That isthmus, whose dividing barriers break
> Into two seas the Ocean's crystal snake,
> So that its head, crowned with Northern light,
> joins not the tail, which the Antarctic night
> Studs with its starry scales].

Balboa's expedition revealed not only the existence of the Pacific, but also the fact that it was separated from the Atlantic by no more than a narrow strip of land. This spurred hopes of finding a strait through central America and a direct sea-route to the Spice Islands in the East, but subsequent exploration made it clear that no such strait would be found.[103] Góngora captures the implications by stating that, because of the isthmus, Ocean is divided from itself, and by describing Ocean, in a conceit, as a crystal serpent, its head coiled in one hemisphere and its lower end in another, unable to bite its own tail and thus form a perfect circle as it would wish.

The ancient image of Ocean is recalled again in the lines concerning the voyage in 1520 of Magellan's ship *Victoria* around Cape Horn (lines 466-76):

> Zodíaco después fue cristalino
> a glorïoso pino,
> émulo vago del ardiente coche
> del Sol, este elemento,
> que cuatro veces había sido ciento
> dosel al día y tálamo a la noche,
> cuando halló de fugitiva plata

la bisagra (aunque estrecha) abrazadora
de un Ocëano y otro, siempre uno,
o las colunas bese o la escarlata,
tapete de la Aurora
[Next, water made the crystal zodiac
Where, in its wandering track,
A glorious pine rivalled the burning flight
Of Phoebus' axle-tree
And reached, after four hundred times the sea
Had made a dais for day, a bed for night,
The fugitive silver of the narrow strait,
The hinge that links two oceans, henceforth found
Ever and only one, whether their brine
Kiss Morning's crimson carpets, or the gate
Hercules' pillars bound].

Magellan showed that a western sea-route to the Spice Islands did exist after all, but that it passed through a narrow and windy strait at the continent's remote end.[104] Góngora's conceit conveys this by comparing the strait to a delicate "hinge of fleeting silver," attained after four hundred days of hard sailing. The hinge brings together the two oceans, which are now acknowledged to be distinct. In doing so, however, it confirms that they are, paradoxically, one, as the ancient view of the world had proclaimed.

Closely connected with Ocean in classical thought was a particular image of the "ends of the Earth" that Góngora also invokes. In Homer and the poetic tradition that followed, the boundaries of the world were marked by the rising and setting of the sun in Ocean's waters.[105] The image occurs also in the Bible.[106] Góngora draws on it in his poem in order to pinpoint the extremes of East and West between which mariners have sailed (lines 386-92). Columbus's three ships are said to have kissed the curtains of the Sun's bedchamber in the West (lines 413-18), while Vasco da Gama is described as having reached the realms of Dawn in the East (lines 453-60). Elsewhere, however, Góngora indicates exactly why the ancient notion could no longer be sustained (lines 403-12):

Piloto hoy la Cudicia, no de errantes
árboles, mas de selvas inconstantes,
al padre de las aguas Ocëano
(de cuya monarquía el Sol, que cada día

nace en sus ondas y en sus ondas muere,

los términos saber todos no quiere)

dejó primero de su espuma cano,

sin admitir segundo

en inculcar sus límites al mundo

[Cupidity now steers across these floods

Not wandering trees, but migratory woods,

Leaving the hoary father of the sea

(Of whose imperial sway

The sun, which every day

Springs from his waves, and in his waves must die,

Sees not how far the utmost limits lie)

To toss the spindrift from his locks, while she

Without a rival charts

The boundaries of earth's remotest parts].

For the early Greeks, the limits to human travel were set by Ocean, the source of all the waters on Earth and in Hades, whose domain stretched an unmeasured distance across the disk of the world to the edge of the celestial dome.[107] Góngora's lines begin accordingly by describing Ocean as "padre de las aguas" (line 405), but they go on to signal that in modern times (*hoy*) natural limits to its vastness no longer exist. In a spherical world, even the Sun cannot discern Ocean's boundaries. Ocean itself, moreover, has become subject to men, whose covetousness (*cudicia*) drives them over its waters, impressing upon it boundaries of their own. In such ways, the poem juxtaposes two contrasting conceptions of the world, and, by highlighting the differences between them, it recreates, in telling conceits, something of the astonishment that the New World provoked.

On first impression, the opinion of seafaring that the old man voices is largely negative. He recognises the part played in its development by daring and inventiveness, but he affirms that its effects have been deadly. The beginnings of navigation in the history of mankind brought disaster to the ancient world (lines 375-78), and the modern voyages of exploration, which have reached every headland and isle (lines 393-96), threaten further calamity in their wake. The Spice Islands, he concludes, should be left untouched in their "uncertain seas" (line 499). Some critics have concluded from this that Góngora was deeply hostile to the imperial ethos of Castile, but others have counselled caution, among them Arthur Terry, who held that we may not assume with any certainty that the old man's opinions are Góngora's own.[108] Two kinds of evidence, it may be argued, lend support to Terry's view. First, criticism of sea travel, its motives, and its results, is a topos in many of the classical texts that underlie Góngora's work. The Roman poets, for instance, including Ovid, "the poet always closest to Góngora's own imagination,"[109] repeatedly lament the invention of ships and the naked pusuit of gain that brought an end to the ancient Age of Gold. Such criticism, moreover, was quite compatible with recognition, even celebration, of the skills seafaring had inspired.[110] Góngora, in imitating the topos, gives it a modern ring, but without dismissing necessarily the Discoveries themselves. His older contemporary, Luis de León, imitated it too in his Fifth Ode, which denounces the greed impelling sea trade between Europe and the East.[111] From his other works, however, we know that he was a firm believer in Spain's imperial role.[112] Second, if we attend to the experience that the speech creates, and not only to what the speaker affirms, we find that it conveys a view of events more complex than some have allowed. Alongside the criticism of *cudicia*, and the accompanying acknowledgement of maritime skill, there is a powerful evocation of the longing and joy that the early explorers knew.[113]

The range of response that the poem invites may be seen in the description of the distant Pacific isles with which the speech concludes (481-90):

> De firmes islas no la inmóvil flota
> en aquel mar del Alba te describo,
> cuyo número, ya que no lascivo,
> por lo bello, agradable y por lo vario
> la dulce confusión hacer podía
> que en los blancos estanques del Eurota
> la virginal desnuda montería,
> haciendo escollos de mármol pario
> o de terso marfil sus miembros bellos,
> que pudo bien Acteón perderse en ellos
> [Of anchored isles, a stationary fleet
> In southern oceans, little need I say,
> Whose numbers—though they wake not lust—display
> Such charm, such beauty, such variety,
> Stirring to soft bewilderment, as when
> The limpid waters of Eurotas greet
> The naked virgins of Diana's train,
> Their lovely limbs like burnished ivory
> Or cliffs of Parian marble –for whose sight
> Actaeon might well hazard life and light].

Through his character, the old man, Góngora begins by saying that he will not describe the islands themselves, and in what follows he is true to his word. He describes instead the other term of his conceit, the encounter between Actaeon and Diana's nymphs recounted in the *Metamorphoses*,[114] dwelling in particular on the moment when Actaeon first beheld them. The moment is not mentioned by Ovid, who goes on at once to describe the screams of the nymphs when Actaeon appeared (lines 177-81). Góngora concentrates instead on the seconds before the screams began, when everyone stood still with surprise. He thus recreates for the reader the wonder (*la dulce confusión*) that mariners had felt when they first reached the islands a century before.

To convey their reaction, Góngora exploits with wit the interplay of similarity and difference that his conceit affords. He invites us to move in imagination between isles surrounded by water and water surrounded by trees, the trees among which, in Ovid's version, Actaeon loses his way and chances on the pools of Eurotas (lines 155-62; 173-76). The numerous islands, he tells us, are, like the nymphs, beautiful, various, and delightful to observe, though, unlike them, they are not *lascivas*; the mariners, unlike Actaeon (lines 141-42), are not guiltless victims of chance, but, like him, they will eventually come to grief. In the last line, Actaeon is said to have become "lost" (*que bien pudo Acteón perderse en ellos*), a phrase with several meanings: "lost in a wood," no doubt, as Ovid relates, but also "lost in wonder," as well as "lost" in the sense of "destroyed."[115]

By using classical myth in this way, Góngora may be said to have changed it: to have given it new life by means of *agudeza* [Wit], and, in doing so, to have extended enormously, through space and in time, its range of reference. The result is a memorable image of the encounter between the Old World and the New. For which islands were as "new" in 1613 as those in the Pacific, many of which Spain had acquired, on its union with Portugal, only a generation before?[116] And which emotion, for a European, could be older than Actaeon's wondering gaze?

BALTASAR GRACIÁN

In *El Criticón* [The Exacting Critic] (1651-57), the allegorical prose epic of Baltasar Gracián, the image of islands at the ends of the Earth is introduced at two key points: at the beginning, when the protagonists, Critilo and Andrenio, meet on the island of St. Helena, and at the end, when they pass together onto the Island of Immortality. Like other images in the work, these are designed to represent in visual terms certain intellectual propositions, to which attention is drawn by incongruities that denote a deeper sense or senses, a technique aptly described, in Gracián's own words, as "disfrazar la verdad para mejor insinuarla" [disguising the truth to convey it more effectively].[117] The contrast drawn between the islands is, in this sense, symbolic, as Mercedes Blanco has pointed out:

> El Criticón sitúa su relato de toda vida humana entre dos límites míticos. El primero es el de una naturaleza sin hombres, desplegada como un espléndido espectáculo, un "teatro del Universo," ante el ojo aislado de Andrenio, Adán en el paraíso de una isla desierta. El segundo límite, la Isla de la Inmortalidad, es el de un universo forjado por el artificio humano, un mundo de personas donde ha sido abolida la naturaleza [...]. Entre los dos espacios insulares diametralmente opuestos, el relato define un itinerario que atraviesa el mapa de las edades de la vida. [El Criticón situates its account of every human life between two mythical limits. The first is that of a natural world without people, laid out as a splendid spectacle, a "theatre of the Universe," before the isolated gaze of Andrenio, who is Adam in the paradise of a deserted island. The second limit, the Island of Immortality, is that of a universe forged by human skill, a world of people where Nature has been abolished [...]. Between these two island locations, diametrically opposed, the narrative traces an itinerary that traverses the map of the stages of life].[118]

Both islands, moreover, reveal in subtle ways the impress of the New World. The opening lines of the tale describe the location of St. Helena and its significance [Crisi I, pp. 103-4]:

> Ya entrambos mundos avían adorado el pie a su universal monarca el católico Filipo; era ya real corona suya la mayor buelta que el sol gira por el uno y otro emisferio, brillante círculo en cuyo cristalino centro yaze engastada una pequeña isla, o perla del mar o esmeralda de la tierra: dióla nombre augusta emperatriz, para que ella lo fuesse de las islas, corona del Occeano [Both worlds had already worshipped at the feet of their universal monarch, Philip the Catholic; his royal crown was already the widest circuit made by the sun as it turns through the two hemispheres, a brilliant circle at whose crystal centre is set a tiny island, either a pearl of the sea or an emerald of the land; it was named after an august empress, so that it might be the empress of islands, the Ocean's crown].

1.11 *Baltasar Gracián* (1601-58). A detail from a portrait formerly in the Jesuit College of Catalayud and now in the Sala de Juntas of La Universidad Nacional de Educación a Distancia in Catalayud (Zaragoza). c.1700. Oil on canvas.

Some elements of traditional cosmography are here retained: the Sun, *pace* Copernicus, revolves around the Earth, and the waters of the world form one Ocean.[119] In other respects, however, the geography implied tallies with the dates of the book's publication during the reign of "el católico Filipo," Philip IV (1621-65), when the Crowns of Castile and Portugal were still united, and the Monarchy's domains extended through both hemispheres. In this empire, justly termed "universal," St. Helena in the South Atlantic is a jewel set at the midpoint of a crown. It is also a pleasant resting place for European travellers (p.104):

> Sirve, pues, la isla de Santa Elena (en la escala del un mundo al otro) de descanso a la portátil Europa, y ha sido siempre venta franca, mantenida de la divina próvida clemencia en medio de inmensos golfos, a las católicas flotas del Oriente [The island of St. Helena (as a port of call between one world and the other) therefore serves as a place of rest for mobile Europe, and it has always been a bountiful wayside inn, maintained by the provident mercy of God amid vast stretches of sea, for the Catholic fleets of the East].

In the lives of the protagonists, the island proves to be a place of rest in senses both literal and figurative. For Critilo, travelling to Spain, from the colonial capital of Goa, in search of his lost love Felisinda, it represents the meeting of sea and land, life and death, as he swims towards its shore against the storm-tossed waves.[120] It was in these waters, we learn, that he was born during an earlier storm, while his parents made their way, in the reign of Philip II, from Spain to the East.[121] For Andrenio, who has lived on the island all his life, it is now the place where he meets Critilo, his father, and discovers what it means to be human, before returning with him to Spain. Later we are told that for Felisinda, too, the island was once a place of blessing, as she journeyed from Goa to Spain, secretly pregnant: in its privacy, she was able to give birth unseen, and thus preserve her good name.[122] It is she, no doubt, who is alluded to in the phrase "la portátil Europa": the island is associated not only with the continent of Europe, nowadays on the move, but also with the classical figure of Europa in flight, to whom Felisinda is compared.[123] In the lives of all these characters, St. Helena is central, a threshold between the New World, where their shared story began, and the Old World, where it subsequently unfolds.

The stereotype of a distant isle is thus amended to make pivotal what was once "on the edge": St. Helena, discovered in 1502,[124] and associated then with the ends of the Earth, is now located on the midline, between two hemispheres and worlds. In other respects, however, the stereotype is reaffirmed. The island is identified, from the start, with uncultivated Nature. It is a place of pristine beauty, but brutish too. No humans live there, apart from Andrenio, who was reared by wild animals in a mountain fastness (*Crisi* I, p.111), and the mariners who visit it are described as an insolent rabble who pause only to hunt and revictual before sailing onwards to Spain. Frightened of them, Critilo and Andrenio pretend to have been left behind accidentally by earlier ships, aware that if they are identified as "outsiders" they will be either killed or enslaved (*Crisi* IV, pp.154-55).[125]

At first, Andrenio seems to be at home in this harsh setting. Naked and unable to speak, he mimics with ease the roaring of beasts and the songs of birds, behaviour which is termed "barbaric," and from which one might reasonably conclude, we are told, that he is a savage.[126] But his civilised potential is indicated by other traits, including the intelligence and compassion with which he greets Critilo, and his physical appearance, which is described as noble, angelic.[127] Attention is drawn specifically to his flowing fair hair and the features of his face, which are said to "inscribe" him as European, in contrast to his complete lack of clothes (p.108):

> Dudara con razón el más atento, ser inculto parto de aquellas selvas, si no desmintieran la sospecha lo inhabitado de la isla, lo rubio y tendido de su cabello, lo perfilado de su rostro, que todo le sobreescrivía europeo: del traje no se podían rastrear indicios, pues era sola la librea de su inocencia [The most attentive observer would have reason to wonder if he was an uncouth offspring of those forests, if the suspicion (that he was) were not gainsaid by the uninhabited state of the island, the fairness and length of his hair, the narrowness of his features, all of which inscribed him as European: from his clothing no clues could be gleaned, for it was simply the livery of his innocence].

As Paul Julian Smith has acutely observed, "he is marked by the differential codes of genealogy ('race') and cultural convention (dress), in spite of his ignorance of these systems. Even the naked body is not innocent of inscription; and nor is the desert island untouched by culture."[128] Elsewhere in the work, as Smith shows, non-Europeans, including Africans, are portrayed as "marooned outside history and indistinguishable from the natural environments they inhabit,"[129] a fate that Andrenio, as the child of Spanish parents, escapes. On the island, he learns from Critilo how to speak, and during the long voyage home their studies range from history and cosmography to astronomy, moral philosophy, and the romance languages, including Spanish, which the narrator describes as "tan universal como su imperio" [as

universal as its empire] (*Crisi* IV, pp.164-65). Civilisation is presented, in such ways, as a European preserve, and when they eventually land it is "este nuestro mundo" [this world of ours] that they are said, significantly, to have reached,[130] far from the island of St. Helena, which is, in cultural terms, still remote.

The Island of Immortality described at the end of the novel also occupies a liminal place between two worlds, in this case the worlds of Time and Eternity.[131] As the ageless Pilgrim (*El Peregrino*) who guides the protagonists explains, it is inhabited only by those whose virtue, wisdom, and valour have merited unending life: "Eternízanse los grandes hombres en la memoria de los venideros, mas los comunes yacen sepultados en el desprecio de los presentes y en el poco reparo de los que vendrán" [Great men are immortalised in the memory of future generations, but those who are undistinguished lie buried in the scorn of the living and in the scant attention of the generations to come].[132] Critilo, when asked, admits to having heard of the island before, but he had always thought of it as a distant place, somewhere in the Antipodes, and he had dismissed it as the stuff of legend in which only the credulous believe (*Crisi* XII, p. 370):

> Ya yo he oydo hablar de ella algunas vezes [. . .] pero como de cosa muy allende, acullá en los antípodas: socorro ordinario de lo fabuloso lo lexos, y como dizen las abuelas, de largas vías cercanas mentiras. Por lo cual yo siempre la he tenido por un espanta vulgo, remitiéndola a su simple credulidad. [I have heard speak of it already from time to time [. . .] but as something very distant, over there in the Antipodes: legend usually draws support from what is remote, and, as old wives say, roads that travel far give rise to local lies. That is why I have always looked upon it as something that fills ordinary people with awe, and atrributed it to their unquestioning credulity].[133]

The Pilgrim, however, insists that it is not legendary but real, and not distant but near, as near, in fact, as death is to immortality.[134]

Having thus reversed some of the traditional associations of the island image, Gracián goes on to retain others in order to evoke the wonder that the island inspires. On hearing the Pilgrim's glowing account of the bliss enjoyed by its inhabitants, who are eternally young and free from the fear of death, Critilo expresses doubts about the prudence of such words: they could induce forgetfulness of the nature of life in Time, which is as fragile as glass (p. 375):

EL CRITICON
PRIMERA PARTE
EN
LA PRIMAVERA
DE LA NIÑEZ,
Y EN
EL ESTIO DE LA IVVENTVD.

AVTOR
GARCIA DE MARLONES.
Y LO DEDICA

A L VALEROSO CAVALLERO
Don PABLO DE PARADA,

DE LA ORDEN DE CHRISTO,
General de la Artilleria , y Governa-
dor de Tortofa.
CON LICENCIA.

En ZARAGOZA, por IVAN NOGVES, y a fu cofta
Año M.DC.LI.

Portada de la primera edición de la Primera Parte de «El Criticón»
(Zaragoza, Juan Nogués, 1651).

1.12 *El Criticón*. The title page of the First Part of *El Criticón* (Zaragoza: Juan Nogues, 1651), which was published under a pseudonym, *García de Marlones*, an anagram of the author's surnames, *Gracián* and *Morales*.

> Por tan dificultoso tengo yo alcançarle solidez a la frágil vida como al delicado vidrio, que para mí, hombre y vidrio todo es uno: a un tris dan un tras, y acábase vidrio y hombre [It is, I think, as difficult to make fragile life durable as it is delicate glass, for to my mind man and glass are one and the same: in a flash they collapse, and man and glass are over].

To make his point, he compares those who, like himself, are still in the world of Time to the Indians Columbus met, who valued so highly the pieces of glass he bestowed that they could not understand his quest for gold (pp. 374-75):[135]

> que si aun desta suerte les dezían los indios a los españoles: "¿Teniendo el vidrio allá en el otro mundo, venís a buscar el oro en éste? ¿teniendo cristales, hazéis caso de metales?" ¿Qué dixeran, si no fuera quebradizo, si le experimentaran durable? [For if the Indians said even this to the Spaniards: "Having glass there in the other world, did you come to seek gold in this one? Having glass, do you pay attention to metal?"; what would they say if it were not breakable, if they found it to be durable?].

Later, the encounter between the Old World and the New is recalled again, this time from the European point of view, as Critilo, Andrenio and their guide voyage in a sailing vessel towards the isle, which gradually becomes visible before their eyes (p. 382):

> Campeavan ya mucho, y de muy lexos dexávanse ver entre brillantes esplendores, unos portentosos edificios, que en divisándolos gritó Andrenio:
> -!Tierra, tierra!
> Y el Inmortal:
> -!Cielo, cielo!
> [Shining brightly now, and visible from very far away amid brilliant brightness, were wondrous buildings, the sight of which made Andrenio cry, "Land, land!," and the Immortal One, "Heaven, heaven!"].

Andrenio's words, as Miguel Romera-Navarro noted, echo those attributed to Rodrigo de Triana, the sailor on board the *Pinta* who first hailed the New World as it came into sight in October 1492,[136] and the passage, like the earlier one concerning *los indios*, draws attention to the perception of similarity and difference long associated with the Discoveries: what for Andrenio is unexplored land at the limit of the world he knows is for the Pilgrim Heaven itself, the "centre of Immortality."[137]

As the narrative proceeds, the scope of the island image is extended to include literature, and the activities of writing and reading which it involves. The travellers are told that to dwell there one must have acquired fame in war, government, or letters, and fame, it is indicated, does not exist unless it is registered in words. For this reason, the food that gives the immortals life is the unending sound of their praise.[138] There follows, logically, a celebration of the arts, in which the conventional dichotomy between Arms and Letters is resolved.[139] Led by the Pilgrim, the travellers reach a blackened sea that the narrator describes as *estraño* [strange].[140] At first they think it may be Lethe, the river where all is forgotten, but their guide assures them that in this place memory is forever preserved. The sources of the sea, he explains, lie in the perspiration that flows from the labours of gods and men, but its blackness is caused by famous writers who have dipped their pens into its waters in order to record great deeds. Among the writers listed, it is the ancients, beginning with Homer, who stand out.[141] Literary allusions multiply as the characters depart from a port significantly named Ostia,[142] and travel across the sea in a vessel made of everlasting cedar that once served to cover famous books. Richly inlaid with inscriptions, embellished with illuminations and covered in emblems, it is propelled by gilded oars that resemble pens, and by sails like painted canvasses that billow with applause.[143] The waters through which it moves denote various features of style which the novel itself exemplifies,[144] while the swans and halcyons that attend its journey represent, respectively, the arts of poetry and history.

The value accorded here to literature helps to explain a further feature of the isle: the comparatively narrow area from which its inhabitants are drawn. There are no women among them, as Francisco Maldonado pointed out,[145] but equally striking is the exclusion of anyone associated with the New World. Many of the heroes mentioned are Spanish or Portuguese, but none of the Iberian explorers, conquistadors or chroniclers is included in their ranks. Fernando of Aragon, *el rey católico* [the Catholic Monarch], is singled out for praise,[146] and so is his grandson, the Emperor Charles V,[147] but although both are said to have ruled vast realms, the nature and extent of their possessions are not detailed. This omission is part of the more general absence of people and places outside Europe. All the Immortals referred to are European, from ancient, medieval, and modern times, and so are most of the place-names cited in the text. After witnessing the guardian of the island, *El Mérito* [Merit], admit certain applicants and refuse others, the travellers hear his wise words echoing throughout time and from province to province in the world [p. 401]:

Repetía aquel eco, no cinco vezes las vozes como éste, sino cien mil, respondiéndose de siglo en siglo y de provincia en provincia, desde la elada Estocolmo hasta la abrasada Ormuz, y no resonava frialdades como suelen otros ecos, sino heroicas hazañas, dichos sabios y prudentes sentencias. Y a todo lo que no era digno de fama, enmudecía [That echo, unlike this one, did not repeat a voice five times, but one hundred thousand times, resounding from century to century and from province to province, from frozen Stockholm to burning Hormuz, and it did not ring out lame jokes, as other echoes usually do, but heroic deeds, wise sayings and prudent remarks (or judgments). And on everything unworthy of fame it was silent].

The provinces mentioned, between Scandinavia and the Persian Gulf, are all located in the Northern hemisphere, and they fall within the confines of the lands known in classical times. *El Criticón* thus ends, as it began, by affirming that "civilisation" and "Europe" are co-extensive, a conviction conveyed by the image of an island on the edge of the world of Time, which far from being "other" or "unknown" is the epitome of Europe's literary tradition and of the values it enshrines.

CONCLUSION

For each of the writers we have considered, the image of mysterious islands located at the ends of the Earth was charged not only with associations bequeathed by the Bible, the Classics, and medieval legend, but also with connotations forged during the voyages of discovery, particularly those of Columbus. In the writings of some, such as Columbus himself, the image was applied to the New World in a literal sense, but always with an ear to its scriptural and mythical overtones, which, for others, from Montalvo to Gracián, were primary. In the process, the image itself developed, like many elements of the rhetoric of travel,[148] and passed into the literatures of other peoples of the Old World. In English writing, for instance, its impact may be traced in works as diverse as Thomas More's *Utopia* (1516), Shakespeare's *The Tempest* (1611), the sermons of John Donne (1622), Francis Bacon's *New Atlantis* (1624), and Daniel Defoe's *Robinson Crusoe* (1719).[149] Detailed study of this legacy lies beyond the confines of the present essay, but one example from the early nineteenth century may be considered briefly, and by way of conclusion, to make a general point:

Much have I travelled in the realms of gold,
    And many goodly states and kingdoms seen;

1.13 Thomas More, *Utopia*. A woodcut illustration from the edition published by Froben in Basle in March 1518.

Round many western islands have I been
Which bards in fealty to Apollo hold.
Oft of one wide expanse had I been told
That deep-browed Homer ruled as his demesne;
    Yet did I never breathe its pure serene
Till I heard Chapman speak out loud and bold:
Then felt I like some watcher of the skies
    When a new planet swims into his ken;
Or like stout Cortez when with eagle eyes
    He stared at the Pacific – and all his men
Looked at each other with a wild surmise –
    Silent, upon a peak in Darien.[150]

On First Looking into Chapman's Homer was composed in 1816, when John Keats was twenty years old and at the start of his poetic career. After a night spent with his friend, Charles Cowden Clarke, leafing through Chapman's translation, he went home at dawn. A few hours later, when Clarke came down to breakfast, the sonnet was waiting on his table.[151] Keats wrote it fast, in other words, relying not on books but on memories of his studies at school, which appear to have included *The History of America* (London, 1777) by William Robertson, as well as the lives of Elizabethan adventurers, keen to emulate their Spanish rivals in pursuit of gold.[152]

When we first read the poem, the "western islands" mentioned in the third line may seem to be those that lie in the Mediterranean Sea. When we read it a second time, however, we become aware that they are also, or instead, those in the Atlantic to which Columbus sailed. The bards who hold them in fealty (line 4) resemble the viceroys who ruled such islands for the Spanish Crown, and the "realms of gold" referred to in the first line turn out to be not only the "golden world" of poetry that Sir Philip Sidney praised, but the fabled *El Dorado* which the Spaniards sought.[153] Then, in the quatrain that follows (lines 5-8), we move from the first stage of the Spanish discoveries to the second. The "one wide expanse" ruled by Homer (lines 5-6) is not named, but we realise, on rereading, that it must be the Pacific. It is, moreover, "his demesne": that is to say, it is not held in trust or fealty, an acknowledgement, no doubt, of Homer's greatness.[154] The poet, we are told, has learnt of it from Chapman (lines 7-8), who returns, like an explorer, to tell of the marvels he has known, enabling others to envisage them in imagination, an experience so intense for the poet that in his description "the senses blur."[155]

In the first tercet, suddenly, the imagery shifts: we are shown that the focus of the poem is not, necessarily, Chapman's text, but the experience of discovery itself. The mention of astronomy achieves this by expanding the frame from the Earth to the cosmos beyond, but a link with navigation is retained: the new planet is said to "swim" (line 10), and the "ken" of the "watcher of the skies" (lines 9-10) draws attention to "seeing," which becomes important in the lines that remain. At the end of the tercet, as Tennyson observed,[156] there appears to be a mistake: the Spaniard who first reached the Pacific was not Cortés but Balboa. Perhaps Keats was thinking, confusedly, of the moment when Cortés and his men looked on the Aztec city and recalled the *Amadís*.[157] If so, his error was inspired, for Balboa is remembered primarily as an explorer, Cortés as a *conquistador*, determined not only to know but to possess.[158] Hence, perhaps, the word "stout," an allusion to his bravery, and the phrase "with eagle eyes" (line 11): he is on a peak, staring like a bird of prey.[159] The poem does not tell what Cortés is seeking, but the closing image gathers force as we recall the relentless quest for the Spice Islands to which his letters refer.[160]

We end, then, with an image of the poet, silent with wonder as he surveys Homer's demesne, and longing not only to explore it but to make it decisively his own.[161] In the words of Helen Vendler:

> As "stout Cortez" stares at the Pacific, the "expanse" of Homer's poetry is shown to be not a land-mass—an island or a state comparable to those the seasoned traveller has already seen—but rather an entire ocean offering innumerable new shores and islands for future exploration.[162]

The sonnet may be said to illustrate the capacity of a great poet, in this case young and in many respects unlearned, to tap into the hidden resources of a language,[163] and Keats's resources here, the metaphors on which he draws, go back ultimately to Castile, and to its encounter with the New World in which ancient images were transformed.

2.1 Jacopino del Conte (1510-98). *Ignatius of Loyola.* 1556. Oil on panel. 17.9 x 13.7 inches. Rome, General Curia of the Society of Jesus. One of the earliest portraits of Ignatius. It was executed shortly after his demise, using the death mask as a model.

Chapter Two

Devotional Writing:
The *Spiritual Exercises* of Ignatius Loyola

More than one hundred years have passed since Henri Watrigant published his pioneering essays on the origin of the *Spiritual Exercises* of St Ignatius Loyola.[1] Since then, our knowledge of their sources has grown in precision and extent, making possible the study of their genesis published by Fathers Calveras and Dalmases in their critical edition of the text.[2] The findings they present indicate that the *Exercises* were composed over a period of more than twenty years, reaching their final state in the early 1540s. They also confirm the testimony of Ignatius's early companions that the main components were selected and ordered, in a rudimentary form at least, within two years of his conversion in 1521.[3] The major literary sources detected are correspondingly small in number and narrow in range: the *Vita Christi* [Life of Christ] of Ludolph the Carthusian, the *Legenda aurea* [Golden Legend] of Jacobus de Voragine, the *Imitation of Christ* by Thomas à Kempis, a confessional manual, and a Book of Hours. Ignatius did not know Latin in the early 1520s, and his reading was restricted, therefore, to writings in the vernacular. Each of the works mentioned was available to him in Spanish, and we know from other evidence that he read or consulted them all at various points during his convalescence in Loyola (June 1521-February 1522), his visit to the Abbey of Montserrat (March 1522), and his largely solitary life in Manresa (March 1522-February 1523).[4] One cannot rule out the possibility, remote though it may seem, that further major sources will come to light, and any conclusions must, therefore, be provisional.[5] There are, none the less, two general observations that may be made.

First, the textual parallels discovered between the *Exercises* and the works Ignatius read are, though significant, occasional and few, and in many parts of the text it is not possible to locate specific sources for his concepts and words. A similar situation arises in the study of other spiritual writers of the period, including San Juan de la Cruz, of whose supposed sources Federico Ruiz has observed:

> Los autores más ponderados y sus críticos terminan siempre reduciendo los hallazgos a proporciones de conjetura y probabilidad: semejanza, pero no sabemos si dependencia; dependencia, pero no

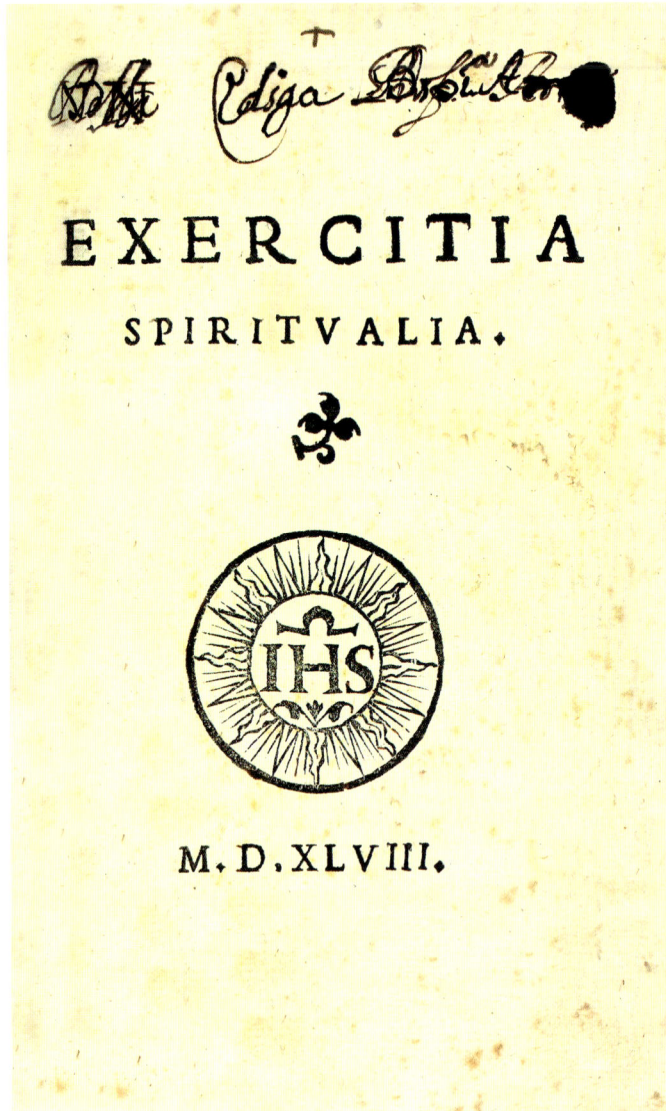

2.2 *The Spiritual Exercises*. The first printed edition of the work (Rome: apud Antonium Bladum, 1548) was a Latin version of the Spanish text prepared by the French Jesuit, André des Freux.

sabemos si directa, o a través de fuentes intermedias, o a través de la mentalidad corriente [The most considered authors and their critics always end by scaling down their findings to the proportions of conjecture and probability: similarity, but we do not know if it is dependence; dependence, but we do not know if it is direct, or transmitted by intermediate sources, or transmitted by the mentality of the time].[6]

For this reason, it is often more helpful, when studying the *Exercises*, to bear in mind the "accumulated tradition"[7] of patristic and medieval theology on which they draw than to focus on specific texts that Ignatius may, or may not, have known. Recent research, for instance, has drawn attention to parallels between the *Exercises* and certain writings of the Eastern Fathers of the Church, few of which we can be sure Ignatius knew directly when the *Exercises* were composed. The lines of transmission, no doubt, were often indirect, and they remain, in most cases, conjectural.[8]

Second, whenever a specific source has been located, the borrowing itself has usually turned out to be less significant than the ways in which it was subsequently altered, combined with other sources, and absorbed into the text. This is so because, as Watrigant noted, "tout le livre a été *vécu* avant d'être écrit" [the whole book was *lived* before being written].[9] When he was asked how the *Exercises* were composed, Ignatius did not refer to the books he had read, but to his own inner experiences, and to his sense of what others might find useful: "algunas cosas que observaba en su alma y las encontraba útiles, le parecía que podrían ser útiles también a otros, y así las ponía por escrito" [some things that he used to observe in his soul and that he found useful could, it seemed to him, be useful also to others, and so he used to write them down].[10] The identification of a possible source, in other words, does not advance necessarily our understanding of the text unless we go further to examine its place and function in the work as a whole.

One aspect of the *Exercises* which confirms the truth of these two points is the use made in them of an ancient conception of the Christian life, rooted in the Bible, according to which spiritual progress involves passing from servile to filial fear. It is alluded to at the very end of the work, in the eighteenth of the rules entitled *Para el sentido verdadero que en la Yglesia militante debemos tener* [For the true attitude of mind that we should have in the Church Militant] (352):

Dado que sobre todo se ha de estimar mucho el seruir a Dios nuestro Señor por puro amor, debemos mucho alabar el temor de la su diuina maiestad; porque no solamente el temor filial es cosa pía y sanctíssima, mas aun el temor seruil, donde otra cosa mejor o más vtil el hombre no alcanze, ayuda mucho para salir del peccado mortal; y salido fácilmente viene al temor filial, que es todo acepto y grato a Dios nuestro Señor, por estar en vno con el amor diuino [Given that above all one should greatly esteem serving God our Lord out of pure love, we must greatly praise the fear of his divine Majesty; for not only is filial fear a pious and most holy thing, but even servile fear, when man does not attain anything better or more useful, greatly helps to move out of mortal sin; and once out he comes easily to filial fear, which is wholly acceptable and pleasing to God our Lord, because it is one with divine love] (370).

It would not be legitimate to assume, without further reason, that this passage contains a direct reference to the *Exercises* themselves. Like the rules that precede it, it was probably added to the text during the late 1530s or early 1540s, with the intention of defending a teaching of the Church that had become controversial, and that the Council of Trent later reaffirmed.[11] Some recent commentators, however, have made a case for the view that the transition from servile to filial fear which the rule concerns may be traced as well in the main body of the work, and they have argued that seen in this light the rule may be fairly described as a "summary" or "recapitulation" of the entire *Exercises*. Jesús Corella, for instance, has interpreted it as "una especie de resumen de todo el proceso" [a sort of résumé of the whole process],[12] while for Javier Melloni, "recapitula el recorrido completo de los *Ejercicios*" [it recapitulates the complete course of the *Exercises*].[13] They have differed, however, in their understanding of the stages in which the transition occurs during the Four Weeks into which the *Exercises* are divided.[14] Nor is it clear, exactly, how Ignatius came to know the tradition that informs the rule when the *Exercises* were originally conceived. He certainly encountered it at Loyola, in the *Vita Christi* of Ludolph the Cartusian, in which it is summarised succinctly,[15] but did he also come across it at Montserrat, in the exercises of Abbot Cisneros, whose *Exercitatorio de la vida spiritual* (Montserrat, 1500) [Book of Exercises of the Spiritual Life] was designed to enable progression from servile to filial fear?[16] The question is not easy to answer. Some scholars have argued that when Ignatius reached Montserrat he was introduced by his confessor, Jean Chanones, either to the *Exercitatorio* itself, or to an abridged version, the *Compendio* [Compendium],[17] but their hypothesis, though plausible, cannot be confirmed, as others have pointed out: the external evidence that Ignatius knew Cisneros's exercises is slight, and the textual parallels, considered alone, are inconclusive.[18]

The pages that follow seek to advance discussion of both the rule and its relation with the text by leaving on one side the quest for specific "sources" in order to examine instead the impact on the *Exercises* as a whole of three broad features of the "accumulated tradition" that were known in the Spain of Ignatius's time: the patristic and medieval concept of the various grades of fear; the biblical imagery associated with it; and the connection of both with other, related schemata of the spiritual life.

THE GRADES OF FEAR

The traditional teaching on the grades of fear and their relationship with love, which finds expression in the eighteenth rule, developed out of attempts by the Fathers of the Church to reconcile an apparent inconsistency in the text of Scripture. In some places, the fear of God is described as a stage through which one passes, and which is left behind as the love of God grows (e.g. Psalm 110:10; I John 4:18). In others it is said to be a necessary part of the spiritual life, one that is pleasing to God and that "abides for ever" (Psalm 18:1). The dilemma was resolved eventually by associating the first fear with terror of being punished for one's sins, a terror expelled as charity grows, and by connecting the second with the love of God that is disinterested or "pure." In his commentary on Psalm 127, St Augustine summed up the accepted view:

> Audistis cum euangelium legeretur: *Ubi uermis eorum non morietur, et ignis eorum non exstinguetur.* Audiunt haec homines; et quia uere futura sunt impiis, timent, et continent se a peccato. Habent timorem, et per timorem continent se a peccato. Timent quidem, sed non amant iustitiam. Cum autem per timorem continent se a peccato, fit consuetudo iustitiae, et incipit quod durum erat amari, et dulcescit Deus; et iam incipit homo propterea iuste uiuere, non quia timet poenas, sed quia amat aeternitatem. Exclusus est ergo timor a charitate, sed successit timor castus [You heard when the Gospel was read out: "where the worm does not perish and the fire is not put out" [Mark 9:48]. Men hear this, and, since it will certainly befall the impious, they fear and abstain from sin. They know fear, and on account of it they do not sin. They are certainly afraid, but they do not love justice. However, when they abstain from sin on account of fear, a habit of justice is engendered, and what was difficult begins to be loved and God becomes attractive; and thus a man begins to live justly, not because he fears punishment but

because he loves eternity. Fear, therefore, has been expelled by charity; but its place has been taken by a fear that is chaste].[19]

Elsewhere, in his commentary on the First Epistle of St. John, he explained that the fear which abides is fear not of punishment but of being parted from God. It is imbued, in fact, with the longing for union that love inspires:

> Ille timor quo times ne in gehennam mittaris cum diabolo, nondum est castus; non enim venit ex amore Dei, sed ex timore poenae: cum autem times Deum, ne deserat te praesentia eius, amplecteris eum, ipso frui desideras. [Your fear of being placed in Hell with the Devil is not yet chaste, for it springs not from love of God but from fear of punishment. But when you fear that God will deprive you of His presence, then you are embracing him and longing to enjoy Him].[20]

This is the fear that Ignatius describes as "at one with" (*en vno con*) divine love (370).

In the East, the teaching had been sketched out earlier, in general terms, in the *Stromata* [Miscellanies] of Clement of Alexandria,[21] and it later became part of the theology of the Cappodocian Fathers, notably Basil the Great, in whose monastic rule it had a prominent place.[22] In the West, it was developed and popularised not only in the works of Augustine, but also in the *Conferences* of John Cassian, who drew his inspiration directly from the writings of Clement and Basil.[23] Through Cassian, it entered the monastic rules of the Master and St. Benedict, and thus became part of the cenobitic tradition of the Western Church.[24] By the time of the Scholastics, it had become a part also of the standard curriculum of the theological schools. It was the Scholastics who established the terms "servile" and "filial," and who distinguished a third grade, *timor initialis* [initial fear], an intermediate stage in which servile and filial fear co-exist. Thomas Aquinas defined the grades precisely:

> Si [...] aliquis convertatur ad Deum et ei inhaereat propter timorem poenae, erit timor *servilis*. Si autem propter timorem culpae, erit timor *filialis*: nam filiorum est timere offensam patris. Si autem propter utrumque, est timor *initialis*, qui est medius inter utrumque timorem [If [. . .] one is converted to God and united with Him through fear of punishment, this will be servile fear; should the fear rather be of offending God, it will be filial, so-called because to fear offending one's father is characteristic of sons. Should it be on

In solitudinem profectus, furente supra orantis caput uarijs serpentum spectris dæmone intrepidus atq̃ inconniuens in precibus perseuerat.

12

2.3   Attributed to Peter Paul Rubens (1577-1640). *Ignatius at Manresa.* From the *Vita beati P. Ignatii Loiolae Societatis Iesu fundatoris* (Rome, 1609), folio 12, a collection of eighty-one images of the life of Ignatius engraved by Jean-Baptiste Barbe, who asked the young Rubens to contribute drawings.

account of both evils, then it is called initial fear, and it is midway between the other two].[25]

For Thomas, as W. J. Hill observed, "filial fear [...] is rooted in filial love," and consequently, "the submission to God which such fear realizes is spontaneous and utterly free."[26] Later in the medieval period, the teaching that he had resumed was propagated in numerous works of devotion, including, as we have seen, two that were well known in the Castile of St. Ignatius: the *Vita Christi* of Ludolph the Carthusian and the *Exercitatorio* of García de Cisneros.

In the main body of the *Exercises*, the traditional teaching on the grades of fear is taken over and adapted in innovative ways. During the opening exercise of the First Week, the retreatant is made aware that his sins have deserved damnation:

> demandar vergüenza y confussión de mý mismo, viendo quántos an sido dañados por vn solo pecado mortal, y quántas veces yo merescía ser condenado para siempre por mis tantos peccados [request shame and confusion on my own account, seeing how many have been harmed by a single mortal sin, and how often I deserved to be condemned for ever for my so many sins] (48).

Later, in the concluding meditation on Hell, an appeal to servile fear is made directly:

> pedir interno sentimiento de la pena que padescen los dañados, para que si del amor del Señor eterno me oluidare por mis faltas, a lo menos el temor de las penas me ayude para no venir en pecado [request an interior sense of the punishment endured by the damned, so that if I should, because of my faults, forget the love of the eternal Lord, at least the fear of punishments may help me not to fall into sin] (65).

This appeal to servile fear, however, occurs in a context of love. Earlier, in the first meditation, the retreatant is reminded that sin involves acting against the goodness of the Creator (52), and in the colloquy that follows God's goodness is highlighted by the reflection that the same Creator took flesh to redeem him:

> Ymaginando a Xpo nuestro Señor de lante y puesto en cruz, hazer vn colloquio; cómo de Criador es venido a hazerse hombre, y de vida eterna a muerte temporal, y así a morir por mis pecados [Imagining Christ our Lord before me and fixed to the cross, make a colloquy:

how he came from being the Creator to become man, and from eternal life to temporal death, and thus to die for my sins] (53).

In the second exercise, the theme of divine goodness is developed further when the retreatant considers that the mercy of God is expressed at every level of Creation. He concludes with an expression of heartfelt gratitude:

> Acabar con un colloquio de misericordia, razonando y dando gracias a Dios nuestro Señor, porque me a dado vida hasta agora [...] [Finish with a colloquy of mercy, conversing with and thanking God our Lord, because he has given me life up to now] (61).

The incipient love that the opening meditations encourage is allowed to deepen in the third exercise in which they are repeated, "haziendo pausa en los punctos que he sentido mayor consolación o desolación o mayor sentimiento spiritual" [pausing at the points at which I have felt greater consolation or desolation or greater spiritual feeling] (62), and in the fourth exercise, in which the third is resumed. When the retreatant comes to meditate on Hell, in other words, he is well aware of God's loving-kindness, and has begun to respond to it. Technically, therefore, the fear that this exercise arouses is not servile but initial, in which servile and filial fear co-exist. As the meditation unfolds, moreover, it is the element of filial fear or love that is encouraged to grow. The second preamble implies clearly that servile fear is not the best motive for avoiding sin: it has its use, but love is better (65). And the meditation ends on a note, not of terror, but of thanksgiving: "y con esto darle gracias, porque no me ha dexado caer en ninguna destas, acabando mi vida" [and with this give him thanks, because he has not let me fall into any of these (categories), ending my life] (71). As Michael Ivens observed:

> Certainly Ignatius recognized, as does the mainstream homiletic tradition, that situations exist where fear must indeed be the first step (370). But the First Week, where the meditation on Hell comes after and not before the person has been touched by God's love (65), is not such a situation. The essential grace of the First Week is that of a conversion arising out of the literally heart-breaking experience of being loved and forgiven.[27]

From the Second Week onwards, the retreatant is encouraged to move away from the stage of initial fear, and to advance to that of filial fear, in which love holds sway.

Caeli aspectu mirifice captus vim lacrymarum profundere, atq̃ exclamare solebat, HEV QVAM SORDET TELLVS, CVM COELVM ASPICIO? *cumq̃ præ lacrymis oculos perderet, imperium in illas à Deo impetrat; nouoq̃ dono donum lacrymarū moderatur.* 68

2.4   Attributed to Peter Paul Rubens (1577-1640). *Ignatius in Ecstasy.* From the *Vita beati P. Ignatii Loiolae Societatis Iesu fundatoris* (Rome, 1609), folio 68.

The transition takes place in response to the love of God, made visible in Christ, which he considers in the course of the meditations on the main events of the Gospel. It may be observed in the gradual changes that occur in the third preamble to the meditations, where he prays for the particular grace he desires. At the start of the Second Week, having considered "el llamamiento del rey temporal" [the call of the temporal king], he prays for an increase in his knowledge and love of the Lord: "[…] demandar conoscimiento interno del Señor, que por mý se ha hecho hombre, para que más le ame y le siga" [request inner knowledge of the Lord, who for my sake has become man, that I may love and follow him more] (104). The preamble remains the same, over the next twelve days, in the meditations that follow, which focus on the Gospel events between the Annunciation and Palm Sunday. As he works through them, the retreatant considers how Christ cast out the fear of his followers in the boat at sea (279, 280), and at the Transfiguration (284). He pauses on the fourth day to make the meditations on *dos banderas* [Two Standards] (136) and *tres binarios* [Three Classes] (149), and then, on the fifth day, he begins *la materia de las electiones* [The matter of the elections] (163). These exercises place before him Christ's call to poverty and humility; they compel him to face the self-interest that impedes his wholehearted response; and they encourage him, in the Election, to make whatever decisions are required to answer the call appropriately in his own life.[28] By the time the Week comes to an end, he is expected to have grown in the knowledge and love he desired.

The change expected is evident in the Third Week when he prays, in the opening exercise on the Passion, for "dolor, sentimiento y confussión, porque por mis peccados ba el Señor a la passión" [pain, feeling and confusion, because on account of my sins the Lord is going to the Passion] (193). In the second exercise he goes further, and begs for a share in the Lord's suffering:

> demandar lo que quiero, lo qual es proprio de demandar en la passión: dolor con Xpo doloroso, quebranto con Xpo quebrantado, lágrimas, pena interna de tanta pena que Xpo passó por mý [request what I desire, namely, what it is fitting to request in the Passion: suffering with Christ suffering, brokenness with Christ broken, tears, inner pain at so much pain that Christ endured for me] (203).

This prayer, which accompanies the remaining meditations of the Week, is informed by a compassion and a generosity of spirit that confirm the purification of motive that has been taking place.

In the Fourth Week, the process comes to a head. As he begins the first exercise, on the Resurrection, the retreatant prays for the gift of joy: "pedir gracia para me alegrar y gozar intensamente de tanta gloria y gozo de Xpo nuestro Señor" [request grace to delight and rejoice intensely in so much glory and joy of Christ our Lord] (221). In the words of William Peters:

> This joy has one cause only, the joy and happiness of the Lord together with His glory [...]. The exercitant's own redemption is passed over in silence as a possible source of joy [...]. No matter what his own sufferings are and, consequently, how great his need of comfort is, his is a most unselfish joy.[29]

The contrast with the First Week could not be greater. The retreatant has passed from initial fear, in which servile fear has a place, to the filial fear which is an expression of disinterested love. In the *Contemplación para alcanzar amor* [Contemplation to attain Love], which follows, he goes on to make his own the prayer set out in the First Point, when, having pondered the unreserved love God has shown him, he resolves to offer Him in return, "todas mis cosas y a mý mismo con ellas" [all the things I have and myself with them] (234).

IMAGERY

The patristic and medieval writers who shaped the teaching on the grades of fear described the transition from servile fear to filial in terms of three main images, each of them derived from Scripture. The first of these was the image of slaves or servants becoming sons, a figure used by St. Paul in the *Epistle to the Romans*: "You did not receive the spirit of slavery to fall back into fear, but you have received the spirit of sonship" (Romans 8:15). In the Church of the West, St. Augustine distinguished the grades of fear by contrasting two men: a servant who is terrified of being punished by beatings, chains, and imprisonment, and a just man who shrinks from giving his father pain because he is assured of his love.[30] Earlier, in the East, St Basil had conveyed the same teaching by means of a threefold comparison with slaves, mercenaries, and children:

> We obey God and avoid vices from the fear of punishment, and in that case we take on the resemblance of slaves. Or we keep the precepts because of the utility we derive from the recompense, thus resembling mercenaries. Or finally, from love of Him who has given us the law, we obey with joy at having been judged worthy of serving so great and good a God, and thus we imitate the affection of children towards their parents.[31]

These similes were cultivated by other Eastern Fathers, among them St. Gregory of Nazianzus,[32] and they were popularised in the West by John Cassian, who reproduced them in his eleventh *Conference*.[33]

The second image was of servants becoming friends, a figure derived from the Gospel of St John: "No longer do I call you servants, for the servant does not know what his master is doing; but I have called you friends, for all that I have heard from my Father I have made known to you" (John 15:15). One of the earliest writers to develop it was Clement of Alexandria, who wrote in his *Stromata*:

> We are told that "the fear of the Lord is pure, enduring for ever." For they who turn to faith and righteousness from fear endure for ever [...]. Fear brings about abstinence from evil, while love prompts us to do good, building us up to a willing mind, in order that one may hear from the Lord the words, "No longer do I call you servants, but friends."[34]

Elsewhere in the same work, which the image pervades, Clement went further and distinguished between two types of servants, "mere" servants and "faithful" ones: "all men belong to Him, but some by way of knowledge, while others have not attained to this; some as friends, some as faithful servants, some as servants merely."[35] This second image, like the first, was taken up, and disseminated in the West, by John Cassian.[36] Bede, in his exegesis, drew a contrast between the fear of a servant (*timor servilis*) and that of a friend (*timor amicabilis*), and his terminology was taken over subsequently in the *Sentences* of Peter Lombard.[37] In the late Middle Ages, Catherine of Siena based on the image a description of spiritual progress which consisted of three stages: mercenary servants, faithful servants, and friends or sons.[38]

The third main image was of lovers. It was popularised by St. Augustine, who conveyed the distinction of fears by describing two women: an unfaithful spouse, who dreads that her husband will punish her, and a faithful one who dreads only to be parted from her beloved.[39] He called the fear of the latter *timor castus* [chaste fear], a term used earlier by Clement of Rome,[40] and evoked it by drawing on the nuptial imagery used in Scripture:

> Audi eam [...] suspirantem, et dicentem, *Psallam et intelligam in via immaculata; quando venies ad me?* Sed in via immaculata merito non timet; quia *perfecta charitas foras mittit timorem.* Et cum venerit ad eius amplexum, timet, sed securiter. Quid timet? Cavebit, et observabit se ab iniquitate sua, ne iterum peccet: non ne mittatur in

ignem, sed ne ab illo deseratur. Et erit in illa, quid? Timor castus, permanens in saeculum saeculi [Listen to her [...] sighing and saying: "I will sing, and I will understand in the unblemished way. When will you come to me?" (Psalm 100:1-2). But she does not fear, and with good reason, in the unblemished way, because "perfect love casts out fear" (I John 4:18). And when she reaches God's embrace she does fear, but she has confidence. What does she fear? She will guard and protect herself against her own wickedness, lest she sin again: not to escape the fire, but to avoid being abandoned by Him. And what will there be within her? "The chaste fear that lasts for ever" (Psalm 18:10)].[41]

Later, Thomas Aquinas took pains to point out that chaste and filial fear were different terms for the same reality, the love of *caritas*:

> habitudo filii ad patrem, vel uxoris ad virum, est e converso per affectum filii se subdentis patri, vel uxoris se coniungentis viro unione amoris. Unde timor filialis et castus ad idem pertinent: quia per caritatis amorem Deus pater noster efficitur [...], et secundum eandem caritatem dicitur etiam sponsus noster [The relationship of a son to father or of a wife to husband is based upon affection, wherein the son submits to his father or the wife joins herself to her husband in loving union. Accordingly, filial fear and chaste fear amount to the same thing, because the love of charity brings it about that we can look upon God as at once our father [...] and even our spouse].[42]

In the course of the Middle Ages, these three main images became intertwined, with the result that writers who wished to allude to the grades of fear had a range of symbols at their disposal. A person moved by servile fear could be described as a slave, a servant, a criminal. One moved by filial fear could be compared to a son, a friend, a spouse. These images are not used in the section on fear in the *Vita Christi* of Ludolph the Carthusian. They do occur, however, in the exercises of García de Cisneros: in the first cycle of his meditations, which appeals to servile fear, the monk sees himself as a prisoner on trial before a harsh judge; in the third cycle, which encourages filial fear, he sees himself as a son or bride.[43]

In the *Spiritual Exercises*, the images associated with the grades of fear are adapted by Ignatius in an original way. The most prominent one is that of servants and friends.

The retreatant is introduced to it in the initial exercise of the First Week, when the nature of a colloquy is explained. It is said to involve addressing the person to whom prayer is directed as one friend addresses another or as a servant speaks to his lord:

> El colloquio se haze propiamente hablando, así como vn amigo habla a otro o vn sieruo a su señor; quándo pidiendo alguna gracia, quándo culpándose por algún mal hecho, quándo comunicando sus cosas, y queriendo consejo en ellas [The colloquy is typically made speaking, as one friend speaks to another or a servant to his lord; at times requesting some favour, at times blaming oneself for something done badly, at times conveying one's concerns, and desiring advice about them] (54).

It is appropriate that servitude and friendship should be mentioned at this stage, for the first exercise, as we have seen, appeals to both servile fear and love, and it is clear from the Fourth Addition that the retreatant is expected to pray in whatever way he feels moved (76). Elsewhere in the Week, the image emphasised is that of a servant who has been unfaithful. The Second Addition indicates that before making the first meditation, on sin, the retreatant should picture himself as an unfaithful knight about to approach his king:

> trayéndome en confusión de mis tantos pecados, poniendo exemplos, así como si vn caballero se hallase delante de su rey y de toda su corte, auergonzado y confundido en hauerle mucho ofendido, de quien primero rescibió muchos dones y muchas mercedes [bringing myself to feel confusion on account of my so many sins, using examples, such as if a knight were to find himself before his king and all his court, shamed and confounded for having greatly offended him from whom he first received many gifts and many favours] (74).

The passage underlines the generosity of the king and the knight's ingratitude, as if to remind the retreatant, who is about to meditate on God's justice, that He is also a loving lord. Later, before the second meditation, he sees himself in a different role: as a prisoner, in chains and deserving of death, on his way to meet a judge:

> haziéndome peccador grande y encadenado, es a saber, que voy atado como en cadenas a parescer delante del sumo Juez eterno, trayendo

> en exemplo cómo los encarçerados y encadenados ya dignos de muerte parescen delante su juez temporal [presenting myself as a great sinner and in chains: that is to say, I go bound, as it were in chains, to appear before the supreme, eternal Judge, bearing in mind as an example how people imprisoned and enchained who are already deserving of death appear before their temporal judge] (74).

In this passage, the accent is on punishment, not mercy, on servile fear, not love, as if to act as a counterbalance to the exercise that follows, in which the emphasis falls on God's mercy.

In the Second Week, it is the image of faithful servants that comes to the fore. During the first part of the exercise on the call of the earthly king, the retreatant is invited to consider the response likely to be made by those of his followers who are loyal, and to contrast it with that of the servant who declines to obey:

> considerar qué deuen responder los buenos súbditos a rey tan liberal y tan humano; y, por consiguiente, si alguno no acceptase la petición de tal rey, quánto sería digno de ser vituperado por todo el mundo y tenido por peruerso caballero [consider the response that good subjects should make to a king who is so generous and humane; and, consequently, if a person were not to respond to the request of such a king, how deserving he would be of everyone's scorn and of being deemed a disreputable knight] (94).

In the second part, when the image is applied to the call of Christ, he considers two groups among the Lord's loyal subjects: those who follow Him prompted by their good judgment and intelligence (96), and others who are moved, in addition, by an ardent desire to serve (97). In this exercise, as in the subsequent meditation on *dos banderas* [Two Standards], the scriptural image of servants is conflated with the ideals and images of chivalry, which Ignatius had come to know intimately in the years before his conversion, through his experience as a courtier and his reading of romances of chivalry, among them *Amadís de Gaula*.[44] The motives ascribed to the king's loyal subjects stem, accordingly, from the code of knightly honour, as Santiago Arzubialde has observed:

> La instancia paradigmática para un hombre de su época era que el Rey llamara a un caballero al servicio de las armas. Y tal llamada era inapelable porque el caballero había recibido de su señor la tenencia de estados o el sueldo estable que le permitían vivir holgadamente,

otorgándole su categoría social. Este hecho le convertía en una persona honorable, precisamente por su *vinculación*, desde el punto de vista humano y divino, al servicio de su Rey. El caballero "se lo debía todo" a su señor y quedaba obligado por ello a un servicio que no podía en modo alguno eludir. De ahí que el eje dialéctico de esta pequeña parábola recaiga, en última instancia, sobre el sentimiento del *honor* y su reverso, la vergüenza, que constituyen la identidad del caballero [The paradigmatic demand for a man of his period was the King summoning a knight to serve him with his arms. And such a summons could not be appealed, because the knight had received from his lord the tenancy of certain estates or the fixed revenue that enabled him to live in comfort and conferred on him his social status. This fact made him a person of honour, precisely because he was *bound*, from a human and divine viewpoint, to serve his King. The knight "owed everything" to his lord, and for this reason was obliged to render a service he could in no way avoid. That is why the logical core of this little parable lies, ultimately, in the sentiment of *honour* and its contrary, shame, which together constitute the knight's identity].[45]

It, therefore, seems self-evident to those with sense that they should serve their king (96), because such service springs naturally from their identity and his. Those who wish to go further are moved, by contrast, not only by their reason but by their affections. They long to respond to him in a spirit of love, and their devotion to him prompts their desire to imitate him in bearing insults and poverty (98). Similarly, it is love that later prompts the retreatant to beg for poverty and insults, when he makes the colloquy that concludes the meditation on *dos banderas* (147).

During the Second Week, the retreatant is not allowed to forget that Christ is followed not only by servants but by friends. In the third point of the meditation on *dos banderas*, he considers, "el sermón que Xpo nuestro Señor haze a todos sus sieruos y amigos, que a tal jornada embía" [the address that Christ our Lord makes to all his servants and friends, whom he sends out on such an expedition] (146). Nevertheless, it is the theme of service that is underlined. The words *servir* and *servicio*, which occur thirty-nine times in the work as a whole, are used on twenty-two occasions during the Week, and they are prominent not only in the material dealing with the Election, but also in the meditations on the life of Christ.[46] In the second of these, the exercise on the Nativity, the retreatant is asked to contemplate the Holy Family in Bethlehem, and to serve them there in all their needs, as if he were their slave:

77

> ver a Nuestra Señora y a Joseph y a la ancilla y al niño Jesú después
> de ser nascido; haziéndome yo vn pobrezito y esclauito indigno,
> mirándolos, contemplándolos y seruiéndolos en sus neccessidades,
> como si presente me hallase, con todo acatamiento y reuerencia
> possible [see Our Lady and Joseph and the servant girl and the child
> Jesus after his birth; making myself a poor and unworthy little slave,
> watching them, contemplating them and serving them in their
> needs, as if I were present, with all possible respect and reverence]
> (114).

In the Third Week, when the retreatant prays to share in the Passion, there is no
development in the images of self with which he is confronted. In the Fourth Week,
however, one notes a change. The images of service fade, and their place is taken by
others associated in the tradition with filial fear. In the first exercise, on the
appearence of the Risen Lord to His mother, the fifth point invites one to consider the
consoling mission of Christ, and to draw a comparison with the consolation offered to
one another by friends (224). In the *Contemplación para alcanzar amor* that follows, the
opening image is that of lovers who make a mutual exchange of gifts:

> el amor consiste en comunicación de las dos partes, es a saber, en dar
> y comunicar el amante al amado lo que tiene, o de lo que tiene o
> puede, y así, por el contrario, el amado al amante [love consists in
> communication between the two parties, namely, in the lover giving
> and communicating to the beloved what he has, or something of
> what he has or can offer, and similarly, on the other hand, the
> beloved to the lover] (231).

As the exercise unfolds, the retreatant is encouraged to apply the image to his
relationship with God, so that, having recognised the gifts he has received, he may
offer in return all that he is and has (234).

The image of lovers recurs later, in the rules *Para el sentido verdadero que en la
Yglesia militante debemos tener* with which the *Exercises* end. Although there is no
indication in the text of how these rules connect with the material included in the
Four Weeks, it is reasonable to suppose, as Pedro de Leturia pointed out, that they
take for granted the transformation of motive that the *Exercises* are intended to
effect.[47] Certainly they are informed by the spirit of disinterested love that fills the
Fourth Week. It is appropriate, therefore, that they should focus on the image of the
Church as the spouse of Christ, "la vera sposa de Xpo nuestro Señor" [the true bride

EODEM DIE APPARET MATRI MARIÆ VIRGINI. 135
cix

A. *Difcedentibus Sanctis, è veftigio venit in montem Sion IESVS, cum cœlefti comitatu, Matri apparet foli in conclaui; iucundifsimè colloquuntur.*

B. *Gerebantur hæc alijs infcijs, & mœrentibus, & mulieribus fe ad fepulcrum vifendum parantibus.*

C. *In fepulcro nulla mutatio.*

2.5 *The Appearance of the Risen Christ to His Mother.* An engraving in Jerome Nadal, S.J., *Adnotationes et meditationes in Evangelia* (Annotations and Meditations on the Gospels) (first published in Antwerp in 1595). Nadal (1507-80), a close collaborator of Ignatius, produced this influential collection of engravings and meditations, based on the Sunday Gospels of the liturgical year, to assist the training of young Jesuit seminarians. From the third edition (Antwerp: Plantin, 1607).

of Christ our Lord] (353). In the thirteenth rule, the retreatant is reminded that the Spirit who rules him is the Spirit who unites Christ and His bride: "entre Xpo nuestro Señor, esposo, y la Yglesia, su esposa, es el mismo espíritu que nos gouierna y rige para la salud de nuestras ánimas" [between Christ our Lord, the bridegroom, and the Church, his bride, is the same Spirit who governs and directs us for the salvation of our souls] (365). The nuptial imagery of the *Contemplación para alcanzar amor* is thereby given a context that is ecclesial: it is as a member of the Church that one is joined to the Lord in the intimate exchange of lovers.[48] Elsewhere in the rules, there are allusions also to the image of sonship. The Church is described on two occasions as a mother, "nuestra sancta madre Yglesia" [our holy mother the Church] (353; 365), and the retreatant is encouraged, by implication, to see himself as an offspring, a child.

OTHER SCHEMATA

In the course of the Middle Ages, the description of spiritual progress in terms of the grades of fear became connected with two other schemata, both rooted in the theology of the Fathers. The first of these was the division of Christians into three groups or classes, which eventually came to be termed "beginners, proficients, and perfect." In the East, it was associated, from the time of Mark the Hermit onwards, with the transition from fear to love, and with the imagery of servants, mercenaries, and sons.[49] In the West, it was disseminated through the writings of Gregory the Great, and it became part of the monastic tradition, where it was developed during the twelfth century by a number of writers, among them the Cistercian, William of St. Thierry, and the Carthusian, Guigo II.[50] Thomas Aquinas, in the *Summa Theologica*, connected it explicitly with the process by which love comes to perfection in the soul:

> diversi gradus caritatis distinguuntur secundum diversa studia ad quae homo perducitur per caritatis augmentum. Nam primo quidem incumbit homini studium principale ad recedendum a peccato et resistendum concupiscentis eius, quae in contrarium caritatis movent. Et hoc pertinet ad incipientes, in quibus caritas est nutrienda vel fovenda ne corrumpatur. Secundum autem studium succedit, ut homo principaliter intendat ad hoc quod in bono proficiat. Et hoc studium pertinet ad proficientes, qui ad hoc princi-paliter intendunt ut in eis caritas per augmentum roboretur. Tertium autem studium est ut homo ad hoc principaliter intendat ut Deo inhaereat et eo fruatur. Et hoc pertinet ad perfectos, qui *cupiunt*

dissolvi et esse cum Christo [Charity may be divided into various degrees which reflect the priorities towards which a person is drawn as it increases. First, the main priority of a person should certainly be to abandon sin and resist the disordered desires that impel one in a direction contrary to charity. This is characteristic of beginners, whose charity needs to be nourished and fostered so that it may not be destroyed. Following this there is a second priority, to strive principally to make progress in what is good. This priority is characteristic of the proficient, who strive principally for charity to grow and become stronger. There is then a third priority, in which a person strives principally towards union with God and enjoyment of Him. This is characteristic of the perfect, who "desire to be dissolved and to be with Christ" (Philippians 1:23)].[51]

The second schema was the division of spiritual progress into three stages or "ways": purgative, illuminative, and unitive. Its roots may be traced, in the East, to Evagrius Ponticus and Dionysius the Pseudo-Areopagite, but it did not become current in the West until the thirteenth century, when it was formulated in two influential works, in both of which it was linked to the gradual perfecting of love: the *Mystica theologica* [Mystical Theology] of Hugh of Balma, and the *De triplici via* [On the Threefold Way] of St. Bonaventure.[52] In the centuries that followed it became common to run the two schemata in parallel, matching each group of Christians with each of the three ways,[53] and at the end of the medieval period the process came to a head in the exercises of García de Cisneros, in which the various schemata are correlated in a systematic way. The three cycles of meditation that the *Exercitatorio* proposes correspond to the three grades of fear, servile, initial, and filial, as well as to the three ways, purgative, illuminative, and unitive; and the monk who makes them is described, in turn, as a beginner, a proficient, and one of the perfect.[54]

In the *Spiritual Exercises,* there are two passages which suggest a connection between the transition from servile to filial fear and the various schemata with which it had become associated. The first of these is the Tenth Annotation, in which Ignatius alludes to the three ways in the course of explaining how to use the rules for discernment during the Second Week:

Quando el que da los exercicios siente al que los rescibe, que es batido y tentado debaxo de especie de bien, entonces es proprio de platicarle sobre las reglas de la segunda semana ya dicha. Porque comúnmente el enemigo de natura humana tienta más debaxo de

especie de bien, quando la persona se exercita en la vida ylluminatiua, que corresponde a los exercicios de la 2a semana, y no tanto
en la vida purgatiua, que corresponde a los exercicios de la 1a
semana [When the one giving the exercises feels that the person
receiving them is being combatted and tempted under the
appearence of good, then it is fitting to talk to him about the rules
of the second week mentioned earlier. For normally the enemy of
human nature tempts more beneath the appearence of good when
the person is exercising himself in the illuminative life, which corresponds to the exercises of the 2nd week, and less so in the purgative
life, which corresponds to the exercises of the 1st week] (10).

The association of the First Week with the purgative way, and of the Second Week
with the illuminative way, recalls the definition of the schema set out by
St. Bonaventure in the *De triplici via*:

> Necesse est [...] per tres gradus ascendere secundum triplicem viam,
> scilicet purgativam, quae consistit in expulsione peccati; illumina
> tivam, quae consistit in imitatione Christi; unitivam, quae consistit
> in susceptione Sponsi [It is necessary [...] to ascend by the three
> ways, namely the purgative, which consists in the expulsion of sin,
> the illuminative, which consists in the imitation of Christ, and the
> unitive, which consists in the reception of the bridegroom].[55]

The second passage occurs later, in the *Examen general de consciencia* [General examen
of conscience], where there is a passing reference to the three groups or classes of
Christian. In the section entitled *De la palabra* [In word] a distinction is drawn
between swearing by the Creator and swearing by a creature:

> es más concedido a los perfectos jurar por la criatura, que a los imper
> fectos; porque los perfectos, por la assidua contemplación y
> ylluminación del entendimiento, consideran, meditan y contemplan
> más ser Dios nuestro Señor en cada criatura, según su propria
> essencia, presencia y potencia; y así en iurar por la criatura son más
> aptos y dispuestos para hazer acatamiento y reuerencia a su Criador
> y Señor, que los imperfectos [the perfect are given greater permission
> to swear by the creature than the imperfect; for the perfect, through
> assiduous contemplation and illumination of the understanding,

consider, meditate and contemplate more the presence of God our Lord in each creature, in his own essence, presence and power; and therefore when swearing by the creature they are more able and disposed to honour and reverence their Creator and Lord than the imperfect] (39).

The description of the "perfect" as those who are aware that "God our Lord is in every creature" calls to mind the *Contemplación para alcanzar amor*, in which the retreatant considers the presence of God throughout Creation:

> mirar cómo Dios habita en las criaturas: en los elementos dando ser, en las plantas vejetando, en los animales sensando, en los hombres dando entender y así en mý dándome ser, animando, sensando, y haziéndome entender [look how God dwells in creatures: in the elements, giving being; in the plants, growing; in the animals, sensing; in men, giving understanding; and so in me: giving me being, animating, sensing, and enabling me to understand] (235).

The parallel suggests a connection between the *Contemplación para alcanzar amor* and the unitive way, the stage associated in tradition with the "perfect" who are moved by love and filial fear.[56] The connection, however, is not explicit.

These two passages indicate that when Ignatius wrote them he was aware of how the various schemata had become linked in late medieval spirituality. They also explain the tendency among his followers to develop the parallels further, and to describe the structure of the *Exercises* almost entirely in their terms. It may be observed among his close companions, notably Jerónimo Nadal, who was one of the first to relate the three ways precisely to the sequence of the Four Weeks, and the unitive way, in particular, to the *Contemplación para alcanzar amor*:

> Hechos los exercicios, tiene el ánima con la gracia de Jesu Xpo. principios de oración en todas las tres vías de que tratan los contemplatiuos: por la primera semana, en la vía purgativa; y por la 2a y 3a, en la vía illuminativa, que es propria contemplación. Y aunque en estas no se aya de separar la vía vnitiua, empero es proprio della la 4a semana en el exercicio de amor con Dios [Once the exercises have been completed, the soul, by the grace of Jesus Christ, has the beginnings of prayer in all of the three ways of which contemplatives treat: as a result of the First Week, in the purgative way; and after

the 2nd and 3rd Weeks, in the illuminative way, which is contemplation itself. And although the unitive way must not be excluded from these (other weeks), it is none the less characteristic of the Fourth Week, in the exercise of the love of God].[57]

With slight differences, connected mainly with the position in the schema of the Third Week, the same correlation was made in the writings of subsequent commentators, and eventually it was incorporated into the Directories of 1591 and 1599.[58] The process came to completion in the *Camino espiritual* (Alcalá de Henares, 1626) [Spiritual Path] of Luis de la Palma, in which the purification of love that the *Exercises* suppose was related systematically not only to the three ways but to the three groups of Christians.[59]

Such developments were understandable, and perhaps legitimate. It may be argued, however, that they failed to take into account the fragmentary nature of the connections Ignatius made. The allusion in the Tenth Annotation to the three ways, for instance, is curious in several respects. It is inexact: the term used is *vida* not *vía* [*life* not *way*]; it is incomplete: there is no mention of the unitive way, or of how the Third and Fourth Weeks relate to it; and it is incidental: the subject of the annotation is discernment, and the ways are mentioned only insofar as they are pertinent to it. The allusion in the *Examen general* is incomplete also: there is no reference to the beginners or the proficient; instead the term *perfectos* [the perfect] is contrasted with an undifferentiated group called *los imperfectos* [the imperfect]. It is also incidental: the focus of attention in the passage is not the three groups of Christians but the morality of swearing. In much the same way, the only allusion in the *Exercises* to the transition from servile to filial fear is oblique: it is couched in general terms and, as we have seen, it does not refer specifically to the *Exercises* themselves, but to a teaching of the Church that required to be defended at the time.

How is one to explain the fact that in all these cases the connections made by Ignatius are partial rather than thorough, and allusive rather than direct? An answer may lie in the explicit definitions of purpose that occur early in the text. When framing them, Ignatius could have drawn on any of the schemata examined here, but he did not do so. Instead, he described a twofold process: first, the removal of affections that are disordered; and second, the quest for God's will in the disposition of one's life. It is announced in the First Annotation:

> todo modo de preparar y disponer el ánima para quitar de sí todas las
> affectiones desordenadas y, después de quitadas, para buscar y hallar
> la voluntad diuina en la disposition de su vida para la salud del

ánima, se llaman exercicios espirituales [all means of preparing and disposing the soul to remove from itself all disordered affections, and, once they have been removed, to seek and find the divine will in the disposition of one's life for the salvation of one's soul, are called spiritual exercises] (1).

In the annotations that follow, it is indicated that this transformation will be effected by God, who may be expected to work directly with his creature [15], while the retreatant, for his part, must go against his disordered affections, and strive for indifference, so that God Himself may reorder his desires [16]. At the end of the annotations, the process is resumed once more in a brief subtitle: "Exercicios espirituales para vencer a sí mismo y ordenar su vida, sin determinarse por affección alguna que desordenada sea" [Spiritual exercises for overcoming oneself and ordering one's life, without being ruled by any affection that is disordered] (21). The same understanding of purpose underlies the *Principio y Fundamento* [Principle and Foundation] (23), as well as the preparatory prayer (46), which prefaces almost every exercise during the retreat. It is intimately connected with the rules for discerning spirits (313-16), and it informs the material dealing with Elections during the Second Week (169-89). Many of the passages in which it is described date, in their present form, from Ignatius's years in France and Italy,[60] but the process itself may be traced back to his conversion, and in particular to his formative experiences in Manresa. It was there that he first encountered the *Imitation of Christ*, in which the removal of disordered affections and obedience to God's will are recurrent themes.[61] For most commentators, both early and modern, it is a defining feature of the *Exercises*, and everything in the text connects with it.[62] Seen in this light, the transition from servile to filial fear, and the schemas with which it was associated, form part of the background to the work, not the foreground. Or, to use a comparison that is scriptural (Matthew 13:33), they are like the ingredients that go into the baking of bread: although present, and essential, they lose their identity in the finished loaf, which has a flavour uniquely its own.

Conclusion

The study of servile and filial fear in the *Spiritual Exercises* reveals how familiar Ignatius was with the "accumulated tradition" of patristic and medieval spirituality, and it illustrates the freedom with which he adapted his sources and combined them in order to articulate what he called, "todo lo mejor que yo en esta vida puedo pensar, sentir y entender, así para el hombre poderse aprovechar a sí mesmo como para poder fructificar, ayudar y aprovechar a otros muchos" [everything best that in this life I can think, feel and understand for enabling a person both to benefit himself and to bring fruit, help and benefit to many others].[63] He took over, and adapted to his own ends, the teaching of the tradition on the grades of fear, a teaching rooted in the exegesis of Scripture, and he incorporated into the structure of his work the biblical images associated with it. It was not, however, the only structuring device that he used, a fact which helps to explain some of the difficulties that have arisen in modern times about the correct interpretation of the work. The transition from servile to filial fear was seen in the late medieval period as a prelude to the intimate union with God that perfect love makes possible.[64] What, then, is the relationship in the *Exercises* between the movement towards union which comes to a head in the Fourth Week, and the discernment of God's will in the disposition of one's life which reaches its climax in the Second Week? Does the work have two goals, one of them explicit, the other implied? Does it have two peak moments, one at the midpoint and the other at the end, or are these different phases of the same experience? Such questions have been debated often, and sometimes with passion, over the last hundred years, yet there has been no clear consensus about the answers.[65] Some commentators have argued that the *Exercises* centre on the election of a state of life which the Third and Fourth Weeks confirm. Others have held to the view that their purpose is the union of the soul with God, to which everything else, including the Election, is subordinate. Others again have sought an interpretation in between these two extremes, and recent commentators, in particular, have stressed that between the midpoint of the *Exercises* and their end there exists an essential continuity.[66] It may be argued that the problem is raised by the text itself, and specifically by the differences, of character and intent, that mark the various traditions on which Ignatius drew. The text, moreover, though it raises the problem, nowhere resolves it explicitly, no doubt because in the early days, when it first circulated among Ignatius's followers and friends,[67] the relationship between the Second Week and the Fourth was not a mystery, but something perfectly understood by those giving the *Exercises* and receiving them.

3.1 Title page of *La vida de Lazarillo de Tormes y de sus fortunas: y adversidades* (Alcalá de Henares: Salzedo, 1554). © British Library Board. All Rights Reserved. C.57.aa.21. This edition of the work and three others of 1554 (Antwerp, Burgos, Medina del Campo) indicate the existence of earlier editions, now lost.

Chapter Three

Prose Fiction: *Lazarillo de Tormes*

The presence in *Lazarillo de Tormes* of allusions to the Bible has long been recognised, and in recent years our knowledge of their extent has grown.[1] Discussion has focused, in particular, on the name of Lázaro himself, and the significance of its New Testament associations.[2] Less attention, however, has been devoted to the numerous parts of the work in which biblical texts are cited, and as a result certain questions concerning them remain unanswered. The first of these has to do with their incidence. In his edition of the text, published in 1963, R. O. Jones identified three passages in which such allusions might be found.[3] Three years later, in 1966, Claudio Guillén noted a total of nine.[4] So did Alberto Blecua in 1972, though his list and Guillén's differed slightly.[5] More recently, in his celebrated edition of 1987, Francisco Rico raised the figure to eleven (see Table 1), and subsequent editors have followed his lead.[6] It is reasonable to ask: are there further passages of the work in which biblical allusions occur? A further question concerns their precise nature. Some of the allusions that have been noted are to specific verses in the Bible. Others, by contrast, evoke phrases that occur repeatedly in both Testaments. Many of these "parallel" texts have been identified by Francisco Rico, but he does not consider them all, nor does he discuss in detail the contexts in which they arise. Is it possible to pinpoint them more precisely? Finally, there is the question of significance. In his study of religious language in the work, Víctor García de la Concha drew a distinction between religious phrases of a conventional kind and others in which a "latent" theological content comes to the fore.[7] How many of the biblical allusions in the text are simply traditional sayings and jokes, designed to make us laugh? And how many are charged, in addition, with a significance that throws light on the themes? The pages that follow seek to answer these questions by examining each of the allusions in turn.[8]

TRATADO PRIMERO

1:12-14. At the beginning of the account of his life, Lázaro tells how his father was imprisoned for theft at the mill where he worked, and he cites two biblical texts:

> Pues siendo yo niño de ocho años, achacaron a mi padre ciertas sangrías malhechas en los costales de los que allí a moler venían, por lo cual fue preso, y confesó y no negó y padeció persecución por justicia. Espero en Dios que está en la Gloria, pues el Evangelio los llama bienaventurados [Now when I was a boy of eight, my father was accused of certain clumsy bloodlettings in the sides of those who came there to use the mill, for which he was imprisoned, and he confessed and did not deny, and he suffered persecution in the cause of justice. I trust in God that he is in glory, since the Gospel calls them blessed] (1:10-14).

The first text, from John 1:20, refers to the words of John the Baptist: "And he confessed and did not deny: and he confessed: I am not the Christ." The second echoes Matthew 5:10 on the Sermon on the Mount: "Blessed are they that suffer persecution for justice's sake: for theirs is the kingdom of heaven" (cf. 1 Peter 3:14). Together they form a two-part joke which amuses because the allusions are incongruous: Lázaro's father, far from being Christlike, was a criminal. The first part (John 1:20) appears to be of the author's own devising. The second part (Matthew 5:10), by contrast, was traditional.[9] For early readers, it would have brought to mind a scene in *Celestina* where the old witch tells Pármeno of his mother's infamy, for which she was pilloried in public:

> el cura [...] viniéndola a consolar, dixo que la Santa Escritura tenía que bienaventurados eran los que padescían persecución por justicia, que aquéllos poseerían el reyno de los cielos. Mira si es mucho passar algo en este mundo por gozar de la gloria del otro. [The parish priest [...] coming to console her, told her that Holy Scripture held that blessed were those who suffered persecution in the cause of justice, that they would possess the kingdom of heaven. Consider if it matters much to suffer a little in this world in order to enjoy the glory of the next].[10]

Here there are the same puns on the meanings of "por" and "justicia."[11]

A few lines earlier in the text, Lázaro refers, indirectly, to another popular work of the time. Explaining why he is called Lázaro de Tormes, he relates:

> Mi padre, que Dios perdone, tenía cargo de proveer una molienda de una aceña, que está ribera de aquel río, en la cual fue molinero más

Biblical Allusions in *Lazarillo de Tormes*
TABLE 1

The following allusions to the Bible are noted by Francisco Rico in his standard edition of *Lazarillo* (Madrid: Cátedra, 1987). References to the text of *Lazarillo* follow the edition of R. O. Jones (Manchester: University Press, 1963), in which the lines are numbered.

Tratado primero
- 12-14: *John 1:20; Matthew 5:10.*
- 104-5: *Acts 3:6.*
- 106-7: *Matthew 15:14; Psalm 31:8.*
- 216 : *Deuteronomy 32:39; Job 5:17-18; Hosea 6:2.*
- 231 : *Proverbs 13:24.*

Tratado segundo
- 42: *1 Corinthians 11:24; Psalm 44:5.*
- 352-53: *Jonah 2:1; Matthew 12:40.*

Tratado tercero
- 194-95: *Deuteronomy 32:39; Job 5:17-18; Hosea 6:2.*
- 199-200: *Romans 11:33.*

Tratado quinto
- 139-40: *Mark 11:25*
- 156-57: *Ezekiel 18:32; 33:11.*

3.2   Table 1. Biblical Allusions in *Lazarillo de Tormes.*

de quince años; y estando mi madre una noche en la aceña, preñada de mí, tomóle el parto y parióme allí: de manera que con verdad me puedo decir nacido en el río [My father, whom God forgive, was responsible for running a water mill, situated on the bank of that river, where he was the miller for more than fifteen years; and one night when my mother was in the mill, and pregnant with me, she went into labour and gave birth to me there: so I can truly say I was born in the river] (1:5-10).

Lázaro's name recalls the romances of chivalry, in which a knight's *nom de guerre* (e.g., Palmerín de Inglaterra) incorporated the place from which he came,[12] and his birth in a river evokes, in particular, Amadís de Gaula, who was born in "una cámara apartada, de bóveda, sobre un río que allí pasaba" [an out-of-the-way chamber, with a vaulted ceiling, above a river that flowed there], and who, set adrift on the river as a baby, was known as "el doncel del mar" [the young knight of the sea] because "en la mar nació" [in the sea he was born].[13] These chivalric references are entertaining because inappropriate: Amadís was a royal prince, Lázaro is the child of poor parents. But they enable Lázaro to make a serious point. At the end of the *Prólogo*, which immediately precedes them, he explains that part of his reason for writing is to describe the misfortunes he has had to face, and in doing so to admonish those of noble birth:

> porque consideren los que heredaron nobles estados cuán poco se les debe, pues fortuna fue con ellos parcial, y cuánto más hicieron los que, siéndoles contraria, con fuerza y maña remando, salieron a buen puerto [so that those who inherited noble estates may consider how little they owe them to themselves, since Fortune favoured them, and how much more was achieved by those who, with Fortune against them, by rowing with vigour and skill, reached a good harbour] (Prólogo: 37-40).

Lázaro's family background is the first instance in his life of hostile fortune, and by stressing his parents' shortcomings (their *deshonra*) he is exalting his own achievement, the "buen puerto" he will reach in the end.[14]

1:42-43. Before telling how he left home to work for a series of masters, Lázaro recounts the fortunes of his mother, who, on learning of her husband's death, moved into Salamanca, where she became involved with a black slave, Zaide. Their child, "un negrito muy bonito" [a very handsome little black boy] (1:34), is the protagonist in a domestic scene that Lázaro recalls vividly:

> Y acuérdome que, estando el negro de mi padrastro trebejando con el mozuelo, como el niño vía a mi madre y a mí blancos, y a él no, huía dél con miedo para mi madre, y señalando con el dedo decía: "¡Madre, coco!"
>
> Respondió él riendo: "¡Hideputa!"
>
> Yo, aunque bien mochacho, noté aquella palabra de me hermanico, y dije entre mí:
>
> "¡Cuántos debe de haber en el mundo que huyen de otros porque no se veen a sí mesmos!"
>
> [And I recall that while my black stepfather was playing with the little lad, the child, on seeing that my mother and I were white and he was not, fled away from him in fear towards my mother, and pointing his finger said, "Mother, a bogeyman!" He replied, laughing, "Son of a bitch!" Though a very young boy, I noted that remark of my little brother, and said to myself, "How many there must be in the world who flee from others so as not to see themselves"] (1: 35-43).

As Jeremy Lawrance has observed,[15] Lázaro's reflection calls to mind Christ's parable of the beam and the mote:

> And why seest thou the mote that is in thy brother's eye; and seest not the beam that is in thy own eye? Or how sayest thou to thy brother: Let me cast the mote out of thy eye; and behold a beam is in thy own eye? Thou hypocrite, cast out first the beam out of thy own eye, and then shalt thou see to cast out the mote out of thy brother's eye (Matthew 7:3-5; cf. Luke 6:41-42).

The allusion, it would appear, is a warning to the reader not to judge Lázaro precipitately: the adventures he is about to narrate may not show him in a good light, but who has the right to cry "Coco"?[16]

1:104-5. The story of Lázaro's first master, which follows, brings together a striking number of biblical allusions in its account of the scene on the bridge in Salamanca, where the blindman taught the child a lesson: "Necio, aprende que el mozo del ciego un punto ha de saber más que el diablo" [Fool, learn that the blindman's boy must know one thing more than the devil] (1:95-96). As they make their way into the countryside, the blindman remarks: "Yo oro ni plata no te lo puedo dar, mas avisos para vivir muchos te mostraré" [I cannot give you gold or silver, but I'll give you many tips for life] (1:104-5). His words are a direct allusion to Acts 3:6, where St. Peter, on healing a crippled beggar, affirms: "Silver and gold I have none; but what I have, I give thee. In the name of Jesus Christ of Nazareth, arise and walk" (cf. 1 Peter 1:18-19). The allusion makes us smile, for it is, in the circumstances, grotesque: the blindman is not healing Lázaro, but corrupting him. The point is underlined by the words, "avisos para vivir muchos te mostraré" [I'll give you many tips for life], which call to mind several Old Testament passages where the acquisition of wisdom is contrasted with the possession of gold and silver: "The finest gold shall not purchase it: neither shall silver be weighed in exchange for it" (Job 28:15. Cf. Wisdom 7:9; Proverbs 3:14; 8:10-11, 19; 16:16).[17]

1:106-7. Reflecting on the blindman's promise, Lázaro writes: "Y fue ansí, que después de Dios éste me dio la vida, y siendo ciego me alumbró y adestró en la carrera de vivir" [And thus it was, for after God this man gave me life, and being blind he gave me light and guided me along the path of life] (1:106-7): just as St. Peter enabled the beggar, literally, to walk, so the blindman taught Lázaro to tread "the path of life."[18] The phrase recalls several passages of the Old Testament in which the Lord promises to guide his people's steps, including Psalm 31:8: "I will give thee under-standing and I will instruct thee in this way, in which thou shalt go" (also see Psalm 118:105,130; Isaiah 48:17).[19] Among such passages there are some that use the term *via vitae*, of which "la carrera de vivir" is a translation. Proverbs 10:17, for instance, promises "the way of life to him that observeth correction" (*via vitae custodienti disci-plinam*), while in Jeremiah 21:8 the Lord proclaims, "Behold I set before you the way of life" (*ecce ego do vobis viam vitae*) (cf. Proverbs 6:23; Psalm 15:11; Acts 2:28). Such allusions undercut Lázaro's claim that his master, after God, gave him life, a claim that evokes several biblical texts in which God is said to be life's author (e.g., Deuteronomy 32:39; 1 Kings 2:6; Wisdom 16:13; 1 Timothy 6:13), and the ironies come to a head in the remark, "siendo ciego me alumbró y adestró" [being blind he gave me light and guided me], a phrase which recalls Luke 6:39: "Can the blind lead the blind? Do they not both fall into the ditch?" (cf. Matthew 15:14).[20]

1:108-110. Lázaro concludes by summing up what the blindman taught him: "Huelgo de contar a V. M. estas niñerías para mostrar cuánta virtud sea saber los hombres subir siendo bajos, y dejarse bajar siendo altos cuánto vicio"

TRACTADO

mal de piedra que cafi tiene forma de
toro, y el ciego mandome que llegaſ
ſe cerca del animal, y alli puefto, me
dixo: Lazaro llega el oydo a efte tó
ro y oyras gran ruydo dentro del.
Yo fimplemente llegue creyendo fer
affi, y como fintio que tenia la cabeça
par dela piedra: afirmo rezio la mano,
y dio me vna gran calabaçada enel
diablo del toro que mas de tres dias
me turo el dolor dela cornada, y dixo
me: Necio aprende que el moço del
ciego vn punto ha de faber mas que
el diablo, y rio mucho la burla. Pa
refciome que en aquel inftante diſ
perte dela fimpleza, en que como ni
ño dormido eftaua, dixe entre mi: ver
dad dize efte, que me cumple abiuar
el ojo y auifar pues folo foy, y penfar
como me fepa valer. Començamos
nueftro camino y en muy pocos dias
me moftro jerigonça, y como me vieſ
ſe de buen ingenio: holgauafe mu
cho y dezia. Yo oro, ni plata no te lo
puedo dar, mas auifos para biuir mu
chos te moftrare: y fue affi que deſ
pues de Dios efte me dio la vida, y
fiendo ciego me alumbro y adeſ
tro en la carrera de biuir. Huelgo de
con

PRIMERO. 7

contara V. M. eftas niñerias para moſ
trar quanta virtud fea faber los hom
bres fubir fiendo baxos: y dexar ſe ba
xar fiendo altos, quanto vicio. Pues
tornando al bueno de mi ciego, y có
tando fus cofas. V. M. fepa que deſ
de que Dios crio el mundo: ninguno
formo mas aftuto ni fagaz, en fu ofi
cio era vn aguila: ciento y tantas ora
ciones fabia de coro, vn tono baxo re
pofado y muy fonable que hazia refo
nar la yglefia donde rezaua, vn roſ
tro humilde y deuoto que con muy
buen continente ponia quando reza
ua, fin hazer geftos ni vifajes, con
boca ni ojos, como otros fuelen ha
zer. Allende defto, tenia otras mil for
mas y maneras para facar el dinero,
dezia faber oraciones para muchos y
diuerfos efectos para mugeres que
no parian, para las que eftauan de par
to, para las que eran mal cafadas que
fus maridos las quifieffen bien. Echa
ua pronofticos a las preñadas fi trayan
hijo o hija. Pues en cafo de Medici
na, dezia Galeno no fupo la mitad
que el, para muelas, defmayos, males
de madre. Finalmente nadie le dezia
decer alguna paffion, que luego no

A 7   le

3.3 The description of the initiation of Lázaro on Salamanca bridge in *La vida de Lazarillo de Tormes, y de sus fortunas y aduersidades* (Antwerp: Martín Nucio, 1554), folios 6v-7r.
© British Library Board. All Rights Reserved. G.10133.
In this passage of the work the biblical allusions are particularly dense.

[I am delighted to tell Your Worship these childish things in order to show how much virtue there is when men manage to rise from the depths, and when they let themselves fall from a height, how much vice] (1:108-10). His words bring to mind a notion, well known in the Golden Age, which Cervantes was later to put succinctly: "El pobre a quien la virtud enriquece suele llegar a ser famoso; como el rico, si es vicioso, puede venir y viene a ser infame" [The poor man whom virtue has made rich usually becomes famous, just as the rich man, if he is given to vice, can and does become infamous].[21] The idea, as scholars have shown, may be traced back to the writings of the Stoic philosophers, notably Seneca:

> Platon ait neminem regem non ex servis esse oriundum, neminem servum non ex regibus. Omnia ista longa varietas miscuit et sursum deorsum fortuna versavit. Quis est generosus? Ad virtutem bene a natura compositus [Plato says: "Every king springs from a race of slaves, and every slave has had kings among his ancestors." The flight of time, with its vicissitudes, has jumbled all such things together, and Fortune has turned them upside down. Then who is well-born? He who is by nature fitted for virtue].[22]

Equally noteworthy, however, and highlighted by the preceding biblical allusions, are its roots in Scripture. In Ecclesiasticus, for instance, we read (10:17): "God hath overturned the thrones of proud princes: and hath set up the meek in their stead"; and in the Psalms (146:6): "The Lord lifteth up the meek: and bringeth the wicked down even to the ground." Such Old Testament passages, of which there are many, underlie, in the New Testament, Christ's teaching on virtue and vice: "whosoever shall exalt himself shall be humbled: and he that shall humble himself shall be exalted" (Matthew 23:12), and they are summed up in the lines of Mary's *Magnificat*: "He hath put down the mighty from their seat and hath exalted the humble" (Luke 1:52).[23] Commenting on Mary's words, the biblical scholar Jaume Pérez de Valencia had observed:

> Sicut iustitia dictat ut superbus humilietur et humilis exaltetur, ita dictat ut ingratus deponatur de sede dignitatis et potestatis, et humilis et gratus exaltetur, et substituatur et succedat in locum eius [Just as justice decrees that the proud be humbled and the humble raised up, so too it commands that the ungrateful be put down from the seat of dignity and power, and that the humble and grateful be raised up to supplant them and take their place].[24]

1:111-13. Lázaro's moral code, learnt from the blindman, is echoed subsequently in the course of his account (e.g. 2:100-102; 6:6-7) and recalled ironically at the end (7:80-81). Immediately after stating it, Lázaro writes: "Pues tornando al bueno de mi ciego y contando sus cosas, V. M. sepa que desde que Dios crió el mundo, ninguno formó más astuto ni sagaz" [Returning then to my good blindman and recounting things concerning him, Your Worship should know that since God made the world he has formed no one more astute or shrewd] (1:111-13). T. Anthony Perry suggested in 1970 that there might be an allusion here to Genesis 3:1, where Satan is described as a serpent: "Now the serpent was more subtle than any of the beasts of the earth which the Lord God had made."[25] Modern editors, on the whole, have not made the suggestion their own, but it has merit in view of the fact that the blindman is associated with Satan elsewhere in Lázaro's tale. His advice to Lázaro, "Necio, aprende que el mozo del ciego un punto ha de saber más que el diablo" [Fool, learn that the blindman's boy must know one thing more than the devil] (1: 95-96) is taken to heart by the child who gets his revenge in the end by being, literally, one step ahead of his master (1:405-15), and in between the initiation and the final scene there are repeated references to the blindman's devilish ways and Lázaro's devilish tricks (cf. 1:138, 152, 161, 277).[26] These references continue into the second *tratado*, where at one point Lázaro relates how he was driven by hunger to become "enemigo de la naturaleza humana" [an enemy of human nature] (2: 69-70), a phrase used of Satan in religious writings of the time,[27] and they reach a climax when the priest identifies the boy as a serpent who has invaded his house (2:350-51) and bids him farewell with the words:

> "Busca amo y vete con Dios, que yo no quiero en mi casa tan diligente servidor. No es posible sino que hayas sido mozo de ciego."
> Y santiguándose de mí como si estuviera endemoniado, tórnase a meter en casa y cierra su puerta ["Seek a master and go on your way with God, for I do not want in my house so diligent a servant. It can only be that you were once a blindman's boy." And blessing himself against me, as if I were possessed, he went back indoors and closed his door] (2:378-82).

1:214-17, 229-32. The biblical allusions between lines 104 and 113 are more closely packed and highly charged than those elsewhere in the book, and compared with them the remaining two allusions in *tratado primero* are straightforward. The first of these occurs when Lázaro reports what his master said on washing him with the wine he had tried to steal:

> Lavóme con vino las roturas que con los pedazos del jarro me había hecho, y sonriéndose decía: "¿Qué te parece, Lázaro? Lo que te enfermó te sana y da salud," y otros donaires que a mi gusto no lo eran [He washed in wine the cuts he had inflicted on me with the pieces of the pitcher, and smiling to himself he said, "What do you think, Lázaro? What made you sick is healing you and restoring health," and other quips that were not to my taste] (1:214-17).

The blindman's quip was a traditional joke whose origins lie, in part, in the Bible, where the image he invokes may be found in three passages, including Job 5:17-18: "Blessed is the man whom God correcteth: refuse not therefore the chastising of the Lord. For he woundeth, and cureth: he striketh, and his hands shall heal" (also see: Deuteronomy 32:39 and Hosea 6:2).[28] The second occurs a short time later when onlookers encourage the blindman to discipline his charge:

> Santiguándose los que lo oían, decían: "¡Mirá, quién pensara de un muchacho tan pequeño tal ruindad!" y reían mucho el artificio, y decíanle: "Castigadlo, castigadlo, que de Dios lo habréis" [Blessing themselves, those listening to him said, "Well, who would have expected such wickedness in a boy so small?", and they laughed heartily at the trick, and said to him, "Punish him, punish him, for your reward will come from God"] (1:229-32).

Francisco Rico has suggested that their advice may have a biblical source, such as Proverbs 13:24: "He that spareth the rod hateth his son: but he that loveth him correcteth him betimes."[29] Similar notions are expressed in several other passages, among them Ecclesiasticus 30:1: "He that loveth his son frequently chastiseth him" (cf. Proverbs 19:18, 23:13, 29:17). None of these biblical verses coincides exactly with the words the onlookers use, but they are indeed similar in sense.

TRATADO SEGUNDO

The allusions to the Bible in the second *tratado* are but one aspect of the use within it of religious terminology, a feature of its style that critics have found hard to interpret. For some, it is deeply significant, but for others it is not so, among them Francisco Rico, who has warned against taking it too seriously. In the notes to his edition, he quotes the view of Eugenio Asensio that it was common in sixteenth-century Spain to draw parallels between everyday events and passages of Scripture and the liturgy, but that usually the parallels were lighthearted. Rico, following him, concludes: "parece anacrónico buscar especial trascendencia en semejante uso de la fraseología y liturgia cristianas" [it seems anachronistic to seek particular significance in such a use of Christian phraseology and liturgy].[30]

2:37-43. Four of the passages in the second *tratado* where religious overtones occur also contain references to Scripture. One is the description of the priest's supper on Saturday nights:

> Los sábados cómense en esta tierra cabezas de carnero, y enviábame por una que costaba tres maravedís. Aquélla le cocía y comía los ojos y la lengua y el cogote y sesos y la carne que en las quijadas tenía, y dábame todos los huesos roídos, y dábamelos en el plato, diciendo: "Toma, come, triunfa, que para ti es el mundo. Mejor vida tienes que el Papa" [On Saturdays in those parts they eat heads of lamb, and he used to send me out for one costing three *maravedís*. This he would cook and eat the eyes and the tongue and the neck and the brains and the meat it had on the jaws, and he would give me all the gnawed bones, and give them me on the dish, saying, "Take, eat, rejoice. You have a better life than the Pope"] (2:37-43).

As Rico observes, the priest's command to the child ("Toma, come, triunfa ...") may be a proverbial saying. Similar phrases occur in *La lozana andaluza* (Venice, 1528), and later in the writings of Cervantes.[31] Parallels may be found also in collections of proverbs, including the anthology compiled in the early seventeenth century by Gonzalo de Correas, who associated one such saying with gluttons: "Komamos i bevamos, i nunka más valgamos (*Es de glotones*)" [Let us eat and drink, and never be respectable again (*a saying of gluttons*)].[32] There is also the twentieth-century compendium by Francisco Rodríguez Marín, who noted a connection with covetousness: "Comamos, bebamos y triunfemos, y con salud los enterremos (*Dicen, o piensan, los que heredan o esperan heredar*)" [Let us eat, drink and rejoice, and in good health let us bury them (*say, or think, those who have or expect an inheritance*)].[33] It is likely that such expressions go back to the Bible, where, in the Old Testament, it is said: "I commend mirth, because there was no good for a man under the sun but to eat and drink and be merry" (Ecclesiastes 8:15). In the New Testament the phrase recurs in Christ's parable of the rich man who, having gathered in all his possessions, prepared foolishly to enjoy them: "I will say to my soul: Soul, thou hast much goods laid up for many years. Take thy rest: eat, drink, make good cheer" (Luke 12:19). The parable, as García de la Concha has observed, is pertinent to the *Lazarillo*, where covetousness and gluttony are hallmarks of the priest.[34]

Another biblical allusion is possible too. According to some critics, the priest's words echo those of Christ at the Last Supper (Matthew 26:26), which are quoted in the Roman Canon of the Mass:

> Accepit panem in sanctas ac venerabiles manus suas, et elevatis oculis in caelum, ad te Deum Patrem suum omnipotentem, tibi gratias agens, benedixit, fregit, deditque discipulis suis, dicens: Accipite et manducate ex hoc omnes. Hoc est enim corpus meum [He took bread into His holy and venerable hands, and with His eyes lifted up to heaven, to You, God, His almighty Father, giving thanks to You, He blessed, broke, and gave to His disciples, saying, "Take and eat, all of you, of this: for this is My body"].[35]

Others, however, have been sceptical, among them García de la Concha, who remarks: "ni la semejanza textual parece estrecha, ni se ajusta al contexto inmediato de la novela" [The textual parallel does not seem close, nor does it fit the immediate context of the novel].[36] When considering the matter, it is helpful to bear in mind various references to the Mass which occur at this point in the tale. On meeting the boy, the priest asks him if he can serve Mass, and accepts him as his servant when he gathers that he can (2:3-7). Later we glimpse the priest during the Offertory, keeping an eye on the collection in the church (2:53-58). Later still, Lázaro mentions his "secreta oración" (2:139) [secret prayer], a phrase that recalls the *oratio secreta* of the liturgy.[37] Repeated references to Lázaro contemplating the bread in the box similarly call to mind the consecrated host in the tabernacle, especially the words, "como vi el pan, comencélo de adorar, no osando recebillo" [when I saw the bread, I started to adore it, not daring to receive it] (2:151-52), where the use of "adorar" and "recibir" makes clear the parallel with Holy Communion. Furthermore, just as Mass ends with a blessing and the words, "Ite, missa est" [Go, the Mass is ended], so the *tratado* concludes when the priest bids Lázaro to leave, blessing himself as he does so (and not, ironically, the child) (2:377-82).[38] These references encourage us to take seriously the possibility that the priest's words ("Toma, come, triunfa ...") contain an allusion to the words of consecration. Like the Last Supper, his meal is of lamb; it takes place on the eve of the Sabbath; and his invitation to the boy to eat is preceded by a string of actions that parallel those of Christ.

2:66-68. The description of the priest's meal, it may be said, combines, in compact form, several biblical allusions, and their point is clearly satirical. They draw attention to the sacramental role of the priest, and to the contrast, in the case of this particular man, between his office and his personal life. Outwardly, and in his words, he seems respectable, even pious, but Lázaro discovers the egoist within. At one point his master explains that, unlike other priests, he practises moderation in food and drink (2:64-65), but Lázaro observes: "el lacerado mentía falsamente, porque en cofradías y mortuorios que rezamos, a costa ajena comía como lobo y bebía más que un saludador" [The wretch was lying treacherously, for when we prayed in confraternities and at funerals, at others' expense he ate like a wolf and drank more than a quack] (2:66-68). The comparison here with a "lobo" [wolf] inevitably calls to mind Christ's warning against wolves in sheep's clothing: "Beware of false prophets, who come to you in the clothing of sheep, but inwardly they are ravening wolves" (Matthew 7:15; cf. Acts 20:29).

2:83-91. The *leitmotif* of death and resurrection, with its eucharistic connotations, is prolonged in later parts of the second *tratado* where biblical allusions occur, including Lázaro's description of the funerals at which he and his master ate well:

> viendo el Señor mi rabiosa y continua muerte, pienso que holgaba de matarlos por darme a mí vida. Mas de lo que al presente padecía, remedio no hallaba, que si el día que enterrábamos yo vivía, los días que no había muerto, por quedar bien vezado de la hartura, tornando a mi cuotidiana hambre, más lo sentía. De manera que en nada hallaba descanso, salvo en la muerte, que yo también para mí como para los otros deseaba algunas veces; mas no la vía, aunque estaba siempre en mí [Seeing my raging and continuous death, the Lord took pleasure, I think, in killing them to give life to me. But for what I was suffering in the present, I found no remedy, for if on a funeral day I had life, on days without a corpse, being used to satiety and returning to my everyday hunger, I felt it all the more. So in nothing did I find rest, except in death, which I sometimes desired, both for myself and for others; but I did not see it, even though it was always in me] (2:83-91).

Here the repeated jokes on the paradoxes of "life in death" and "death in life" evoke a scriptural theme summed up in the words, "he that findeth his life shall lose it: and he that shall lose his life for me shall find it" (Matthew 10:39), a theme echoed in

St. Paul's description of himself "as dying and behold we live" (*quasi morientes et ecce vivimus*: 2 Corinthians 6:9). Lázaro's remark about desiring death but not finding it (2:89-90) brings to mind passages in Job and the Apocalypse where such suffering is described (Job 3:21; Apocalypse 9:6), and his closing comment that death "estaba siempre en mí" [was always in me] (2:90-91) may carry an ironical reference to 2 Corinthians, where St Paul writes of finding death within himself: "we were pressed out of measure above our strength, so that we were weary even of life. But we had in ourselves the answer of death"; "for we who live are always delivered unto death for Jesus's sake: that the life also of Jesus may be made manifest in our mortal flesh. So then death worketh in us" (2 Corinthians 1:8-9; 4:11-12).

2:352-353. The *tratado* concludes with Lázaro's description of the days that followed his beating by the priest: "De lo que sucedió en aquellos tres días siguientes ninguna fé daré, porque los tuve en el vientre de la ballena" [Of what happened in those following three days I will give no account, because I spent them in the belly of the whale] (2:352-53). As Rico notes, this appears to be an allusion to the story of Jonah and the whale (Jonah 2:1), which Jesus applies in St. Matthew (12:40) to His Passion and raising from the tomb: "as Jonas was in the whale's belly three days and three nights: so shall the Son of man be in the heart of the earth three days and three nights."[39] Like the biblical allusions that precede it, this observation of Lázaro draws attention, ironically, to the ideal that underpins the vocation of the priest, an ideal that his life contradicts.

Tratado tercero

In the third *tratado*, references to Scripture are less frequent, a reflection, perhaps, of the character of Lázaro's new master, the squire. He hears Mass devoutly (3:32-35), and wears, at his waist, a rosary of large beads (3:179-80), but in his inner life, it seems, religion plays no part. The biblical allusions that do occur, moreover, are found together in a passage that voices the thoughts of the child, not his master. One morning, after watching the squire dress with care, Lázaro looks on as he strides up the street and reflects:

> ¡Bendito seáis vos, Señor, [...] que dais la enfermedad y ponéis el remedio! ¿Quién encontrara a aquel mi señor que no piense, según el contento de sí lleva, haber anoche bien cenado y dormido en buena cama, y aunque agora es de mañana, no le cuenten por muy bien almorzado? ¡Grandes secretos son, Señor, los que vos hacéis y las gentes ignoran! ¿A quién no engañara aquella buena disposición

y razonable capa y sayo, y quién pensara que aquel gentil hombre se
pasó ayer todo el día sin comer, con aquel mendrugo de pan que su
criado Lázaro trujo un día y una noche en el arca de su seno, do no
se le podía pegar mucha limpieza, y hoy, lavándose las manos y cara,
a falta de paño de manos, se hacía servir de la halda del sayo? Nadie
por cierto lo sospechara. ¡Oh Señor, y cuántos de aquéstos debéis vos
tener por el mundo derramados, que padecen por la negra que
llaman honra lo que por vos no sufrirían! [Blessed be to you, Lord,
[...] who give the illness and apply the remedy! Who, on seeing that
master of mine, would not think, so satisfied with himself does he
seem, that last night he dined well and slept in a good bed, and
though it is now morning, who would doubt that he has eaten an
excellent meal? Great are the hidden things, Lord, that you perform
and people do not see! Who would not be fooled by that good disposition and reasonable-looking cape and tunic, and who would think
that gentleman spent the whole of yesterday without eating, with
merely that crust of bread which his servant Lázaro bore for one day
and one night in the ark of his bosom, where it cannot have picked
up much cleanness, and that today, on washing his hands and face, for
want of a hand-towel he used the hem of his tunic? No one, certainly,
would suspect this. O Lord, and how many people of that kind must
you have, scattered through the world, who suffer for the curse they
call honour what they would not suffer for you!] (3:194-209).

3:194-95. His thoughts begin with another version of the biblical adage cited in the
first *tratado* (1:216-17): "Blessed is the man whom God correcteth: refuse not therefore
the chastising of the Lord. For He woundeth, and cureth: He striketh, and His hands
shall heal" (Job 5:17-18. Cf. Deuteronomy 32:39, Hosea 6:2). Now, however, there is
a difference of tone. Lázaro's words express not so much amusement as wonder and
concern, and they form the preamble to a heartfelt prayer. The opening phrase,
"¡Bendito seáis vos, Señor...!," was an accepted formula of devotion. It may be found,
for instance, in the *Libro de la vida* (1565) of St. Teresa of Ávila: "¡Bendito seáis vos,
Señor, que tanto me havéis sufrido! . . . ¡Bendito seáis vos, Señor, que tan inhábil y sin
provecho me hecistes! . . . ¡Bendito seáis vos, Señor, que ansí me remediastes!" [Blessed
be to you, Lord, who have put up with me so much! . . . Blessed be to you, Lord, who
made me so incompetent and useless! . . . Blessed be to you, Lord, for thus did you correct
me!].[40] The phrase itself was based on prayers in the Old Testament and the New,
including Psalm 118:12, "Blessed art thou, O Lord: teach me Thy justifications," and the

first verse of the *Benedictus*: "Blessed be the Lord God of Israel: because He hath visited and wrought the redemption of His people" (Luke 1:68).[41]

3:199-200. Lázaro's reflections then move on to the omnipotence and omniscience of God: "¡Grandes secretos son, Señor, los que vos hacéis y las gentes ignoran!" [Great are the hidden things, Lord, that you perform and people do not see!] (3:199-200). His remark brings to mind several verses of Scripture that dwell on God's mysterious ways. One of them is Romans 11:33: "O the depth of the riches of the wisdom and of the knowledge of God! How incomprehensible are His judgments, and how unsearchable His ways!" There is also Job 5:8-9: "I will pray to the Lord, and address my speech to God. Who doth great things and unsearchable and wonderful things without number."[42] A further verse, of particular interest, is Ecclesiasticus 11:4: "Glory not in apparel at any time, and be not exalted in the day of thy honour: for the works of the Highest only are wonderful, and His works are glorious, and secret, and hidden." This last allusion is pertinent in several ways. First, the focus on clothing is apt in the case of the squire, whose garments as "un hombre de bien" [gentleman] are frequently mentioned. As Lázaro puts it in what immediately follows: "¿A quién no engañara aquella buena disposición y razonable capa y sayo?" [Who would not be fooled by that good disposition and reasonable-looking cape and tunic?] (3:200-201). Second, the warning against being "exalted in the day of thy honour" is a reminder of the blindman's moral code, and connects with Lázaro's wish that the squire would "lower" his pretensions: "Sólo tenía dél un poco de descontento: que quisiera yo que no tuviera tanta presunción, mas que abajara un poco su fantasía con lo mucho que subía su necesidad" [I was displeased with him only a little: I would prefer if he did not have so much presumption, but lowered a little his pretensions to match the great rise in his need] (3:347-49). The verse occurs in a context that is relevant too: the tenth and eleventh chapters of Ecclesiasticus concern the nature of true honour, which does not depend, they affirm, on externals: "Praise not a man for his beauty: neither despise a man for his look" (Ecclesiasticus 11:2). Its basis is, instead, virtue, and it is conferred, not by men, but by God, who alone has the power to raise up and cast down: "Many tyrants have sat on the throne: and he whom no man would think on hath worn the crown. Many mighty men have been greatly brought down: and the glorious have been delivered into the hand of others" (Ecclesiasticus 11:5-6).[43] In his commentary on Ecclesiasticus 11:4, Denis the Carthusian underlined such points and concluded:

> Pauca vidimus operum eius. Et apostolus ait: *Quam incomprehensibilia sunt iudicia eius, et investigabiles viae eius.* Qui superbos potest subito

dejicere, et humiles exaltare. Interea si tam periculosum est in die proprii honoris extolli, etiam his qui ad honores promoventur inviti, quantum periculum imminet eis qui directe aut indirecte ad promotionem suam aspirant, aut eam aliquo modo procurant [Of His works we glimpse little. As the Apostle says, "How incomprehensible are his judgments, and how unsearchable his ways!" He who can suddenly put down the proud and raise up the meek. If, indeed, it is so dangerous to be exalted in the day of one's honour, even in the case of those who are invited to accept honours, how much danger must threaten those who, directly or indirectly, seek their own promotion, or somehow procure it?].[44]

3:207-9. The child's prayer concludes: "¡O Señor, y cuántos de aquéstos debéis vos tener por el mundo derramados, que padecen por la negra que llaman honra lo que por vos no sufrirían!" [Oh Lord, and how many people of that kind must you have, scattered through the world, who suffer for the curse they call honour what they would not suffer for you!] (3:207-9). In this remark, Marcel Bataillon discerned a possible reminiscence of the fourth rule of Erasmus's *Enchiridion*, "que el fin de todas nuestras obras, oraciones y devociones ha de ser sólo Jesu Christo" [the end of all our works, prayers and devotions must be Jesus Christ alone], a rule summed up in the phrase, "la summa honrra es aplazer a Jesu Christo" [the highest honour is to please Jesus Christ].[45] In the life of his master, Lázaro seems to affirm, honour has taken the place due to Christ: he is guilty, that is, of idolatry. This insight into the squire's spiritual state helps to explain the curious phrase, "por el mundo derramados." In the Old Testament being "scattered through the world" was the standard punishment for presumption. It is first mentioned in Genesis 11:4, where the rebellious citizens of Babel resolve to win renown by raising a tower to Heaven: "let us make our name famous, before we be scattered abroad into all lands." Their punishment is, as they fear, to be scattered throughout the world: "And so the Lord scattered them from that place into all lands, and they ceased to build the city" (Genesis 11:8). When, subsequently, the Chosen People sin, they suffer the same fate, and are threatened with exclusion from the Promised Land, often because they have become idolators: "I will disperse thee in the nations and will scatter thee among the countries" (Ezekiel 22:15).[46] In the New Testament the theme recurs in the *Magnificat*: "He hath shewed might in His arm: He hath scattered the proud in the conceit of their heart" (Luke 1:51). The squire, it would seem, is one of those "por el mundo derramados" by the Lord, who suffers, because of his presumption, the hardship of exile from his home.[47]

Tratado quinto

5:86-88. In the first three *tratados*, many of the allusions to Scripture have a thematic role: they draw our attention to Gospel teachings that each master, in his own way, flouts. This is not the case in *tratado quinto*, which differs from them in other ways too,[48] but it does contain a number of biblical allusions, each voiced by the pardoner in scenes that take place within the parish church. The first four occur in the remarks he makes after listening to the denunciations of the *alguacil* [constable]. Addressing God directly in prayer, he says: "Señor Dios, a quien ninguna cosa es escondida, antes todas manifiestas, y a quien nada es imposible, antes todo posible, tú sabes la verdad y cuán injustamente yo soy afrentado" [Lord God, from whom nothing is hidden, rather all things known, and to whom nothing is impossible, rather all things possible, you know the truth and how unjustly I am insulted] (5:86-88). Here there are echoes of the liturgy, in particular of a prayer associated specifically with divine inspiration, the Collect of the Mass of the Holy Spirit, which was also said privately by every celebrant before Mass began:

> Deus, cui omne cor patet, et omnis voluntas loquitur, et quem nullum latet secretum: purifica per infusionem sancti Spiritus cogitationes cordis nostri, ut te perfecte diligere, et digne laudare mereamur [O God, to whom every heart lies open, and every wish speaks, and from whom no secret lies hidden; purify the thoughts within our hearts by the outpouring of the Holy Spirit, so that we may be worthy to love you perfectly and to give you fitting praise].[49]

The liturgical echoes may be traced back in turn to passages in the Bible which declare that nothing is hidden from God (e.g., Ecclesiasticus 17:13, 39:24; Jeremiah 16:17) and that for Him all things are possible (e.g., Genesis 18:14; Jeremiah 32:17, 27; Zacharias 8:6; Luke 1:37; Mark 10:27).

5:88-99. The pardoner goes on to affirm, "En lo que a mí toca, yo lo perdono porque tú, Señor, me perdones" [For my part I forgive him, so that You, Lord, may forgive me] [5:88-89], an allusion, it would seem, to Matthew 6:14: "if you will forgive men their offences, your heavenly Father will forgive you also your offences." He adds, sanctimoniously, "No mires a aquél que no sabe lo que hace ni dice" [Do not look on that man, for he does not know what he does or says] (5:90), a reference to Christ's prayer on the Cross, "Father, forgive them, for they know not what they do" (Luke 23:34). Then, to prove his innocence, he calls on Heaven for a sign: "Si es verdad lo que aquél dice y que yo traigo maldad y falsedad, este púlpito se hunda comigo y meta siete estados debajo de tierra, do él ni yo jamás parezcamos" [If what that man says is true, and I am a carrier of evil and falsity, let this pulpit sink with me, and lie seven *estados* (= approximately 40 feet) beneath the earth, neither he nor I ever reappearing] (5:96-99). His words, as Claudio Guillén observed, allude to the Old Testament scene in which Moses called down a curse on the sons of Korah, who had questioned his authority: "if the Lord do a new thing, and the earth opening her mouth swallow them down, and all things that belong to them, and they go down alive into hell, you shall know that they have blasphemed the Lord" (Numbers 16:30; cf. 16:28).[50]

5:139-40, 153-60. The two remaining allusions arise later in the tale when the pardoner is roused from prayer to tend the *alguacil*, who has collapsed in a fit. To the bewildered parishioners, he says of the Almighty: "él nos manda que no volvamos mal por mal y perdonemos las injurias" [He commands us not to return evil for evil, and to forgive injuries] (5:139-40). Rico finds here a reference to Mark 11:25: "when you shall stand to pray, forgive, if you have aught against any man: that your Father also, who is in heaven, may forgive you your sins."[51] Pertinent also are Proverbs 20:22 ("Say not: I will return evil for evil"), and three passages in the New Testament: "to no man rendering evil for evil" (Romans 12:17), "see that none render evil for evil to any man" (1Thessalonians 5:15), and "not rendering evil for evil [...] but contrariwise, blessing" (1Peter 3:9). Then, before healing the *alguacil* by placing, on his head, the papal bull, the pardoner offers a moving prayer:

> comienza una oración no menos larga que devota, con la cual hizo
> llorar a toda la gente como suelen hazer en los sermones de Pasión
> de predicador y auditorio devoto, suplicando a Nuestro Señor, pues
> no quería la muerte del pecador, sino su vida y arrepentimiento, que
> aquel encaminado por el demonio y persuadido de la muerte y
> pecado, le quisiese perdonar y dar vida y salud, para que se arrepin-
> tiese y confesase sus pecados [He began a prayer as long as it was
> devout, with which he made all the people weep, as they usually do
> in Passion sermons with a preacher and a devout congregation,
> beseeching Our Lord, since he did not want the sinner to die but to
> live and repent, to deign to grant pardon, life and health to that man
> led astray by the devil and persuaded by death and sin, so that he
> might repent and confess his sins] (5:153-60).

His words allude to several passages in Scripture, notably Ezekiel 18:23: "Is it My will that a sinner should die, saith the Lord God, and not that he should be converted from his ways and live?"[52] The reference is appropriate, for the Ezekiel verse was associated at the time with those whose salvation was most at risk. It was invoked, for instance, on Good Friday, in the Church's prayers for pagans:

> Omnipotens sempiterne Deus, qui non mortem peccatorum sed vitam semper inquiris: suscipe propitius orationem nostram, et libera eos ab idolorum cultura, et agrega Ecclesiae tuae sanctae, ad laudem et gloriam nominis tui [Almighty and eternal God, who always seek not the death but the life of sinners: mercifully hear our prayer, and deliver them from the worship of idols, and for the praise and glory of your name, admit them into your holy Church].[53]

The Inquisition invoked it too when sparing a life, a point noted by Guillén, who cites the sentence delivered in 1529 in the case of Pedro Ruiz de Alcaraz:

> queriendo usar con él de nuestra misericordia, teniendo alguna esperanza de su conversión, siguiendo la doctrina de Nuestro Salvador y Redentor Jesucristo, que no quiere la muerte del pecador, salvo que se convierta y viva [. . .]. [wishing to treat him in accord with our mercy, having some hope of his conversion, following the teaching of Our Saviour and Redeemer, Jesus Christ, who does not wish the sinner to die, but to be converted and live [. . .]].[54]

All the biblical allusions in the *tratado* serve the purpose of depicting the pardoner's cool hypocrisy, and in doing so they heighten the hilarity of the events Lázaro recounts. They are apposite also in a further sense: most of them concern the forgiveness of sins, the end that a plenary indulgence was intended to serve, and the theme, presumably, of the pardoner's preaching.

TRATADO SÉPTIMO

7:15-18. In the seventh and last *tratado* there are two biblical allusions, both of which refer back to earlier passages in the book. The first occurs early on when Lázaro describes the duties that his "oficio real" (7:12) [royal post] involves:

> Y es que tengo cargo de pregonar los vinos que en esta ciudad se venden, y en almonedas y cosas perdidas, acompañar los que padecen persecuciones por justicia y declarar a voces sus delitos:

pregonero, hablando en buen romance [And it (my job) is that I am responsible for making proclamation of the wines sold in this town and things for sale and lost, for accompanying those suffering persecution in the cause of justice, and for shouting out their crimes: a town crier, to speak frankly] (7:15-18).

The reference to criminals as "los que padecen persecución por justicia" [those suffering persecution in the cause of justice] reminds us of Matthew 5:10, and its application in the first *tratado* to his father. Now, however, the tone is less jesting. Lázaro has a serious point: with the help of God, as he puts it, he has risen above his origins at last: "quiso Dios alumbrarme y ponerme en camino y manera provechosa" [God willed to give me light and to set me on my path and in a profitable way] (7:8-9; cf. 1:107). His claim is undermined, however, by what follows: the description of his marriage to the archpriest's mistress, which makes him a public cuckold. Despite his efforts, it would appear, he has failed to shake off the *deshonra* of his roots.[55]

7:80-81. Lázaro, ostensibly at least, does not see it so. In the closing lines of the tale he affirms:

> Esto fue el mesmo año que nuestro victorioso Emperador en esta insigne ciudad de Toledo entró y tuvo en ella cortes, y se hicieron grandes regocijos, como vuestra merced habrá oído. Pues en este tiempo estaba en mi prosperidad y en la cumbre de toda buena fortuna [This was the same year in which our victorious Emperor entered this famous town of Toledo and summoned a parliament in it, and great celebrations took place, as Your Worship will have heard. For at this time I was in my prosperity and at the height of all good fortune] (7: 77-81).

Having begun his account with a contrast between his family, plagued by misfortune, and the royal birth of Amadís, Lázaro now ends with a parallel between his achievements, which Fortune has blessed, and those of the Emperor Charles V,[56] and his image of rising to a summit or peak takes us back to the summary, in the first *tratado*, of the moral code he learnt from the blindman: "Huelgo de contar a V. M. estas niñerías para mostrar cuánta virtud sea saber los hombres subir siendo bajos, y dejarse bajar siendo altos cuánto vicio" [I am delighted to tell Your Worship these childish things in order to show how much virtue there is when men manage to rise from the depths, and when they let themselves fall from a height, how much vice] (1:108-10).

Reread in the light of his practice, these words are now charged with irony. For Lázaro honour is not a matter of noble birth: his prologue made that clear. Nor does it depend, simply, on appearance and reputation: he rejected the notions of the squire. Instead it derives from integrity, and to this, with mock seriousness, he lays claim.[57] But in what does his integrity consist? When, at the end, we reconsider his moral code, as the text invites us to do, we discover in it a meaning that we had not, perhaps, first observed. Lázaro, strictly speaking, does not describe "rising" as the reward of virtue and "falling" as the punishment of vice, as the Bible, like the Stoics, had affirmed. Instead, as R. W. Truman noted, he indicates that to rise *is* virtue and that to fall *is* vice,[58] a statement that runs counter to the wisdom of the Bible and empties its words of their sense.

CONCLUSION

The number of passages in *Lazarillo* that contain allusions to the Bible is in excess of twenty (see Table 2), a greater total than has been supposed. The allusions themselves vary greatly in kind. Some recall specific verses; others carry vaguer reminiscences of biblical turns of phrase; others again are to themes and images that occur in several parts of Scripture. They vary also in their sources. A number appear to derive directly from the Bible itself, but others, a majority, are drawn from it indirectly, through popular sayings, traditional jokes and familiar passages of the liturgy. These features are consistent with the style of the book, in which popular material and learned references are combined, in accordance with a humanist taste for "witty sayings," and "well rounded phrases, adages or apothegms."[59] In the work as a whole, moreover, the biblical allusions play a significant part. All of them, one way or another, contribute to the comedy of the tale, but many, in addition, reinforce its satire, by reminding the reader of the values that Lázaro and his masters subvert.

It remains to ask: do the allusions throw light on the beliefs of the anonymous author? The question is a compelling one, but the answer has to be "no," for at no point does the author speak in his own voice. He creates, by means of irony, a point of view which is often at odds with the literal sense of Lázaro's words, and which therefore encourages a sceptical response to his claims.[60] This point of view, which conveys the stance of the "implied" author of the tale, has been associated by critics with various responses to the crises of early sixteenth-century Spain, including illuminism, protestantism, *converso* scepticism and *comunero* dissent. Despite prolonged debate, however, it has not proved possible to identify it convincingly with any one movement of thought, not even with the Erasmianism that flourished in Spain during the years in which it was composed.[61] Even if this were possible, it would still not be clear how far the implied author's viewpoint coincides with the real author's personal convictions. The continuing anonymity of the work, and the ambiguities that make its interpretation problematic, have ensured that the matter remains open to debate.[62] What may be said is that the real author, by ironically invoking the Bible at key points, allows the characters he depicts, and the society they represent, to be judged by the standard of the sacred texts whose authority they profess to accept, and that this device provides much of the work's comedy, as well as its satirical bite.

Biblical Allusions in *Lazarillo de Tormes*
TABLE 2

Note: an asterisk indicates that the biblical verse cited forms part of a chain of parallel references, details of which may be found in the text and notes of the present chapter.

Tratado primero
- 12-14: *John 1:20; Matthew 5:10.*
- 42-43: *Matthew 7:3-5.*
- 104-5: *Acts 3:6; Job 28:15.**
- 106-7: *Psalm 31:8*; Proverbs 10:17*; Deuteronomy 32:39*; Luke 6:39.*
- 108-10: *Ecclesiasticus 10:17*; Matthew 23:12*; Luke 1:52.**
- 111-13: *Genesis 3:1.*
- 214-17: *Job 5:17-18.**
- 229-32: *Proverbs 13:24; Ecclesiasticus 30:1.**

Tratado segundo
- 37-43: *Ecclesiastes 8:15; Luke 12:19; Matthew 26:26.*
- 66-68: *Matthew 7:15.*
- 83-91: *Matthew 10:39; 2 Corinthians 6:9; Job 3:21; Apocalypse 9:6; 2 Corinthians 1:8-9; 4:11-12.*
- 352-53: *Jonah 2:1; Matthew 12:40.*

Tratado tercero
- 194-95: *Job 5:17-18* ;Psalm 118:12*; Luke 1:68.**
- 199-200: *Romans 11:33; Job 5:8-9; Ecclesiasticus 11:4.*
- 207-9: *Genesis 11:4*; Ezekiel 22:15*; Luke 1:51.**

Tratado quinto
- 86-88: *Ecclesiasticus 17:13*; Genesis 18:14.**
- 88-89: *Matthew 6:14.*
- 90: *Luke 23:34.*
- 96-99: *Numbers 16:30.*
- 139-40: *Mark 11:25; Proverbs 20:22; Romans12:17; 1Thessalonians 5:15; 1Peter 3:9.*
- 153-60: *Ezekiel 18:23.**

Tratado séptimo
- 15-18: *Matthew 5:10.*
- 80-81: cf. *Tratado 1: 108-110*

3.4   Table 2. Biblical Allusions in *Lazarillo de Tormes.*

4.1 *Fray Luis de León*. A portrait by Francisco Pacheco (1564-1644), from the *Libro de descripción de verdaderos retratos de ilustres y memorables varones*. The biblical passage cited is an adaptation of Ecclesiasticus 15:5: "The Lord filled him with the spirit of wisdom and understanding."

Chapter Four

Poetry: Luis de León and the Ascension of Christ

The writings of Luis de León bear witness to his conviction that to understand the Bible one must study it in the languages in which it was originally composed. He defended this conviction throughout his trial before the Spanish Inquisition, arguing, with eventual success, that it was compatible with due reverence for the Vulgate, which the Council of Trent had decreed.[1] Unlike some of his contemporaries, however, whose interests were primarily philological, he did not consider that determining the literal sense of Scripture was important as an end in itself.[2] It was, though crucial, but one element in a process of enquiry that had as its goal the spiritual or mystical sense of the sacred words, in which the mystery of Christ (*el mysterio de Christo*) was concealed.[3] To discover this hidden sense, he held, it was necessary to draw not only on knowledge of the ancient languages involved, but on two disciplines of a theological kind: the biblical exegesis of the Fathers of the Church, and the scholastic learning of the medieval schoolmen.[4] His ideas on the subject are set out in a document from his trial: "Dije que para el entero entendimiento de la Escritura era menester saberlo todo: la Teología escolástica, lo que escribieron los Santos, las lenguas griega y hebrea" [I said that for the complete understanding of Scripture it was necessary to know everything: Scholastic theology, the writings of the Saints, the Greek and Latin languages].[5] Of particular value, to his mind, were the teachings of the Fathers, and the traditions of exegesis to which they had given rise. Accused during his trial of having treated them disrespectfully, he replied that on the contrary he had always sought in them a guide to Scripture's meaning: "Nunca me mofé, sino estimé en mucho, las declaraciones del común de los santos. No dije que no sabían escritura, antes enseñé que de ellos se había de tomar el entendimiento della" [I never ridiculed, but greatly esteemed, the interpretations of the generality of Saints. I did not say that they did not know Scripture, instead I taught that from them one should take its understanding].[6] He later summed up his views in *Los nombres de Cristo* [The Names of Christ], in the course of an attack on so-called "theologians" who were blind to the nature of their calling:

> No tienen la theología; de la qual, como se entiende, el principio son
> las questiones de la Escuela, y el crecimiento la docrina que escriven

los sanctos, y el colmo y perfección y lo más alto de ella las letras sagradas, a cuyo entendimiento todo lo de antes, como a fin necesario, se ordena [They do not have theology, whose beginning, as it is agreed, is in the questions of the Schools, and whose growth is in the teaching written by the Saints, and whose summit and perfection and highest point is Sacred Scripture, to the understanding of which everything aforementioned is ordered, as to a necessary end].[7]

The approach to the Bible in which Fray Luis believed had a shaping influence on his prose, as modern scholars have shown, especially on the three great works of exegesis that he completed late in life: the *Exposición del Libro de Job* [Explanation of the Book of Job], the Latin commentary on the *Song of Songs*, and *Los nombres de Cristo*.[8] Its impact on his poetry, however, is less obvious, and it has been left, on the whole, unexplored. A case in point is his ode on the Ascension of Christ, which survives in two versions, the longer of which is generally considered apocryphal.[9] The biblical passages on which the shorter version is based, and others to which it alludes, have been identified and discussed in a number of studies, but its connections with patristic and medieval thought have been examined in few. The present essay will consider in turn two exegetical traditions that appear to have left their mark on the shorter version, and it will then review, in their light, the longer version's authenticity. Both traditions figure prominently in patristic and medieval sermons on the Ascension, whose relevance to the ode Senabre has underlined,[10] and both, significantly, stem in part from the corpus of writings associated with St. Augustine, the patron of the religious order to which Fray Luis belonged.

THE DISTRESS OF THE DISCIPLES

The five stanzas of the ode, in the shorter version, dramatise the events described briefly in one verse of the *Acts of the Apostles*: "And when He had said this, as they were looking on, He was lifted up, and a cloud took Him out of their sight" (Acts 1:9). The ode begins (stanza 1) with Christ rising up into the sky, and it ends (stanza 5) with His occlusion by the cloud. The viewpoint from which it is narrated is that of the disciples, who watch Him ascend and disappear, and who experience, as they do so, the anguish of loss. This interpretation of their feelings is not found in *Acts*, which dwells on the fact that they gazed into the sky (Acts 1:9-11) but not on the emotions they felt. *Acts* does, however, underline their limited understanding of Jesus and His mission by noting the inappropriate question they asked him beforehand (verse 6: "Lord, wilt Thou at this time restore again the kingdom of Israel?") and their need for guidance once he had disappeared (verses 10-11).[11] Their lack of understanding, and the weakness of faith that it implies, is the subject of Fray Luis's poem.

To describe the disciples' feelings when their master left them, the Fathers turned to another part of the New Testament in which the subject is explored: the discourse of Jesus at the Last Supper, recorded in the Gospel of St. John (chapters 14-17), in which he tells them of His approaching departure and seeks to allay their distress: "Do not let your hearts be troubled or afraid. . . . I have told you this now, before it happens, so that when it does happen you may believe" (John 14: 27, 29). The most influential Western commentary on His words was that of St. Augustine, who considered them at length in his homilies on the Gospel. It was necessary, he argued, that the disciples should lose sight of Jesus, because they were too attached to His physical presence. By ascending into heaven, He was preparing them for the descent of the Holy Spirit at Pentecost, when He would become present within them in a new and more intimate way. On hearing these things, however, they did not understand and were afraid:

> Videbat utique quid illa sua uerba in eorum cordibus agerent: spiritalem quippe nondum interius habentes consolationem, quam per Spiritum sanctum fuerant habituri, id quod exterius in Christo uidebant, amittere metuebant [...] contristabatur humanus affectus, quia carnalis desolabatur adspectus. Nouerat autem ille quid eis potius expediret, quia uisus interior ipse est utique melior, quo eos consolaturus fuerat Spiritus sanctus; non cernentium corporibus ingesturus corpus humanum, sed seipsum credentium pectoribus infusurus [He was fully aware of the effect that His words were having on their hearts: because they did not yet have within them the spiritual joy which they would later receive through the Holy Spirit, they were afraid of losing what they could see outwardly in Christ [...] their human feelings were sorrowful, because they were going to lose the sight of him in the flesh. But He knew what was better for them, for the inner seeing by which the Holy Spirit would console them was preferable: it would not bring a physical body before their bodily sight, but instead it would infuse Himself into their believing hearts].[12]

Elsewhere, in the *De Trinitate* [On the Trinity], Augustine made a distinct but related point: the Ascension made it possible for the disciples to grasp that Jesus was not only fully human but divine:

Oportebat ergo ut auferretur *ab oculis eorum forma serui* quam intuentes hoc solum esse Christum putabant quod uidebant. Inde est et illud quod ait: *Si diligeretis me, gauderetis quoniam eo ad patrem, quia pater maior me est* (John 14:28), id est propterea me oportet ire *ad patrem* quia dum me ita uidetis, et ex hoc quod uidetis aestimatis *minor* sum *patre*, atque ita circa creaturam susceptumque habitum occupati aequalitatem quam cum patre habeo non intelligitis [It was appropriate for the *form of a slave* (Philippians 2:7) to be removed from their sight, since looking on Him they thought that Christ was no more than what they could see. Hence His words, *If you loved Me you would be glad that I am going to the Father, for the Father is greater than I* (John 14:28), by which he meant: It is necessary, therefore, that I go to the Father, for while you see Me like this you deduce, from what you can see, that I am less than the Father, and, preoccupied with something created and with the form I have assumed, you do not comprehend the equality with the Father that I enjoy].[13]

Later medieval commentators, both monastic and scholastic, developed the theme that Augustine had set out, including two whose writings Fray Luis knew and esteemed. In his sermons on the Ascension, St. Bernard of Clairvaux dwelt repeatedly on the Last Supper scene, noting the dismay of the disciples and their excessive attachment to the world of the senses, which Christ's departure was intended to transform:

Quidni concuterentur viscera, turbaretur affectus, haesitaret animus, haereret vultus, paveret auditus, nec omnino aequanimiter discessionis eius sermo posset admitti, ut relinqueret eos, pro quo omnia reliquissent? Ceterum non ut maneret in carne, sed ut transferretur ad spiritum, totus ab eo in illam carnem Discipulorum fuerat collectus affectus, ut dicere esset aliquando: *Etsi cognovimus Christum secundum carnem, sed nunc iam non novimus* [Must not their bowels have been shaken, their emotions confused, their minds disturbed, must not their faces have fallen and their ears been horrified, totally unable to accept with equanimity His talk of going away and leaving them who had left all for Him? None the less, He did not draw all the love of the disciples towards His flesh for it to remain in the flesh (cf. Philippians 1:2), but so that it might be transferred to the Spirit, and they might eventually say: "Even if we once knew Christ according to the flesh, now we know Him thus no longer" (2 Corinthians 5:16)].[14]

St. Thomas Aquinas drew the same contrast between carnal and spiritual love in the *quaestio* devoted to the Ascension in the *Summa Theologica*, in which, quoting Augustine, he rebutted the argument that it would have been better for Christ's followers if He had not ascended: "ascensio Christi in caelum, qua corporalem suam praesentiam nobis subtraxit, magis fuit utilis nobis quam praesentia corporalis fuisset" [the ascension of Christ into heaven, by which He withdrew from us His physical presence, was more helpful to us than His physical presence had been].[15] The Lord's departure, he affirmed, deepened faith and hope, and raised love up to heaven:

> Et quia Spiritus Sanctus est amor nos in caelestia rapiens, ideo Dominus dicit discipulis, *Expedit vobis ut ego vadam. Si enim non abiero, Paraclitus non veniet ad vos; si autem abiero, mittam eum ad vos* (John 16:7). Quod exponens Augustinus dicit: *Non potestis capere Spiritum quandiu secundum carnem nosse persistitis Christum. Christus autem discedente corporaliter, non solum Spiritus Sanctus, sed et Pater et Filius illis affuit spiritualiter* [And because the Holy Spirit is the love that carries us up to heavenly things, the Lord tells His disciples: "It is expedient for you that I go; for if I do not go, the Paraclete will not come to you." Commenting on this, Augustine observes: "You cannot receive the Spirit as long as you persist in knowing Christ according to the flesh. But when Christ withdrew physically, not only the Holy Spirit, but also the Father and the Son became spiritually present within them"].[16]

Mediated by such authorities, St. Augustine's interpretation of the disciples' distress became familiar to Fray Luis's contemporaries in Spain, and many of them drew on it in their writings, including Juan de Valdés, Pedro de Alcántara, and Alonso Orozco.[17] San Juan de Ávila, an attentive reader of St. Augustine, proclaimed it in his sermons:

> la causa por que no vino el Espíritu Santo a los apóstoles estando acá Jesucristo en este mundo fue porque estaban ellos colgados de la presencia de su Maestro y estaban contentos con aquello solo; y aunque la presencia de nuestro Señor era tan santa y tan buena, pero estorbaba a los apóstoles de no ser perfectos, y por eso Jesucristo se quiso ir [the reason why the Holy Spirit did not come to the Apostles while Jesus Christ was here in this world is that they clung to the presence of their Teacher and were content with that alone;

and though the presence of Our Lord was so holy and so good, none the less it was preventing the Apostles from being perfect, and therefore Jesus Christ willed to depart].[18]

Bartolomé Carranza, following St. Thomas, resumed it in his *Catechismo christiano* [Christian Catechism], where he observed of the apostles: "cuando le tenían presente, le amaban como a hombre, y sus afetos eran muy humanos, como parece por la historia del Evangelio [...]. Así que era necesaria su ausencia y que se subiese a los cielos, para la perfeción de los Apóstoles" [when they had him present, they loved him as a man, and their affections were very human, as the Gospel story makes clear (...). It was therefore necessary that he should absent himself and ascend into Heaven, for the perfecting of the Apostles].[19] Similarly, Francisco de Osuna invoked the tradition in his *Tercer abecedario espiritual* [Third Spiritual Alphabet] in order to underpin his teaching that contemplatives seeking to know Christ in His divinity should suspend meditation on His humanity:

> todos los que han hablado sobre la ida del Señor al cielo para que viniese el Espíritu Santo, se conforman a San Cipriano, diciendo que los apóstoles estaban detenidos en el amor de la sacra humanidad, la cual era menester que les quitasen para que así volasen a mayores cosas, deseando la venida del Espíritu Santo, que les enseñase a conocer a Cristo, no según la carne, sino según el espíritu [...]. Pues que a los apóstoles fue cosa conveniente dejar algún tiempo la contemplación de la humanidad del Señor, para más libremente se ocupar por entero en la contemplación de la divinidad, bien parece convenir también aquesto algún tiempo a los que quieren subir a mayor estado [All those who have spoken about the Lord's going to Heaven so that the Holy Spirit might come, have followed St. Cyprian in saying that the Apostles were stuck in the love of the sacred humanity, which had to be taken from them so that they might fly to greater things, desiring the coming of the Holy Spirit, who would teach them to know Christ, not according to the flesh, but according to the Spirit [...]. Since it was suitable for the Apostles to relinquish for a while the contemplation of the Lord's humanity, so that, in greater freedom, they might give themselves wholly to the contemplation of His divinity, it would seem to suit also, for a while, those who wish to rise to a higher state].[20]

Osuna's teaching later became controversial when St. Teresa de Ávila, reluctant to relinquish devotion to the humanity of Christ, dissented from it in her autobiography, a text that Luis de León, as the first editor of her works, prepared for publication.[21]

THE SHORTER VERSION

The ode of Fray Luis makes many allusions to this exegetical tradition, and it is clearly meant to be read in its light. The anonymous speaker who gives expression to heartfelt grief is presented as "neither omniscient nor reliable," as Elias Rivers has observed: like the apostles, whose viewpoint he shares, he is unaware of the impending joy of Pentecost.[22] He is also forgetful of Jesus's loving words of warning at the Last Supper. The result is a series of subtexts that point to an alternative truth.

> 1. ¿Y dexas, Pastor santo,
> tu grey en este valle hondo, escuro,
> con soledad y llanto,
> y tú, rompiendo el puro
> ayre, te vas al inmortal seguro?
> [And, holy Shepherd, are You leaving / Your flock in this deep, dark
> valley, / in loneliness and tears, / while You, cleaving the pure / air,
> go away to the everlastng haven?]

The reproachful question directed to the ascending Christ in stanza one introduces a stark contrast between two images: a shepherd moving upwards into light, and a flock of sheep foresaken in a dark valley, uncertain and bereaved. The contrast, and the prominence given in the opening line to the verb *dexas*, call to mind the Old Testament curse of the shepherd who abandons his sheep (Zechariah 11:16-17), which Jesus Himself took up in the New Testament (John 10:12). There is, however, no reference to the reassurance Jesus immediately gave His disciples: "I am the good shepherd" (John 10:14).[23] Nor is there any recollection of His departing promise to remain with them always (Matthew 28:20), a promise recalled by St. Leo the Great in a well-known sermon:

> spondet nobis Dominus praesentiam suam, dicens: *Ecce ego vobiscum
> sum omnibus diebus usque ad consummationem saeculi.* Non enim
> frustra per Isaiam dixerat Spiritus sanctus: *Ecce virgo in utero accipiet
> et pariet filium; et vocabunt nomen ejus Emmanuel, quod est interpre-
> tatum, nobiscum Deus.* Implet ergo Jesus proprietatem nominis sui, et

qui ascendit in coelos non deserit adoptatos [The Lord promises us his presence, saying, "Lo! I am with you all days, even till the end of the age." For not in vain had the Holy Ghost said by Isaiah: "Behold, a virgin shall conceive and shall bear a Son, and they shall call his name Emmanuel, which is, being interpreted, God with us" (Isaiah 7:14; Matthew 1:23). Jesus, therefore, fulfils the proper meaning of His name, and in ascending into the heavens He does not foresake His adopted bretheren].[24]

The *valle hondo, escuro* in line two no doubt contains an allusion to the valley of death evoked in Psalm 22:4 (*in valle mortis*) and echoed in a phrase of the *Salve Regina* (*in hac lachrimarum valle*), but absent is the Psalm's countervailing affirmation, "I shall fear no evil, for you are with me."[25] These omissions indicate a lack of faith, on the speaker's part, in the divinity of Christ, which continued to be present once His body had disappeared, as San Juan de Ávila, following Aquinas, pointed out: "la divinidad de Cristo no se iba, como no descendió del cielo; la divinidad tampoco subió ahora al cielo; lo que se ausentaba era el ánima y el cuerpo" [the divinity of Christ was not departing, since it did not come down from Heaven; nor did it rise to Heaven now; what was going away was the soul and body].[26]

> **2. Los antes bienhadados,**
> **y los agora tristes y afligidos,**
> **a tus pechos criados,**
> **de ti desposseidos,**
> **¿a dó convertirán ya sus sentidos?**
> [Those who before were blessed, / and who now are sad and afflicted,
> / nourished at Your breasts, / and by You abandoned, / where will
> they now direct their senses?]

The agitation of the disciples is conveyed in stanza two by contrasting images and tenses: those who were once happy and fulfilled are now fraught with anguish and grief (lines 1-4), and face an unknown future (line 5). In line one, they are described as having formerly been *bienhadados*, a reference, perhaps, to the Beatitudes (Matthew 5:1-12),[27] though the speaker seems oblivious of Christ's assurance, "Blessed are those who mourn, for they shall be comforted" (verse 4), and forgetful too of His prediction, "You shall be made sorrowful, but your sorrow shall be turned into joy" (John 16:20). They are also described (lines 2-3) as children once nourished at Christ's breast but now abandoned, an image with several New Testament associations (e.g. Matthew

10:42, 11:25), including Matthew 9:15, where Jesus, in the Vulgate version, refers to his disciples as *filii sponsi* (children of the bridegroom). Sixteenth-century commentators, such as Juan Maldonado, recognised that the Latin phrase was a literal rendering of a Hebraism meaning "the bridegroom's companions," but they were aware that some of the Fathers, notably St. Jerome, had seen in it a mystical sense: spiritually speaking, the disciples were, indeed, Christ's offspring.[28] In the poem, the image of breastfeeding calls to mind also, as Colin Thompson has noted, three passages in the Epistles, where Christian believers are likened to babes who must be fed milk because they cannot eat meat (1 Corinthians 3:1-2; Hebrews 5:12; 1 Peter 2:2).[29] The implication that to grow spiritually one must be weaned is explicit in the Old Testament text from which all three derive: "Whom will He teach knowledge, and to whom will He explain the message? Those who are weaned from the milk, those taken from the breast" (Isaiah 28:9). For the speaker, however, the disciples are being deserted, not weaned, despite the firm promise of Christ, "I will not leave you orphans" (John 14:18). Here the patristic allusions are dense, as Joseph F. Chorpenning has shown.[30] The image of Christ as a nursing mother was developed by the Fathers, among them St. Augustine, whose commentary on the Last Supper discourse draws an extended comparison between the weaning of infants and the Ascension. Paraphrasing the Gospel text, he imagines Christ telling the disciples that so far He has consoled them by His physical presence because they are "little ones" (*parvuli*), but now He desires to "wean" them from their carnal attachment and, in doing so, to prepare them for the Spirit's "solid food":

> caro quidem factum Verbum habito in uobis, sed nolo me carnaliter adhuc diligatis, et isto lacte contenti semper infantes esse cupiatis [...]. Si alimenta tenera quibus uos alui non subtraxero, solidum cibum non esurietis; si carni carnaliter haeseritis, capaces Spiritus non eritis [As the Word made flesh, I am living among you, but I do not want you to go on loving Me with a carnal love and, content with this milk, to happily remain babies [...]. If I do not take away the delicate food with which I have nourished you, you will have no appetite for solid food; if you remain attached, with a carnal love, to what is flesh, you will not be able to receive the Spirit].[31]

Judging when to wean, Augustine adds, is no easy matter, for a point of balance must be found between love of Jesus in His humanity, which milk symbolises, and faith in His divinity, which deepens once milk is withdrawn.[32] At the Last Supper, he implies, the disciples lacked such balance, and they were therefore dismayed by Christ's words.

During the Middle Ages, the nursing imagery on which Augustine drew became a commonplace of exegesis, and many of Luis de León's contemporaries made use of it, including San Juan de Ávila, who urged his listeners to wean themselves if they wished to receive the Spirit: "gozarán de este Espíritu Santo y saldrán sus discípulos los *ablactatos a lacte, avulsos ab uberibus: los que están ya destetados y apartados de los pechos de sus madres* (Isaiah 28:9); a estos tales enseña el Espíritu Santo, con éstos se comunica, a éstos se da" [those will enjoy this Holy Spirit and become His disciples who are *ablactatos a lacte, avulsos ab uberibus: already weaned and taken from their mothers' breasts*: such people the Spirit teaches, with these He communicates, to these He gives Himself].[33] The second stanza ends with a question which sums up the nature of the disciples' distress as Augustine had defined it: *¿a dó convertirán ya sus sentidos?* The bewidered tone, and the prominence accorded, by position and rhyme, to the key word *sentidos*, pinpoint their reliance on sense-knowledge rather than faith, and the panic they consequently felt when Jesus, ascending, passed beyond their ken.

> **3. ¿Qué mirarán los ojos**
> **que vieron de tu rostro la hermosura,**
> **que no les sea enojos?**
> **Quien oyó tu dulçura,**
> **¿qué no tendrá por sordo y desventura?**
> [On what will the eyes gaze / that saw the beauty of Your face, / without being vexed? / To one who heard Your sweetness, / what will not seem silent and misfortune?]

The future tense with which the second stanza concludes is taken up in the antitheses of stanza three, which contrast the bliss the disciples enjoyed in Christ's company with the desolation that will afflict them once He has gone, and the image of children now overlaps with that of companions as the prophetic words are recalled: "Can the children [or companions] of the bridegroom mourn as long as the bridegroom is with them? But the days will come when the bridegroom shall be taken away from them, and then they shall fast" (Matthew 9:15). St. Augustine had associated this prophecy with the state of post-Ascension Christians, yearning to behold in the flesh the beauty of Jesus, the divine bridegroom,[34] and St. Bernard, in the same vein, had applied it to the misery of the disciples at the Ascension:

> Dolor ergo nimius erat, quia videbant illum, propter quem omnia reliquerant, a suis sensibus et aspectibus tolli, ut non possent, ablato a se sponso, sponsi filii non lugere [Their anguish was intense, for

they were seeing Him, for whom they had left everything, being taken away from their senses and beyond their sight, with the result that once the bridegroom had been removed, His children/companions could not fail to weep].[35]

Of the senses mentioned collectively in stanza two, sight and hearing are now singled out, in accord with a patristic tradition, noted by Senabre, which St. Bernard had resumed: "in corporis sensibus visus quidem ceteris omnibus, auditus vero reliquis tribus dignior est" [among the senses of the body, sight is, indeed, finer than all the rest, while hearing is finer than the remaining three].[36] Sight and hearing are paired also in various passages of the Bible (e.g., Ecclesiasticus 17:11; Isaiah 6:9-10, 64:4; John 12:40; 1 Corinthians 2:10), one of which concerns the disciples directly: "Blessed are your eyes, for they have sight; blessed are your ears, for they have hearing. And, believe me, there have been many prophets and just men who have longed to see what you see and never saw it, to hear what you hear, and never heard it" (Matthew 13:16-17). These words of Jesus are echoed in stanza three. Commenting on them, St. Augustine had contrasted the joy that Christ's physical presence inspired with the misery experienced by Christians since its withdrawal,[37] and St. Bernard, taking the contrast further, had remarked that when the disciples first loved Jesus, in His humanity, they were drawn by what they could see and hear: "Beati siquidem oculi qui videbant Dominum maiestatis in carne praesentem [...]. Beatae aures quae verba vitae ab ipsius incarnati Verbi ore percipere merebantur" [Blessed were the eyes that saw the Lord of majesty present in the flesh [...]. Blessed were the ears judged worthy to hear the words of life from the mouth of the incarnate Word Himself]. Naturally, therefore, they were distraught when he told them of his departure: "Quid mirum, fratres, si implebat tristitia cor eorum, cum ab eis sese pronuntiaret iturum?" [What wonder is it, brothers, if their hearts were filled with sorrow when He told them He would be going away?].[38]

> Aqueste mar turbado,
> ¿quién le pondrá ya freno? ¿quién concierto
> al viento fiero, ayrado?
> Estando tú encubierto,
> ¿qué norte guiará la nave al puerto?
> [That stormy sea, / who will now restrain it? Who will temper / the wild, angry wind? / With You concealed, / which lodestar will guide the ship to port?]

In stanza four, the antitheses between a happy past and an uncertain future become sharper, and the note of anxiety deepens, as the moment of Christ's disappearence, which stanza 5 will evoke, draws near. Just as the third stanza had developed the allusion to *sentidos* at the end of the second, so now the fourth carries further the mention of *desventura* at the end of stanza three, by calling to mind a specific event in the Gospels, the stilling of the storm. Small details point to a figurative sense: *aqueste* in line one implies that the storm is raging now, metaphorically, in the disciples' lives, while *nave* in line five identifies them as the Church, heading through time towards heaven.[39] The stilling of a storm by Jesus is narrated twice in the Gospels. The first account, found in the Synoptics only, is set during the day, and tells how Jesus had to be roused from sleep in order to check the winds (Matthew 8:23-27; Mark 4:36-41; Luke 8:22-25). The second, retailed by John (6:16-21) as well as by Matthew (14:22-36) and Mark (6:45-52), is set in "the fourth watch of the night" (Matthew 14:25; Mark 6:48), when the winds ceased after He walked on the sea and came to His disciples' aid. In the poem, the closing image of a ship unable to navigate in the dark (line 5) indicates that the latter event is the one being recalled. St. Augustine's exegesis of the incident, in his commentary on the Gospel of St. John, connects with the poem's images in several ways. He describes the boat in which the disciples were travelling as the Church, and the darkness and stormy weather around them as the tribulations in this world to which *Ecclesia* is exposed:

> nauicula illa ecclesiam praesignabat. Si non hoc primo in ecclesia intelligimus, quod illa nauicula patiebatur, non erant illa significantia, sed simpliciter transeuntia [...]. Crescunt tenebrae, et nondum uenit Iesus. Crescentibus tenebris, refrigescente caritate, abundante iniquitate, ipsi sunt fluctus nauem turbantes; tempestates et uenti, clamores sunt maledicorum. Inde caritas refrigescit, inde fluctus augentur, et turbatur nauis [That boat foreshadowed the Church. If its tribulations are not understood primarily of the Church, then those events were not significant, but of passing importance only [...]. The darkness deepens, and Jesus has yet to arrive. The growing dark, the cooling of charity, the flourishing of wickedness: these are the waves that toss the boat; the stormy weather and the winds are the cries of those who insult her. Thus charity cools; thus waves rise, and the boat is shaken].[40]

He also comments on the mysterious ending of John's account, in which, as Jesus approaches, the boat suddenly reaches its destination, a moment evoked, it would seem, at the stanza's close (line 5): "*Et statim fuit navis ad terram, in quam ibant. Factus est finis ad terram: de humido ad solidum, de turbato ad firmum, de itinere ad finem*"[*And immediately the boat was at the place to which they were going* (John 6:21): thus they reached land, passing from liquid things to solid, from disturbance to solidity, from their journey to their goal].[41] St. Augustine's exegesis was later taken up by Aquinas, and linked directly with the Ascension. In his commentary on Matthew's account, St. Thomas dwells on the detail that while the boat was floundering at sea Jesus was on the mountain praying (verses 23-24), and he compares the scene to the Ascension, when Christ disappeared into heaven, leaving the Church at the mercy of the waves: "Per naviculam significatur Ecclesia, per mare mundus [...]. Et haec Ecclesia, Christo ascendente, remansit in mari, et in periculis maris mundi" [The boat signifies the Church, the sea the world [...]. And when Christ ascended, this Church remained in the sea, amid the perils of the sea of the world]. However, he continues, the Church that the disciples represent need not fear, for in the troubles of this world it is supported invisibly by the Lord: "Quando enim aliquis magnus impugnat Ecclesiam, tunc agitatur fluctibus [...]. Sed quia Christus orat, non potest submergi, quamvis fluctuet et elevetur" [When, then, something great assails the Church, it is tossed by the waves [...]. But because Christ is praying, it cannot go under, however much it may rock and be thrown up in the air].[42] The reassuring faith in Christ's presence that Aquinas counselled is lacking in the poem's speaker, for whom the storm is an image of the perils that the Church must now face on its own.

> 5. ¡Ay nube embidiosa!:
> aun deste breve gozo, ¿qué te aquexas?
> ¿Dó buelas presurosa?
> ¡Quán rica tú te alexas!
> ¡Quán pobres y quán ciegos, ay, nos dexas!
> [O envious cloud!: / why do you begrudge even this brief joy? / Where are you flying in haste? / How rich you are as you recede! / How poor and, O, how blind you leave us!]

The distress to which the poem gives expression becomes acute in stanza five, at the moment when Jesus disappears from view, depriving the onlookers of joy (*gozo*), riches (*pobres*), and sight itself (*ciegos*). The speaker, who can no longer address Jesus, directs his remarks instead to the receding cloud, and his recourse to metonymy at this point creates a moving anticlimax, of the sort used by Fray Luis elsewhere.[43] His tone changes too, from anxiety and bewilderment to hopeless anger, and it is on a note of anguish that the poem concludes, "with its question unanswered and the perplexity and fear of the disciples unallayed."[44] In the stanza's last line, the identity of the speaker becomes clear. The use of the personal pronoun *nos* confirms that he is not only an observer of the scene but one of the followers of Christ. The question then arises: is he an apostle, or a Christian of the poet's time, meditating on the biblical event?[45] The answer lies in the poem itself, where the final phrase, *nos dexas* (line 5), recalls the opening words of stanza one: *dexas [...] tu grey*. The speaker is part of Christ's flock, a member of his Church, and, therefore, a traveller too in the *nave* of stanza four. His voice, moreover, though personal, is anonymous, and collective as well as singular, the voice of an individual whose poetic identity is ecclesial.[46] Seen thus, his role helps to explain the rather complex response that his words invite. He is not, necessarily, a contemporary of the disciples, and he, therefore, remains distinct from them in time, but because he is a fellow Christian he is able to enter fully into their pain. San Juan de Ávila urged his listeners to be present at the Ascension in precisely such a way:

> Así estaban los santos apóstoles del Señor en este santo tiempo: y así, hermanos, es muy gran razón que estemos nosotros, pues somos una cosa con ellos, una Iglesia y una unión con Cristo. Todos aquellos que sirven a Jesucristo, que están en su servicio, todos son una misma cosa, la Iglesia de Dios, y la congregación de los cristianos [Thus were the holy apostles of the Lord at this holy time: and thus, brothers and sisters, we have very good reason to be ourselves, for we are one thing with them, one Church and one unity with Christ. All those who serve Jesus Christ, who are in His service, all are one thing, the Church of God, and the congregation of Christians].[47]

Guided by the speaker, the reader empathises with the disciples in their plight, and acknowledges the passionate love that moves them, while recognising their lack of faith, and therefore hope, to which attention is constantly drawn. The combination of compassion and detachment that this entails was evoked vividly in the first Ascension sermon of Leo the Great:

> illa trepida sollicitudo et curiosa cunctatio nostrae fidei fundamenta jecisset. Nostris igitur perturbationibus, nostrisque periculis in apostolis consulebatur [...]. Nos illorum instruxit aspectus, nos erudivit auditus, nos confirmavit attactus. Gratias agamus divinae dispensationi et sanctorum Patrum necessariae tarditati. Dubitatum est ab illis, ne dubitaretur a nobis [Their trembling anxiety and careful hesitation laid the foundations of our faith. It was our perplex-

ities and our dangers that were provided for in the apostles [...]. We have been instructed by what they saw; we have been taught by what they heard; we have been convinced by what they touched. Let us give thanks to divine providence and to the holy Fathers' necessary slowness of belief. They doubted so that we might not doubt].[48]

WITNESSES OF THE ASCENSION

The second exegetical tradition that appears to have shaped the poem was not concerned with the emotions of the disciples during the Last Supper, but with their reactions to the Ascension itself. The writings of the Fathers, as Senabre has noted, advanced two different interpretations of the event, one of which emphasised the sorrow of the disciples, the other their happiness, and the latter interpretation became part of the liturgy of the feast.[49] In the breviary of the Council of Trent, for instance, the patristic readings at First Vespers affirm: "ita sunt veritate perspicua roborati, ut, Domino in caelorum eunte sublimia, non solum nulla afficerentur tristitia, sed etiam magno gaudio replerentur" [they were so strengthened by the clear truth (they beheld), that, as the Lord rose into the heights of heaven, they were not only untouched by any sadness, but were rather filled with a great joy].[50] Both interpretations may be found in the sermons of St. Bernard, which in places assume that the distress of the disciples was still present at the Ascension scene, but elsewhere imply that by the time the Ascension took place their faith and understanding had grown.[51] Devotional writings in the Middle Ages also reflected both views: the *Meditationes vitae Christi* [Meditations on the Life of Christ], for instance, depicted the disciples rejoicing at Christ's ascent, while Ludolph of Saxony described them as moved by a mixture of delight and grief.[52] In his poem, Luis de León follows the sorrowful interpretation exclusively. In doing so, however, he develops it in a distinctive way: he focuses on the event as the disciples witnessed it, making their feelings present to the reader, and he dramatises their response, expressing it in a crescendo of queries and exclamations. His portrayal of the Ascension is not, in these respects, characteristic of Augustine, but elements of it may be found in two conventions by which the sorrowful interpretation, which Augustine had articulated, survived into the Middle Ages and beyond.

The first convention is iconographic. Colin Thompson has related the ode to medieval and Renaissance representations of the "disappearing Christ," in which Jesus is shown entering the cloud while His disciples look on in consternation.[53] The motif first appeared around the year 1000 in illustrations produced in Anglo-Saxon England, from where it spread at once to the continent, becoming widespread in the late Middle Ages throughout Europe, including Spain.[54] Robert Deshman traced its sources back to the writings of St. Augustine, and specifically to his teaching that the disciples needed to be deprived of Christ's physical presence, a teaching given currency in England by a movement of monastic reform which was eager to renew contemplation of Christ's divinity.[55] Although there is no indication in the poem that Fray Luis took a particular painting as his model,[56] it is feasible that he had this pictorial convention in mind, and assumed that his readers would know it too.

The second convention is connected with sacred oratory, and the influence of the Ascension sermons of the pseudo-Augustine, which were included in sixteenth-century editions of the saint's works.[57] In these, the sorrowful interpretation is prominent. The fourth sermon opens with a description of the disciples' disarray:

> Vident hoc praesentes Apostoli, et paulatim semetipsum ad superna tollentem, pectore pavidi, mente confusi, oculis trepidi consequuntur, donec ultro solutam nubem serena dies exciperet, et fulgore corrusco vallatum humanis conspectibus occultaret [The apostles, who are present, see this, and as He raises Himself gradually into the heights, they are left with panic-stricken hearts, confused minds and anxious looks, until the sunny day swallows up the cloud, and hides Him, behind bright light, from human eyes].[58]

The fifth sermon goes further and dramatises the emotions they felt, putting into their mouths a series of questions and requests:

> Domine, inquiunt, quare nos derelinquis ascendens, qui nos elegisti in ripa praecedens? Domine, quando sumus verba tua super mel et favum eminus percepturi, et stillantis rorantisque gratiae balsamum de tuis labiis ac faucibus libaturi? Aut instrue quo ascendis, aut ne deseras cum ascendis: quasi scuto benignitatis tuae remansimus in aperto nudati, tanquam pulli matris amplectentis pennatae velamine destituti [Lord, they ask, why are You ascending and abandoning us, whom You chose as You walked before us by the sea? Lord, when will we hear Your words, sweeter than honey and the honeycomb, and when will we taste the balm of grace that moistens and flows from Your lips and mouth? Either tell where You are ascending, or do not forsake us when You ascend: we have been left exposed, as if stripped of the shield of Your kindness, like chicks deprived of the protection of their mother's enclosing wings].[59]

4.2   Juan de Flandes (active from 1496; died 1519). *The Ascension of Christ*. c.1500. Tempera on wood. 110 x 84 cm. Museo del Prado, Madrid.

This passage is an example of *amplificatio*, as Fray Luis's contemporaries understood it: the visualisation by a preacher "of a dramatic scene, replete with vivid and concrete detail," in order to animate his hearers' "flagging imaginations, engage their sympathetic attention and control their emotional temperature."[60] Often *amplificatio* was combined with antitheses to intensify the feelings the preacher wished to evoke.[61] Luis de Granada defined it as follows in his *Ecclesiasticae Rhetoricae* [Sacred Rhetoric] (Lisbon, 1576): "habiéndose inventado la amplificación para conmover los afectos, nada los conmueve más que el pintar una cosa con palabras, de manera que no tanto parezca que se dice cuanto que se hace y se pone delante los ojos" [amplification having been invented to move the affections, nothing moves them more than painting something in words in such a way that it seems not so much recounted as happening and placed before one's eyes].[62] Like a sermon, the poem uses *amplificatio* to place the Ascension before the reader's eyes, reinforcing it with *sermocinatio*, the attribution to an individual of imaginary words, appropriately phrased.[63] Its presentation of the scene, moreover, follows the norms of *narratio*, which according to Granada should be not only clear, persuasive, and pleasing, but brief and to the point:

> Podremos narrar una cosa *brevemente* si empezáremos a referirla desde donde fuere necesario, y no desde su primer principio; si sumariamente, y no por menudo, la contáremos; si no la continuáremos hasta el fin, sino hasta allí donde convenga; si no usáremos de transiciones; si de tal suerte expusiéremos el éxito de las cosas que pueda saberse también lo que pasó antes, aunque nosotros lo callemos [We shall manage to narrate something *briefly* if we start to recount it from a point that is necessary, rather than from its first beginning; if we relate it summarily, rather than in detail; if we continue it, not to the end, but to wherever is fitting; if we make no use of transitions; if we reveal how things turned out in such a way as to make clear also what happened beforehand, though we ourselves do not describe it].[64]

In accord with such precepts, the poem's account is succinct: it begins *in medias res*, ends abruptly, and excludes extraneous facts, leaving the reader to supply the broader context, including earlier and later events. In addition, it makes effective use of *interrogatio*, *apostrophe* and *exclamatio*, devices which Granada recommends as ways of arousing in the listener emotions appropriate to the scene portrayed.[65]

4.3   Albrecht Dürer (1471-1528). *The Ascension of Christ*. c.1510. Woodcut print on paper. 126 x 97 mm.
© Trustees of The British Museum.

SANTO TOMÁS DE VILLANUEVA

The poem's use of such rhetorical techniques to evoke the Ascension was not without parallel in sixteenth-century Spain. Granada himself had recourse to them in his *Meditaciones de la vida de Cristo* [Meditations on the Life of Christ] in order to evoke the disciples' doubts:

> todos a una voz le dirían: ¿Cómo, Señor, nos dejáis solos y huérfanos entre tantos enemigos? ¿Qué harán los hijos sin padre, los discípulos sin maestro, las ovejas sin pastor y los soldados flacos sin su capitán? ¿Dónde vais, Señor, sin nosotros? ¿Dónde quedaremos sin vos? ¿Qué vida será la nuestra faltándonos tal arrimo, tal guía y tal compañía? [all of them would say to Him with one voice: "How is it, Lord, that You are leaving us alone and orphans among so many enemies? What will the children do without a father, the disciples without a teacher, the sheep without a shepherd, and the faint-hearted soldiers without their captain? Where are you going, Lord, without us? What will become of us without You? What will our life be like without such a support, such a guide and such company?"]

In his account, Jesus dispels their anxieties, and they behold His ascension with equanimity.[66] Closer to the approach of the ode is the third Ascension sermon of Santo Tomás de Villanueva, Fray Luis's older contemporary and fellow Augustinian,[67] which begins by raising the issue with which the poem is also concerned: why did Jesus leave those he had come to save?

> Justa quaedam in devotis mentibus, fratres, dubitatio surgit, quid hoc sit, quod filius Dei unigenitus, qui ex ardentissimo amore suae flagrantissimae charitatis, e sinu patris descendens, terras lustrare, et miserias nostras subire dignatus est, ut nobis coelestia regna donaret, post resurrectionem suam nobis in hoc exilio relictis, post modicum tempus ipse in coelos sine nobis redierit. An sicut vita, ita et animo in resurrectione mutatus est, ut gloriosus effectus, mortalium oblivisceretur, quos sanguine suo et morte redemerat? [A certain proper doubt arises in devout minds, brothers and sisters: why is it that the only-begotten Son of God, who came down from the bosom of the Father out of a most ardent desire of His most burning love, and deigned to travel to earth and undergo our miseries that He might bestow on us the heavenly kingdom, would, after a brief time

4.4 Juan de Juanes (Vicente Juan Masip) (c.1523-79). *Santo Tomás de Villanueva* (1486-1555). In the collection of the Stirlings of Keir. Photo: Warburg Institute. © National Galleries of Scotland.

following His resurrection, return to heaven without us, leaving us in this exile? Or, just as He was changed in life at His resurrection, so was He changed in soul that, having been made glorious, He forgot the mortals whom He had redeemed by His blood and death?][68]

Immediately, it makes explicit the answer that the poem implies, invoking the Scriptural image of a parent unable to desert its child: "*Quis hoc dicat? cum ipse per prophetam clamet: Nunquid oblivisci potest mulier infantem suam, ut non misereatur filio uteri sui? Et si illa oblita fuerit, ego tamen non obliviscar tui. Ecce in manibus meis descripsi te*" [Who could say this when he himself cries out with the prophet: "Can a woman forget her infant, so as not to have pity on the son of her womb? and if she should forget, yet will not I forget thee. Behold, I have graven thee in My hands" (Isaiah 49:15-16)].[69] Despite this explanation, the sermon goes on to address to Jesus, the good shepherd, a string of further questions which voice the perplexity that the poem explores:

> Quid ergo bone Jesu, cur tam cito redisti, cur sine nobis ascendisti? Secura tibi tua gloria erat, cur non expectasti nos, ut in ultimum diem tecum in caelestia regna gaudentes migraremus? An non melius esset, ut socius itineris et peregrinationis nostrae, gregis tui tunc consolator et custos existens, postmodum ductor iter panderes ante eum, et cum gloria et triumpho tuis comitantibus, supernam illam civitatem intrares? [Why then, good Jesus, why did You return so quickly, why did You ascend without us? Your own glory was secure, why did You not wait for us, that we might all travel rejoicing with You to the heavenly kingdom? Would it not be better for You, the companion on our journey and pilgrimage, to comfort Your flock, to stand guard as a guide after You opened the way before it (Micah 2:13), and to enter that supernal city in glory and triumph with Your followers?][70]

It indicates, as the poem does, that if Jesus had remained with His flock, the trials of life could have been endured:

> Quantum solatii, quantum securitatis et gaudii, ovibus tuis haec tua praesentia contulisset? Te praesente non graves fuissent persecutiones, tormenta omnia tyrannorum et vitae hujus discrimina nobis tolerabilia viderentur: nihil tam durum, nihil tam acerbum, quod

4.5 *Santo Tomás de Villanueva*. The reverse of a medal struck for Pope Alexander VII (1655-67), during whose reign the Augustinian friar was canonised (in 1658).
© Warburg Institute.

non tuo eloquio molliretur. Vita haec calamitosa et tristis, levis nobis et facilis tua jucunda societate fuisset: si quid scrupuli incidisset, consuleremus te; si quid periculi, fugeremus ad te: si quid doloris et amaritudinis, recrearemur a te: essesque nobis etiam nunc omnia in omnibus, in quibus indigeremus te [How much solace, how much security and joy Your presence could have given Your sheep! With You present, no persecution would have been severe; all the torments of tyrants and the dangers of this life would seem bearable to us; nothing would be so difficult, nothing so bitter, that it would not be attempted at Your command. This life of misfortune and sadness would have seemed light and easy to us in Your pleasant company. If a doubt had assailed us, we would have consulted You; if a danger, we would have fled to You; if anything of sorrow and hardship, we would have been refreshed by You. Even now You would be for us "all in all" (1 Corinthians 15:28) in those things for which we need You].[71]

The interrogation then resumes, and becomes intense. The first query recalls the contrast in the poem's opening stanza between sheep forsaken in a perilous place and a shepherd travelling safely towards heaven: "Oves, inquam, tuas, quas tanto pretio comparasti, inter atroces lupos et bestias crudelissimas relinquis, et tu ad caelestia tutus migras?" [Do You, I say, leave Your sheep, whom You have gathered at such a great cost, among savage wolves and most cruel beasts, while You travel safely to the heavens?][72] Others, equally reproachful, follow, including one that presents the image of children abandoned in "this vale of tears": "Filiolos tuos miseros et aerumnolos in hac lachrymarum valle relinquis, et solus ad regni solatia vadis? Quaenam haec impatientia regni, ut tuos deseras in aerumnis?" [Do You abandon Your miserable and troubled children in this valley of tears, while You go alone to the comforts of the kingdom? What is this impatience for the kingdom, that You leave Your own in hardships?][73] At this point, the questioning comes to a halt, and the sermon begins to provide answers, something the poem does not do. The explanation offered, however, is consonant with the poem's theme: it was expedient for His followers that Jesus should depart, and He ascended with their needs in view: "Qui propter nos venerat, propter nos rediit; nos illi adventus causa, nos causa regressus. Sic utique nobis expediebat, sic oportebat, ut cito rediret" [He who had come for us also returned for us; we were the cause of His coming, and we were the cause of His returning. Thus it was beneficial for us, thus it was necessary, that He left quickly].[74]

In its argument and rhetorical construction, the sermon is so similar to the ode that it is hard to avoid the conclusion that Fray Luis used it as a model and source. Santo Tomás was revered within his order, which decided after his death to gather and publish his works. A royal licence to print his sermons was granted in 1569, and three years later, in 1572, the first edition of the *Conciones* appeared in Alcalá de Henares, edited by a confrere and friend of Fray Luis, Pedro de Uceda y Guerrero.[75] It is possible that the poem was intended as an act of homage to a great Augustinian whom Fray Luis admired. If so, the year in which the sermons were published may be a clue to when it was composed.

The Longer Version

The longer version of the ode, which consists of four additional stanzas, is found in the family of manuscripts known as Merino. It does not figure in the manuscript tradition known as Quevedo, which most modern critics have accepted as authoritative.[76] There is general agreement that it is less successful, poetically, than the shorter version, but views are divided about its authorship. Some have not hesitated to ascribe it to Fray Luis, but others, a majority, have dismissed it as apocryphal, and most modern editions omit it. In the absence of external evidence, its authenticity has to be decided by analysis of the text itself, two aspects of which have proved crucial in the debate so far. The first concerns continuity of theme. Sarmiento considered the additional stanzas to be "a real completion, and more consonant with Christian thought than a stop at *nos dexas*,"[77] but most subsequent writers have disagreed. Macrí believed that they were the work of "un teólogo" [a theologian] who held that the sentiments expressed in the shorter version were unchristian and should, therefore, be "corrected," while Senabre has argued, similarly, that they alter the poem's drift: "modifican sustancialmente el sentido global de la composición" [they make a substantial change in the poem's overall sense].[78] The second has to do with coherence of form. Sarmiento noted parallels in the longer version between the later stanzas and the earlier ones, and he saw in its movement of thought the lineaments of an Ignatian meditation. His views, however, have not won acceptance. For Senabre, in particular, the changes of addressee in the additional stanzas are artificial, and dissipate, pointlessly, the intensity of the ode.[79] Both aspects deserve to be reconsidered in the light of the patristic context of the work. Is the interpretation of the Ascension on which the shorter version draws broken or developed in stanzas six to nine? And are the added stanzas incorporated formally into the poem as a whole?

6. **Tú llevas el tesoro**
que solo a nuestra vida enriquecía,
que desterraba el lloro,
que nos resplandecía
mil veces más que el puro y claro día

[You are taking the treasure / that alone enriched our life, / that banished sorrow, / that shone upon us / a thousand times more brightly than the pure, clear day].

Stanza six prolongs the reproaches addressed in stanza five to the cloud, and it makes effective two images which stanza five introduced: that of treasure, now lost, which the earlier allusion to wealth (¡Quán rica tú te alexas!) anticipated, and that of light, now extinguished, by which the previous reference to blindness (¡quán ciegos, ay, nos dexas!) is recalled. Both images are scriptural, and associated in exegesis with the Ascension. In his second sermon on the feast, St. Bernard, following St. Paul, described the ascending Christ as *thesaurus noster* [our treasure], in whom the wealth of divinity resides.[80] The image is invoked too in the Ascension *quaestio* of the *Summa Theologica*, which cites Matthew 6:21: "Where your treasure is, there will your heart be also."[81] Carranza, in his catechism, made Aquinas's meaning clear:

> fue más provechosa su ausencia para levantar nuestro amor al cielo y para espiritualizarle haciendo divino y espiritual al que antes era un amor humano. Porque, como dijo el mismo Cristo, *donde está tu tesoro, allí está tu corazón*. Y nuestro tesoro y todo nuestro bien se subió al cielo [His absence was more beneficial in that it raised our love to heaven, and spiritualised it by making divine and spiritual what was previously a human love. For, as Christ Himself said, "where your treasure is, there your heart is too." And our treasure and all our good went up to heaven].[82]

The pseudo-Augustine, in the fourth Ascension sermon ascribed to him, portrayed the cloud that concealed Christ as removing bright sunlight from the disciples' eyes,[83] and a similar comparison was drawn by St. Bede:

> ascensurus ad caelos unicam se mundi lucem monstrauit, *Ego sum*, inquiens, *lux mundi, qui sequitur me non ambulat in tenebris sed habebit lumen vitae*. Vnde a propheta sol iustitiae uocatur quia ipse nimirum cunctas mundi partes a solis ortu usque ad occasum ab aquilone

usque ad meridiem gratia fidei et ueritatis inlustrare dignatus est [He, when on the point of ascending into heaven, pointed out that He was the unique light of the world, saying: "I am the light of the world; one who follows Me does not walk in darkness but will have the light of life" (John 8:12). Hence He is called "the sun of right-eousness" by the prophet (Malachi 4:2), since He deigned to enlighten all parts of the world, from the rising of the sun to its setting, from the north even to the south, by the grace of His faith and truth].[84]

St. Bernard, too, compared the ascending Lord to the sun, and he drew parallels with the Transfiguration, quoting Matthew 17:2, "refulsit facies eius ut sol" [His face did shine as the sun], a verse to which the closing line of the stanza may allude.[85] Within the broader context of the ode, stanza six forms a contrast with stanza four. The cloud travelling heavenwards with hidden treasure parallels the boat carrying the disciples in the storm, and the brightness of the divine sun, now shrouded, balances the pole star covered in cloud.

> 7. ¿Qué lazo de diamante,
> ¡ay alma!, te detiene y encadena
> a no seguir tu amante?
> ¡Ay, rompe y sal de pena!
> Colócate ya libre en luz serena
> [What adamantine bond, / O soul, holds you back, enchained, / from following your lover? / O, break loose and escape from pain! / Place yourself, once free, in serene light].

In stanza seven, the speaker berates his own soul, and urges it to cast off the impedi-ments that prevent it following its beloved. The theme is patristic. St. Augustine, in an Ascension homily, called on his hearers to ascend, in their hearts, with the Lord,[86] and he added that to follow Him, even in the flesh, should be easy, unless one is weighed down by sin.[87] In the poem, the speaker imagines his soul held back by a *lazo de diamante* (line 1). For Senabre, the image is not connected with its context, and he suggests that it was introduced simply to provide a rhyme.[88] In fact, it is drawn from the Old Testament, where adamant represents hardness of heart: "They made their heart as the adamant stone, lest they should hear the law and the words which the Lord of hosts sent" (Zechariah 7:12). St. Jerome, in his commentary on Zechariah, had made its meaning clear: "duritiam cordis ostendit, et cor lapideum, quod noluerint Dei verba suscipere" [it indicates hardness of heart, and a heart of stone, for they were unwilling to accept the words of God].[89] As the stanza concludes, the speaker commands his soul to break free from the constraints that make it suffer, and follow Jesus into the light (lines 4-5). His words call to mind the second Ascension sermon of the pseudo-Augustine, where the same idea is expressed in similar terms:

> si post Medicum desideramus ascendere, debemus vitia vel peccata deponere. Omnes enim quasi quibusdam compedibus nos premunt, et peccatorum nos retibus ligare contendunt: et ideo cum Dei adjutorio, secundum quod ait Psalmista, *Dirumpamus vincula eorum*; ut securi possimus dicere Domino, *Dirupisti vincula mea, tibi sacrificabo hostiam laudis* [If we wish to ascend after the Physician, we must lay aside vices or sins. For all these weigh us down like so many fetters, and strive to bind us with the nets of sins; and so with God's help, as the psalmist says, "let us break their bonds" (Psalm 2:3), so that, fearless, we may say to the Lord, "You have broken my bonds, I will offer You a sacrifice of praise" (Psalm 115:16-17)].[90]

At this point in the poem, the parallels are with stanza three. Both stanzas centre on nuptial images applied to Christ, who is the bridegroom (3) and the lover (7). The attachment to his physical presence, which stanza three concerns, is the bond, described in stanza seven, which stops the soul following him to heaven, and which must be broken if it is to recover its joy.

> 8. ¿Qué temes la salida?
> ¿Podrá el terreno amor más que la ausencia
> de tu querer y vida?
> Sin cuerpo, no es violencia
> vivir, mas lo es sin Cristo y su presencia
> [Why do you fear to escape? / Is earthly attachment more powerful than the absence / of your love and life? / Life without a body does one no violent harm, but such harm does result from living without Christ and his presence].

Stanza eight continues the address to the soul, which is fearful. Torn between love of sensible things (*el terreno amor*) and devotion to Jesus (*tu querer y vida*), it hesitates to claim the freedom it desires. In the last two lines, the speaker confronts such vacillation robustly. The meaning he attaches to "cuerpo," however, is not immediately clear. Sarmiento took it as a reference to the body,[91] but it may equally signify the life according to "the flesh" which St. Paul affirms must perish if one is to find new life in Christ. Commenting on Paul's words, "I live, now not I, but Christ lives in me" (Galatians 2:20), St. Gregory the Great observed in a famous passage: "Ac si aperte dicat: Ego quidem a memetipso extinctus sum, quia carnaliter non uiuo; sed tamen essentialiter mortuus non sum, quia in Christo spiritaliter uiuo" [It is as if he were to say explicitly: I have, in truth, deprived myself of life, for I am not living according to the flesh; and yet, in what is essential, I have not died, for spiritually I am living in Christ].[92] The opposition between flesh and spirit runs through the first five stanzas, as we have seen. Now the poem, in its penultimate verse, makes the theme explicit, in ways that take us back to stanza two. The spiritual state of the disciples described there is that of the soul in stanza eight, and the question with which stanza two concludes (*¿a dó convertirán ya sus sentidos?*) is now answered. The senses are no longer the means by which Jesus is known. He has ascended, and henceforth He dwells within His followers, who have access, through faith, to His life-giving presence.

9. Dulce señor y amigo,
dulce padre y hermano, dulce esposo:
en pos de ti yo sigo,
o puesto en tenebroso,
o puesto en lugar claro y glorïoso
[Sweet lord and friend, / sweet father and brother, sweet spouse: / after you I follow, / whether I am in a dark place, / or in a place that is bright and glorious].

In the ninth stanza, the crisis within the speaker's soul is resolved as he determines to follow Jesus, in both the darkness of the present life and the bright glory of the next. His words recall, and at the same time respond to, the prayer that formed the liturgical collect of the feast, before and after the Council of Trent: "Concede, quaesumus, omnipotens Deus: ut qui hodierna die Unigenitum tuum Redemptorem nostrum ad caelos ascendisse credimus, ipsi quoque mente in caelestibus habitemus" [Grant, we beseech you, almighty God, that we, who believe your only-begotten Son our Redeemer to have this day ascended into heaven, may ourselves dwell in mind amid heavenly things].[93] The epithets he addresses to Jesus in the first two lines have been described as arbitrary and flat: "[son] apelaciones conventuales y hasta heterogéneas [...] sin función clara en el contexto" [they are appeals of a pious and even heterogeneous sort [...] with no clear function in the context].[94] It may be argued, however, that they express the balanced faith in the two natures of Christ which the disciples, according to Augustine, initially lacked. He is said to be Lord as well as friend (*señor y amigo*), a parent as well as a brother (*padre y hermano*), and the divine bridegroom (*esposo*), whose spouse is humanity itself. Each of these images is evoked or implied earlier in the ode. Above all, He is *dulce* (the adjective is used thrice): not the neglectful pastor or parent imagined at the poem's start, but a loving and beloved presence in whom the speaker delights. The poem's end matches its beginning. Like the first stanza, the last one begins by addressing Christ, and then goes on to draw a contrast between time and eternity, darkness and light. But now the mood is different. The bewilderment expressed in stanza one has been replaced by understanding and acceptance, and the opening note of complaint has given way to earnest resolve, a contrast reflected in the two main verbs, *dexas* (1) and *sigo* (9).

MEDITATION

The longer version of the ode, it would seem, was not intended to undermine the shorter one, but to complete it. The problem posed in stanzas one to five is resolved in stanzas six to nine, and the poem is organised in a chiastic structure, like other odes of Fray Luis.[95] The unity of theme and form that it displays makes it likely that Fray Luis was its author, and other features point in the same direction, including diction and tone.[96] As Sarmiento noted, "there is no internal evidence to discredit the suggestion that it is by Fray Luis himself, it is well within his idiom and range of imagery and ideas."[97] Its unity, moreover, helps to account for the changes of addressee that it contains. In stanzas seven and eight, the lesson to be drawn from the disciples' doubts is applied to the soul, which appropriates it wholeheartedly in stanza nine. This progression of thought, as Sarmiento noted, "conforms to the general scheme of a religious meditation [...] of which the Ignatian [...] is usually taken as the type."[98] The poem, however, is not influenced specifically by the Ignatian *Exercises*, where the account of the Ascension makes no reference to Patristic interpretations of the scene.[99] It has more in common with the Ascension meditation proposed by San Pedro de Alcántara in his popular *Tratado de la oración y meditación* [Treatise on Prayer and Meditation]. This affirms that Jesus prepared His disciples for His departure so that they might accompany His ascent in their hearts, and it draws a parallel with Christians since who have found themselves bereft of devotion:

> Donde verás, que a aquellos desampara muchas veces la presencia
> corporal de Cristo (esto es, la consolación sensible de la devoción),
> que pueden ya con el espíritu volar a lo alto y estar más seguros del
> peligro. En lo cual maravillosamente resplandece la providencia de

Dios y la manera que tiene en tratar a los suyos en diversos tiempos: cómo regala los flacos y ejercita los fuertes; da leche a los pequeñuelos y desteta a los grandes; consuela los unos y prueba los otros, y así trata a cada uno según el grado de su aprovechamiento [From this you will see that the bodily presence of Christ (that is, the sensible consolation of devotion) often deserts those who can then fly upwards in the spirit and be safer from danger. In this, we see shining wonderfully the providence of God and the way in which He treats His own at various times: how He cherishes the weak and exercises the strong; feeds the little ones with milk and weans the great; consoles some and tests others, and thus treats each person in accord with their degree of progress].[100]

It adds that Jesus wanted His disciples to grieve as they watched Him ascend so that their longing might prepare them for Pentecostal grace, and it commends contemporary Christians who yearn, similarly, for His presence:

Quiso también que le viessen subir a los cielos para que le siguiessen con los ojos y con el spíritu, para que sintiessen su partida, para que les hiziesse soledad su ausencia, porque este era el más conveniente aparejo para recibir su gracia [...]. Pues aquellos serán herederos del spíritu de Christo, a quien el amor hiziere sentir la partida de Christo, los que sintieren su ausencia y quedaren en este destierro sospirando siempre por su presencia [He also wanted them to see Him rise up to heaven so that they might follow Him with their eyes and their spirit, so that they might regret His departure, so that His absence might make them lonely, because this was the best preparation for receiving His grace [...]. For the heirs of Christ's spirit will be those whom love causes to regret Christ's departure, those who feel His absence and who remain in this desert sighing unendingly for His presence].[101]

In one respect, however, Alcántara's approach differs sharply from that of the poem. Like Osuna and others before him, he applied the exegesis of St. Augustine to a particular aspect of religious experience, in this case consolation in prayer. The Ascension ode, by contrast, does not "accommodate" Scripture to a specific situation or need. Instead, it remains close to the biblical account, as interpreted by the Fathers and their successors. Taking as its starting point the events narrated in *Acts*, it elaborates the interpretation of them that Augustine had proposed, and considers its implications for the Christian believer now, before ending with an allusion to the liturgy. The movement of thought this exemplifies is that of *lectio divina*, the reading in an ecclesial context of a scriptural text in order to discover its hidden meaning.[102]

The fact remains, none the less, that the longer version, though cogent in its theology, does not work well as a poem. Once the emotional climax of stanza five has passed, the ode loses momentum. The added stanzas lack the tight construction and the cumulative tensions that make the shorter version so compelling, and they convey the theme less persuasively than the earlier ones, which gain in power by refraining from direct statement.[103] Probably, therefore, it was a first draft, which Fray Luis later revised and shortened.[104] In spite of their differences, however, both versions may be said to reflect their author's familiarity with patristic and medieval exegesis, and his keen interest in the spiritual or mystical sense of Scripture, as St. Augustine, in particular, understood it.

5.1 The view from the balcony in the *Corral del Príncipe* in Madrid [Carlos Dorremochea]. An artist's impression of the interior of a Spanish playhouse of the seventeenth century. From John J. Allen, *The Reconstruction of a Spanish Golden Age Playhouse: El Corral del Príncipe, 1583-1744* (Gainesville: University Presses of Florida, 1983), 68-69.

Reprinted with permission of the University Press of Florida.

Chapter Five

Drama: *El condenado por desconfiado*

Scholars interested in the theological sources of *El condenado por desconfiado* [The Man Condemned for Lack of Trust] have sometimes sought them in Counter-Reformation debates about the relation between grace and free will.[1] Their search, however, has proved inconclusive, a fact which reinforces the view, argued cogently by Terence May, that the work "expounds no particular theory of grace."[2] It has also led to the neglect of other writings and traditions that form the background to the play. One of these is the Bible. As May pointed out, "we must react to the play first of all as ordinary playgoers who know a few biblical texts and have our wits about us"; otherwise our theological arguments "will never escape from muddle."[3] Another, related part of the background is the pastoral theology of the time, shaped by the Council of Trent, which applied biblical themes and images to the practical problems of Christian living. It found expression in works of devotion and catechesis, and it was disseminated, at parish level, by popular preaching. The audiences who first saw the play may not have been uniformly versed in the niceties of theological controversy, but they would have been familiar, before entering the *corral*, with the pastoral *topoi* that it reworks. As Jonathan Thacker has observed:

> A dramatization of the issues of sin and redemption, free will, good works, and divine grace would echo some of the points heard more dryly from the pulpit in church, and probably engaged members of the audience by teaching them through *admiratio*, that is through engaging them with lively, spectacular and thought-provoking stories. The theatre was a centre for entertainment but also a place where one could learn important lessons for life.[4]

The pages that follow examine three of the lessons that *El condenado*, it would seem, was designed to impart: the nature of the fear of God, the experience of despair, and the value of wisdom.

THE FEAR OF GOD

The role of fear in Paulo's life was described vividly by Alexander Parker: "La clave del carácter de Paulo es el temor. Teme el infierno. Se entierra en un desierto para escaparse de él" [The key to the character of Paulo is fear. He fears Hell. He buries himself in a desert to flee from it].[5] The fear from which he suffers was known in patristic and scholastic theology as *timor servilis*, or servile fear. San Francisco de Borja defined it as arising, "cuando se teme la pena que se merece por la culpa, como [...] los pecadores, que por temor del infierno se convierten" [when one fears the punishment merited by one's guilt, like […] sinners who, through fear of Hell, are converted].[6] An earlier chapter examined its biblical roots, and the three images conventionally used to convey it: a servant or slave in the employ of a lord, a criminal facing his judge, and a soldier fighting for an award rather than an ideal.[7] Each of these images appears to inform the portrayal of Paulo. His fear is evident in his opening prayer, not only in his longing to behold heaven itself (21-24), but also in the self-interest that underlies his decision to become a hermit (65-66), and the image of God which emerges from his words is of a distant but omniscient master, whose servant he wishes to be. In the dream which intensifies his fear, God appears as the judge, Paulo as the plaintiff (161-76). Later as a bandit, he acts with ruthless cruelty, moved once again by mercenary self concern.[8] At no point does Paulo refer to God as his Father. Instead he addresses him as his Lord (*Señor*) and Creator (26, 37, 63-64, 71), a tendency that the *Catechism of the Council of Trent*, commenting on the *Pater Noster*, had associated with fear rather than love:

> Nam etsi Salvator noster divinam hanc orationem praetexere potuit aliquo verbo, quod plus maiestatis haberet, exempli causa, Creatoris aut Domini; tamen haec omisit, quae timorem simul nobis afferre possent; illud autem adhibuit, quod orantibus et aliquid a Deo petentibus, amorem fiduciamque conciliat. Quid enim iucundius est patris nomine, quod indulgentiam sonat et charitatem? [Our Saviour, it is true, might have commenced this divine prayer with some word more expressive of majesty, such as "Creator" or "Lord"; yet did He omit these, as they might be associated with ideas of fear, choosing rather an expression that inspires love and confidence in those who pray to and petition God; for what sweeter name than that of Father?—a name which sounds indulgence and love].[9]

However, although Paulo's selfishness is appalling, the play does not imply that his motive for becoming a monk was mistaken. Servile fear does not figure in the Devil's list of his sins (207-36), and Paulo's final entry on stage, wrapped in flames, demonstrates that God is indeed just as well as merciful (2945-74). Nor does Anareto, in order to convert his son, hesitate to insist on the torments of Hell (2485-86). In this the play reflects the orthodoxy of its time. The Council of Trent, in its *Decree on Justification* (1547), had insisted that good works prompted by servile fear, though lacking in merit, were not displeasing to God: "Si quis dixerit, gehennae metum, per quem ad misericordiam Dei, de peccatis dolendo, confugimus vel a peccando abstinemus, peccatum esse aut peccatores peiores facere: anathema sit" [If anyone says that the fear of hell, because of which we seek refuge in God's mercy by expressing sorrow for sins, or refrain from committing sin, is itself a sin or makes sinners worse: let him be anathema].[10] It had also argued that no one could expect to be sure of his own salvation: "cum nullus scire valeat certitudine fidei, cui non potest subesse falsum, se gratiam Dei esse consecutum" [since no one can know, by that assurance of faith which excludes all falsehood, that he has obtained the grace of God]; and that therefore, "quilibet, dum se ipsum suamque propriam infirmitatem et indispositionem respicit, de sua gratia formidare et timere potest" [it is possible for anyone, while he regards himself and his own weakness and lack of dispositions, to be anxious and fearful about his own state of grace].[11] If Paulo had been fully aware and fearful of his weakness, would he have trusted the Devil's prophecy so readily? The Council had affirmed, in addition, that repentant sinners should be led by servile fear towards hope and love:

> peccatores se esse intelligentes, a divinae iustitiae timore, quo utiliter concutiuntur, ad considerandam Dei misericordiam se convertendo, in spem eriguntur, fidentes, Deum sibi propter Christum propitium fore, illumque tamquam omnis iustitiae fontem diligere incipiunt [acknowledging that they are sinners, they turn from fear of divine justice, which profitably strikes them, to thoughts of God's mercy; they rise to hope, with confidence that God will be favourable to them for Christ's sake; and they begin to love him as the fount of all justness].[12]

If Paulo is criticised, it would seem, it is because he fails to develop spiritually, for his fear does not issue in hope and love, but in loss of hope and indifference to others.

Fear also makes Paulo pusillanimous. Once his confidence in God has been shaken, he abandons his life of penance in disgust, a move deplored by the *pastorcillo* [young shepherd] whom he encounters in the second act. When the shepherd comes on stage, he is weaving a *corona* of flowers for the lost sheep he hopes to retrieve (1598-1608),

5.2   Italian School. *The Council of Trent, 4 December 1563.* 16th century. Oil on canvas. 117 x 176 cm.
Louvre, Paris, France. Lauros, Giraudon. The Bridgeman Art Library. The Council was convened
by Pope Paul III in December 1545, and met on three separate occasions before closing in
December 1563.

CATECHISMVS,

Ex Decreto Concilii Tridentini,

AD PAROCHOS,

PII QVINTI PONT. MAX.
IVSSV EDITVS.

ROMAE,
In ædibus Populi Romani,
apud Paulum Manutium,
M D L X V I.
CVM PRIVILEGIO PII V. PONT. MAX.

5.3 *Catechism of the Council of Trent.* The title page of the first edition (Rome: Manutius, 1566).
The *Catechism* had a formative influence on the devotional and catechetical literature by which
the teachings of the Council were disseminated in Spain and the New World.

153

but when he returns in Act Three, convinced that Paulo will never repent, he destroys the *corona* with the words:

> Volved, bellas flores
> a cubrir la tierra,
> pues que no fue digna
> de vuestra belleza.
> Veamos si allá
> con la tierra nueva
> la pondrán guirnalda
> tan rica y tan bella
> [Go back, lovely flowers, / to cover the land, / for she was not worthy
> / of your loveliness. / Let's see if there, / in the new land, / they give
> her a garland / so rich and so lovely] (2728-35).

The image of the *corona* is used in several parts of Scripture to denote the reward reserved for those who persevere to the end. In the Book of Wisdom (5:16-17), it is affirmed: "the just shall live for evermore: and their reward is with the Lord [...]. Therefore shall they receive a kingdom of glory and a crown of beauty." Later, in the New Testament, the image recurs in the Epistles of Paul (2 Timothy 4:8), James (1:12) and Peter (1 Peter 5:4), and in the promise recorded in the Apocalypse (2:10): "Be thou faithful unto death, and I will give thee the crown of life." The Council of Trent cited the image in its *Decree on Justification* after urging Christians, in the words of St. Paul, not to lose their confidence, "which has a great reward":[13]

> Bene operantibus usque in finem et in Deo sperantibus proponenda
> est vita aeterna, et tamquam gratia filiis Dei per Christum Iesum
> misericorditer promissa, et tamquam merces ex ipsius Dei promis-
> sione bonis ipsorum operibus et meritis fideliter reddenda. Haec est
> enim illa corona iustitiae, quam post suum certamen et cursum
> repositam sibi esse aiebat Apostolus a iusto iudice sibi reddendam,
> non solum autem sibi, sed et omnibus, qui diligunt adventum eius
> [To those who work well right to the end (Matthew 10:22) and keep
> their trust in God, eternal life should be held out, both as a grace
> promised in His mercy through Jesus Christ to the children of God,
> and as a reward to be faithfully bestowed, on the promise of God
> Himself, for their good works and merits. This, then, is that crown
> of righteousness which the Apostle says is laid up for Him after his

fight and his race, and will be awarded by the righteous judge not
only to him but to all who love his appearing (2 Timothy 4:7-8)].[14]

If Paulo errs because his fear is excessive, Enrico errs because he does not fear
enough. Yet his boast, "A nadie temí en mi vida" [I have feared no one in my life]
(1275) is untrue. He is afraid of displeasing his father Anareto, whom he describes as,
"un hombre eminente / a quien temo solamente / y en esta vida respeto" [an eminent
man / whom alone I fear / and respect in this life] (1220-22). This fear is not servile,
for Anareto is old and crippled, and would be unable to punish him, even if he wished
to. Its nature becomes clear in the third act, when Enrico's resistance to confession is
demolished, not by the threat of Hell, but by the prospect of being disowned:

> Si quieres mi hijo ser
> lo que te digo has de hacer;
> si no (de pesar me aflijo),
> no te has de llamar mi hijo
> ni yo te he de conocer
> [If you wish to be my son / you must do what I say; / else (the distress
> of it pains me) / you may not call yourself my son / nor will I know you]
> (2502-6).

In the event, his love of Anareto is so disinterested that he is more upset by his
father's distress than by his own:

> Bueno está, padre querido,
> que más el alma ha sentido
> (buen testigo de ello es Dios),
> el pesar que tenéis vos,
> que el mal que espero afligido
> [Very good, beloved father, / for my soul has felt more keenly / (as God
> well knows) / the distress you feel / than the evil I await in anguish]
> (2507-11).

The relationship between Enrico and Anareto recalls many descriptions of a type
of fear often contrasted with *timor servilis*, and known as *timor castus* or *filialis*. As an
earlier chapter showed, this was commonly defined as the fear of God which stems, not
from aversion to Hell, nor from longing for Heaven, but from love, and it was conventional to compare the person moved by it to a lover or son.[15] In a work published in

1553, the Dominican Pablo de León described it succinctly, in terms drawn from two medieval writers of his order, William Peraldus and St. Thomas Aquinas:

> Así como el buen hijo no sirve a su padre por lo que le ha de dar, ni le deja de honrar por miedo ni por pena que le dará, sino porque es su padre, que todo se lo debe y porque es muy bueno para él [. . .]: a esta semejanza se llama temor filial [Just as the good son does not serve his father because of gifts he expects to receive, and does not cease to honour him out of fear or because of any punishment he might inflict, but because he is his father, to whom he owes everything and because he is very good to him [. . .]: on the basis of this comparison it is called servile fear].[16]

St. Francis de Sales, writing in 1616, near the time of the play, made the same point more dramatically, by comparing the person moved by such fear to a son in the prime of life whose father is (like Anareto) enfeebled by age: "encore que le père serait vieux, impuissant et pauvre, il ne laisserait pas de le servir avec égale diligence, ains [. . .] il l'assisterait avec plus de soin et d'affection" [even if the father were aged, incapacitated and poor, he would not cease to serve him with as much diligence as ever. Indeed [. . .] he would look after him more carefully and more lovingly].[17] Until his conversion, Enrico's relationship with his father is, admittedly, far from ideal: despite his avowals of affection, he tries to deceive him about his crimes. None the less, the image of his filial devotion, however limited, serves a thematic purpose: just as Anareto's paternity suggests an alternative to Paulo's image of God as Judge, so Enrico's love suggests an alternative to Paulo's terror; and at the end, after his change of heart, Enrico utters a prayer to the Virgin which reveals that his love of God, too, has become unselfish:

> Decilde que yo quisiera,
> cuando comencé a gozar
> entendimiento y razón,
> pasar mil muertes y más
> antes que haberle ofendido
> [Tell him that I would prefer, / since beginning to enjoy / understanding and reason, / to die a thousand deaths and more / rather than to have offended him] (2562-66).

His state of soul at this point is one of perfect contrition, as a passage in Luis de la Palma makes clear:

5.4 The title page of the *Guía del Cielo* by Pablo de León, O.P. (Alcalá de Henares: Juan de Brocar, 1553). The book, probably written c. 1520, was published two decades after the author's death (1531).

Cuando el alma con la gracia divina se levanta al conocimiento de Dios, y al reconocimiento de su majestad y bondad, y de lo que merece ser amado y servido, y se mueve a aborrecer el pecado por ser ofensa de este Señor, más que por otra ninguna fealdad que tenga en sí, o daño que me haga a mí; ésta se llama verdadera contrición [When the soul, by divine grace, rises up to the knowledge of God, and to the recognition of His majesty and goodness, and of how much He deserves to be loved and served, and is moved to abhor sin because it is an offence to this Lord, rather than because of any ugliness it may possess, or any harm it may do me: this is called true contrition].[18]

The figure of Anareto, it may be said, has a twofold identity, to both parts of which Enrico appears to respond when he finally repents: "Anareto is both the 'dear old father' of his human affections, and the representative of a divine fatherhood."[19] The connection between parents and God, which the play dramatises in this way, was underlined by the *Catechism of the Council of Trent* in its comments on the Fourth Commandment, "Honour thy father and thy mother":

Si parentes, quos secundum Deum diligere debemus, non veneramur et colimus, quum in conspectu nobis fere semper sint; Deo, summo parenti et optimo, qui nullum sub aspectum cadit, quem honorem, quem cultum tribuemus? [. . .] Ex quo fit, ut honor quem parentibus habemus, Deo potius, quam hominibus haberi videatur. Sic enim apud sanctum Matthaeum est [. . .]: *Qui recipit vos, me recipit* [. . .]. Sunt enim immortalis Dei quasi quaedam simulacra, in iisque ortus nostri imaginem intuemur [If we do not honour and reverence our parents, whom we ought to love next to God, and whom we have almost continually before our eyes, how shall we reverence and honour God, the supreme and best of parents, whom we cannot see? [. . .] The honour we give our parents would seem to be given to God rather than to men, for so it is in [Mt 10:40] [. . .]: "he that receives you, receives Me" [. . .]. They are, as it were, so many images of the immortal God, and in them we behold the likeness of our origin].[20]

DESPAIR

Many aspects of the play become significant when seen in the light of traditional views on despair. It was a medieval belief that if servile fear was untempered it could result in loss of hope. Pablo de León warns people who derive profit from meditating on the pains of Hell to be careful: "Débense guardar que no les hagan desesperar y afligir por tanto habituarse en ellas que siempre estén en ellas pensando, que olviden las grandezas de Dios y su gran gloria y lo que debemos" [They should make sure that they [the pains of Hell] do not make them despairing and distressed through becoming so familiar to them that they think about them always and forget the greatness of God, and His great glory, and how much we owe Him].[21] Luis de la Palma writes in similar terms of meditation on the Last Judgement and the fear it can arouse: "Este temor se debe siempre templar con la esperanza, para que no venga en desesperación, como lo aconsejó el Eclesiástico (2:9), cuando dijo: 'Los que teméis a Dios, esperad en Él'"[22] [This fear must always be tempered with hope, so that it does not end up in despair, as Ecclesiasticus counselled in the words: "You who fear God, hope in Him"]. Another, related cause of despair was *acedia*, the sin from which Paulo appears to be suffering at the time of his dream.[23] In the dream, Paulo sees Death, who lays aside his scythe to shoot him with a bow and arrow:

> Tiróme el golpe con el brazo diestro,
> no cortó la guadaña. El arco toma:
> la flecha en el derecho, y el siniestro
> el arco mismo que altiveces doma
> [He fired the shot at me with his right hand, / the scythe did not cut.
> He takes the bow: / the arrow in his right hand, and in the left / the
> bow itself that conquers pride] (153-56).

Daniel Rogers suggested that this change of weapon probably means that Paulo will die "an untimely and violent end,"[24] and indeed in the third act Paulo is pursued to his death by bowmen (2826-29). His end also calls to mind the figure of Cain, a traditional type of despair, who was killed, according to legend, by an archer.[25] Cain's words, "My sin is greater than His mercy" (Genesis 4:13) are echoed repeatedly in Paulo's disbelief that God will pardon Enrico's sins or his own. The mark set on Cain by God (Genesis 4:15) was commonly interpreted as a tormented spirit, full of fear, as Tirso's contemporary, the Jesuit Cornelius à Lapide, observed,[26] and it was recognised that despair could lead to the kind of reckless sins that Paulo commits as a bandit: "Sin freno pecan los hombres que no esperan alcanzar perdón de sus pecados. Y así a la muerte desesperan; son sin remedio" [They sin without restraint, men who do not hope to be forgiven for their sins. And so, when death comes, they despair; they are without remedy].[27] In Paulo's dream, moreover, the figure of Death seizes the bow in his left hand, a small detail which is also prophetic, for the left hand of God, in medieval exegesis, was the side of the damned.[28]

The playwright appears to have been influenced, in addition, by some of the texts used in pastoral literature to remedy despair. The *Catechism of the Council of Trent* urged parish priests to reassure their flocks of the divine willingness to pardon by recalling the examples of those to whom, when repentant of the most grievous crimes, God granted forgiveness,[29] and the procedure was adopted by devotional writers keen to encourage hope. In his *Examen de conciencia* [Examination of Conscience] (Alcalá de Henares, 1570), for instance, St. Alonso de Orozco wrote:

> Hijos de Caín son los que dicen como él dijo: "Mayor es mi maldad que la misericordia divina" (Genesis 4:13). Dios infinito es en poder, y no sólo los pecadores del mundo, mas aún de millares de mundos, basta a perdonar. Confió la Magdalena, aunque pecadora, y fuéronle perdonados sus pecados (Luke 7:47). Confió el ladrón estando en el palo por sus robos, y alcanzó perdón general y firme para en el día poseer el cielo (Luke 23:43). Confió San Pedro, habiendo tres veces negado al Señor, y no sólo fue perdonado, mas aún le fue encomendado la Iglesia para ser príncipe de ella (John 21:15-17). Dime, pues, ¡oh pecador!, ¿de qué temes? [. . .] Vete a los pies del confesor, manifiéstale tu conciencia, que allí hallarás lo que tu alma desea [Sons of Cain are those who say, as he did: "My wickedness is greater than divine mercy." God is infinitely powerful, and He is capable of forgiving not only the sinners of the world, but even of thousands of worlds. Mary Magdalene trusted, though she was a sinner, and her sins were forgiven her. The thief trusted, while on the cross for his thefts, and he received a pardon, general and secure, that enabled him to possess heaven on that day. St. Peter trusted, having denied the Lord thrice, and he was not only pardoned, but even given charge of the Church, to rule over it. Tell me, then, O sinner, what do you fear? [. . .] Go to the feet of the confessor, make your conscience known to him, for there you will find what your soul desires].[30]

In Act Two, the *pastorcillo* cites such examples in an attempt to infuse Paulo with *confianza*:

> Y si os guiáis por ejemplo,
> decid: ¿no fue pecador
> Pedro, y mereció después
> ser de las almas pastor?

5.5   *Christ on the Cross, with the Virgin Mary and St John the Evangelist.* An illustration in a popular
collection of writings by San Alonso de Orozco (1500-91), *Recopilación de las obras […] Agora
nueuamente emendadas por el mismo auctor* (Alcalá de Henares: Andrés de Angulo, 1570), opposite
folio 1r.

Mateo, su coronista,
¿no fue también su ofensor?
....
¿no fue pecador Francisco?
....
¡La pública pecadora,
Palestina no llamó
Magdalena, y fue santa
por su santa conversión?
Mil ejemplos os dijera
a estar espacio, señor
[And if you find guidance in examples, / tell me: was not Peter / a
sinner who later merited / to be a shepherd of souls? / Matthew, His
chronicler, / did he not also sin against Him? / [. . .] Was not Francis
a sinner? [. . .] / Was not the public sinner / known in Palestine as
Magdalene / a saint through her holy conversion? / I'd give you a
thousand examples, / if I had time, sir] (1573-94).

Great sinners who became saints were commonly listed also in *ars moriendi* writings, in
order to encourage the dying person who might be tempted to despair. Jaime Montañés,
for instance, in his *Espejo de bien vivir y para ayudar a bien morir* [A Mirror of the Good
Life and an Aid to a Good Death] (1573), encouraged the reader thus:

Toma ejemplo de San Pedro, el cual negó a Jesucristo, y a San Pablo
que perseguía la Iglesia y a los cristianos, y a San Mateo, María
Magdalena y la mujer presa en adulterio [. . .] y otros grandes
pecadores, los cuales son agora grandes santos en la gloria eterna,
porque supieron pedir perdón y tuvieron contrición, y confiaron y
esperaron de Dios el perdón y ninguno desesperó [Follow the
examples of St. Peter, who denied Jesus Christ, and St. Paul who
persecuted the Church and Christians, and St. Matthew, Mary
Magdalene and the woman taken in adultery [. . .] and other great
sinners, who are now great saints in eternal glory, because they chose
to beg forgiveness and were contrite, and trusted and hoped for
pardon from God, and none of them despaired].[31]

One scriptural passage cited frequently in such texts was Ezekiel, chapter 18. Its
central theme is the purport of the *pastorcillo's* message: "Is it My will that a sinner

should die [. . .] and not that he should be converted from his ways and live?" (Ezekiel 18:23).[32] The same chapter also contains a striking contrast between two men: a just man who suddenly turns to evil and commits all the wickedness of the sinner, and a sinner who abandons evil and repents. All the good works of the just man are forgotten; all the wickedness of the sinner is blotted out:

> If a wicked man turns away from all his sins which he has committed and keeps My statutes and does what is lawful and right, he shall surely live: he shall not die. None of the transgressions which he has committed shall be remembered against him [. . .]. But when a righteous man turns away from his righteousness and commits iniquity, and does the same abominable things that the wicked man does, shall he live? None of the righteous deeds which he has done shall be remembered; for the treachery of which he is guilty and the sin he has committed, he shall die (Ezekiel 18: 21-24; also see 33:12-20).

Here, perhaps, is one source of the image of *las suertes trocadas* in the play, to which Pedrisco alludes after Paulo's death: "Las suertes fueron trocadas: / Enrico, con ser tan malo, / se salvó, y este al infierno / se fue por desconfiado" [The destinies were exchanged: / Enrico, though so evil, / was saved, and this man went / to Hell, for lack of trust] (2908-11; cf. 3005). Another source may lie in the writings of San Juan de Ávila, whose *Audi, Filia* [Listen, Daughter] (Toledo, 1574) draws a similar distinction between two kinds of sinners: those who give way to despair and end badly, and those who trust in God's mercy and repent. The distinction matches the fates of Paulo and Enrico as the play draws to a close:

> Ahora sabed que en una de dos maneras se han los hombres que mucho han pecado. Unos, *desesperados* de remedio, como Caín, vuelven las espaldas a Dios, y *entréganse*, como dice San Pablo, *a toda suciedad* y pecado (Ephesians 4:19) [. . .] lo que a éstos acaecerá es lo que la Escritura dice: *Al corazón duro, mal le irá en sus postrimerías* (cf. Ecclesiasticus 3:27,29). ¡Y ay de aquel que este mal ha de probar, que muy mejor le fuera no haber nacido! Otros hay que, habiendo hecho muchos pecados, tornan sobre sí con el socorro de Dios, y hiriendo su corazón con dolor, y llenos de confusión y vergüenza, humíllanse delante de la misericordia de Dios, tanto con mayor humildad y gemido cuanto han sido sus pecados más y mayores [. . .]. Y la ocasión de ello fue haber pecado muchos pecados, los cuales ellos confiesan

LIBRO ESPIRITVAL,
SOBRE EL VERSO AVDI
FILIA, ET VIDE, &c.

Compuesto por el padre Maestro Iuan
de Auila, Predicador en el
Andaluzia.

DIRIGIDO A DON ALONSO
de Aguilar, Marques de Pliego, señor
de la casa de Aguilar.

Con priuilegio de Castilla, y Aragon.

En Madrid, en casa de Luis Sanchez,
Año M. D. XCV.

5.6 The title page of the *Audi, filia* of San Juan de Ávila (1500-1569) in *Primera parte de las obras del padre maestro Iuan de Ávila* (Madrid: Luis Sánchez, 1595). The first edition of the *Audi, filia* (Alcalá de Henares, 1556) was included in the Inquisition Index of 1559. The revised edition, published in 1574, became a bestseller.

y gimen; mas no desesperan, y alegan, delante la misericordia de Dios, que, pues su miseria y daño es muy grande, sea con ellos la misericordia de El copiosa y muy grande [Know that men who have sinned greatly behave in one of two ways. Some, *despairing* of a remedy, like Cain, turn their backs on God, and *give themselves*, as St Paul says, *to every kind of filth* and sin [. . .] to these will happen what Scripture says: *For the hard heart it will go badly at the last.* And alas for him who will experience this evil, for it would be much better for him if he had not been born! Others there are who, after committing many sins, come to their senses with the help of God, and, piercing their hearts with pain, and filled with confusion and shame, humble themselves before God's mercy, with all the more humility and grief the greater and more numerous their sins have been [. . .]. The occasion of this is their having committed many sins, which they confess and bemoan; yet they do not despair, and they plead, in the presence of God's mercy, that since their wretchedness and harm are very great, his mercy towards them may be abundant and very great].[33]

Enrico's story balances Paulo's exactly. As Daniel Rogers observed: "every excessive inference we might be tempted to draw from one side of the action is checked and balanced by the message of the other."[34] His faith in God's mercy is a contrast to Paulo's despair, but it is, none the less, reprehensible. Just before the final meeting with Anareto he scornfully refuses confession:

> ¿Yo tengo de confesarme?
> Parece que es necedad.
> ....
> Dios es piadoso y es grande;
> su misericordia alabo,
> con ella podré salvarme
> [Must I confess? / It seems to be folly. / [. . .] / God is compassionate
> and great; / I praise His mercy, / with it I can be saved] (2396-2406).

His refusal flies in the face of the teaching of Trent, which had affirmed in its canons concerning justification: "Si quis dixerit [. . .] posse quidem, sed sola fide, amissam iustitiam recuperare sine sacramento paenitentiae [. . .] anathema sit" [If anyone says [. . .] that a person can recover lost justice by faith alone, and without the sacrament of penance, [. . .] let him be anathema].[35] Anareto, accordingly, is quick to point out that he is wrong:

> Aqueso es tomar venganza
> de Dios: el poder alcanza
> del empíreo cielo eterno.
> Enrico, ved que hay infierno
> para tan larga esperanza
> [That is taking revenge / on God: it attacks the power / of the eternal
> empyrean heaven. / Enrico, see that Hell awaits / a hope so long
> deferred] (2481-85).

Enrico, in fact, is guilty of presumption, a sin at the other extreme from despair, but equally opposed to confidence in God. For biblical commentators, the *locus classicus* concerning it was Ecclesiasticus 5:6-9:

> And say not: The mercy of the Lord is great: He will have mercy on
> the multitude of my sins. For mercy and wrath quickly come upon
> Him: and His wrath looketh upon sinners. Delay not to be
> converted to the Lord: and defer it not from day to day. For His
> wrath shall come on a sudden: and in the time of vengeance He will
> destroy thee.[36]

Pablo de León considered that presumption occurs, "cuando el hombre sin méritos presume de haber la gloria en el cielo" [when the man without merits presumes that he will have glory in heaven],[37] and the excessive trust in divine mercy that it supposes was roundly condemned in the *Guía de pecadores* [A Guide for Sinners] (Salamanca, 1567) of Luis de Granada:

> ¿Estás tú vanamente confiado, creyendo que con todo esto estás
> seguro? Yerras, hermano mío, yerras si crees que eso sea esperar en
> Dios. No es ésa esperanza, sino presunción, porque esperanza es
> confiar que arrepintiéndote y apartándote de pecado te perdonará
> Dios, por malo que hayas sido; mas presunción es creer que perse-
> verando siempre en mala vida todavía tienes tu salvación segura. Y
> no pienses que es éste cualquier pecado, porque él es uno de los
> pecados que se cuentan contra el Espíritu Santo [. . .] los cuales
> pecados dice el Salvador que no se perdonan en este siglo ni en el
> otro (Matthew 12:31-32) [Are you trustful without reason, believing

that despite all this you are secure? You are mistaken, my brother, you are mistaken if you believe that is hope in God. That is not hope, but presumption, because hope is trusting that if you repent and abandon sin God will forgive you, however evil you may have been; but presumption is believing that if you persevere ceaselessly in an evil life your salvation is none the less secure. And do not think that this is any kind of sin, for it is one of the sins included in those against the Holy Spirit [. . .] such sins, according to the Saviour, are not forgiven in this age, or any other].[38]

Until the closing moments of Act Three, both protagonists lack the virtue of hope, though in contrasting ways. The difference between their respective faults is neatly defined by Pablo de León, who writes of *la esperanza*: "Esta virtud se pierde o por esperar más de lo que es menester, que es esperar sin méritos; o dejar de esperar cuando es menester, que es desesperar" [This virtue is lost either by hoping more than one should, which is to hope without merits; or by failing to hope when one should, which is to despair].[39] In dramatic terms, however, it is Paulo, rather than Enrico, who is the object of censure, a fact which appears to reflect the view, defended by St. Thomas Aquinas, that, although both faults are worthy of blame, excessive hope is preferable to despair: "praesumptio est peccatum. Minus tamen quam desperatio: quanto magis proprium est Deo misereri et parcere quam punire, propter eius infinitam bonitatem" [Presumption is a sin. But it is less sinful than despair, because taking pity and forgiving are more characteristic of God, in His infinite goodness, than inflicting punishment].[40]

WISDOM

Fear of God is connected with wisdom in several parts of the Old Testament, particularly the Book of Proverbs: "The fear of the Lord is the beginning of wisdom" (1:7; 9:10; Psalm 110:10; Sirach 1:16, 25). According to tradition, the fear from which wisdom springs could be servile or filial. Paulo's fear of Hell, which might have saved him, issues instead in folly, and the playwright drives the point home by making him, at certain moments, look ridiculous.[41] Apart from the semi-allegorical *pastorcillo*, the character who most clearly exemplifies wisdom is Anareto, particularly during his last meeting with his son. Terence May argued that, despite our first impression, he is far from being a foolish father, blind to his son's misdeeds. He is, on the contrary, aware of Enrico's failings, but he chooses to conceal his knowledge, and to wait in patience for a change of heart.[42] This reading is strengthened by several allusions in the play to the Wisdom literature of the Old Testament.

5.7   Fray Luis de Granada, O.P. An eighteenth-century print by Jerónimo Andrade. The writings of
       Luis de Granada (1504-88) were popular throughout Europe in the late sixteenth and early
       seventeenth centuries.

Anareto's cryptic words to Enrico, "Eres crisol / donde la virtud se apura" [You are a crucible / in which virtue is refined] (1112-13) are, for May, full of irony: "His son is a crucible in which his own soul is being tested to the extreme of patience [. . .]. Enrico's own poor shred of natural virtue is being tried too."[43] The image of precious metals refined by fire occurs often in the Old Testament, particularly the Wisdom books, and in exegesis it was normally applied to the trials of the just man. In the words of Cornelius à Lapide: "Quod [. . .] ignis est auro, hoc tribulatio est justo" [What fire is to gold, tribulation is to the just].[44] An example of such a just man is Job, who declared in his affliction: "He has tried me as gold that passeth through the fire" (Job 23:10). Like Job, Anareto has been rendered immobile by physical infirmity, and he bears his trial with resignation, saying simply: "La divina voluntad se cumpla" [May the divine will be done] (1151-52). Unlike Job, however, he is a repentant sinner. As a younger man he spoilt his son, a parental fault admonished in the Book of Proverbs (13:24; 22:15; 29:17), and in doing so he launched him on a life of crime (722-37). Now, in old age, he is making satisfaction for his past by bearing without complaint the sufferings God sends. A passage in Ecclesiasticus (2:3-5) evokes his state:

> Hold fast to the Lord and do not leave Him, so that you may be
> honoured at the end of your days. Whatever happens to you, accept
> it, and in the uncertainties of your humble state be patient, since gold
> is tested in the fire, and the chosen in the furnace of humiliation.

The virtue that Anareto exemplifies is, appropriately, the hope that the two protagonists lack, a virtue that St. Alonso de Orozco associated directly with the image of the *crisol*:

> El Eclesiástico dice que, "como el oro se prueba en el fuego, así los
> hombres son examinados en el horno de la humillación" (cf.
> Ecclesiasticus 2:5). Y está bien dicho, porque el oro se purifica y sube
> en quilates en el fuego [...]. De aquí es lo que dijo aquella santa viuda
> Judith, consolando a los ciudadanos de Bethulia: "Como les puso a
> ellos en el crisol para sondear sus corazones, así el Señor nos hiere a
> nosotros, los que nos acercamos a él, no para castigarnos, sino para
> amonestarnos" (cf. Judith 8:27). De esta probación, como de padre,
> nace otra virtud maravillosa, y es la esperanza. Quiere San Pablo
> decir: cuando el justo es probado por la tribulación, teniendo sufrim-
> iento y loando a Dios que se la envió, luego le da el Señor una
> prenda de gran valor, y es confianza que se ha de salvar, y que Dios

le es padre y defensor en sus trabajos. De aquí es que viene a decir aquellas palabras del rey David: "Vos, Señor, singularmente me pusisteis en esperanza" (Psalm 4:10) [Ecclesiasticus says that "as gold is tried in the fire, so are men examined in the furnace of humiliation." And this is well said, for gold is refined and increases in value in fire [. . .]. Hence what was said by that holy widow Judith, when consoling the inhabitants of Bethulia: "Just as He placed them in the crucible to probe their hearts, so the Lord wounds us who draw near to Him, not to punish but to admonish us." From this test, as from a father, is born another wonderful virtue, namely hope. St. Paul's meaning is: when the just man is tested by tribulation, experiencing suffering and praising God who sent it to him, then God gives him a token of great value, namely trust that he will be saved, and that God is for him a father and defender in his trials. Hence he is able to say those words of King David, "You, Lord, have singularly settled me in hope"].[45]

A few lines later, Anareto urges Enrico to marry, giving him advice on how to choose and treat a bride.[46] His words call to mind the fatherly counsels in Proverbs and Ecclesiasticus on how to treat a wife (Proverbs 31:11-12; Ecclesiasticus 9:1-2, 25:18-26). As an example of worldly wisdom they are unremarkable, but understood figuratively they express the message of the play. The most striking advice is to trust the beloved:

> Y nunca entienda de ti
> que de su amor no te fías,
> que viendo que desconfías,
> todo lo ha de hacer ansí
> [And may she never gather from you / that you do not trust her love,
> / for on seeing your lack of trust, / she is sure to behave accordingly]
> (1186-89).

As Daniel Rogers indicated, "there is a significant analogy between what Anareto says here [...] and what the whole play has to say about the need to trust God."[47] Anareto's other advice is also significant. First, he warns Enrico not to be unduly influenced by good looks when he seeks his spouse:

> No busques mujer hermosa,
> porque es cosa peligrosa

 ser en cárcel mal segura

 alcaide de una hermosura

 donde es la afrenta forzosa

[Do not seek a beautiful woman, / for it is a dangerous thing / to be, in an insecure prison, / the keeper of a beauty / from which dishonour is sure to result] (1180-84).

One theme of the play (which has been called a dramatisation of the notion that appearances deceive)[48] is that God does not judge a person simply on good works. Finally, as he falls asleep, Anareto urges caution in timing the marriage proposal, a remark that Enrico describes as "la mejor lición" [the best lesson]:

 No declares tu pasión

 hasta llegar la ocasión

[Do not declare your love / until the occasion arises] (1195-96).

His words, understood figuratively, may explain the curious scene later in the play when Enrico, facing death, wishes to repent, but cannot:

 Vénguese en mí el justo cielo,

 que quisiera arrepentirme,

 y cuando quiero no puedo

[Let righteous heaven have revenge on me, / for I should like to repent, / and when I wish to do so, I cannot] (1775-77).

To account for this twist in the plot, it is not necessary to invoke the distinctions between sufficient and efficient grace.[49] It was a common theme in devotional literature that a deathbed repentance was a gift of God, and could not be planned. To rely on it was presumption. In the words of Pablo de León: "¿Qué mayor presunción puede ser que presumir de hacer mal con intención de salir de él cuando quisiere, como aquel salir no sea en su poder?" [What greater presumption can there be than to presume to do evil with the intention of withdrawing from it when one so wishes, when that withdrawal is not in one's power?][50] For Luis de Granada, such behaviour was deranged:

 ¿qué mayor locura que disponer un hombre por su autoridad lo que

 ha de ser adelante, como si tuviese en su mano la presidencia de los

 tiempos y momentos que el padre eterno tiene puestos en su poder?

 [. . .] Sólo este atrevimiento merece ser castigado con este castigo—

para que el loco por la pena sea cuerdo—: que no halle adelante tiempo de penitencia el que no quiso aprovecharse del que Dios le daba [What is more mad than a man arranging on his authority what will happen in the future, as if he had in his remit the overseeing of times and moments that the eternal father has reserved for his own power? [. . .] This rashness deserves to be castigated only with the following punishment—so that by suffering the madman might be made sane: that no opportunity for repentence be available in the future to one who declined to take the opportunity offered him by God].[51]

Enrico, in the end, is granted contrition, but at the appropriate moment, when death is certain, and in the presence of Anareto, the person through whom he hears God's declaration of love. On reaching Enrico's prison cell, Anareto hails the *ocasión* that has impelled him to come:

> La cama, Enrico, dejé,
> y arrimado a este bordón
> por quien me sustento en pie,
> vengo en aquesta ocasión
> [I left my bed, Enrico, / and leaning on this staff / which enables me
> to stand, / I come on this occasion] (2457-60).

The occasion is, indeed, momentous. Enrico, regretting his decision not to escape, has just called on the Devil to return, and is about to rebel once more. Anareto's arrival at this point, as Nicholas Round has noted, is "a free gift, an act of grace."[52]

The image of married love which Anareto invokes is used throughout Scripture to describe God's dealings with humankind, a point to which the *Catechism of the Council of Trent* drew attention:

> Quum enim Christus dominus vellet arctissimae illius necessitudinis, quae ei cum ecclesia intercedit, suaeque erga nos immensae charitatis certum aliquod signum dare, tanti mysterii dignitatem hac potissimum maris et feminae sancta coniunctione declaravit [When Christ the Lord would give some sign of that very close union which subsists between Him and His Church, and of His boundless love towards us, He made known the dignity of so great a mystery principally by this holy union of man and wife].[53]

In the action of the play, by contrast, the fidelity Anareto counsels is wholly absent. In the first act, Lisardo asks Celia to compose a poem for a woman who deserted him to marry another man (441-44), and Octavio asks her to do the same for a woman who loved him when he was well off and left him when he became poor (455-58). Later, in act three, Enrico discovers that Celia has abandoned him to marry Lisardo instead (2129-32). Her betrayal, as Oakley notes, is one of a series of events that lead, ultimately, to his repentance.[54] These instances of infidelity throw into relief the ideal to which Anareto points, an ideal which in the play only divine love fulfils.

At the end of Act Three, Paulo appears before the audience and confesses his folly. Greater wisdom, he now sees, would have protected him against the Devil's deceit:

> Forma de un ángel tomó
> y engañóme; que a ser sabio
> con su engaño me salvara
> [He assumed the guise of an angel / and deceived me; yet had I been
> wise, / his deception would have saved me] (2961-63).

He then goes on to curse his parents:

> ¡Malditos mis padres sean
> mil veces, pues me engendraron!
> [Cursed be my parents / a thousand times, for they conceived me!]
> (2971-72)

His words recall several passages in Scripture which proclaim that such a curse deserves death, among them Leviticus 20:9: "If a man curses father or mother, his life must pay for it; he has put himself beyond hope of pardon."[55] For most of the play, Enrico, in his presumption, is as foolish as Paulo. He has, however, one claim to wisdom: the filial love that bears fruit eventually in his conversion. In this respect, his story is an antidote to Paulo's, and illustrates the wise advice offered in Ecclesiasticus (3:12-15):

> My son, support your father in his old age [. . .]. Even if his mind
> should fail, show him sympathy, do not despise him in your health
> and strength: for kindness to a father shall not be forgotten, but will
> serve as reparation for your sins. In the days of your affliction it will
> be remembered of you; like frost in sunshine, your sins will melt away.

The nature of the wisdom that the work commends is underscored towards the end when Paulo returns to Hell, having explained why his condemnation was just. One of the characters on stage (*el juez*) exclaims: "Misterios son del Señor" [They are mysteries of the Lord] (2975). The phrase is apt, for the play has focused our attention on enigmas, and "if its enigmas are carefully made fathomless, that is because reality itself is ultimately fathomless."[56] The Council of Trent had done likewise. In its *Decree on Justification* it had stated that for a person to be saved both free will and grace were essential, but it had refrained altogether from probing the interplay between them.[57] Reticence about the workings of the Almighty, whose providence is inscrutable, is also a biblical theme, vigorously expressed in the Book of Job, where God enquires: "Do you know the order of heaven? And can you set down the reason of it on the earth?" (Job 38:33). Commenting on these words in his *Moralia in Iob* [Morals on the Book of Job], St. Gregory the Great had observed:

> Rationem uidelicet coeli in terra ponere, est supernorum iudiciorum mysteria uel considerando discutere, uel loquendo manifestare. Quod utique facere in hac uita positus nullus potest [To set down, namely, the reason of heaven on the earth, is either to examine the mysteries of the heavenly judgments by consideration, or to make them manifest in words. Which certainly no one can do who is placed in this life].[58]

To illustrate the point, he had gone on to give examples of such "mysteries," including the case of two men, one of them evil in conduct, the other apparently good:

> Quis intelligat cur [. . .] alius male uiuens diu reseruatur, ut corrigat, alius uero bene quidem uidetur uiere, sed in hac uita eo usque durat, quoad peruersa prorumpat? [Who can understand why [. . .] one who is an evil liver is spared for a long time, in order that he may improve, while another seems to be living properly, but continues in this life till he breaks out into evil ways?][59]

He had concluded:

> Quis ergo ista iudiciorum caelestium secreta discutiat? Quis intelligat discretam lancem aequitatis occultae? Ad cognoscendos quippe istos iudiciorum secretorum sinus nullus ascendit [Who then can examine into these secrets of the heavenly judgments? Who can

understand the secret balance of hidden equity? For no one attains
to understand these recesses of secret judgments.][60]

Did the author of *El condenado por desconfiado* find in this text about true wisdom a seed from which his drama grew? Certainly he took pains to ensure that his characters, faced with the judgments of God, would appear to be caught up in events far beyond their grasp: "Paulo, shrunk within the limits of his earth-reason, rebels against something which he does not understand. Enrico transcends reason also to follow something which he does not intellectually understand. And most important of all, Tirso sees to it that they really seem not to understand."[61] The wisdom that Paulo and Enrico need, and that only Enrico acquires, is shown, in this way, to depend not on reason but on faith, a lesson that the Devil, ironically enough, voices clearly:

> porque es la fe en el cristiano
> que sirviendo a Dios y haciendo
> buenas obras, ha de ir
> a gozar de él en muriendo
> [for it is the Christian's faith / that if he serves God and performs /
> good works, he will surely go / to enjoy him, when he dies] (209-12).

6.1   Diego Rodríguez de Silva y Velázquez (1599-1660). *Kitchen Scene with Christ in the House of Martha and Mary*. 1618. Oil on canvas. 60 x 103.5 cm. Bequeathed by Sir William H. Gregory, 1892. © The National Gallery, London.

Chapter Six

Painting: The Biblical *bodegones* of Velázquez

In an article entitled *Enigmas*, published to mark the fourth centenary of Velázquez's birth, the Spanish art historian Alfonso Pérez Sánchez observed that many of his paintings remain hard to interpret despite the scholarly attention they have received, and he suggested that this may be so because they have not been related precisely to the thought and literature of his time, including the *conceptismo* that his contemporaries prized.[1] Among the enigmatic canvases to which he alludes, one that stands out is the early *bodegón* [a genre scene combined with a still-life] entitled in English, *Kitchen Scene with Christ in the House of Martha and Mary*, which has hung since 1892 in the National Gallery in London (Plate 6.1). A fragmentary date uncovered in the course of restoration indicates that it was completed in 1618, when the artist was living in Seville and entering into the humanist and ecclesiastical circles with which his father-in-law, Francisco de Pacheco, was familiar. In composition it is similar to another *bodegón* of his, *Kitchen Maid with the Supper at Emmaus* (Plate 6.16), which is now in the National Gallery of Ireland in Dublin, and it has been suggested that originally the two paintings hung together.[2] However, the precise circumstances in which they were produced are unrecorded, and we have no accounts by contemporaries of how they were received.[3] In modern times, by contrast, they have been the subject of much debate, especially *Christ in the House of Martha and Mary*, of which Enriqueta Harris has observed, "nearly as remarkable [as the work itself] is the amount of ink spilt [...] in attempts to read meaning into the painting as a whole and into every detail."[4] In spite, or perhaps because, of this debate, critics continue to vary in their views, and there exists no consensus about the interpretation of either *bodegón*. The purpose of the pages that follow is to reconsider the enigmatic features of both works in the light of various types of writing, devotional, exegetic, and rhetorical, by which biblical themes and images were disseminated in the Spain of Velázquez's time.[5]

CHRIST IN THE HOUSE OF MARTHA AND MARY

Christ in the House of Martha and Mary presents us with two scenes that differ in content, period, and style. The first is contemporary and secular. In the foreground, on the left, are two women who are dressed in seventeenth-century clothes, and portrayed in a kitchen beside food and utensils that have been painted with "heightened physicality."[6] The second is historical and religious. In the background, on the right, we see, through a frame, a relatively small and sketchy rendition of two women. They are in the presence of Jesus inside a room: the house of Martha and Mary. The differences between the two scenes imply a reversal of the roles traditionally accorded to the sacred and the profane: the religious event is reduced to an inset, and the secular setting becomes prominent.[7] This feature of the painting has led some to conclude that its subject is not religious at all. For Ortega y Gasset, the background scene had "una irreal presencia" [an unreal presence] which showed that Velázquez was reluctant to paint religious subjects,[8] and, more recently, Lawrence Gowing concluded: "the Martha and Mary subject seen through the hatch and painted so feebly is surely no more than a laudable footnote [...] supplying at best a reminder of the honour done to household life by a mention in Scripture."[9] It may be argued, however, that the matter looks different when we bear in mind the artistic conventions on which Velázquez drew and how he transformed them.

The technique of inversion, as it has been termed, was pioneered in the Netherlands by Pieter Aertsen, who during the 1550s made three paintings of the Bethany scene. In the second of these, which has been dated to 1553, there is a striking contrast between the secular foreground, filled with an abundant display of food and utensils, and the religious background, where Christ is seated with Martha and Mary (Plate 6.2).[10] It is a contrast, above all, of atmosphere: the people in the foreground (apostles to the right, sixteenth-century figures to the left) are absorbed in their revelry, apparently unaware of the sacred conversation taking place close by. Similar contrasts may be observed in the work of Aertsen's relative, Joachim Beuckelaer, who made several versions of the same subject, in one of which, dated 1568, the foreground is dominated by the cooks, busy with their tasks, and by the food they are preparing, while the Gospel story unfolds in a far room, glimpsed through an arch (Plate 6.3).[11] The same pattern recurs in the many works by which the convention was disseminated throughout Europe in the late sixteenth century, among them the painting by the Lombard artist, Vincenzo Campi (Plate 6.4), and the engravings of Jacob Matham.[12]

When, with these examples in mind, we examine again Velázquez's version of the theme, we are likely to be struck not only by similarity but by difference.[13] First, in place of profusion there is simplicity: the ingredients and utensils are still prominent, but they are modest and few. Second, the deep recession of the background is eliminated, and, as a result, the Gospel scene is brought closer, in an interior that is more intimate and confining. Third, and, above all, there is a different atmosphere.

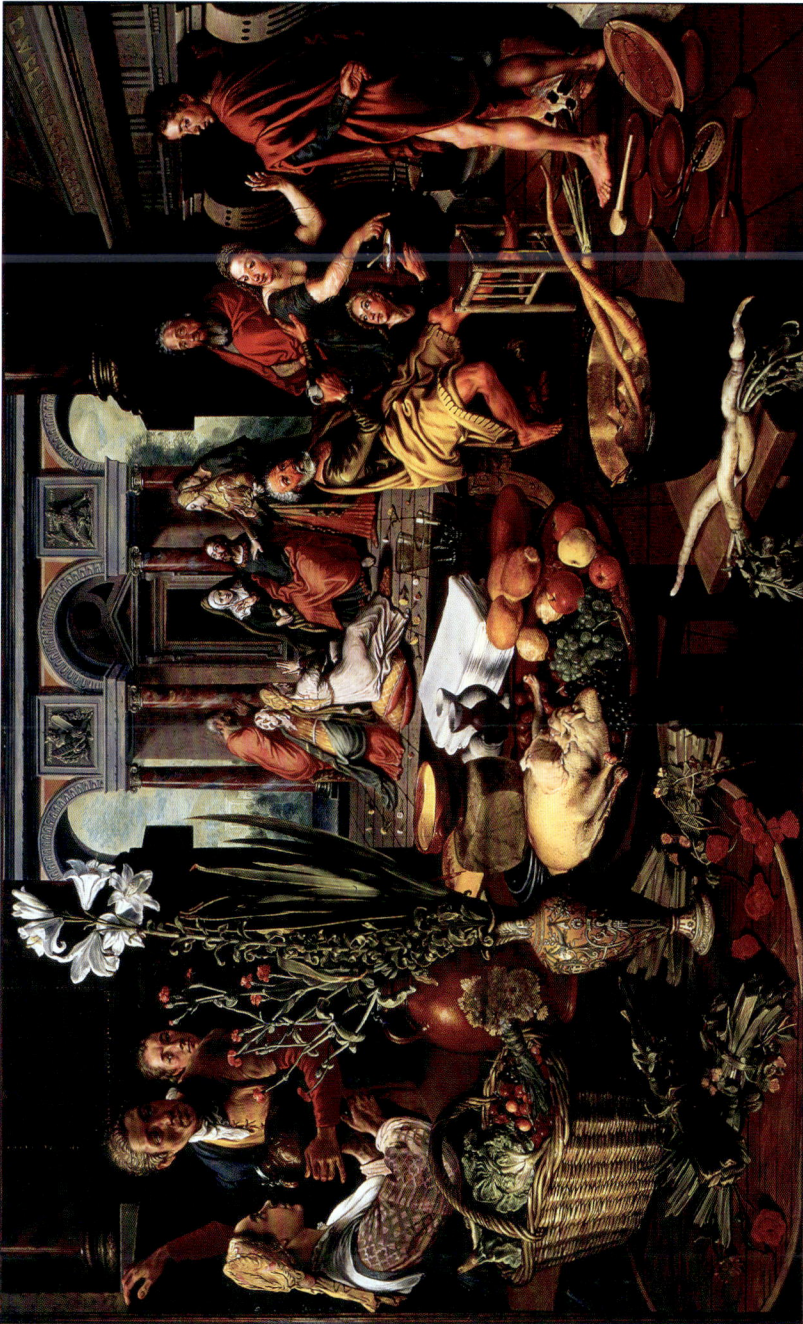

6.2   Pieter Aertsen (Lange Pier) (1507/8-75). *Christ in the House of Martha and Mary.* 1553. Oil on canvas.
© Museum Boijmans Van Beuningen, Rotterdam.

6.3 Joachim Beuckelaer (active 1560-74). *Kitchen Scene with Christ in the House of Martha and Mary.* 1568. Oil on canvas. Museo del Prado, Madrid.

6.4 Vincenzo Campi (1536-91). *Martha Preparing the Meal for Jesus* or *Jesus at the House of Martha and Mary*. Oil on canvas. Galleria e Museo Estense, Modena, Italy. Alinari. The Bridgeman Art Library.

The foreground figures are no longer portrayed, with moralising intent, in a light-hearted or comic mode. Instead, they have about them a certain gravity and stillness.[14] Nor do they appear to be oblivious to the sacred events nearby. As Aidan Weston-Lewis has noted, "[the] pensive kitchen maids seem to betray an awareness, however elliptic, of the event illustrated in the subsidiary scene," and instead of a stark contrast between the religious and secular elements there is now, as he remarks, "an implicit harmony" of a subtle kind.

In making these changes to a well-known convention, Velázquez may have been influenced by other traditions, both iconographic and literary, that are now not easy to recover. Some of them, it may be argued, inform a striking miniature in a fifteenth-century Book of Hours in which Mary of Burgundy, for whom the book was made, is shown seated in a room and reading. Behind her there is a window overlooking a Gothic chapel, where the Virgin is seated with Mary at her side. As Virginia Reinburg has noted, the background and the foreground are intimately linked: "what we see is Mary's visualization of the act of prayer. Through prayer Mary imagines herself in the Madonna's presence" (Plate 6.5).[15] Underlying the miniature, and taken for granted in it, is a meditation practice widely cultivated at the time: the technique of imagining scenes from the life of Christ as if they were present, not past. It was described vividly by, among others, Ludolph of Saxony, whose *Vita Christi* was popular throughout Europe when the miniature was made. In the famous Spanish version by Fray Ambrosio Montesino, his words read:

> assi esta presente a las tales cosas que assi por el mesmo Señor fueron dichas o hechas como si con tus propias orejas las oyesses i con tus ojos las viesses [...]. E porende aunque muchas dellas se cuentan como ya passadas: cata que las pienses como si todas te fuessen presentes [...] lee las cosas ya hechas como si agora se fiziessen: i pon ante tus ojos los fechos passados como si fuessen presentes: i assi te paresceran los mysterios de xpo mas sabrosas i mas alegres [Be present to such things as were said or done thus by the Lord Himself as if you were hearing them with your own ears and seeing them with your own eyes [...]. And although, therefore, many of them are recounted as now having passed, be careful to think about them as if they were all present to you [...] read things now passed as if they were happening now, and place before your eyes events that occurred in the past as if they were present; and in this way the mysteries of Christ will seem to you more delightful and joyful].[16]

6.5 *Mary of Burgundy Praying from Her Book of Hours*. An illustration in *The Hours of Mary of Burgundy*, folio 14v. Codex Vindobonensis 1857. Österreichische Nationalbibliothek, Vienna.
© Austrian National Library Vienna, Picture Archive.

In Velázquez's day, over a century later, the practice continued to be recommended in the numerous meditation manuals that were written and published in Spain, and various ways of "being present" to biblical events were advised.[17] One of them, made popular by the *Spiritual Exercises* of St Ignatius of Loyola, was to imagine oneself in Palestine at the place and time of the events being meditated.[18] Another involved imagining the sacred events occurring here and now, in one's own surrounds. Fray Luis de Granada recommended the latter option in his famous *Libro de la oración y meditación* [Book of Prayer and Meditation]:

> Cuando el misterio que queremos pensar es de la vida y pasión de Cristo, o de alguna otra cosa que se puede figurar con la imaginación [. . .] debemos figurar cada cosa de éstas con la imaginación de la manera que ella es, o de la manera que pasaría, y hacer cuenta que allí, en aquel mismo lugar donde estamos, pasa todo aquello en presencia nuestra [When the mystery that we wish to consider concerns the life and Passion of Christ, or something else that can be pictured with the imagination [. . .] we should picture each of these things in our imagination as it is, or as it would occur, and be aware that there, in that very place where we are, it is all happening in our presence].[19]

Both these methods were set out by St. Francis of Sales in his *Introduction à la vie dévote* [Introduction to the Devout Life], which became a bestseller in Spain after it was published there in translation in 1618.[20]

Such precepts can help us to understand the curious depiction of time and space in Velázquez's painting. The two women in the foreground belong to the Spain of his time, but the figures glimpsed beyond them are from the New Testament age. This juxtaposition of two worlds makes sense if we suppose that in the inset we are shown the subject of the women's thoughts: they are considering the scene in Bethany by imagining that it is happening in their own period and place. The scene, in this sense, is both there and not there; it is "una irreal presencia" as Ortega termed it,[21] but a presence nevertheless.

The use in this way of a background scene to portray thoughts would not have been unfamiliar to Velázquez's contemporaries, for it was sanctioned by an iconographic convention that was well established by the fifteenth century. It may be observed, for instance, in a fresco by the School of Fra Angelico, *Christ Mocked in the Presence of the Virgin and St. Dominic*, where the saint is portrayed in the foreground, absorbed in *lectio divina* [sacred reading], while behind him we behold the subject of his prayerful meditation: the image of Jesus blindfolded, with symbols of violence and derision around his head (Plate 6.6).[22] In the *Portrait of a Young Man* by his contemporary, Petrus Christus, the figure in the foreground, who gazes out of the canvas, is holding an open volume, perhaps a work of devotion or a Book of Hours, while behind him hangs a sheet of parchment, fixed to a board, which indicates the subject of his thoughts: a prayer to St. Veronica. The prayer, well known at the time, carried with it an indulgence, provided that it was recited before an image of Christ's face, of the kind shown on the board above the text itself (Plate 6.7).[23] Again, in a French miniature of the period, by Jean Colombe, which depicts Boethius in his study, the framed scene on the left makes visible the interior life of the writer, seated on the right, who is shown calling to mind a past event: the visit to his bedside of Lady Philosophy (Plate 6.8).[24]

In paintings of a later period, the convention recurs. It may be seen in the portrait by Lorenzo Lotto of Fra Gregorio Bela da Vicenza (1547), in which the friar, holding a book in one hand and beating his breast with the other, looks out of the picture towards the viewer, lost in thought. Behind him, a small scene shows Christ on the Cross, the subject of his meditation (Plate 6.9).[25] It is apparent, too, in the portrayal of St. Stephen in the Temple by Juan de Juanes (c. 1565), where the framed inset at the back places before us the vision of Christ in glory that Stephen was granted, but that the Sanhedrin around him could not see (Plate 6.10).[26] Similarly, the painting of Sts. Sebastian and Irene (1616) by Francisco Pacheco, Velázquez's father-in-law, includes a background scene, glimpsed through a window, which explains to us the actions of the two figures in the foreground. Without it, we might not guess their identities or their thoughts. To the right, we see St. Irene, and to the left St. Sebastian, the man she had earlier rescued from death in the gruesome scene that the inset depicts. They are silent and withdrawn, yet united by a tenderness which their gestures express. The framed scene behind them enables us to understand why, and in this way gives us access to their inner lives (Plate 6.11).[27]

In Velázquez's painting, the two women in the foreground are also absorbed in their thoughts, and, unlike the figures in the inset, they do not speak. As Leo Steinberg has remarked, in a memorable phrase, their faces "seem stilled from within as if restrained by an earnestness too deep for externalization."[28] This detail, too, may be connected with meditation. The manuals often made the point that the goal of meditation was not speculation or discussion, but a deeper wisdom, sought in recollection, and attained, not by analysis, but by looking and listening with attention. Luis de Granada writes:

> No aciertan este camino los que de tal manera se ponen en la
> oración a meditar los misterios divinos como si lo estudiasen para

6.6 School of Fra Angelico (c.1387-1455). *Christ Mocked in the Presence of the Virgin and St. Dominic.*
Fresco. Church of San Marco, Florence, Italy. Alinari.
The Bridgeman Art Library.

6.7   Petrus Christus (d. 1475/1476). *Portrait of a Young Man*. 1450-60. Oil on oak. 35.4 x 26 cm.
Salting Bequest, 1910.
© The National Gallery London.

6.8 Jean Colombe (c.1430-c. 1493). *Boethius and Philosophy*. British Library Harley MS. 4335, folio 1.
© The British Library Board.

6.9   Lorenzo Lotto (c.1480-1556). *Brother Gregorio Belo of Vicenza*. 1547. Oil on canvas. 87.3 x 7.1 cm.
The Metropoilitan Museum of Art, Rogers Fund, 1965 (65.117).
© The Metropolitan Museum of Art.

6.10 Juan de Juanes (Vicente Juan Masip) (c.1523-79). *St. Stephen in the Temple*. c.1565. Oil on canvas. 160 x 125 cm. Museo del Prado, Madrid.

6.11 Francisco Pacheco (1564-1644). *St. Sebastian in Bed, Attended by St. Irene*. Formerly in Alcalá de Guadaira: Hospital of St Sebastian. Destroyed in 1936.

predicar: lo cual más es derramar el espíritu que recogerlo, y andar más fuera de sí que dentro de sí […]. Debrían los tales considerar que en este ejercicio más nos llegamos a escuchar que a parlar; pues, como dijo el profeta, *los que se llegan a los pies del Señor, recibirán de su doctrina* (Deuteronomy 33:3), como la recibía aquel que decía: *Oiré lo que hablare dentro de mí el Señor Dios* (Psalm 84:9) [Those people fail to find this path who, when they pray, begin to meditate on the divine mysteries as if they were studying the matter in order to preach; to act in this way is to pour the spirit out rather than to gather it in, and to move outside oneself rather than within […]. Such people should consider that in this practice we come to listen rather than to chatter; for, as the prophet said, "they that approach to the feet of the Lord shall receive of His doctrine," just as he received it who said, "I will hear what the Lord God will speak within me"].[29]

THE FOREGROUND FIGURES

The two women in the foreground are looking out of the picture towards the place in which the viewer stands. The older is pointing, with her right hand, in the direction of her companion and the inset behind. The younger is pensive, and, it appears, rather sullen and puzzled too. The painting invites us to wonder at the meaning of their actions and expressions, and it impels us to seek an answer in the scene occupying their thoughts, which is recounted in the Gospel of St. Luke (10: 38-41):

> Now it came to pass, as they went, that He entered into a certain town: and a certain woman named Martha received Him into her house. And she had a sister called Mary, who, sitting also at the Lord's feet, heard His word. But Martha was busy about much serving. Who stood and said: Lord, hast Thou no care that my sister hath left me alone to serve? Speak to her therefore, that she help me. And the Lord answering, said to her: Martha, Martha, thou art careful and art troubled about many things: But one thing is necessary. Mary hath chosen the best part, which shall not be taken away from her.[30]

The story of Bethany has been read in many different ways over the centuries, as Giles Constable, who has studied its interpretation, makes plain: "every generation, almost since the beginning of Christianity, has tried to fit the story of Martha and Mary to its needs and to find in it a meaning suited to the Christian life of its time."[31] In order, therefore, to understand its role in this particular painting, it is helpful for us to enquire how it was interpreted in early seventeenth-century Spain.

The two most influential commentaries on St. Luke in Velázquez's day were by Spaniards. Juan Maldonado, a native of Extremadura, wrote a study of the Gospels which appeared posthumously in 1597 and soon became popular, going through seven editions between then and 1619.[32] Francisco de Toledo, who was born in Cordoba, left his Lucan commentary unfinished at chapter twelve on his death in 1596, but it was published four years later in Paris, Venice, and Rome, and in 1611 it was reissued in Cologne.[33] Both these writers were members of the Society of Jesus, an influential order in the Seville of Velázquez's time, and one with which his father-in-law had close relations; and both left their mark on Catholic theology, not only directly, in the formation of priests, but indirectly, too, through popular preaching.[34] Their commentaries throw light on several aspects of the background scene, especially three.

First, there is the contrasting age of the two female figures. Critics have agreed that the young woman seated must be Mary, listening to the Lord, but they have differed about the identity of the woman standing. Many have considered her to be Martha, Mary's sister, but some have argued that, because of her greater years, this cannot be so, and they have suggested that she may be, instead, an anonymous figure introduced into the scene on Velázquez's initiative.[35] Maldonado's commentary resolves the issue. In his view, the Gospel account implies, in several small details, that Martha was indeed older than Mary. When Christ visited their home, he notes, she was the one who welcomed Him and who seemed to be in charge, acting as His hostess to ensure that all His needs were met. Moreover, he adds, Mary is described as her sister, not *vice-versa*, an implicit recognition of seniority.[36]

Second, there are the postures of the three figures in the room. These correspond exactly with how Maldonado describes them. Mary sat at Christ's feet, he observes, the more easily to hear His words. He too was seated, and at once began to teach (in the picture His chair is imposing: it is a *cathedra*, from which instruction is dispensed), but Mary was seated lower down, as befitted a disciple and a woman. Martha, by contrast, stood before Christ, because such is the stance one adopts when addressing a judge, and she wished Him to reprimand her sister, whom she accused of neglecting her work.[37]

Third, there is the depiction of Martha and Jesus. The scene, considered closely, portrays, not just a group of people in a room, but a specific moment: Jesus and Martha face each other, gazing intently, each with a hand raised, as if to indicate that both have spoken. Their exchange, no doubt, is the one recorded in the Gospel. Martha has made her complaint, and is hearing Christ's reply: "Martha, Martha, thou art careful and art troubled about many things." Both Maldonado and Toledo interpret His words as a rebuke, loving but firm: she had failed to grasp a central point in His teaching, and so He reproached her by repeating her name. In the picture He raises His left hand, not His right, a traditional sign of censure.[38]

The young woman in the foreground, it would seem, is pondering their exchange and trying to understand it. She looks perplexed and slightly resentful, a response that reminds us of the reaction of Martha. The implication appears to be that she is trying to apply to her own situation the lesson that Martha was taught. But what was that lesson? If she is puzzled, it may be because, like Martha, she is involved in a practical task. Do the Lord's words imply that to be perfect one must desist from activity, like Mary? The question is raised by Maldonado and Toledo. Both reply that Martha was chided, not for being busy, for she was doing a good work and her motive was love, but for being distracted: she had become over-anxious, and had lost her peace of soul. The lesson Christ wished her to learn was not to give up her work of service, but to combine it with attentiveness to Him; to integrate, in other words, the lives of contemplation and action. The point is well made in a passage, attributed to St. Gregory the Great, that Toledo cites in full:

> Quo profecto exemplo instruimur ut qui fratribus ministeria exhibemus, si per moram sedere ad redemptoris pedes non possumus, per aliquantulam morulam redemptori adsistere debeamus. Sed bene ei adsistimus si transeundo et serviendo videamus. Quid est autem transeundo Dominum cernere, nisi in omni nostro boni opere ad ipsum dirigere cordis intentionem? Transimus enim quando, huc illucque discurrendo, in membris suis Domino ministramus, sed transiendo Dominum cernimus si per omne quod agimus praesentem nobis ipsum cui placere cupimus contemplamur [By this example, clearly, we are taught that if we who serve our brethren cannot sit undisturbed at our Redeemer's feet, we should find a little time to be in the Redeemer's presence. This, indeed, we can do if we look on Him while we move around and serve. And what does it mean to look on the Lord as we move around, if not to direct towards Him, in all our good works, the intention of our hearts? For we move around when, dashing here and there, we serve the Lord in His members; but we look on the Lord as we move around if, in all we do, we contemplate Him, present to us, whom we desire to please].[39]

In the early seventeenth century this lesson had a particular appeal. For over one hundred years, devotional writers in Spain had sought to provide a literature suitable for lay people living in the world, and one purpose of the meditation manuals was to provide methods of drawing work and prayer into harmony. In them, we find the story of Bethany cited as an example of the need to integrate the two. Luis de Granada writes:

> Así como impiden los cuidados y congojas del espíritu, así también impiden las ocupaciones y trabajos del cuerpo cuando son demasiados; porque los unos embarazan el espíritu para que no pueda orar, y los otros ocupan el tiempo para que no haya lugar de orar […]. .Mas en las unas y en las otras ocupaciones conviene tener medida, porque no impida lo menos a lo más; conviene saber: la obra de Marta a la de María [Just as the cares and anguish of the spirit become impediments, so also do the labours and sufferings of the body when they are excessive; for the former prevent the spirit from praying, while the latter take up so much time that none is left for prayer […] But in both these activities (of the spirit and the body), we should be moderate, so that what is lesser, namely the work of Martha, may not impede what is greater: the work of Mary].

A similar point is made by St. Francis de Sales.[40]

To learn such a lesson, however, takes time, as the presence of the older woman seems to imply. Her thoughtful gaze indicates that, like her companion, she is considering the Gospel scene, but, unlike her, she does not look perplexed. Her finger points towards the younger woman as if to say, in the words of the Latin tag, "de te fabula narratur" [the story is about you].[41] She has about her, in addition, as Ruth Fainlight has observed, a certain air of wisdom,[42] and we surmise that she has long lived with the problem illustrated in the Bethany tale and explored in her companion's gaze: the difficulty of doing one's work without neglect of the one thing necessary that Christ praised.

THE STILL-LIFE

The still-life that fills the lower section of the painting to the right has attracted much attention, not only because it is painted magnificently, but also because it seems charged with an elusive significance, difficult to define. John Moffit has argued that each of the objects on the table has a symbolic role: the fish represent Christ, the jug of wine, His blood, the eggs, His resurrection; the garlic stands for worldliness renounced, and the mortar and pestle call to mind the manna of Old Testament times in which the Eucharist was prefigured.[43] This detailed allegorical reading has been echoed, in some respects, by others, but on the whole it has not been well received.

Jonathan Brown, for instance, has criticized it for imposing on the picture, "a set of associations extrinsic to the visual data," and he has affirmed that "the reconstruction of the cultural associations of a given motif does not mean that these associations are automatically to be invoked whenever and wherever they are encountered"; a master painter, like Velázquez, "deliberately orders his composition to focus the viewer's attention on matters he considers to be essential."[44]

The point made by Brown is undoubtedly correct, but it does not follow necessarily that the still-life is no more than a realist scene, bereft of symbolic significance. Three aspects of the painting, indeed, suggest otherwise. First, the composition. The ingredients and utensils on the table in the middle of the canvas are immediately underneath the Bethany scene. In the upper part, we see the figure of Jesus talking, and, in the lower part, the meal that the young woman has been preparing.[45] Considered in the light of exegesis, the juxtaposition is fitting. Maldonado notes that before Jesus received from the sisters food for His body he fed their spirits with His word.[46] The same contrast is made by Toledo.[47] The bringing together of these images at the centre of the painting draws attention to a contrast around which the Gospel story revolves. It also links the two scenes that make up the composition. The fish in the platter point upwards in two directions: on one side, they match the motion of Jesus's hand while He talks; on the other, they lead the viewer's eyes towards the hand of the young woman on her work.[48] In this sense, the still-life may be said to link the painting's elements both in structure and in theme.

Second, there is the simplicity of the meal being prepared. The garlic, pimento, eggs, and fish constitute a modest meal of perhaps one dish, and the temperance, even abstinence, that they denote take us back once again to Bethany.[49] In his discussion of Christ's words to Martha, Toledo cites various authorities to argue that she was "troubled about many things" because she was preparing many courses. Jesus, however, who valued a simple diet, urged her to prepare only one, and thus leave time for matters spiritual. This was "the one thing necessary" that Christ praised.[50]

Third, there are the main ingredients. Fish and eggs are mentioned in St. Luke's Gospel (11:11-13) shortly after the account of the meal in Bethany:

> And which of you, if he ask his father bread, will he give him a stone? Or a fish, will he for a fish give him a serpent? Or if he shall ask an egg, will he reach him a scorpion? If you then, being evil, know how to give good gifts to your children, how much more will your Father from heaven give the good Spirit to them that ask Him?[51]

In this passage, as in the Bethany scene, food becomes an image of prayer. The fish and the egg are examples of hospitality, the good work with which Martha was concerned. They point also to the generosity of God, who cares like a father for those who bring Him their needs, a generosity evident at Bethany in Jesus, at whose feet Mary sat. In this respect they may be seen as emblems of the two kinds of nourishment, corporal and spiritual, on which the painting dwells. In his commentary on the parable, Toledo comments that fish and eggs are everyday ingredients, good for one's health as well as tasty, and he singles out eggs as the food of the poor, noting that Christ took as His examples those things that make up a meal of moderation.[52] His words confirm David Davies's observation that the women in the foreground are instances of the profound sympathy Velázquez shows in his *bodegones* for those who are lowly in class.[53] They are also a further indication of the subtle harmonies that exist between foreground and background in the painting.

THE FRAME

Scholarly discussion of the painting has been characterised by fierce disagreements about the nature of the frame around the background scene. For some, including Maravall and Ortega, it encloses a picture hanging on the kitchen wall.[54] For others, notably López Rey, it is the surround of a mirror.[55] For others, again it is the opening of a hatch.[56] The question was resolved to the satisfaction of many by the restoration carried out in the 1960s which apparently showed that what we see is an embrasure giving into another room.[57] More recently, David Davies and Enriqueta Harris have adduced further reasons for supposing that this is, indeed, the case.[58] None the less, there are scholars who remain unconvinced, among them Odile Delenda who has observed, "on ne peut discerner avec certitude s'il s'agit d'un miroir, d'un tableau ou, plus vraisemblablement, d'une fenêtre de la cuisine, ouverte vers l'extérieur" [One cannot tell with certainty if it is a mirror, a painting, or, more likely, a kitchen window, open outwards].[59]

The long debate to which the issue has given rise may be attributed, in part, to the fact that in places the painting has suffered damage and become worn. There was also, it has emerged, an earlier restoration, in which extensive repainting was carried out. It is, therefore, difficult to ascertain the original state of the canvas.[60] Further reasons, however, may be connected with the work's design. Is it possible that the background scene was deliberately planned to create ambiguity, and thus provoke thought? Certain features suggest that this may be so. First among them is the nature of the frame itself, which abuts on the top and side of the picture, and is, therefore, only partly visible. The viewpoint is to the left of the foreground table, as Davies and

Harris have pointed out,[61] so if a recessed shutter to the right were there it should be visible. Its absence keeps open, at least initially, the possibility that what we see is not a hatch at all, but a painting or a mirror.

Second, there is the curious fact, noted by Peter Cherry, that the lines of perspective in the foreground table do not concur exactly with those in the inset, and that, as a result, each scene is observed from a slightly different angle. Instead of one implied viewpoint, there are two.[62] This detail no doubt explains the impression recorded by Ortega, and noted earlier, that when the background scene is perceived from the viewpoint of the kitchen it seems, in some sense, *irreal*. It also lends support to the notion that the image within the frame may be a painting, in which a divergent perspective of this type would be feasible. On the other hand, the image differs in its brightness from how Velázquez portrays paintings elsewhere. In the contemporary *bodegón*, *The Berlin Musical Trio*, for instance, a painting may be glimpsed behind the singing figures, but although the frame is visible, the picture it encloses is not.[63] Similarly, in *Las Meninas*, the pictures on the walls of the room are portrayed in shadow, and their subjects, as a result, cannot easily be discerned.[64]

Third, there is the scene inside the frame. The left-handed gestures of two of the figures, Jesus and Mary, is the detail that led José López Rey to conclude that what we are shown is a reversed image of the sort a mirror provides, and, more recently, Thomas L. Glen has argued on similar lines that the inset is "a reflection of a scene set in the viewer's space to the left."[65] The theory is made plausible, at first, by certain similarities with mirrors in *Las Meninas* and the *Rokeby Venus*: their frames, too, are dark, and enclose images that are luminous, reversed, and rather sketchy.[66] It is weakened, however, when we recall the iconographic models on which Velázquez drew. In Aertsen's first painting on the subject, completed in 1552, Jesus raises His left hand before Martha in much the same way (Plate 6.12),[67] and in Dürer's *Melancholia*, which lies behind the depiction of Mary, it is again a raised left hand that is portrayed (Plate 6.13).[68] There is, in addition, the telling fact, observed by Tanya Tiffany, that in the background scene light enters from the right, and not from the left, as one would expect if the inset were a mirror.[69] None the less, further details serve to keep doubt alive. Why, for instance, is the mantle of Christ's tunic draped over His right arm, and not over the left, as other pictures of Christ by Velázquez and his contemporaries might lead one to expect? It is on the left arm in the painting attributed to Velázquez of Christ breaking bread at Emmaus (Plate 6.14),[70] and in the version of the theme painted by Caravaggio in 1601 (Plate 6.17)[71] the same detail occurs. Other paintings of Christ's blessing, by Zurbarán (Plate 6.15)[72] and Ribera,[73] observe the convention, and it is respected even when Christ is shown rebuking, as in Zurbarán's depiction of St Jerome being scourged.[74]

6.12 Pieter Aertsen (Lange Pier) (1507/8-75). *Christ with Mary and Martha*. 1552. Oil on panel.
60 x 101.5 cm. Kunsthistorisches Museum, Vienna, Austria.
The Bridgeman Art Library.

6.13 Albrecht Dürer (1471-1528). *Melancholia*. 1514. Print from an engraving, on paper. 241 x 189 mm. © Trustees of the British Museum.

6.14 Diego Rodríguez de Silva y Velázquez (1599-1660). *The Supper at Emmaus*. 1622-23. Oil on canvas. 123.2 x 132.7 cm. The Metropolitan Museum of Art. Bequest of Benjamin Altman, 1913. © The Metropolitan Museum of Art.

6.15 Francisco de Zurbarán (1598-1664). *The Saviour Blessing*. 1638. Oil on canvas. 99 x 71 cm. Museo del Prado, Madrid.

In ways such as these, Velázquez appears to delight in what Julián Gállego has termed "las ambigüedades de la óptica" [the ambiguities of optics].[75] His composition raises questions in our mind, and then provides evidence that points in contrary directions, making a firm answer impossible. However, the process of reflection that this fuels is not wasted. It prompts us to suspect that the ontological status of the background scene is uncertain, a suspicion that other features of the work confirm; and it draws us into an enquiry that goes further, as other and deeper enigmas open up.

COHERENCE

A number of scholars have lamented that the meaning of the painting is obscure. N. MacLaren and A. Braham have written that it "seems to portray immaturity in the confusion of its subject matter," and Jonathan Brown considers that, despite its merits, it is "compromised by a lack of narrative clarity." Others have voiced similar views.[76] It may be argued, however, that a lack of clarity was part of the artist's purpose; that he wished to create a *misterio* [mystery], as the word was understood in his time.

Alexander Parker noted in 1977 that *misterio* is regularly used in Spanish writings of the early seventeenth century to designate, "a statement or juxtaposition of ideas so enigmatic at first sight that the reader senses a significance that he feels compelled to unravel." This is the meaning it has in Góngora's defence of the *Soledades*, in the *autos sacramentales* [sacred dramas] of Calderón, and in the *Agudeza y arte de ingenio* [Wit and the Art of Ingenuity] of Gracián,[77] and it is one of the definitions of the term in the later *Diccionario de Autoridades*, where the phrase *hablar de misterio* is said to mean: "afectar obscuridad en lo que se dice para dar en qué entender y qué discurrir a los que oyen" [to affect obscurity in what one says so that those listening may have something to make sense of and ponder].[78] An analogous approach to lack of clarity may be found in biblical exegesis of the same period. Since Patristic times, the Latin word *mysterium* had been used to designate the secret, spiritual sense of the sacred text that the letter concealed, a notion expressed by St. Ambrose in eloquent terms: "foris littera est, intus mysteria" [the letter is without, the mystery within] (*Epistola* 26, 15); "quam profunda latent misteriorum secreta in litteris!" [how deeply lie, within the letters, the secrets of the mysteries!] (*De Cain et Abel* 1, 4, 13).[79] In the *De doctrina cristiana* [On Christian Teaching], moreover, St. Augustine had defended the obscurity of certain parts of Scripture on the grounds that those who fail to find what they seek suffer from hunger, while others, who do not seek because they have it in front of them, often die of boredom. He had reflected also on the pleasure it gives to learn lessons through imagery, and to struggle with difficulties in order to find meaning.[80] These arguments recur in the *Laurea Evangélica* [The Laurel Tree of the

Gospel] (Salamanca, 1614), a work by Velázquez's older contemporary, the Cistercian Ángel Manrique, in which one detects the influence, not only of the Fathers, but of a metaphysical taste for difficulty.[81] Jesus, he writes, used an enigmatic language, informed by imagery, in order to communicate His teaching because He wished His listeners to be stimulated by perplexity in the quest for truth:

> Quiere que le procuren entender con gran cuidado, para que la misma dificultad de su sentido les haga apetecer más la inteligencia de él, para que engendrándose de la privación el apetito le tengan mejor de llegar a entender lo que les dice [He wishes them to strive most earnestly to understand Him, so that the very difficulty of His meaning might make them hunger more to grasp it, and so that, being born of privation, their appetite for understanding His words to them might increase].[82]

Velázquez's painting, it may be argued, is designed to provoke us in this way. As we stand before it, we are confronted by something which, at first sight, we do not understand. We behold the gaze of a young woman, puzzling over a scene in which Christ is addressing another woman, who is puzzled by His words. For us, the mystery (or *misterio/misterium*) is the exact relation between the two scenes. To solve it, we must ponder the connection between the Gospel story and everyday life, and that, as has been seen, is precisely the problem exercising the young woman. We look at the image of the biblical event that she can see in her mind's eye, and as she thinks it over so do we. We thus become involved in the painting in a personal way. The gestures and expressions of the women in the foreground seem addressed to us, and, to explain the painting, we need the kind of insight that they are concerned to attain.

Velázquez, however, does not leave us without help. By means of compositional devices, he directs our eye to patterns of similarity and difference through which the painting's theme is disclosed. Of particular importance are the parallels and contrasts that exist between the two groups of women. The parallels are clear: in both groups there is an older woman standing partly in shadow, and a younger woman, seated, on whose face light is falling; and, in both, the older woman is turning inwards and gesturing with her right hand. These parallels are reinforced by certain coincidences of colour and design between their various clothes.[83] There are contrasts too. The older woman in the background is busy, complaining, mistaken; her counterpart in the foreground, however, is observant rather than active, supportive rather than complaining, and apparently wise. Similarly, the young woman in the background is inactive, lost in contemplation, and content, unconcerned; her counterpart, on the other hand, is busy, questioning, and preoccupied. At the centre, as we have seen, there is the same play of likeness and distinction between the two types of nourishment placed before the viewer's eye.

To note such parallels and contrasts, and to seek through them a deeper, hidden sense, requires the exercise of *ingenio*, *agudeza* or wit, as the seventeenth century understood it: "the intellectual agility to see similarities in apparently dissimilar things, detecting 'correspondences' that are not self-evident, as well as the inventiveness that can express these 'correspondences' imaginatively."[84] In Velázquez's time, the theory of wit was developed primarily in discussions of poetic language,[85] but, as Michael Woods has noted, the possibility of *agudeza* in other fields, including the visual arts, was not ruled out.[86] An important part of Velázquez's achievement, it may be held, was to realize this possibility in painting, and the *Kitchen Scene with Christ in the House of Martha and Mary* indicates that he had begun to do so while he was still a young artist in Seville.

THE SUPPER AT EMMAUS

Many of the features that distinguish *Christ in the House of Martha and Mary* recur in Velázquez's other religious *bodegón*, *Kitchen Maid with the Supper at Emmaus* (Plate 6.16). Foremost among them is the use of inversion to shape an enigma.[87] We are shown, in the foreground, a young serving girl of African origin, bending over a table on which kitchen utensils are arranged. Her dress indicates that she belongs to the world of Velázquez's time. Behind her, through a hatch (whose shutter is visible, unambiguously, to the right) we glimpse a New Testament event, depicted sketchily: Christ breaking bread with His disciples at Emmaus. The contrast between the secular and the sacred prompts us to ask: what is the connection between the two scenes? In what sense is the Gospel story present in the young woman's workplace? And what is the significance of the expression on her face? Is she lost in thought, and unaware of her surrounds, as she appears to be in the other version of the work, now in Chicago, which omits the background scene?[88] Or is she responding, in some way, to the Gospel event? The answers to such questions are to be sought, once again, in the traditions, pictorial and literary, on which the painting draws.

EMMAUS

The canvas has suffered damage over time, and it has been cut down by several centimetres on both sides.[89] As a result, the face and torso of the disciple on the left have disappeared. None the less, enough survives for us to reconstruct the story that the inset depicts, which is recounted in the Gospel of St. Luke: "And it came to pass, whilst He was at table with them, He took bread, and blessed, and broke, and gave it to them. And their eyes were opened, and they knew Him: and He vanished out of their sight" (Luke 24:30-31).[90] The inset focuses our attention on one moment: Christ has bread in His left hand, which He is blessing with his right, and the disciples, as their postures indicate, are beginning to realise who He is: the one on the left holds out his hand in acclamation, while the one on the right sits forward attentively. These details recur in an earlier and well-known representation of the scene completed by Titian in the early 1530s, and now in the Louvre (Plate 6.18),[91] where the disciple on the left, sitting back in amazement, has his right hand slightly raised, while his companion to the right sits forward with his hands joined, looking on. The disciples react in much the same way in Caravaggio's depiction of the event painted in 1606, now in the Galleria Brera in Milan (Plate 6.19).[92] In his other version of the scene, painted five years earlier, and now in London, Caravaggio dramatised the disciples' response: now it is the one on the right who stretches out his arms, while the one on the left sits back in awe, gripping his chair with both hands (Plate 6.17).[93]

Velázquez's version of the event, however, differs from these precedents in one notable respect. Both Titian and Caravaggio include figures in the scene that the Gospel account does not mention. Titian depicts an innkeeper behind the table, next to Christ, with a boy servant on the extreme left, while beneath the table a small dog plays. The standing innkeeper recurs in the London painting of Caravaggio, while the Milan version shows him accompanied by an elderly woman servant. In the person of his kitchen maid, Velázquez, it would seem, takes over this motif, and in doing so he transforms it: he retains one servant only, makes her female rather than male, and places her beside, rather than within, the New Testament scene. He also alters the nature of the servant figure's response. In the Milan Caravaggio, the innkeeper and the female servant seem unaware of the event to which the disciples are reacting: the eyes of the servant are downcast and averted, and the innkeeper, though looking at Christ, is unseeing. In the London version he looks impassively at Christ once again, unlike the disciples, who have been galvinised.[94] In the Titian, the innkeeper stares at a disciple, not at Christ, while the little dog pursues his own concerns and the servant stands quietly by. Similarly, in a Dürer print of about 1510, which Titian no doubt knew, the disciples turn to Jesus, wholly absorbed, while a figure on the far left looks away, his gaze distracted (Plate 6.20).[95]

The explanation of this motif may lie in the Latin liturgy of Easter Monday, when the Emmaus story supplied the Gospel, both at Mass and in the Office of Matins.[96] In the Office, it was accompanied by a reading from the Homilies of St. Gregory the Great, which related what the disciples saw, and did not see, to their degree of faith:

6.16 Diego Rodríguez de Silva y Velázquez (1599-1660). *Kitchen Maid with the Supper at Emmaus.* Oil on canvas. 55 x 118 cm. National Gallery of Ireland, Beit bequest, 1987. Photograph courtesy of the National Gallery of Ireland.

6.17 Michelangelo Merisi da Caravaggio (1571-1610). *The Supper at Emmaus*. 1601. Oil and tempera on canvas. 141 x 196.2 cm. Presented by Hon. George Vernon, 1839.
© The National Gallery, London.

6.18 Titian (Tiziano Vecellio) (c.1488-1576). *The Supper at Emmaus*. c.1535. Oil on canvas. 169 x 244 cm. Louvre, Paris, France. Giraudon.
The Bridgeman Art Library.

6.19 Michelangelo Merisi da Caravaggio (1571-1610). *The Supper at Emmaus*. 1606. Oil on canvas. 141 x 175 cm. Pinacoteca di Brera, Milan, Italy. The Bridgeman Art Library.

6.20 Albrecht Dürer (1471-1528). *The Supper at Emmaus*. 1510. Woodcut print on paper. 126 x 96 mm.
© Trustees of the British Museum.

"Hoc ergo egit foris Dominus in oculis corporis quod apud ipsos agebatur intus in oculis cordis" [The Lord thus behaved before the eyes of their bodies in accord with what was going on inwardly before the eyes of their hearts].[97] When He first met them on the road, their love of Him was mixed with doubt. He chose, therefore, to be present to them outwardly, in response to their love, but, because of their doubt, He refrained from showing them who He really was. Later, however, the situation changed. After He had explained the Scriptures to them as they walked, they urged Him to stay and dine, and He responded to their offer of hospitality by revealing His identity in full:

> Mensam ponunt, cibos afferunt, et Deum quem in scripturae sacrae expositione non cognouerant, in panis fractione cognoscunt [...]. Ecce Dominus non est cognitus dum loqueretur, et dignatus est cognosci dum pascitur [They set the table, brought food, and recognised in the breaking of bread the God they had not known as He explained the sacred scriptures [...]. The Lord was not recognised when He was speaking, but He deigned to be recognised while He was eating].[98]

In the Emmaus scenes of Dürer, Titian, and Caravaggio, the lesson taught by Gregory is underlined by the presence of the servants, whose blindness to the revelation taking place before their eyes indicates that they lack the inner faith and love by which the disciples are moved.

In Velázquez's painting, by contrast, the serving girl seems aware of the miracle beginning behind her. She has paused in her work, and, with one hand on a jug, she is turning towards the hatch, her face half-lit, like that of Christ, by light falling from the left. What does her reaction mean? For Gregory, like St. Augustine before him,[99] the theme of the Emmaus tale was hospitality:

> Hospitalitatem ergo, fratres carissimi, diligite, caritatis opera amate. Hinc enim per Paulum dicitur: *Caritas fraternitatis maneat et hospitalitatem nolite obliuisci. Per hanc enim placuerunt quidam, angelis hospitio receptis.* Hinc Petrus ait: *Hospitales in inuicem sine murmurationibus.* Hinc ipsa Veritas dicit: *Hospes fui et suscepistis me* [...]. Ecce in iudicium ueniens dicit: *Quod uni ex minimis meis fecistis, mihi fecistis.* Ecce ante iudicium cum per membra sua suscipitur, susceptores suos etiam per semetipsum requirit, et tamen nos ad hospitalitatis gratiam pigri sumus. Pensate, fratres, quanta hospitalitatis uirtus sit. Ad mensas uestras Christum suscipite, ut uos ab eo suscipi ad conuiuia

aeterna ualeatis. Praebete modo peregrino Christo hospitium [Dearly beloved, love hospitality, love the works of charity. Paul said: "Let the charity of the brotherhood remain, and do not forget hospitality; it was by this that some have been made acceptable, having entertained angels hospitably" [Hebrews 13:1-2]; and Peter told us to be "hospitable before one another, without complaint" [1 Peter 4:9]; and Truth Himself said: "I needed hospitality, and you welcomed Me" [Matthew 25:35]. [...] You know that before the judgment He will say, "What you did to one of these, my least ones, you did to Me" [Matthew 25:40]. You know that before the judgment, when He is received in His members, He is Himself searching for those who will receive Him. And yet we are disinclined to offer the gift of hospitality. Consider, my friends, how great the virtue of hospitality is. Receive Christ at your tables so that you may be received by Him at the eternal banquet. Offer hospitality now to Christ the stranger].[100]

Velázquez's painting, it may be argued, illustrates the truth of these words. The humble maid, dutifully serving a guest in the next room, is about to discover in a stranger the presence of Christ, as the disciples did during the Emmaus meal.

The *Paterfamilias*

The interpretation of the painting on these lines is confirmed by a story that Gregory included in his homily to illustrate the point he wished to make:

Quidam paterfamilias cum tota domo sua magno hospitalitatis studio seruiebat; cumque cotidie ad mensam suam peregrinos susciperet, quodam die peregrinus quidam inter alios uenit, ad mensam ductus est. Dumque paterfamilias ex humilitatis consuetudine aquam uellet in eius manibus fundere, conuersus urceum accepit, sed repente eum in cuius manibus aquam fundere uoluerat non inuenit. Cumque hoc factum secum ipse miraretur, eadem nocte ei Dominus per uisionem dixit: Ceteris diebus me in membris meis, hesterno autem die me in memetipso suscepisti [A certain head of a family (*paterfamilias*) with his entire household zealously practised hospitality. Every day he received strangers at his table, and on a certain day a nameless stranger came among them and was brought to table. As was his humble custom, the head of the family wished to pour water for his

213

hands. He turned and took hold of the jug, but suddenly he could not find the person on whose hands he had intended to pour the water. He wondered at what had happened; and on that same night the Lord said to him in a vision: "On other days you received Me in My members; yesterday you received Me in person".[101]

The significant detail here is what happens immediately before the stranger disappears: the *paterfamilias* turns and seizes a jug, only to find, on turning back, that his guest has gone. The same detail recurs in a story about St. Gregory himself which was recorded in the ninth-century life by John the Deacon, and reproduced in the thirteenth century in the *Legenda aurea* of Jacobus of Voragine.[102] In the Spain of Velázquez's day it was probably known most widely in the version by Pedro de Ribadeneira:

> Su caridad para con los pobres fue maravillosa, y por ella recibió grandes dones de Dios. Combidáualos a comer a su mesa: y queriendo una vez por su humildad dar él mismo agua a manos a un pobre peregrino, mientras que tomaua el jarro, para hazer este oficio tan humilde, el peregrino desapareció, y la noche siguiente Christo nuestro Señor le apareció en sueños, y le dixo: *Otras vezes me has recibido en mis miembros, mas ayer me recebiste en mi persona* [His charity towards the poor was wonderful, and through it he received great gifts from God. He would invite them to eat at his table; and wishing on one occasion, in his humility, to himself pour water on the hands of a poor pilgrim, while he was taking hold of the jug to carry out this most humble office, the pilgrim disappeared, and that night Christ Our Lord appeared to him in his dreams and said to him, "On other occasions you have received Me in My members, but yesterday you received Me in person"].[103]

The image in Velázquez's painting of the serving girl holding a jug in her left hand as she turns towards the hatch, connects the kitchen scene with both stories, and the moral that they teach. The literary allusions are reinforced, in turn, by the composition and the use of colour in the work. Our eye is invited to move across from the white cloth on the right, in the basket on the wall, to the white turban of the maid in the centre, and then to descend to the white sleeve of her blouse and the crumpled cloth or paper on the table, before coming to rest, finally, in the jug itself.

EXEGESIS

A further puzzle remains. In the two stories, by and about Gregory, it is implied that the miracles took place when the guests arrived in the house, and before food was served. In Velázquez's picture, however, the bare table, the upturned jug, and the pile of crockery washed and left to dry indicate that the meal prepared earlier in the kitchen is now over, and the maid's work almost done.[104] The puzzle is resolved when we consult the Gospel commentary of Maldonado, whose reflections on the meal at Emmaus include a lengthy discussion of the blessing Christ gave at table, just before He broke the bread. Erasmus, in his *In Evangelium Lucae Paraphrasis* [Paraphrase of the Gospel of St Luke], published in 1523, had described it as the blessing Christ normally gave before a meal began, and he had interpreted the breaking of bread, symbolically, as a sharing of the word of God.[105] Maldonado was aware that this reading had been followed subsequently by certain Protestant divines, and he rejected it energetically. For him, the bread broken by Christ was the Eucharist, and the blessing took place not before the meal but at its close:

> Cum communem benedicebat cibum, non in fine, non in medio nimirum prandii, sed initio, antequam quisquam quidquam gustaret, benedicebat. At hic, non initio, sed in fine, ut indicat Evangelista, benedixit. Hoc enim est [...] *et factum est cum recubuisset*, id est coenasset. Sicut cum Eucharistiam instituit, non initio, sed in fine coenae panem benedixit, ut Matth.26, 26 probavimus [When He blessed ordinary food, He did so, not at the end of the meal, and certainly not during it, but at its start, before anyone had tasted anything. But, as the Evangelist makes clear, He blessed this food not at the start but at the end. For the meaning [of the Greek text] here is, *et factum est cum recubuisset*: that is, "when He had dined." In the same way, when He instituted the Eucharist He blessed bread not at the start of the meal but at its end, as we showed [in the account of the Last Supper] in Matthew 26:26].[106]

The exegesis Maldonado defended became normative in Catholic commentaries of the early seventeenth century, including that of his fellow Jesuit, Cornelius à Lapide.[107] Seen in its light, the moment depicted in the foreground of Velázquez's painting is not anomalous, but in accord with the action of Christ in the Emmaus meal behind.

CONCLUSION

The *Supper at Emmaus* shows the same taste for "wit" that we noticed earlier in *The House of Martha and Mary*. It functions rather like a conceit, as Helen Gardner defined the term: "A conceit is a comparison whose ingenuity is more striking than its justness, or, at least, is more immediately striking. All comparisons discover likeness in things unlike: a comparison becomes a conceit when we are made to concede likeness while being strongly conscious of unlikeness."[108] On first seeing the painting, we are likely to be struck by the difference, of status, epoch and location, in the two scenes portrayed. But when we ponder them in the light of their sources, we are led to concede that, despite their remoteness, they are connected in unexpected ways that throw light on the teaching of the Gospel.

In their subject matter, also, the two works have much in common. Both focus on the relationship between contemplation and action. The London painting underlines that Mary chose the better part: to recognise Christ's presence, and to listen to His word, is what matters, even in the midst of activity. The Dublin painting places the emphasis elsewhere: to recognise Christ's presence, it is not enough to listen to His word; one must put it into action. This is the lesson the two disciples were taught: "audiendo ergo praecepta Dei illuminati non sunt, faciendo illuminati sunt" [they were enlightened, therefore, not on hearing God's commandments, but through their actions].[109] It has been surmised that the two pictures were conceived as a "working pair," and designed to "speak" to each other.[110] If so, their silent dialogue presents the viewer with two contrasting teachings, at first sight hard to reconcile: a further *misterio*.[111]

In both cases, moreover, the Gospel story framed in the inset has to do with the practice of hospitality, a fact which makes plausible the suggestion of Enriqueta Harris and Rosemarie Mulcahy that originally the two pictures hung together in the refectory or guest-room of a nunnery.[112] Convents in Seville at the time regularly employed coloured servants of the sort the Dublin painting depicts, and the work may have been influenced, as Tanya Tiffany has shown, by contemporary debates in Seville about the conversion of African slaves.[113] Equally plausible is the conjecture of Alfonso Pérez Sánchez that they were commissioned for the private gallery of a devout humanist or aristocrat in the city.[114] Such a patron might have belonged to the circle of scholarly friends cultivated by Francisco Pacheco. In the absence of documentary evidence, however, neither theory can be proved. What may be said is that whatever their origins may have been, both *bodegones* presuppose a viewer who is familiar with the traditions of piety and learning on which they draw, and equipped to appreciate with relish the *conceptismo* they display.

Epilogue

In Protestant Europe during the sixteenth and seventeenth centuries, the availability of vernacular translations of the Scriptures and the custom of reading them privately created a common biblical culture to which everyone who was literate had access, whether they were formally educated or not. In Spain of the same period, a common biblical culture existed as well, but it was different in character. It was shaped and sustained by the interaction of two subcultures, one learned and latinate, the other popular and vernacular. The first was centered on the study of the Latin Bible and its patristic and medieval commentators. The second was based on a knowledge of Scripture that was partial and indirect but ubiquitous. The distinction between them was inherited from the Church of the late Middle Ages, which in this respect, as in others, lasted longer in Spain than elsewhere. In the course of the sixteenth century, however, both were transformed by a series of events that marked the emergence of the early modern world: the discovery and colonisation of Spanish America, which Columbus, and many Spaniards after him, strove to interpret in biblical terms; the renewal of biblical studies inspired by the recovery of the original languages of Scripture; the irruption of movements of reform within the Church, among clergy, religious, and laity; and the dissemination throughout society of printed books.

In the latinate subculture, these developments bore fruit towards the end of the sixteenth century in a body of biblical commentaries by Spanish writers which became well known throughout Europe. We have had occasion to mention three Spanish exegetes of the period whose writings were particularly distinguished: Luis de León, Francisco de Toledo, and Juan Maldonado. The work of such authors, at its best, brought together two kinds of scholarship that had begun to flourish earlier in the century: first, the study of the Latin Bible alongside the original texts of Scripture, in Hebrew and Greek, and the ancient translation of the Old Testament into Greek known as the Septuagint; and second, the study of the biblical exegesis of the Church Fathers, notably Origen, Jerome, and Augustine, which Erasmus and his fellow humanists had edited and published.[1] The influence of the commentaries is pervasive in the literature and art of seventeenth-century Spain, when the cultivation of difficulty and Wit spread to all genres. It is apparent, as we have seen, in the biblical *bodegones* of Velázquez, which create enigmas that can be resolved only by invoking certain passages of Scripture and their generally accepted exegesis.

In the vernacular subculture, the arrival of the printing press prompted a demand for religious writings in Castilian which was met in the reign of Ferdinand and Isabella by the publication of devotional works of two kinds, both based on Scripture: late medieval classics, such as the *Vita Christi* of Ludolph of Saxony, and writings penned by Spanish authors, among them García Jiménez de Cisneros, abbot of Montserrat. This literature, as we noted in Chapter Two, had a formative influence, both direct and indirect, on the *Spiritual Exercises* of Ignatius Loyola, who, having no Latin at the time, drew his knowledge of the Bible almost exclusively from such texts. Ignatius went on, after his solitary life in Manresa, to study theology in Paris, and when the Society of Jesus was founded he insisted that its professed members should make the study of the Bible in Hebrew, Greek, and Latin a primary concern. Later in the century, Spanish Jesuits took a leading part in the renewal of biblical studies at university level.[2] None of this, however, led Ignatius or his successors to modify the popular and apocryphal elements in the *Exercises*, which the Society gave to people of all social classes, both educated and unlettered.[3] In this respect, the *Exercises* and the history of their practice offer a vivid example of how the two subcultures, latinate and vernacular, were connected. Their close connection is evident, too, in the vernacular writings of Luis de León, in which his biblical and patristic learning found full expression.

During the reign of Charles V, various movements of Church reform in Spain found a voice in the moral and devotional writings of Erasmus, many of which were translated into Castilian. The anonymous author of *Lazarillo de Tormes* may not have been an Erasmian himself, and his work is not specifically Erasmian in character, but the radical literature informed by scriptural themes that Erasmus inspired forms the backdrop to his book, in which biblical allusions are deployed with skill to provoke laughter, and in doing so to satirise a society out of touch with its spiritual roots. After the *Index* of 1559, when Erasmian writings were banned, a new devotional literature developed, informed by the decrees of the Council of Trent, and influenced by the renewal of biblical preaching that the Council had promoted. Its richness and diversity are apparent in *El condenado por desconfiado*, a *comedia* that makes powerful theatre out of biblical themes and images that writers such as Juan de Ávila, Luis de Granada, and Alonso de Orozco had popularised.

Despite their differences, the two subcultures had one thing in common: in both of them the Bible was read and interpreted in the light of tradition. The Council of Trent, in its fourth session (8 April 1546), rejected the Protestant view that the word of God should be "emancipated from the oppressive authority of church and tradition, and set free to work directly on human hearts and minds."[4] It affirmed instead that the teachings of Christ were transmitted not only in Scripture but in unwritten traditions inherited from the apostles, and that the two channels were subject to the teaching authority of the Church.[5] The Tridentine decree helps us to understand the importance accorded in both subcultures to the scriptural exegesis of the Church Fathers, who were held to have preserved in their writings the apostolic legacy.[6] It follows from this that in order to interpret accurately the literature and art of early modern Spain we need to know more about the devotional writings and the latin commentaries of the time, in which Scripture and tradition were combined. At present, it is true, we lack critical editions and scholarly studies of many of the important works, but, as our knowledge of them grows, we will be better placed to describe both the reception of the Bible in Spain and its impact on the literary imagination of the age.

Notes

PREFACE

1. "Golden Age Studies: Spain and Spanish America in the sixteenth and seventeenth centuries," in Catherine Davies, ed., *The Companion to Hispanic Studies* (London: Arnold, 2002), 50-67.
2. It was published subsequently as an article, "El tránsito del temor servil al temor filial en los 'Ejercicios Espirituales' de san Ignacio," in Juan Plazaola, S.J., ed., *Las fuentes de los Ejercicios Espirituales de San Ignacio* (Bilbao: Mensajero, 1998), 223-40.

A NOTE ON BIBLICAL REFERENCES

1. I have used two editions of the Vulgate Bible: Robert Weber, ed., *Biblia sacra iuxta vulgatam versionem*, 4th edition prepared by Roger Gryson (Stuttgart: Deutsche Bibelgesellschaft, 1994), and *Biblia sacra Vulgatae editionis Sixti V Pontificis Maximi iussu recognita et Clementis VIII auctoritate edita* (Milan: Edizioni San Paolo, 2003)
2. *The Holy Bible Translated from the Latin Vulgate and Diligently Compared with Other Editions in Divers Languages (Douay, A.D. 1609; Rheims, A.D. 1582)* (London: Burns Oates and Washbourne, 1914).

INTRODUCTION

1. See Edward M. Wilson, "Continental Versions to c.1600: Spanish Versions," in *The Cambridge History of the Bible*, vol. 3, ed. S.L. Greenslade (Cambridge: Cambridge University Press, 1963), 125; Guy Bedouelle and Bernard Roussel, eds., *Le Temps des Réformes et la Bible* (Paris: Beauchesne, 1989), 536-37. The *Index* of 1559 was the third produced by the Spanish Inquisition. The first (1551) was an expanded edition of the Index published by the University of Louvain in 1550; the second (1554) was concerned specifically with editions of the Bible. All three are edited in J. M. de Bujanda, *Index de livres interdits: Index de l'Inquisition espagnole, 1551, 1554, 1559* (Sherbrooke: Université de Sherbrooke, 1984). On these and later Indices, see Joseph Pérez, *The Spanish Inquisition: A History*, trans. Janet Lloyd (London: Profile Books, 2004), 181-87.
2. A recent study is Sergio Fernández López, *Lectura y prohibición de la Biblia en lengua vulgar: defensores y detractores* (León: Universidad de León, 2003).
3. Wilson, "Continental Versions to c. 1600," 127. The Bible of Casiodoro de Reina, which included the Apocrypha, was first published in Basle in 1569. On the translation and its background, see A. Gordon Kinder, *Casiodoro de Reina, Spanish Reformer of the Sixteenth Century* (London: Tamesis, 1975).
4. Wilson, "Continental versions from c.1600 to the present day," 354. The translation of the Vulgate by Scío de San Miguel was published in Valencia in ten volumes between 1790 and 1793.
5. Wilson, "Continental Versions to c.1600," 127. On translations of the Psalms, see Laurie Kaplis-Hohwald, *Translation of the Biblical Psalms in Golden Age Spain* (Lewiston: Mellen, 2003).

6. The popularity of devotional writings in Spain and the New World is discussed in Trevor Dadson, *Libros, lectores y lecturas. Estudios sobre bibliotecas particulares españolas del Siglo de Oro* (Madrid: Arco/Libros, 1998), 51-70.

7. H. Outram Evennett, *The Spirit of the Counter-Reformation*, eds. John Bossy (Cambridge: Cambridge University Press, 1968), 41.

8. See Bedouelle and Roussel, eds., *Le Temps des Réformes et la Bible*, 81-83, 262-69.

9. "The Golden Century of Spain was marked by a great florescence of Scripture studies in that land, the Spanish exegetes of the period from 1560 to 1630 surpassing those of other lands." F. J. Crehan, S.J., "The Bible in the Roman Catholic Church from Trent to the Present Day," in *The Cambridge History of the Bible*, vol. 3, ed. S.L. Greenslade (Cambridge: Cambridge University Press, 1963), 213.

10. On the teaching and knowledge of Latin during the Golden Age, see Luis Gil Fernández, *Estudios de humanismo y tradición clásica* (Madrid: Universidad Complutense, 1984), 67-79, and on the universities of the period, Antonio Domínguez Ortiz, *The Golden Age of Spain, 1516-1659* (London: Weidenfeld and Nicolson, 1971), 230-35, and Henry Kamen, *Spain 1469-1714. A Society of Conflict* (London: Longman, 1991), 152-55. The emergence of a secular elite equipped to read the Bible in Latin or Greek is considered in José Ignacio Tellechea, "Bible et théologie en 'langue vulgaire,' discussion à propos du *Catéchisme* de Carranza," in *L'Humanisme dans les lettres espagnoles*, ed. A. Redondo (Paris: Urin, 1979), 219-32.

11. A thoughtful overview of the question is provided in Jeremy Robbins, "Renaissance and Baroque: continuity and transformation in early modern Spain," in David T. Gies, ed., *The Cambridge History of Spanish Literature* (Cambridge: Cambridge University Press, 2004), 146-47. The sixteenth-century context is examined in R.W. Truman, *Spanish Treatises on Government, Society and Religion in the Time of Philip II. The 'De regimine principum' and Associated Traditions* (Leiden: Brill, 1999). On the seventeenth century, see Robbins, *Arts of Perception: The Epistemological Mentality of the Spanish Baroque, 1580-1720*, a special issue of *Bulletin of Spanish Studies* 82 (2005).

12. Mary Midgley, *The Myths We Live By* (London: Routledge, 2004), 1,4.

13. The term and its scope are discussed in Diana de Armas Wilson, *Cervantes, the Novel and the New World* (Oxford: Oxford University Press, 2000), 24-28, and Jorge Checa, "Didactic prose, history, politics, life writing, convent writing, *Crónicas de Indias*," in Gies, *The Cambridge History of Spanish Literature*, 283-90.

14. See Marcel Bataillon, *Erasmo y España. Estudios sobre la historia espiritual del siglo xvi*, trans. Antonio Alatorre (Mexico: Fondo de Cultura Económica, 1966), 44-51, and Alison P. Weber, "Religious literature in early modern Spain," in Gies, ed., *The Cambridge History of Spanish Literature*, 150-51.

15. On the history of Spanish humanism in these years, see Jeremy N. H. Lawrance, "Humanism in the Iberian Peninsula," in *The Impact of Humanism on Western Europe*, ed. Anthony Goodman and Angus MacKay (London: Longman, 1990), 220-58. On Erasmus's critics in Spain see Alejandro Coroleu, "Anti-Erasmianism in Spain," in Erika Rummel, ed., *Biblical Humanism and Scholasticism in the Age of Erasmus* (Leiden and Boston: Brill, 2008), 73-92.

16. "Regardless of the author's name, *Lazarillo* is a work from the pen of a highly learned individual, probably a scholar trained in the Bible, the classics, and the best of vernacular literature." E. Michael Gerli, "The antecedents of the novel in sixteenth-century Spain," in Gies, ed., *The Cambridge History of Spanish Literature*, 197.

17. José Caso González, ed., *La vida de Lazarillo de Tormes y de sus fortunas y adversidades* (Madrid: Boletín de la Real Academia Española, anejo XVII, 1967), 9. See too Alberto Martino, *Il "Lazarillo de Tormes" e la sua ricezione in Europa (1554-1753)*, 2 vols. (Pisa and Rome: Istituti Editoriali e Poligrafici Internazionale, 1999), 1: 1.

18. R. W. Truman, "Lazarillo de Tormes," in *The Continental Renaissance, 1500-1600*, ed. A. J. Krailsheimer (Hassocks: Harvester Press, 1978), 336.

19. Jorge de Montemayor, *Omelías sobre Miserere mei Deus*, ed. Terence O'Reilly (Durham: University of Durham, 2000). On the date of the first edition of Montemayor's religious verse,

see Juan Montero Delgado, "Sobre imprenta y poesía a mediados del xvi (con nuevos datos sobre el *princeps* de *Las obras* de Jorge de Montemayor," *Bulletin Hispanique* 106 (2004): 81-102.

20. See Luis Gómez Canseco and Valentín Núñez Rivera, *Arias Montano y el "Cantar de los cantares." Estudio y edición de la "Paráfrasis en modo pastoril"* (Kassel: Reichenberger, 2001), 14-16. The authors surmise that Montano began to compose the *Paráfrasis* in the summer of 1552, and probably completed it by early 1553.

21. Gómez Canseco and Núñez Rivera, 4.

22. Luis de León, *Obras propias, y traduciones latinas, griegas y italianas. Con la paráfrasi de algunos psalmos de y capitulos de Iob [...] Dalas a la Impressión don Francisco de Quevedo Villegas* (Madrid: Imprenta del Reyno, 1631).

23. Melveena McKendrick, *Theatre in Spain, 1490-1700* (Cambridge: Cambridge University Press, 1989), 122.

24. T.E. May, "*El condenado por desconfiado,*" *Bulletin of Hispanic Studies* 35 (1958): 138-56, reprinted in *The Wit of the Golden Age. Articles on Spanish Literature* (Kassel: Reichenberger), 134-53 (p. 145).

CHAPTER ONE
DISTANT ISLES: THE LITERARY IMPACT OF THE DISCOVERIES

1. Henry Kamen, *Spain 1469-1714. A Society of Conflict*, 96: "Spanish culture made its mark [on America] obviously in language, religion and architecture, less obviously in technology [...]. By contrast, the impact of America on Spain was muted." See too Dadson, *Libros, lectores y lecturas*, 71-92, and J. H. Elliott, *The Old World and the New: 1492-1650* (Cambridge: Cambridge University Press, 1970). The influence of Las Casas is considered by Anthony Pagden in his introduction to Bartolomé de las Casas, *A Short Account of the Destruction of the Indies*, ed. and trans. Nigel Griffin (London: Penguin, 1992), and by Hugh Thomas, *Rivers of Gold. The Rise of the Spanish Empire* (London: Weidenfeld and Nicholson, 2003), passim. On the literary impact of the New World in Castile, see the essays collected in Valentín de Pedro, *América en las letras españolas del Siglo de Oro* (Buenos Aires: Editorial Sudamericana, 1954) and Ingrid Simson, ed., *América en España: influencias, intereses, imágenes* (Madrid/Frankfurt: Iberoamericana/Vervuert, 2007).

2. On Ercilla's epic poem, see Alonso de Ercilla, *La Araucana*, ed. Isaías Lerner (Madrid: Cátedra, 1993); Frank Pierce, *Alonso de Ercilla y Zúñiga* (Amsterdam: Rodopi, 1984); Isaías Lerner, "América en la poesía épica áurea: la versión de Ercilla," *Edad de Oro* 10 (1991): 125-40; David Quint, *Epic and Empire: Politics and Generic Form from Virgil to Milton* (Princeton: Princeton University Press, 1993), 157-85; J. H. Elliott, *Empires of the Atlantic World. Britain and Spain in America, 1492-1830* (New Haven and London: Yale University Press, 2006), 270, 278, 280. The figure of the *indiano* is discussed in Héctor Brioso Santos, *Cervantes y América* (Madrid: Fundación Carolina and Marcial Pons, 2006), 125-74.

3. Francisco Ruiz Ramón, *América en el teatro clásico español. Estudios y textos* (Pamplona: Universidad de Navarra, 1993), 13. On the phenomenon and its causes, see Joseph E. Gillet, *Torres Naharro and the Drama of the Renaissance*, ed. Otis H. Green (Philadelphia: University of Pennsylvania Press, 1961), 164-69; Otis H.Green, *Spain and the Western Tradition. The Castilian Mind in Literature from El Cid to Calderón*, 4 vols. (Madison and Milwaukee: University of Wisconsin Press, 1963-65), 4:27-52; F. Morales Padrón, "L'Amérique dans la littérature espagnole," in M. Ballesteros, ed., *La Découverte de l'Amérique* (Paris: Vrin, 1968), 279-98; the essays collected in *Edad de Oro* 10 (1991); Ignacio Arellano, ed., *Las Indias (América) en la literatura del Siglo de Oro. Homenaje a Jesús Cañedo* (Kassel: Reichenberger, 1992); Dadson, *Libros, lectores y lecturas*, 71-92; Ingrid Simson, *Amerika in der spanischen Literatur des Siglo de Oro: Bericht, Inszenierung, Kritik* (Frankfurt am Main: Vervuert, 2003), and the extended discussion in Brioso Santos, *Cervantes y América*, 43-124, 345-58.

4. Barry W. Ife, "The Literary Impact of the New World: Columbus to Carrizales," *Journal of the Institute of Romance Studies* 3 (1994-95): 65-85; Barry W. Ife and John W. Butt, "The literary

heritage," in J.H. Elliott, ed., *The Hispanic World* (London: Thames and Hudson, 1991), 204-7; Diana de Armas Wilson, *Cervantes, the Novel and the New World* (Oxford: Oxford University Press, 2000), reviewed by Barry W. Ife in *The Times Literary Supplement*, 1 June 2001, 6, and, critically, by Daniel Eisenberg in *Bulletin of Hispanic Studies* 80 (2003): 130-31; Diana de Armas Wilson, "Cervantes and the New World," in Anthony J. Cascardi, ed., *The Cambridge Companion to Cervantes* (Cambridge: Cambridge University Press, 2002), 206-25. See too Stelio Cro, *Realidad y utopía en el descubrimiento y conquista de la América Hispana, 1492-1682* (Madrid: Fundación Universitaria Española, 1983), 109-31.

5.   Ángel Rosenblat, *La primera visión de América y otros estudios* (Caracas: Ministerio de Educación, 1969), 37, cited in Martín de Riquer, "California," in A. Sotelo Vázquez and M. C. Carbonell, eds., *Homenaje al profesor Antonio Vilanova* (Barcelona: Universidad de Barcelona, 1989), 1: 599.

6.   On the influence of the classical and medieval traditions see especially E. O'Gorman, *La invención de América* (Mexico: Fondo de Cultura Económica, 1958); H. Levin, *The Myth of the Golden Age in the Renaissance* (London: Faber, 1970), 58 onwards; Claudio Sánchez-Albornoz, *La Edad Media española y la empresa de América* (Madrid: Ediciones Cultura Hispánica de Cooperación Iberoamericana, 1983), 123-37; Anthony Pagden, *The Fall of Natural Man. The American Indian and the Origins of Comparative Ethnology* (Cambridge: Cambridge University Press, 1986); J. Gil, *Mitos y utopías del Descubrimiento. Vol. 1: Colón y su tiempo* (Madrid: Alianza, 1989); Wolfgang Haase and Meyer Reinhold, ed., *The Classical Tradition and the Americas. Vol. 1: European Images of the Americas and the Classical Tradition* (Berlin and New York: Walter de Gruyter, 1994). The influence of biblical traditions is discussed by Marc Venard, "La Bible et les Nouveaux Mondes," in Bedouelle and Roussel, eds., *Le Temps des Réformes et la Bible*, 489-514. See too Enrique Pupo-Walker, *La vocación literaria del pensamiento histórico en América. Desarrollo de la prosa de ficción: siglos XVI, XVII, XVIII y XIX* (Madrid: Gredos, 1982), 33-64.

7.   "En la abundancia retórica generada por los justos debates de la conmemoración del cuarto centenario del descubrimiento del continente americano por los europeos, creo que el esfuerzo otorgado al estudio del impacto que este descubrimiento tuvo en el pensamiento europeo sigue siendo relativamente menor." Isaías Lerner, "La visión humanística de América: Gonzalo Fernández de Oviedo," in Arellano, ed., *Las Indias (América) en la literatura del Siglo de Oro*, 3. See also Anthony Pagden, *European Encounters with the New World. From Renaissance to Romanticism* (New Haven and London: Yale University Press, 1993); Stephen Greenblatt, ed., *New World Encounters* (Berkeley: University of California Press, 1993); David A. Lupher, *Romans in the New World. Classical Models in Sixteenth-Century Spanish America* (Ann Arbor: University of Michigan Press, 2003), 320-21. The role of cartography in the assimilation of the New World by the Old is examined in Ricardo Padrón, *The Spacious Word. Cartography, Literature and Empire in Early Modern Spain* (Chicago: University of Chicago, 2004).

COLUMBUS

8.   J. H. Parry, *The Spanish Seaborne Empire* (Berkeley: University of California Press, 1990), 40-42; Henry Kamen, *Spain's Road to Empire. The Making of a World Power 1492-1763* (London: Penguin, 2003), 11-13; Felipe Fernández-Armesto, *Before Columbus. Exploration and Colonisation from the Mediterranean to the Atlantic, 1229-1492* (London: Macmillan, 1987). On views of cosmography current in Spain among mariners and *letrados*, see Francisco Rico, "El nuevo mundo de Nebrija y Colón," in Victor García de la Concha, ed., *Nebrija y la introducción del Renacimiento en España* (Salamanca: Universidad de Salamanca, 1983), 157-85, and *El sueño del humanismo (De Petrarca a Erasmo)* (Madrid: Alianza, 1993), 70-72. The impact of these and later discoveries on the genre of *isolarii* or island books (manuscript or printed maps of islands and coastlands) is examined in George Tolias, "*Isolarii*, Fifteenth to Seventeenth Century," in David Woodward, ed., *Cartography in the Renaissance* (Chicago: University of Chicago Press, 2007), 263-84.

9.   "Y para ello me hizieron grandes merçedes y me anobleçieron que dende en adelante yo me llamase Don y fuesse Almirante Mayor de la Mar Occéana y Visorey e Governador perpetuo

de todas las yslas y tierra firme que yo descubriese y ganase, y de aquí adelante se descubriesen y ganasen en la mar Occéano." Christopher Columbus, *Journal of the First Voyage (Diario del primer viaje) 1492*, ed. and trans. B. W. Ife, with an essay on Columbus's language by R. J. Penny (Warminster: Aris and Phillips, 1990), 2.

10. "estas yslas son aquellas innumerables que en los mapamundos en fin de oriente se ponen." Columbus, *Journal of the First Voyage*, 82. On medieval *mappaemundi*, see J. B. Harley and David Woodward, eds., *Cartography in Prehistoric, Ancient and Medieval Europe and the Mediterranean* (Chicago: University of Chicago Press, 1987); Marc Venard, "La Bible et les Nouveaux Mondes," 492; Pauline Moffit Watts, "Prophecy and discovery," *American Historical Review* 90 (1985): 73-102; Margarita Zamora, *Reading Columbus* (Berkeley: University of California Press, 1993), 102-7; Alessandro Scafi, "Mapping Eden: cartographies of the Earthly Paradise," in Denis Cosgrove, ed., *Mappings* (London: Reaktion, 1999), 65, and *Mapping Paradise. A History of Heaven on Earth* (London: British Library, 2006), 84-124.

11. Columbus, *Journal of the First Voyage*, 226, 228, and 259 n.252. His belief that he had found Eden is discussed by Juan Pérez de Tudela y Bueso, *"Mirabilis in altis." Estudio crítico sobre el origen y significado del proyecto descubridor de Cristóbal Colón* (Madrid: Consejo Superior de Investigaciones Científicas, 1983), 249 onwards, and 417-19; Cro, *Realidad y utopía en el descubrimiento y conquista de la América Hispana*, 6-12; Zamora, *Reading Columbus*, 95-151. On the Earthly Paradise and the Americas, see J. Prest, *The Garden of Eden* (New Haven: Yale University Press, 1981), 27-37.

12. See the comments of Barry Ife in his introduction to Columbus, *Journal of the First Voyage*, xix-xxv.

13. Columbus, *Journal of the First Voyage*, 40-41. See P. Henríquez Ureña, "El descubrimiento del Nuevo Mundo en la imaginación europea," in *Las corrientes literarias en la América hispánica* (Mexico: Fondo de Cultura Económica, 1969), 11: "En esta afirmación Colón se dejó engañar por el gran número de plantas parásitas que puede padecer un árbol tropical"; and Stephen Greenblatt, *Marvellous Possessions. The Wonder of the New World* (Oxford: Clarendon, 1991), 75-76.

14. Columbus, *Journal of the First Voyage*, 42-43.

15. Columbus, *Journal of the First Voyage*, 28-29.

16. The interplay in such passages of similarity and difference is discussed by Antonello Gerbi, *Nature in the New World. From Christopher Columbus to Gonzalo Fernández de Oviedo*, trans. Jeremy Moyle (Pittsburgh: University of Pittsburgh Press, 1985), 1-22, and the sense of wonder experienced by Columbus is considered in Lorraine Daston and Katherine Park, *Wonders and the Order of Nature, 1150-1750* (New York: Zone books, 2001), 146-47. On the "production of wonder" as a "calculated rhetorical strategy" see Greenblatt, *Marvellous Possessions*, 72-85, and Rosa Pellicer, "La 'maravilla' de las Indias," *Edad de Oro* 10 (1991): 141-54.

17. Christopher Columbus, *The Book of Prophecies*, ed. Roberto Rusconi and trans. Blair Sullivan (Berkeley: University of California Press, 1997). The influence on Columbus of biblical prophecy is considered in the introduction by Roberto Rusconi. Also see J. S. Cummins, "Christopher Columbus: crusader, visionary and *servus Dei*," in *Medieval Hispanic Studies presented to Rita Hamilton*, ed. A. D. Deyermond (London: Tamesis, 1976), 45-55, reprinted in his collection of essays, *Jesuit and Friar in the Spanish Expansion to the East* (London: Variorum, 1986); Moffit Watts, "Prophecy and discovery"; Valerie Flint, *The Imaginative Landscape of Christopher Columbus* (Princeton: Princeton University Press, 1992); Djelal Kadir, *Columbus and the Ends of the Earth. Europe's Prophetic Rhetoric as Conquering Ideology* (Berkeley: University of California Press, 1992); Zamora, *Reading Columbus*; and the review by L. J. Woodward of Christopher Columbus, *Libro delle Profezie*, trans. William Melczer (Palermo, 1992), *Bulletin of Hispanic Studies (Liverpool)* 71 (1994): 503-5.

18. Columbus, *The Book of Prophecies* 19-21, 136-37.

19. Columbus, *The Book of Prophecies*, 136. Rusconi comments (20) that in this annotation Columbus omitted to observe "the elementary rules of Latin grammar," and that, as a result, "the emphasis was shifted from his personal role to the universal significance of the events for

which he was a protagonist, and in particular to the evangelization of the peoples who had been destined to enter into the inheritance of the Hebrews."

20. On the classical tradition, see James S. Romm, *The Edges of the Earth in Ancient Thought. Geography, Exploration and Fiction* (Princeton: Princeton University Press, 1992). The biblical and early medieval background is discussed in Jennifer O'Reilly, "The art of authority," in Thomas Charles-Edwards, ed., *After Rome* (Oxford: Oxford University Press, 2003), 141-43, and "Islands and idols at the ends of the earth: exegesis and conversion in Bede's *Historia Ecclesiastica*," in Stéphane Lebecq, Michel Perrin, and Olivier Szerwiniack, eds., *Bède le Vénérable entre tradition et postérité* (Lille: University of Lille, 2005), 119-45.

21. *Epistola* 199:47, in *Patrologia Latina*, 33:922-23. I have followed the translation of Sr. Wilfrid Parsons in Augustine, *Letters*, vol. 4 *(165-203)*, trans. Sister Wilfrid Parsons, S.N.D. (New York: Fathers of the Church, 1955), 393.

22. Columbus, *The Book of Prophecies*, 316-17: "*De futuro. In novissimis.*"

23. *The Book of Prophecies*, 346-47.

24. *The Book of Prophecies*, 28.

25. Denis the Carthusian, *Opera omnia*, 42 vols. (Montreuil, Tournai and Parkminster, 1896-1935), 1: 200 [*In Genesim*].

26. *Opera omnia*, 8: 65 [*In Isaiam*].

27. Colin P. Thompson, *The Strife of Tongues. Fray Luis de León and the Golden Age of Spain* (Cambridge: Cambridge University Press, 1988), 97-101, 118, 131, 161, 202; A. Moreno Mengíbar, and J. Martos Fernández, "Mesianismo y Nuevo Mundo en fray Luis de León: *In Abdiam Prophetam Expositio*," *Bulletin Hispanique* 98 (1996): 261-89. Sixteenth-century attempts to locate native Americans within the plan of history as Christians understood it are discussed by Marcel Bataillon, "Les Indes occidentales, découverte d'un monde humain," in M. Ballesteros, ed., *La Découverte de l'Amérique* (Paris: Vrin, 1968), 7-10, and Levin, *The Myth of the Golden Age in the Renaissance*, 175-76, 183-84.

28. "Prima nascentis ecclesiae de gentibus tempora designat quando et parua erat numero credentium populorum et ad praedicandum Dei verbum minus idonea remanebat." Bede, *In Cantica Canticorum*, ed. D. Hurst, O.S.B., Corpus Christianorum Series Latina, vol.119B (Turnhoult: Brepols, 1983), 349. On the medieval exegetical tradition, see Cornelius à Lapide, *Commentaria in Scripturam Sacram*, 21 vols. (Paris: Vivès, 1868-76), 8: 227.

29. Gilbert Génébrard, *Canticum Canticorum Salomonis Regis* (Paris: apud M. Iuuenum, 1570), 77-78; Cipriano de la Huerga, *Comentario al Cantar de los Cantares (1582)*, ed. Avelino Domínguez García, in *Obras completas*, vols. 5 and 6 (León: Universidad de León, 1991), 6: 383-87. The traditional interpretation may be found also in the early seventeenth-century commentaries of Luis de Sotomayor, O.P. *Cantici Canticorum Salomonis interpretatio* (Paris: apud M. Sonnium, 1605), 1511-18, and Luis de la Puente, S.J., *Expositio moralis et mystica in Canticum Canticorum* (Cologne: I. Kinckium, 1622), 557-64. On Luis de León's studies under Huerga, see Thompson, *The Strife of Tongues*, 6, 156.

30. Luis de León, *Cantar de los Cantares. Interpretaciones: literal, espiritual, profética*, ed. José María Becerra Hiraldo (Real Monasterio del Escorial: Ediciones Escurialenses, 1992), 432.

31. Quoted from the translation of the Vulgate text by Ronald Knox, *The Old Testament, newly translated from the Latin Vulgate*, 2 vols. (London: Burns Oates and Washbourne, 1949).

32. Columbus, *The Book of Prophecies*, 322-23 and 330-31.

33. "Desde la Española, que el mismo Almirante Colón, autor de tan gran descubrimiento, supone sea la mina de oro del Ophir de Salomón, pasó a otra provincia." Pedro Mártir de Anglería, *Cartas sobre el Nuevo Mundo*, trans. Julio Bauzano, with an introduction by Ramón Alba (Madrid: Polifemo, 1990), 54 (in a letter dated 9 August 1495). On the announcement and initial reception of Columbus's discoveries, see Barry W. Ife, "Las dos cartas de Colón de 1493: transmisión y público," *Edad de Oro* 12 (1993): 131-39.

34. "Esta isla es Tharsis, es Cethia, es Ohir y Ophaz e Çipanga, y nos le havemos llamado Española." Christopher Columbus, *Textos y documentos completos. Relaciones de viajes, cartas y memoriales*, ed. Consuelo Varela (Madrid: Alianza, 1982), 311.

35. *El libro del famoso Marco Polo*, trans. and ed. Rodrigo Fernández de Santaella (Seville: Polono and Cromberger, 1503). F. J. Norton, *A Descriptive Catalogue of Printing in Spain and Portugal 1501-1520* (Cambridge: Cambridge University Press, 1978), 48, 549, describes the first edition and notes the later ones of Toledo, 1507, and Seville, 1518 and 1520. On the nature and impact of the book itself, see the comments of Rusconi in *The Book of Prophecies*, 7, and W. G. L. Randles, "Classical models of world geography and their transformation following the discovery of America," in Haase and Reinhold, eds., *The Classical Tradition and the Americas*, 48; on the translator, see Thomas, *Rivers of Gold*, 466, who also notes (142) the scepticism with which Columbus's claims were greeted in some Court circles.

36. Pedro Mártir de Anglería, *Décadas del Nuevo Mundo*, trans. Joaquín Torres Asensio (Buenos Aires: Bajel, 1944), 6. The early chapters of the First Book of the *De Orbe Novo*, in which the passage occurs, date from 1493. The first *Decade* was published in 1511 (Seville: Cromberger), and republished, with the remaining *Decades*, in 1516 (Alcalá de Henares: Guillén de Brocar): see the introduction by Hipólito Escolar Sobrino to Pedro Mártir de Anglería, *De orbe novo decades: A facsimile reprint of the edition of 1516* (Alicante: Rembrandt, 1986). On the legendary isles of Antilla, see Rosenblat, *La primera visión de América y otros estudios*, 18, 33, and Louis-André Vigneras, *The Discovery of South America and the Andalusian Voyages* (Chicago: University of Chicago Press, 1976), 3-4.

37. Toribio de Benavente, *Memoriales o libro de las cosas de la Nueva España y de los naturales de ella*, ed. E. O'Gorman (Mexico: U.N.A.M, 1971), 235, cited in Jean-Pierre Sánchez, "Myths and legends in the Old World and European expansionism on the American continent," in Haase and Reinhold, eds., *The Classical Tradition and the Americas*, 198. On the millenial vision of Benavente and his companions, see Elliott, *Empires of the Atlantic World*, 185.

38. Gonzalo Fernández de Oviedo, *Historia general y natural de las Indias*, ed. Juan Pérez de Tudela Bueso, 5 vols., Biblioteca de Autores Españoles, vols. 117-21 (Madrid: Real Academia Española, 1959), 1: 17-20. The objections to this notion advanced by Hernando Colón and Fray Bartolomé de las Casas, and the later modification in Oviedo's views, are considered by Álvaro Félix Bolaños, "The historian and the Hesperides: Fernández de Oviedo and the limitations of imitation," *Bulletin of Hispanic Studies (Liverpool)* 72 (1995): 273-88. See also Lupher, *Romans in the New World*, 215-17, and, on the *Historia general* as a whole, Isaías Lerner, "La visión humanística de América: Gonzalo Fernández de Oviedo," in Arellano, ed., *Las Indias (América) en la literatura del Siglo de Oro*, 3-22.

39. "Ophir insula est remotissima à sinu Ellantico: nam tertio demum anno reuertebātur inde. Vocatur hodie Spagniola, sic nominata à Christophoro Colmbo: in Occidente est, in terra inuenta nuper, est enim illic aurum laudatissimum." François Vatable, *Biblia* (Paris: Robert Estienne, 1545), fol. 50r. The annotation was retained without change in the edition of the Vatable Bible published in Salamanca nearly forty years later: Vatable, *Biblia sacra*, 2 vols. (Salamanca: apud Gaspard de Portonariis suis et Rouillii, Benedictus Boierii expensis, 1584-85), 1: fol. 214v. On the Vatable Bible itself, see Bedouelle and Roussel, eds., *Le Temps des Réformes et la Bible*, 168-69, and on its presence in Spanish America, see Elliott, *Empires of the Atlantic World*, 206.

40. *Phaleg, sive De gentium sedibus primis orbisque terrae situ* (1572), 11, in Benito Arias Montano, *Biblia Sacra*, 8 vols. (Antwerp: Plantin, 1569-73), vol. 8. See Venard, "La Bible et les Nouveaux Mondes," 502, and Zur Shalev, "Sacred geography, antiquarianism and visual erudition: Benito Arias Montano and the maps in the Antwerp Polyglot Bible," *Imago Mundi* 55 (2003), 69-71.

41. "No podía venir acá la flota de Salomón, sin passar toda la India Oriental, y toda la China, y otro infinito mar, y no es verisimil que atravessasen todo el mundo para venir a buscar acá el oro [...] y mostraremos después que los antiguos no alcançaron el arte de navegar que agora se usa, sin el qual no podian engolfarse tanto." José de Acosta, *Historia natural y moral de las Indias* (Seville: Juan de León, 1590), 51. On the sceptical reception accorded to Montano's theory by his contemporaries Abraham Ortelius and Joseph Scaliger, see Shalev, "Sacred geography, antiquarianism and visual erudition," 71. A generation later, José Pellicer de Salas y Tovar likewise rejected "la común opinión" which identified Ophir with Peru: see Melchora

Romanos, "El discurso contra las navegaciones en Góngora y sus comentaristas," in Arellano, ed., *Las Indias (América) en la literatura del Siglo de Oro*, 41.

42. *Historia natural y moral de las Indias*, 51.

AMADÍS DE GAULA

43. E. Michael Gerli, "The antecedents of the novel in sixteenth-century Spain," in Gies, ed., *The Cambridge History of Spanish Literature*, 181-86; Frank Pierce, *Amadís de Gaula* (Boston: Twayne, 1976). On Cervantes's opinion of the *Amadís* and its role in *Don Quixote*, see Daniel Eisenberg, *Romances of Chivalry in the Spanish Golden Age* (Newark, Del.: Juan de la Cuesta, 1982), 131-45; E.C. Riley, *Don Quixote* (London: Allen and Unwin, 1986), 35-42; Edwin Williamson, *The Halfway House of Fiction. Don Quixote and Arthurian Romance* (Oxford: Clarendon, 1984); Anthony Close, *Cervantes and the Comic Mind of his Age* (Oxford: Oxford University Press, 2000), 57-58, 110, 139; and Bienvenido Morros, "Amadís y Don Quijote," *Criticón* 91 (2004): 41-65.

44. See, in particular, the argument advanced in Irving A. Leonard, *Books of the Brave*, with a New Introduction by Rolena Adorno (Berkeley: University of California Press, 1992), 42-45. The views of such critics are summarised and discussed by Armas Wilson, *Cervantes, the Novel and the New World*, 123-26. See too Thomas, *Rivers of Gold*, 224-25 and 454, and Kathleen Ross, "Historians of the conquest and colonisation of the New World: 1550-1620," in Robert González Echavarría and Enrique Pulpo-Walker, eds., *The Cambridge History of Latin America* (Cambridge: Cambridge University Press, 1996), 1:117-18.

45. Bernal Díaz del Castillo, *Historia verdadera de la conquista de la Nueva España*, ed. Carmelo Sáenz de Santa María, with an introduction and notes by Luis Sáinz de Medrano (Barcelona: Planeta, 1992), 248.

46. Ife, "The literary impact of the New World: Columbus to Carrizales," 82-83. See too the comments of Rolena Adorno in Leonard, *Books of the Brave*, xxii: "The evidence suggests that the novels of chivalry inspired neither Bernal Diaz's actions of soldiering nor his act of narrating. Instead, they became a solution to his search for a way to communicate the magnificence and splendor of his first sight of Tenochtitlán." The edition of *Amadís* published in 1508 (Zaragoza) is described in Norton, *A Descriptive Catalogue of Printing in Spain and Portugal 1501-1520*, 231-32. On the likelihood of an earlier edition, now lost, see Garci Rodríguez de Montalvo, *Sergas de Esplandián*, ed. Carlos Sainz de la Maza (Madrid: Castalia, 2003), 25-26.

47. Garci Rodríguez de Montalvo, *Amadís de Gaula*, ed. Juan Manual Cacho Blecua, 2 vols. (Madrid: Cátedra, 1987), 1: 660. The page references that follow are to this edition.

48. Book 4, Chapter 84, in *Amadís de Gaula*, 2:1318.

49. María Rosa Lida de Malkiel, "La visión del trasmundo en las literaturas hispánicas," an appendix in Howard Rollin Patch, *El otro mundo en la literatura medieval* (Mexico: Fondo de Cultura Económica, 1956), 412. The classical and medieval legends mentioned are discussed by Patch, 25-26 and 36, who also considers Eden and its association with the Fortunate Isles, 152. See also A. Bartlett Giamatti, *The Earthly Paradise and the Renaissance Epic* (Princeton: Princeton University Press, 1966), 32-33; José Lara Garrido, "Las ínsulas extrañas de San Juan de la Cruz," in Jesús Montoya Martínez and Juan Paredes Núñez, eds., *Estudios románicos dedicados al Profesor Andrés Soria Ortega*, 2 vols. (Granada: Universidad de Granada), 2: 294-95. On the topography of Dante's island-mountain of Purgatory, see Marcello Aurigemma, "Purgatorio," in *Enciclopedia Dantesca*, 4:745-50; Dorothy L. Sayers, "The physical aspect of the Mountain," in *The Comedy of Dante Alighieri the Florentine, Cantica II : Purgatory* (Harmondsworth: Penguin, 1955), 69-71; Scafi, *Mapping Paradise*, 182-83.

50. See the remarks of Carlos Sainz de la Maza in his introduction to Rodríguez de Montalvo, *Sergas de Esplandián*, 20-26, and Hugh Thomas, *Rivers of Gold*, 125. The development of views about dating may be traced by comparing the remarks of Juan Manuel Cacho Blecua in his monograph, *Amadís: heroísmo mítico cortesano* (Madrid: Cupsa, 1979), 407-8, with those in his edition of *Amadís de Gaula*, 2 vols. (Madrid: Cátedra, 1987), 1: 76-81; see too Susana Gil-

Albarellos, *Amadís de Gaula y el género caballeresco en España* (Valladolid: Universidad de Valladolid, 1999), 129-30.

51. Juan Bautista Avalle-Arce, *Amadís de Gaula: el primitivo y el de Montalvo* (Mexico: Fondo de Cultura Económica, 1990), 194-96.

52. Lida de Malkiel, "La visión del trasmundo en las literaturas hispánicas," 413; Leonardo Olschi, *Storia letteraria delle scoperte geografiche* (Florence: Olschi, 1937), 53-54; Pierce, *Amadís de Gaula*, 151-55.

53. Rodríguez de Montalvo, *Sergas de Esplandián*, 727 (Chapter 157).

54. Martín de Riquer, "California," in *Homenaje al profesor Antonio Vilanova*, ed. A. Sotelo Vázquez and M.C. Carbonell (Barcelona: Universidad de Barcelona, 1989), 1: 589-90; Leonard, *Books of the Brave*, 38-42. Avalle-Arce, *Amadís de Gaula: el primitivo y el de Montalvo*, 52-54, 196, discusses Montalvo's debt to the *Historia destructionis Troiae* (1287) by Guido de Columnis, and traces the influence of the Discoveries on his depiction of California.

55. Cited in Riquer, "California," 585-86. On Montalvo's use of traditional Trojan material, and the precise meaning in this description of the phrase *al diestro*, see Rodríguez de Montalvo, *Sergas de Esplandián*, 43; on the impact in the New World of the Amazon legend, see K. March and K. Passman, "The Amazon myth and Latin America," in Haase and Reinhold, eds., *The Classical Tradition and the Americas*, 285-338, and Armas Wilson, *Cervantes, the Novel and the New World*, 126-30

56. The dates of composition of *Sergas* are discussed by Edwin B. Place in his edition of Garci Rodríguez de Montalvo, *Amadís de Gaula*, 4 vols. (Madrid: Consejo Superior de Investigaciones Científicas, 1959-69), 4: 1343-46; Riquer, "California," 581-82; and Sainz de la Maza in *Sergas de Esplandián*, 22-23, 25.

57. Columbus, *Journal of the First Voyage*, 182, 193, 196, 201, 255-56. On the Amazons in the *De Orbe Novo* of Peter Martyr, see Cro, *Realidad y utopía en el descubrimiento y conquista de la América Hispana*, 31-33.

58. The edition of 1510 (Seville) is described in Norton, *A Descriptive Catalogue of Printing in Spain and Portugal 1501-1520*, 708.

59. Thomas, *Rivers of Gold*, 292-93; Kamen, *Spain's Road to Empire*, 86; Venard, "La Bible et les Nouveaux Mondes," 499 n.25.

60. Rosenblat, *La primera visión de América y otros estudios*, 27-28; Riquer, "California," 584; Thomas, *Rivers of Gold*, 424; Lupher, *Romans in the New World*, 9.

61. Riquer, "California," 586-87.

62. Lida de Malkiel, "La visión del trasmundo en las literaturas hispánicas," 417-18, 430; José Lara Garrido, "Las ínsulas extrañas de San Juan de la Cruz," 294-96, and *Los mejores plectros. Teoría y práctica de la épica culta en el Siglo de Oro* (Málaga: Universidad de Málaga, 1999), 416-41. See too Nieves Barand, "El espejismo del Preste Juan de las Indias en su reflejo literario en España," in *Actas del X Congreso de la Asociación Internacional de Hispanistas*, ed. Antonio Vilanova, 4 vols. (Barcelona: Promociones y publicaciones universitarias, 1992), 1: 359-64.

63. In *Las lágrimas de Angélica* (1586), for instance, an epic poem by Luis Barahona de Soto, the influences of Ariosto and Camões come together in a setting that extends from Europe to the Pacific isles. This aspect of the work has been studied by José Lara Garrido, "Las ínsulas extrañas de San Juan de la Cruz," 295.

64. Bernardo de Balbuena, *El Bernardo*, in *Poemas épicos I*, ed. Cayetano Rosell, *Biblioteca de Autores Españoles*, vol.17 (Madrid: Real Academia Española, 1945), 250, cited and discussed by Lara Garrido, "Las ínsulas extrañas de San Juan de la Cruz," 295. On Balbuena's poem see Arthur Terry, *Seventeenth-Century Spanish Poetry. The Power of Artifice* (Cambridge: Cambridge University Press, 1993), 188-93; Frank Pierce, *The Heroic Poem of the Spanish Golden Age. Selections* (Oxford: Dolphin, 1947), 167-69, and *La poesía épica del Siglo de Oro* (Madrid: Gredos, 1968), 276-79; Margarita Peña, "Epic Poetry," in González Echaverría and Pulpo-Walker, eds., *The Cambridge History of Latin America*, 1: 247-50.

65. Armas Wilson, *Cervantes, the Novel and the New World*, 150-57, and "Cervantes and the New World," in *The Cambridge Companion to Cervantes*, 218; Close, *Cervantes and the Comic Mind*

of his Age (Oxford: Oxford University Press, 2000), 30, 59. See too Olschi, *Storia letteraria delle scoperte geografiche*, 41-42; Lida de Malkiel, "La visión del trasmundo en las literaturas hispánicas," 412; Cro, *Realidad y utopía en el descubrimiento y conquista de la América Hispana*, 112-15; and Brioso Santos, *Cervantes y América*, 285-315.

66. Book 2, Chapter 15, in Miguel de Cervantes, *Los trabajos de Persiles y Sigismunda*, ed. Carlos Romero Muñoz (Madrid: Cátedra, 2002), 379-87. On this episode, see Joaquín Casalduero, *Sentido y forma de "Los trabajos de Persiles y Sigismunda"* (Buenos Aires: Sudamericana, 1947), 151-54, and Alban K. Forcione, *Cervantes' Christian Romance. A study of "Persiles y Sigismunda"* (Princeton: Princeton University Press, 1972), 81-84. The influence on the *Persiles* as a whole of the Chronicles of the New World is considered in Cro, *Realidad y utopía en el descubrimiento y conquista de la América Hispana*, 115-31.

67. Miguel de Cervantes, *Los trabajos de Persiles y Sigismunda*, 381-82.

68. "las perlas del Sur, los diamantes de las Indias y el oro del Tíbar" (382). A note (n.7) discusses the associations in Cervantes's time of *Tíbar*. According to Covarrubias (s.v. *oro*), the term *Tíbar* in the phrase *oro de Tíbar* denotes, "río que los árabes llaman Etar, según Tamarid." Sebastián de Covarrubias Orozco, *Tesoro de la lengua castellana o española*, ed. Felipe C. R. Maldonado and rev. Manuel Camarero (Madrid: Castalia, 1995), 790.

SAN JUAN DE LA CRUZ

69. The image has been studied by Hugo Rahner, *Greek Myths and Christian Mystery* (London: Burns and Oates, 1963), 341-53, and Bernard McGinn, "Ocean and desert as symbols of mystical absorption in the Christian tradition," *Journal of Religion* 74 (1994): 155-81.

70. Marcel Bataillon, "Sobre la génesis poética del *Cántico Espiritual* desde la estética de su recepción," in *Varia lección de clásicos españoles* (Madrid: Gredos, 1964), 167-82, and *Erasmo y España*, 47; Colin P. Thompson, *St John of the Cross. Songs in the Night* (London: S.P.C.K., 2002), 5, 155, 158, 170.

71. *Patrologia Latina* 40: 895, in *Patrologiae cursus completus. Series Latina*, ed. Jacques-Paul Migne (Paris: Garnier, 1844-64).

72. Luis de Granada *Guía de pecadores (texto definitivo)*, ed. Herminio de Paz Castaño (Madrid: Fundación Universitaria Española y Dominicos de Andalucía, 1995), 185. See Green, *Spain and the Western Tradition*, 3: 27.

73. Fray Agustín Antolínez O.S.A., *Amores de Dios y el alma*, ed. A. Custodio Vega (Madrid: El Escorial, 1956), 19-20. The passage occurs in his commentary on the opening words of the *Cántico* of San Juan de la Cruz. See Eulogio Pacho, "Agustín Antolínez, O.S.A. (1554-1626)," in *Diccionario de San Juan de la Cruz*, ed. Eulogio Pacho (Burgos: Monte Carmelo, 2000), 119-20.

74. Francisco de Aldana, *Poesías castellanas completas*, ed. José Lara Garrido (Madrid: Cátedra, 1985), 450. On this remarkable poem, see, in particular, José Bergamín, "*Hombre adentro y las Indias de Dios*," in *Beltenebros y otros ensayos sobre literatura española* (Barcelona: Noguer, 1973), 151-64; Michel de Certeau, *La Fable mystique. XVI-XVII siècle* (Paris: Gallimard, 1982), 267; Alexander A. Parker, *The Philosophy of Love in Spanish Literature 1480-1680*, ed. Terence O'Reilly (Edinburgh: Edinburgh University Press, 1985), 68-71; Robert Archer, "The overreaching imagination: the structure and meaning of Aldana's *Carta para Arias Montano*," *Bulletin of Hispanic Studies* 65 (1988): 237-49; Terence O'Reilly, "Friendship and contemplation in the *Carta para Arias Montano*," *Calíope* 14 (2008): 47-60.

75. On the history of this mission, see Eulogio Pacho, "Méjico," in *Diccionario de San Juan de la Cruz*, 945-47.

76. Alonso de la Madre de Dios, O.C.D., *Vida, virtudes y milagros del santo padre Fray Juan de la Cruz*, ed. Fortunato Antolín, O.C.D. (Madrid: Editorial de Espiritualidad, 1989), 511.

77. Thompson, *St John of the Cross. Songs in the Night*, 104-8.

78. San Juan de la Cruz, *Obras completas*, ed. Eulogio Pacho (Burgos: Monte Carmelo, 1997), 1137, 1140 (cited from the first redaction of the poem, CA). The references that follow are to this edition. The translation is the one provided in Colin P. Thompson, *The Poet and the Mystic. A*

Study of the "Cántico espiritual" of San Juan de la Cruz (Oxford: Oxford University Press, 1977), 173-77.

79. José María de Cossío, "Rasgos renacentistas y populares en el *Cántico Espiritual* de San Juan de la Cruz," *Escorial* 25 (1942): 220; Arturo Marasso, "Aspectos del lirismo de San Juan de la Cruz," *Boletín de la Academia Argentina de Letras* 14 (1945): 593; José Constantino Nieto, *Místico, poeta, rebelde, santo* (Mexico: Fondo de Cultura Económica, 1982), 97; Thompson, *St. John of the Cross. Songs in the Night*, 169-70; San Juan de la Cruz, *Cántico espiritual y poesía completa*, ed. Paola Elia and María Jesús Mancho (Barcelona: Crítica, 2002), 477. But see the dissenting views of José L. Morales, *El Cántico Espiritual de San Juan de la Cruz. Su relación con el Cantar de los Cantares y otras fuentes escriturísticas y literarias* (Madrid: Editorial de Espiritualidad, 1971), 152-53, and Domingo Ynduráin in *San Juan de la Cruz. Poesía*, ed. Domingo Ynduráin (Madrid: Cátedra, 1984), 94.

80. s.v. *extraneus* in Charlton T. Lewis and Charles Short, *A Latin Dictionary* (Oxford: Clarendon, 1879).

81. Margherita Morreale, "Sobre algunas acepciones de 'extraño' y su valor ponderativo," *Revista de Filología Española* 36 (1952): 310-17; María Jesús Mancho Duque, *Palabras y símbolos en San Juan de la Cruz* (Madrid: Fundación Universitaria Española y Universidad Pontificia de Salamanca, 1993), 73-84; María de los Ángeles López García, "El léxico de la maravilla en la obra de San Juan de la Cruz," in *Estado actual de los estudios sobre el Siglo de Oro*, ed. M. García Martín (Salamanca: Universidad de Salamanca, 1993), 2: 576-77. The close link in San Juan's time between the words *extrañeza* and *novedad* was noted by Ermanno Caldera: "la *extrañeza* está íntimamente conectada al concepto de *novedad* hasta el punto que, mientras confiere a esta última rasgos típicos de la época, constituye, en cierto modo, su explicación o su premisa, cuando no se identifica incluso con ella." "El manierismo en San Juan de la Cruz," in *En torno a San Juan de la Cruz*, ed. J. Servera Baño (Madrid: Júcar, 1986), 66. See, too, Thompson, *The Poet and the Mystic*, 169-70.

82. Cited by Gillet, *Torres Naharro and the Drama of the Renaissance*, 165.

83. Hernán Pérez de Oliva, *Historia de la invención de las Yndias*, ed. José Juan Arrom (Bogotá: Instituto Caro y Cuervo, 1965), 53-54, cited in Elliott, *The Old World and the New: 1492-1650*, 15.

84. Acosta, *Historia natural y moral de las Indias*, 9; cf. 52: "[...] el uso y lenguaje nuestro nombrando Indias, es significar unas tierras muy apartadas y muy ricas, y muy *extrañas* de las nuestras."

85. See, for instance, Ynduráin in *San Juan de la Cruz: Poesía*, 94; Garrido, "Las ínsulas extrañas de San Juan de la Cruz," 296-97; Mancho Duque, *Palabras y símbolos en San Juan de la Cruz*, 82: "[...] el arcaísmo 'ínsula' remite a épocas pretéritas, vagas y caballerescas."

86. Eulogio Pacho, *San Juan de la Cruz. Historia de sus escritos* (Burgos: Monte Carmelo, 1998), 104-5.

87. "No fewer than fifteen Carmelite breviaries appeared during the sixteenth century, though in 1585 the Discalced changed to the Roman breviary [...]. Which of the earlier ones San Juan used is not known." Thompson, *The Poet and the Mystic*, 17.

88. It has been shown that the late medieval Carmelite tradition, which underlies the sixteenth-century breviaries San Juan could have used, was characterised by a high degree of liturgical uniformity, due to the influence of the Ordinal of Sibert de Beka (promulgated c.1312) which stipulated the *incipits* for all chants, prayers, readings and psalms: see James Boyce, O. Carm., "From Rule to Rubric: the impact of Carmelite liturgical legislation upon the order's Office tradition," *Ephemerides Liturgicae* 108 (1994): 262-98, and "The Carmelite feast of the Presentation of the Virgin: a study in musical adaptation," in *The Divine Office in the Latin Middle Ages*, ed. Margot E. Fassier and Rebecca A. Baltzer (Oxford: Oxford University Press), 485-86.

89. I have consulted the copy in the British Library (catalogue number 844.c.2): *Breviarium Carmelitarum* (Venice, 1504).

90. "¿Estas islas tan lueñes, no serán un recuerdo del versículo de Jeremías tantas veces cantado por el Santo: *annuntiate in insulis quae procul sunt?*" Rafael María de Hornedo, S.J., "El humanismo de San Juan de la Cruz," *Razón y Fe* 129 (1944): 145.

91. Two other passages of the Vulgate that San Juan may have recalled are Isaiah 41:5 and 66:19: see the observations of María Rosa Lida de Malkiel in her review of Dámaso Alonso, *La poesía de San Juan de la Cruz (desde esta ladera)* (Madrid, 1942), in *Revista de Filología Hispánica* 5

(1943): 381; Morales, *El Cántico Espiritual de San Juan de la Cruz: su relación con el Cantar de los Cantares y otras fuentes escriturísticas y literarias*, 152; Nieto, *Místico, poeta, rebelde, santo*, 97.

92. On "mixed" *imitatio* see Anne J. Cruz, *Imitación y transformación. El petrarquismo en la poesía de Boscán y Garcilaso de la Vega* (Amsterdam/Philadelphia: John Benjamins, 1988); and on San Juan's approach to imitation, Cristóbal Cuevas, "Estudio literario," in *Introducción a la lectura de San Juan de la Cruz*, ed. Salvador Ros et. al. (Salamanca: Junta de Castilla y León, 1991), 135-36 and 147-48.

93. Thompson, *St. John of the Cross. Songs in the Night*, 104, 111-12.

LUIS DE GÓNGORA

94. Luis de Góngora, *Soledades*, ed. Robert Jammes (Madrid: Castalia, 1994). All references to the poem, and quotations from it, are taken from this edition. The English version cited is Gilbert F. Cunningham, trans., *The Solitudes of Luis de Góngora*, with a Preface by A.A. Parker and an Introduction by Elias L. Rivers (Baltimore: Johns Hopkins Press, 1969).

95. María Rosa Lida de Malkiel, "El hilo narrativo de las *Soledades*," in *La tradición clásica en España* (Barcelona: Ariel), 243-51. For the Greek text, with a translation into English, see "The Euboean Discourse, or The Hunter," in *Dio Chrysostom*, trans. J. W. Cohoon (London: Heinemann and New York: Putnam, 1932), 1: 286-373.

96. Elias L. Rivers, "'Góngora y el Nuevo Mundo," *Hispania* 75 (1992): 856-57.

97. See the comments of Robert Jammes in Luis de Góngora, *Soledades*, 132-34; 270.

98. Romm, *The Edges of the Earth in Ancient Thought*, 12; Randles, "Classical models of world geography and their transformation," 7-10.

99. *Iliad*, Book 8, lines 607-8. See Romm, *The Edges of the Earth in Ancient Thought*, 13-14, and Jerry Brotton, "Terrestrial globalism: mapping the globe in Early Modern Europe," in Cosgrove, *Mappings*, 74.

100. Romm, *The Edges of the Earth in Ancient Thought*, 41, 43; Randles, "Classical models of world geography and their transformation," 7-8; Góngora, *Soledades*, ed. Jammes, 278.

101. "Oceanum Graeci et Latini ideo nominant eo quod in circuli modum ambiat orbem [...]. Iste est qui oras terrarum amplectitur." Isidore of Seville, *Etimologías*, ed. José Oroz Reta and Manuel C. Diaz y Diaz , 2 vols. (Madrid: Biblioteca de Autores Cristianos, 1982), 2: 144 [Book 13:15]: See Randles, "Classical models of world geography and their transformation," 15-16, 74.

102. Fernández-Armesto, *Before Columbus*, 246.

103. J. H. Parry, *The Spanish Seaborne Empire* (Berkeley: University of California Press, 1990), 52; Randles, "Classical models of world geography and their transformation," 58-59; Kamen, *Spain's Road to Empire*, 86; Thomas, *Rivers of Gold*, 241, 292-94.

104. Randles, "Classical models of world geography and their transformation," 59; Kamen, *Spain's Road to Empire*, 198; Thomas, *Rivers of Gold*, 44. On the dispute between Spain and Portugal over the islands of the Moluccas to which Magellan's voyage gave rise, see Brotton, "Terrestrial globalism: mapping the globe in Early Modern Europe," 82-84.

105. Romm, *The Edges of the Earth in Ancient Thought*, 10-12, 15.

106. E.g. Psalm 49:1, 112:3; Isaiah 45:6, 59:19; Malachi 1:11.

107. *The Oxford Classical Dictionary*, ed. N. G. L. Hammond and H. H. Scullard (Oxford: Clarendon), 744-45 (*s.v.* 'Oceanus'); Romm, *The Edges of the Earth in Ancient Thought*, 15-16; Góngora, *Soledades*, ed. Jammes, 278. The poem alludes to the waters of Hades in lines 443-46.

108. Terry, *Seventeenth-Century Spanish Poetry*, 84. The debate may be traced in Dámaso Alonso, "Góngora y América," in *Estudios y ensayos gongorinos* (Madrid: Gredos, 1955); Luis de Góngora, *Poems*, ed. R. O. Jones (Cambridge: Cambridge University Press, 1966), 26-27; Robert Jammes, *Etudes sur l'oeuvre poétique de Don Luis de Góngora y Argote* (Bordeaux: Féret, 1967), 140-44, 601-5; Luis de Góngora, *Soledades*, ed. John Beverley (Madrid: Cátedra, 1980), 96; Lorna Close, "The play of difference: a reading of Góngora's *Soledades*," in *Conflicts of Discourse: Spanish Literature of the Golden Age*, ed. Peter Evans (Manchester: Manchester University Press, 1990), 184-98; Ignacio Arellano, "La imagen de las Indias y los puntos de

vista de la escritura," in Arellano, ed., *Las Indias (América) en la literatura del Siglo de Oro*, 309-10; Melchora Romanos, "El discurso contra las navegaciones en Góngora y sus comentaristas," in Arellano, ed., *Las Indias (América) en la literatura del Siglo de Oro*, 47-49; Rivers, "Góngora y el Nuevo Mundo," 857.

109. Terry, *Seventeenth-Century Spanish Poetry*, 82.

110. The classical tradition and Góngora's use of it have been studied in detail by Lía Schwartz Lerner, "Quevedo junto a Góngora: recepción de un motivo clásico," in *Homenaje a Ana María Barrenechea*, ed. Lía Schwartz Lerner and Isaías Lerner (Madrid: Castalia, 1984), 313-25, and "El motivo de la *auri sacra fames* en la sátira y en la literatura moral del siglo xvii," in Arellano, ed., *Las Indias (América) en la literatura del Siglo de Oro*, 51-72; Georgina Sabat-Rivers, "Interpretación americana de tópicos clásicos en Domínguez Camargo: la navegación y la codicia," *Edad de Oro* 10 (1991): 187-98; Romanos, "El discurso contra las navegaciones en Góngora y sus comentaristas," 37-49.

111. Luis de León, *Poesías completas: propias, imitaciones y traducciones*, ed. Cristóbal Cuevas (Madrid: Castalia, 2001), 103-5.

112. Colin P. Thompson *The Strife of Tongues. Fray Luis de León and the Golden Age of Spain* (Cambridge: Cambridge University Press, 1988), 15-17, 98-101.

113. On the complexity of the views implicit in the speech, see Jammes, *Etudes sur l'oeuvre poétique de Don Luis de Góngora y Argote*, 602; Romanos, "El discurso contra las navegaciones en Góngora y sus comentaristas," 49; and the sustained argument of Richard Hitchcock, "Góngora and the Hyrcanian tigress," in *What's Past Is Prologue. A Collection of Essays in Honour of L.J. Woodward*, ed. Salvador Bacarisse, Bernard Bentley, Mercedes Clarasó and Douglas Gifford (Edinburgh: Scottish Academic Press, 1984), 82-87.

114. Book 3, lines 138-252, in Ovid, *Metamorphoses*, ed. and trans. Frank Justus Miller, rev. G. P. Goold, 2 vols. (Cambridge, Massachusetts: Harvard University Press and London: Heinemann, 1977), 1: 134-42.

115. In the phrase "perderse en ellos," "ellos" refers back to the lovely limbs (*sus miembros bellos*) that Actaeon sees (line 489), limbs that are described in turn as reefs (*escollos*) in line 488. The suggestion of shipwreck is clear.

116. Kamen, *Spain's Road to Empire*, 301-5. R. O. Jones, in his introduction to Góngora, *Poems*, 27 n.1, drew attention to the possibility that Góngora's lines were influenced by the *Conquista de las islas Molucas* (Madrid, 1609) by Lupercio Leonardo de Argensola.

BALTASAR GRACIÁN

117. See Robert Pring-Mill, "Some techniques of representation in the *Sueños* and *Criticón*," *Bulletin of Hispanic Studies* 45 (1968): 270-84, especially 283-84; Jeremy Robbins, *The Challenges of Uncertainty. An Introduction to Seventeenth-Century Spanish Literature* (London: Duckworth, 1998), 63-77; Fernando Lázaro Carreter, "El género literario de *El Criticón*," in *Clásicos españoles. Desde Garcilaso a los niños pícaros* (Madrid: Alianza, 2003), 371. The novel was published in three parts: 1651 (*Primera Parte*), 1653 (*Segunda Parte*), 1657 (*Tercera Parte*). References are to Baltasar Gracián, *El Criticón*, ed. M. Romera-Navarro, 3 vols. (Philadelphia: University of Pennsylvania Press, 1938-40).

118. Mercedes Blanco, "*Homo homini lupus*. Estado de naturaleza y hombre artificial en Baltasar Gracián y Thomas Hobbes," *Insula* 655-56 (2001): 15.

119. Gracián's ambiguous reaction to the ideas of Copernicus is noted by Romera-Navarro in his edition of *El Criticón*, 1: 121-22 n.28.

120. *Primera Parte, Crisi I*, 107: "Fluctuando estava entre uno y otro elemento, equívoco entre la muerte y la vida."

121. *Crisi IV*, 155: "En medio destos golfos nací, como te digo, entre riesgos y tormentas."

122. *Crisi XII*, 353: "Executáronla los dolores del parto en una isla, deviendo al cielo dobladas providencias, con que pudo salvar su crédito, no fiándolo ni de sus mismas criadas, enemigas mayores de un secreto."

123. *Crisi XII*, 353-54: "¡Ah, qué linda era, y aun por esso tan poco venturosa! ¡O qué gran muger y qué discreta! Pero ¿qué Danae escapó de un engaño? ¿qué Elena de una fuga? ¿qué Lucrecia de una violencia y qué Europa de un robo?"

124. E. Uriz Echaleco, "Santa Elena, isla de," in *Gran Enciclopedia Rialp* (Madrid: Rialp, 1974), 20: 820.

125. "Los demás hombres, los extraños, como incapaces de la noble conversación y exilados del lenguaje, serán fieras." Mercedes Blanco, "*Homo homini lupus*. Estado de naturaleza y hombre artificial en Baltasar Gracián y Thomas Hobbes," 16.

126. *Crisi I*, 10. The combination in Andrenio of brutishness and innocence, both features of St. Helena itself, is discussed by Theodore L. Kassier, *The Truth Disguised. Allegorical Structure and Technique in Gracián's "Criticón"* (London: Tamesis, 1976), 13-15. On the image of the barbarian at the time of the Discoveries, see Pagden, *The Fall of Natural Man*, 15-26, and P. Mason, "Classical ethnography and its influence on the European perception of the peoples of the New World," in Haase and Reinhold, eds., *The Classical Tradition and the Americas*, 135-72.

127. *Crisi I*, 107: "[...] un gallardo joven, ángel al parecer y mucho más al obrar, alargó sus braços para recogerle en ellos."

128. Paul Julian Smith, *Representing the Other. "Race," Text and Gender in Spanish and Spanish American Narrative* (Oxford: Clarendon, 1992), 68.

129. *Crisi I*, 91.

130. *Crisi IV*, 165: "al tiempo acostumbrado aportaron a este nuestro mundo." As Francisco Vivar has observed: "Europa es el mundo, posee una cultura universal, lo que convierte a la experiencia europea en única; 'las naciones bárbaras' simplemente se excluyen de nuestra historia y forman parte de la expansión de Europa." "Representación y símbolo de la frontera en *El Criticón*," *Bulletin of Hispanic Studies* 75 (1998): 431.

131. The correspondences that exist between the beginning and end of the work, among which the island image figures prominently, are considered by Kassier, *The Truth Disguised*, 31, and Aurora Egido, *La rosa del silencio. Estudios sobre Gracián* (Madrid: Alianza 1996), 65 n.37.

132. *Tercera Parte, Crisi XII*, 370. On the triad of wisdom, virtue and valour, see Aurora Egido, *Humanidades y dignidad del hombre en Baltasar Gracián* (Salamanca: Universidad de Salamanca), 117.

133. In the phrase "un espanta vulgo," the verb *espantar* is synonymous with *asombrar*, as M. Romera-Navarro observed (3: 370 n.10); it denotes, appropriately, awe and wonder rather than fear.

134. *Crisi XII*, 370: "Isla ay de la Inmortalidad, bien cierta y bien cerca, que no ay cosa más inmediata a la muerte que la inmortalidad: de la una se declina a la otra."

135. Gracián uses the same New World image, and to similar effect, in aphorism 198 of the *Oráculo manual*: "Un alfiler pudo conseguir estimación, passando de un mundo a otro, y un vidrio puso en desprecio al diamante porque se trasladó. Todo lo extraño es estimado, ya porque vino de lexos, ya porque se logra hecho y en su perfección." Baltasar Gracián, *Oráculo manual y arte de prudencia*, ed. Emilio Blanco (Madrid: Cátedra, 1997), 210-11. See Robbins, *The Challenges of Uncertainty*, 113. Other references to the Indies made by Gracián are discussed by Alessandro Martinengo, "Gracián, las Indias y la interpretación de un pasaje de *El Criticón* (II,3)," in Arellano, ed., *Las Indias (América) en la literatura del Siglo de Oro*, 23-35.

136. *El Criticón*, 3: 382 n.103. The scene had been immortalised a century before by Francisco López de Gómara in his history of the Indies (Zaragoza, 1552): "Al día siguiente, que era 11 de octubre del año de 1492, dijo Rodrigo de Triana: '¡Tierra, tierra!,' y a tan dulce palabra acudieron todos a ver si decía verdad; y como la vieron, comenzaron el *Te Deum laudamus*, hincados de rodillas y llorando de alegría." Francisco López de Gómara, *Historia general de las Indias*, ed. Pilar Guibelaide, 2 vols. (Barcelona: Iberia, 1954), 1: 33. See too Bartolomé de Las Casas, *Historia de las Indias*, ed. J. Pérez de Tudela and E. López Oto, Biblioteca de Autores Españoles, vol. 95 (Madrid: Real Academia Española, 1957), 140; Thomas, *Rivers of Gold*, 83.

137. The island is termed "centro de inmortalidad" in the closing lines of the work (412). On parallels between *El Criticón* and utopian writings of the Renaissance influenced by the Discoveries, see Nilo Palenzuela, "*El Criticón*: entre viejo y nuevo mundo," *Insula* 655-56 (2001): 39-42.

138. *Crisi XII*, 373. See Aurora Egido, *La rosa del silencio*, 63-64.

139. Aurora Egido, *Las caras de la prudencia y Baltasar Gracián* (Madrid: Castalia, 2000), 226-29, and *Humanidades y dignidad del hombre en Baltasar Gracián*, 132: "son las letras las que, en definitiva, consiguen que los héroes y los gobernantes sean inmortales [...] sin letras no hay fama que valga."

140. *Crisi XII*, 375: "Sacólos finalmente a la orilla de un mar tan estraño que creyeron estar en el puerto si no de Hostia, de Víctima de la Muerte, y más quando vieron sus aguas, tan negras y tan obscuras."

141. *Crisi XII*, 376-77. On Gracián's notion of literary immortality, see Ricardo Senabre, *Gracián y "El Criticón"* (Salamanca: Universidad de Salamanca), 45-56.

142. "El topónimo 'Ostia' se elige en virtud de la cercanía de ese puerto a Roma, a la vez centro radiante de una cultura que es para Gracián la cultura por antonomasia, y capital del orbe católico." Mercedes Blanco, *"Homo homini lupus.* Estado de naturaleza y hombre artificial en Baltasar Gracián y Thomas Hobbes," 15. On the importance of the Humanist and Classical traditions for Gracián, see Jeremy Robbins, "Baltasar Gracián (1601-2001)," *Bulletin of Hispanic Studies* 80 (2003): 52, 54.

143. *Crisi XII*, 377-78. The sources of the image are noted by Egido, *Humanidades y dignidad del hombre en Baltasar Gracián*, 130-31.

144. *Crisi XII*, 378: "Fuéronse ya engolfando por aquel mar en leche de su eloqüencia, de cristal en lo terso del estilo, de ambrosía en lo suave del concepto, y de bálsamo en lo odorífero de sus moralidades."

145. In *El ocaso de los héroes en "El Criticón"* (Zaragoza, 1945), cited in Smith, *Representing the Other*, 73. On the treatment of women generally in the work, see Kassier, *The Truth Disguised*, 12-13.

146. *Crisi XII*, 397: Fernando is described as "[el] mayor rey del mundo, pues fundó la mayor monarquía que ha avido ni avrá."

147. *Crisi XII*, 388: "Todos aquellos otros [castillos] que allí ves los erigió el inmortal Carlos Quinto para defensa de sus dilatados reynos, digno empleo de sus flotas y millones."

CONCLUSION

148. Michel de Certeau, *Heterologies: Discourse on the Other*, trans. Brian Massumi, with a foreword by Wlad Godzich (Minneapolis: University of Minnesota, 1986); Luce Giard, "Epilogue: Michel de Certeau's heterology and the New World," in Greenblatt, *New World Encounters*, 313-22.

149. The impact of the Spanish discoveries on each of these works is considered in Armas Wilson, *Cervantes, the Novel and the New World*, with the exception of John Donne's sermon "to the Honourable Company of the Virginia Plantation" (13 November 1622), which may be seen in John Donne, *Selected Prose*, ed. Neil Rhodes (Harmondsworth: Penguin, 1987), 202-5.

150. John Keats, *The Complete Poems*, ed. John Barnard, with an introduction by Andrew Motion and engravings by Simon Brett (London: Folio Society, 2001), 43.

151. John Middleton Murry, *Keats* (London: Cape, 1955), 145-46.

152. Carl Woodring, "On looking into Keats's Voyagers," *Keats-Shelley Journal* 14 (1965): 16-17; Lawrence Lipking, *The Life of the Poet. Beginning and Ending Poetic Careers* (Chicago: University of Chicago Press, 1981), 5.

153. Lipking, *The Life of the Poet*, 7. On the viceroyalties of the Spanish Empire see Elliott, *Empires of the Atlantic World*, 125-29.

154. Woodring, "On looking into Keats's Voyagers," 20.

155. Lipking, *The Life of the Poet*, 8: "he looks until he hears a voice that lets him breathe"; also see Paul McNally, "Keats and the rhetoric of association. On looking into the Chapman's Homer sonnet," *Journal of English and Germanic Philology* 79 (1980): 530-40.

156. John Barnard, *John Keats* (Cambridge: Cambridge University Press, 1987), 18.

157. Fiona Robertson, "Keats' New World: on emigrant poetry," in Michael O'Neill, ed., *Keats: Bicentenary Readings* (Edinburgh: Edinburgh University Press, 1997), 31-32.

158. Leon Waldoff, *Keats and the Silent Work of Imagination* (Urbana: University of Illinois Press, 1985), 78-79.

159. Helen Vendler, *Coming of Age as a Poet: Milton, Keats, Eliot, Plath* (Cambridge, Mass.: Harvard University Press, 2003), 56, who notes that "stared" is "a word of riveted fixation rather than of traveled contemplation or telescopic wonder."

160. Hernán Cortés, *Letters from Mexico*, trans. and ed. A. R. Pagden with an introduction by J. H. Elliott (Yale: Yale University Press, 1986), 444-45, 508-9, 526-27.

161. Waldoff, *Keats and the Silent Work of Imagination*, 193-94; J. R. Watson, "Keats and silence," in O'Neill, ed., *Keats: Bicentenary Readings*, 77-78.

162. Vendler, *Coming of Age as a Poet*, 55.

163. Marjorie Levinson, *Keats's Life of Allegory. The Origins of a Style* (Oxford: Blackwell, 1988), 11-14; Vendler, *Coming of Age as a Poet*, 55, 155.

CHAPTER TWO
DEVOTIONAL WRITING:
THE *SPIRITUAL* EXERCISES OF IGNATIUS LOYOLA

1. Henri Watrigant, S.J., "La genèse des *Exercices* de saint Ignace," *Études* 71 (1897): 506-29; 72 (1897):195-216; 73 (1897): 199-228.

2. J. Calveras, S.J., and C. Dalmases, S.J., eds., *Exercitia spiritualia. Textuum antiquissimorum nova editio* (Rome: Institutum Historicum Societatis Iesu, 1969). Quotations from the *Exercises* are taken from this edition, and refer in parentheses to the numbered subdivisions of the text.

3. Calveras and Dalmases, *Exercitia spiritualia*, 27-32.

4. Ibid., 34-54. On works that may have influenced the text of the *Exercises* between 1523 and 1541 see Javier Melloni, S.J., "Ejercicios espirituales: génesis del texto," in José García de Castro and others, eds., *Diccionario de Espiritualidad Ignaciana* (Bilbao: Mensajero / Santander: Sal Terrae, 2007), 685-89.

5. Recent research may be seen in Juan Plazaola, ed., *Las fuentes de los Ejercicios Espirituales de San Ignacio* (Bilbao: Mensajero, 1998).

6. Federico Ruiz Salvador, *Introducción a San Juan de la Cruz* (Madrid: Biblioteca de Autores Cristianos, 1968), 90.

7. The phrase was coined by Colin Thompson to describe his approach to the sources of San Juan: "It is usually impossible to locate his sources precisely, because he is indebted to the accumulated tradition rather than to specific authors." *The Poet and the Mystic*, 8-9. See too the discussion of methodology in Santiago Arzubialde, S.J., *Ejercicios Espirituales de San Ignacio. Historia y análisis* (Bilbao: Mensajero / Santander: Sal Terrae, 1991), 123-29, and Marko Ivan Rupnik, "Paralelismos entre el discernimiento según San Ignacio y el discernimiento según algunos autores de la *Filocalia*," in Plazaola, ed., *Las fuentes de los Ejercicios Espirituales de San Ignacio*, 276-77.

8. See, in particular, Tomáš Špidlík, *Ignazio di Loyola e la spiritualità orientale. Guida alla lettura degli Esercizi* (Rome: Studium, 1994), and the studies of Lothar Lies, S.J., "La doctrina de la discreción de espíritus en Ignacio de Loyola y Orígenes de Alejandría," in Plazaola, ed., *Las fuentes de los Ejercicios Espirituales de San Ignacio*, 101-21; Santiago Arzubialde, "Casiano e Ignacio. Continuidad y ruptura. Una original aportación de Ignacio a la historia de la tradición espiritual," in Plazaola, 123-86; and José María Lera, S.J., "Influjos patrísticos en la *Contemplación para alcanzar amor* en los *Ejercicios* de San Ignacio," in Plazaola, 207-22.

9. Watrigant,"La genèse des *Exercices* de saint Ignace," *Études* 71 (1897): 511.

10. His remarks were recorded by Fr Luis Gonçalves da Cámara in his transcript of Ignatius's autobiographical account: see Ignatius Loyola, *Obras. Edición manual*, ed. Ignacio Iparraguirre, S.J., Cándido de Dalmases, S.J., Manuel Ruiz Jurado, S.J., 5th ed. (Madrid: Biblioteca de Autores Cristianos), 175.

11. L.Teixidor, "Algo sobre la regla 18," *Manresa* 8 (1932): 312-26; Calveras and Dalmases, *Exercitia spiritualia*, 33; Jesús Corella, S.J., *Sentir la Iglesia. Comentario a las reglas ignacianas para el sentido verdadero de la Iglesia* (Bilbao: Mensajero / Santander: Sal Terrae, 1995), 107-8;

Arzubialde, *Ejercicios Espirituales de San Ignacio*, 809-10.

12. Corella, *Sentir la Iglesia*, 207.

13. Javier Melloni, S.J., *La mistagogía de los Ejercicios* (Bilbao: Mensajero / Santander: Sal Terrae, 2001), 271.

14. Corella, *Sentir la Iglesia*, 207-9; Melloni, *La mistagogía de los Ejercicios*, 270-71.

15. Ludolph of Saxony, *Vita Cristi Cartuxano*, trans. Fray Ambrosio Montesino, 4 vols. (Alcalá de Henares: Stanislao de Polonia, 1502-03), part 1, chapter 53 (fols 71v-73r); see Arturo Codina, S.J., *Los orígenes de los Ejercicios Espirituales de San Ignacio de Loyola. Estudio histórico* (Barcelona: Balmes, 1926), 150, and Paul Shore, "Ludolfo de Sajonia," in García de Castro, ed., *Diccionario de Espiritualidad Ignaciana*, 1149-53.

16. The *Exercitatorio* has been edited, with detailed notes on its sources, in García Jiménez de Cisneros, *Obras completas*, ed. C. Baraut, O.S.B., 2 vols. (Montserrat: Abadía de Montserrat, 1965). On the structure of the work, see Terence O'Reilly, "The structural unity of the *Exercitatorio de la vida spiritual*," *Studia Monastica* 15 (1973): 287-324, and "Meditation and contemplation: monastic spirituality in early sixteenth-century Spain," in *Faith and Fanaticism: Religious Fervour in Early Modern Spain*, ed. Lesley K. Twomey (Aldershot: Ashgate, 1997), 38-41.

17. See the bibliography in Calveras and Dalmases, *Exercitia spiritualia*, 50 n.15, and, in addition, Manuel Ruiz Jurado, S.J., "¿Influyó en S. Ignacio el *Exercitatorio* de Cisneros?," *Manresa* 51 (1979): 65-75; Aimé Solignac, S.J., "Le *Compendio Breve* de l'*Exercitatorio* de Cisneros et les *Exercices Spirituels*," *Archivum Historicum Societatis Iesu* 63 (1994): 141-59; Javier Melloni, S.J., "Las influencias cisnerianas en los *Ejercicios*," in Plazaola, ed., *Las fuentes de los Ejercicios Espirituales de San Ignacio*, 353-77, and *The Exercises of St Ignatius Loyola in the Western Tradition*, trans. Michael Ivens, S.J. (Leominster: Gracewing); Otger Steggink, "Iñigo López de Loyola, el peregrino vasco de Montserrat, y la *devotio moderna*," in *Fuentes neerlandesas de la mística española*, ed. Miguel Norbert Ubarri and Lieve Behiels (Madrid: Trotta, 2005), 71-79. The relationship between the *Exercitatorio* and the *Compendio* is studied in detail in the introduction to *Compendio breve de ejercicios espirituales, compuesto por un monje de Montserrat entre 1510-1555*, ed. Javier Melloni, S.J. (Madrid: Biblioteca de Autores Cristianos, 2006).

18. Calveras and Dalmases, *Exercitia spiritualia*, 47-52. The presence of the grades of fear in other writings by Ignatius is considered in Terence O'Reilly, "Temor," in García de Castro, ed., *Diccionario de Espiritualidad Ignaciana*, 1676-80.

THE GRADES OF FEAR

19. *Psalm 127:7* in St. Augustine, *Enarrationes in psalmos ci-cl*, ed. Eligius Dekkers O.S.B. and Iohannes Fraipont, Corpus Christianorum Series Latina, vol. 40 (Turnhout: Brepols, 1956), 187-88.

20. *In epistolam Ioannis ad Parthos*, tractatus 9:5, in *Patrologia Latina*, 35: 2049.

21. *Stromata 7*, chapters 11:67 and 12:79, in Clement of Alexandria, *Miscellanies: Book VII*, ed. and trans. Fenton John Anthony Hort and Joseph B. Mayor (London: MacMillan, 1902), 115-17, 137.

22. Basil, *Les Règles monastiques*, ed. Léon Lèbe, O.S.B. (Maredsous: Editions de Maredsous, 1969), 35, 57.

23. Conference XI, in John Cassian, *Conférences vii-xvii*, ed. and trans. E. Pichery (Paris: Editions du Cerf, 1958), 100-119.

24. *La Règle de Saint Benoît*, vol. 1, ed. Adalbert de Vogüé and Jean Neufville (Paris: Editions du Cerf, 1972), 474-75, 488-91, and *The Rule of St. Benedict: A Guide to Christian Living*, ed. George Holzherr (Dublin: Four Courts, 1994), 98, 111; Adalbert de Vogüé, *La Règle de Saint Benoît: Commentaire historique et critique*, 3 vols. (Paris: Editions du Cerf, 1971), 1: 344-70, and *La Règle de Saint Benoît: Commentaire doctrinal et spirituel* (Paris: Editions du Cerf, 1977), 171-83.

25. *Summa Theologiae*, 2a-2ae, q.19.a.2, in Thomas Aquinas, *Summa Theologiae, cura fratrum eiusdem Ordinis*, 5 vols. (Madrid: Biblioteca de Autores Cristianos, 1961-65), 3:118. I have followed, with slight amendments, the translation in Aquinas, *Summa Theologiae, vol. 33: Hope*

(*2a-2ae. 17-22*), ed. and trans. W.J. Hill, O.P. (London:Blackfriars and Eyre and Spottiswoode, 1966), 49.

26. Aquinas, *Summa Theologiae, vol. 33: Hope (2a-2ae. 17-22)*, 172.

27. Michael Ivens, S.J., *Understanding the Spiritual Exercises. Text and Commentary. A Handbook for Retreat Directors* (Leominster: Gracewing, 1998), 44.

28. On decision-making in the *Exercises*, and the role of the Election, see Ivens, *Understanding the Spiritual Exercises*, 128-32, and Alfredo Sampaio Costa, S.J., "Elección," in García de Castro, ed., *Diccionario de Espiritualidad Ignaciana*, 726-34.

29. William A. M. Peters, S.J., *The Spiritual Exercises of St Ignatius. Exposition and Interpretation* (Jersey City: Program to Adapt the Spiritual Exercises, 1968), 147. See too Ivens, *Understanding the Spiritual Exercises*, 162-63.

IMAGERY

30. *Sermo* 161:9, in *Patrologia Latina*, 38: 885.

31. Basil, *Les Règles monastiques*, 37; see too Friedrich von Hügel, *The Mystical Element of Religion as Studied in Saint Catherine of Genoa and her Friends*, 2 vols. (London: Dent and Clarke, 1961), 2: 165-66.

32. Gregory of Nazianzus, *Discours 38-41*, ed. Claudio Moreschini and trans. Paul Gallay (Paris: Editions du Cerf, 1990), 225.

33. Conference XI: 7, in Cassian, *Conférences vii-xvii*, 105-7.

34. *Stromata* 7, chapter 12:79, in Clement of Alexandria, *Miscellanies: Book VII*, 137.

35. *Stromata*, chapter 2:5, in *Miscellanies: Book VII*, 11.

36. Conference XI:12, in Cassian, *Conférences vii-xvii*, 114.

37. *Sentences*, Book 3, *distinctio* 34, in *Patrologia Latina* 192: col. 824. St. Anselm's understanding of fear and love of God may be seen in his *Liber de similitudinibus*, chapter 169, in *Patrologia Latina* 159: col. 693, and in his *Orationes*, *Patrologia Latina* 158: cols 884-85.

38. Catherine of Siena, *The Dialogue of the Seraphic Virgin, Catherine of Siena*, trans. Algar Thorold (London: Kegan Paul, Trench, and Trübner, 1896), 122-53.

39. *In epistolam Ioannis ad Parthos*, tractatus 9: 6-7, in *Patrologia Latina*, 35: 2049-50.

40. Jacques Farges and Marcel Viller, "La charité chez les Pères," *Dictionnaire de Spiritualité*, vol. 2.i: 534.

41. *In epistolam Ioannis ad Parthos*, tractatus 9:8, in *Patrologia Latina*, 35: 2050-51.

42. *Summa Theologiae*, 2a-2ae, q.19.a.2.

43. *Exercitatorio*, chapter 12, lines 70-73, and chapter 27, lines 7-10.

44. See Pedro de Leturia, S.J., *El gentilhombre Iñigo López de Loyola en su patria y en su siglo* (Barcelona: Labor, 1949), and Rogelio García Mateo, S.J., "Amadís de Gaula," in García de Castro, ed., *Diccionario de Espiritualidad Ignaciana*, 132-36.

45. Arzubialde, *Ejercicios Espirituales de San Ignacio*, 232. Parallels between the language of chivalry used in the exercise and certain patristic and monastic traditions are discussed in the same author's "Casiano e Ignacio. Continuidad y ruptura. Una original aportación de Ignacio a la historia de la tradición espiritual," in Plazaola, ed., *Las fuentes de los Ejercicios Espirituales de San Ignacio*, 123-86.

46. *s.v. servicio* and *servir*, in Seppo A. Teinon, *Concordancia de los Ejercicios Espirituales de San Ignacio de Loyola* (Helsinki: Academia Scientiarum Fennica, 1981), and Ignacio Echarte, ed., *Concordancia ignaciana. An Ignatian Concordance* (Bilbao: Mensajero / Maliaño: Sal Terrae, 1996).

47. Pedro de Leturia, S.J., *Estudios ignacianos*, ed. I. Iparraguirre, S.J., 2 vols. (Rome: Institutum Historicum Societatis Iesu, 1957), 2: 162.

48. On the nuptial imagery of the *Exercises* see Michael Buckley, S.J., "Misticismo eclesial en los *Ejercicios Espirituales*: dos notas sobre Ignacio, la Iglesia y la vida en el Espíritu," in Juan M. García Lomas, ed., *Ejercicios Espirituales y mundo de hoy. Congreso Internacional de Ejercicios, Loyola, 20-26 setiembre de 1991* (Bilbao: Mensajero / Santander: Sal Terrae, 1992), 175-95, and "Ecclesial Mysticism in the *Spiritual Exercises* of Ignatius," *Theological Studies* 56 (1995): 441-63.

Other Schemata

49. Farges and Viller, "La charité chez les Pères," 535-36.
50. Pierre Pourrat, "Commençants", *Dictionnaire de Spiritualité*, 2.i: 1144.
51. *Summa Theologiae*, 2a-2ae, q.24.a.9.
52. Aimé Solignac, S.J, "Voies (purificative, illuminative, unitive)," *Dictionnaire de Spiritualité* 16: cols 1202-7.
53. Karl Rahner, "Reflections on the problem of the gradual ascent to Christian perfection," in *Theological Investigations*, vol. 3 (London: Darton, Longman and Todd, 1967), 8.
54. See O'Reilly, "The structural unity of the *Exercitatorio de la vida spiritual*," 310-11, and Solignac, "Voies (purificative, illuminative, unitive)," 1207, who considers Cisneros to be, "celui qui a le plus fait pour diffuser le schéma des trois voies par son *Exercitatorio*."
55. *De triplici via*, chapter 3:1, in *Obras de San Buenaventura*, vol. 4, ed. Bernardo Aperribay, O.F.M., and Miguel Oromi, O.F.M. (Madrid: Biblioteca de Autores Cristianos, 1963), 124.
56. Michael Buckley, S.J., "The Contemplation to Attain Love," *The Way Supplement* 24 (1975): 92-94; Ivens, *Understanding the Spiritual Exercises*, 146 n.1.
57. J. Nadal, *Epistolae IV* (Madrid: Monumenta Historica Societatis Iesu, 1905), 673.
58. Ignacio Iparraguirre, S.J., ed., *Directorium Exercitiorum Spiritualium (1540-1599)* (Rome: Monumenta Historica Societatis Iesu, 1955), 246 n.12; Brian O'Leary, S.J., "Third and Fourth Weeks: what the Directories say," *The Way Supplement* 58 (1987): 15-19; Arzubialde, *Ejercicios Espirituales de San Ignacio*, 407-10; Gaston Fessard, S.J, *La dialectique des Exercices Spirituels de Saint Ignace de Loyola*, 2 vols. (Paris: Aubier, 1956 and 1966), 1: 27-29, 32; Ivens, *Understanding the Spiritual Exercises*, 10-11; Miguel Lop Sebastià, S.J., *Los Directorios de Ejercicios 1540-1599* (Bilbao: Mensajero/Santander: Sal Terrae, 2000), 698 (on the Tenth Annotation).
59. "La división de las tres vías que corresponden a los tres estados de incipientes, proficientes y perfectos, es la misma que la de las cuatro semanas, aunque los nombres sean diferentes." Luis de la Palma, S.J., *Obras*, ed. Francisco X. Rodríguez Molero, S.J. (Madrid: Biblioteca de Autores Cristianos, 1967), 461-62.
60. Calveras and Dalmases, *Exercitia spiritualia*, 32-33.
61. Manuel Ruiz Jurado, S.J., "Fuentes de las Elecciones," in Plazaola, ed., *Las fuentes de los Ejercicios Espirituales de San Ignacio*, 339-51; Calveras and Dalmases, *Exercitia spiritualia*, 46-47; Henri Bernard-Maitre, S.J., "Saint Ignace de Loyola mystique et les anciennes traductions espagnoles de l'*Imitation de Jésus-Christ*," *Ons Geestelijk Erf* 30 (1956): 25-42; Rogelio García Mateo, S.J., "Imitación de Cristo," in García de Castro, ed., *Diccionario de Espiritualidad Ignaciana*, 994-1001.
62. Lop Sebastià, *Directorios de Ejercicios 1540-1599*, 651-53; Arzubialde, *Ejercicios Espirituales de San Ignacio*, 48-54; Brian O'Leary, S.J., "Foundational values in the *Spiritual Exercises* of St. Ignatius," *Milltown Studies* 33 (1994): 5-7; Luis María García Domínguez, S.J., "Orden/desorden," in García de Castro, ed., *Diccionario de Espiritualidad Ignaciana*, 1378-87.

Conclusion

63. Letter to Manuel Miona, 16 November 1536, in Loyola, *Obras. Edición manual*, 736.
64. Such is clearly the understanding that informs the *Exercitatorio*: see O'Reilly, "The structural unity of the *Exercitatorio de la vida spiritual*," 290-95.
65. On this debate see J. de Guibert, S.J., *The Jesuits: Their Spiritual Doctrine and Practice* (St. Louis: Institute of Jesuit Sources, 1972), 122-32; Joseph Veale, S.J., "Dominant orthodoxies," *Milltown Park Studies* 30 (1992): 43-65; Herbert Alphonso, "La vida diaria como oración," in García Lomas, ed., *Ejercicios Espirituales y mundo de hoy*, 272; Gilles Cusson, S.J., "Breve historia de la interpretación de los *Ejercicios*. Escuelas y tendencias," *Manresa* 66 (1994): 87-103.
66. The three approaches mentioned are outlined, with a bibliography, in Loyola, *Obras. Edición manual*, 227-28 n.21. Among recent commentators see Ivens, *Understanding the Spiritual Exercises*, 146-48, and Alphonso: "Se podría [...] afirmar que hay dos momentos cumbre en los *Ejercicios*: la *Elección* y la *Contemplación para alcanzar amor*. Pero en realidad no son dos cimas: son la misma y única cumbre considerada desde dos ángulos distintos." "La vida diaria como

oración," 272. Javier Melloni characterises his approach thus: "quisiéramos poder superar el debate de los años 20-50 sobre si los *Ejercicios* conducían a la unión con Dios o a la mera elección." *La mistagogía de los Ejercicios* (Bilbao: Mensajero / Santander: Sal Terrae, 2001), 24.

67. On the *Exercises* in this period, see Ignacio Iparraguirre, S.J., *Práctica de los Ejercicios de San Ignacio de Loyola en vida de su autor (1522-56)* (Bilbao: Mensajero/Rome: Institutum Historicum Societatis Iesu, 1946).

CHAPTER THREE
PROSE FICTION: *LAZARILLO DE TORMES*

1. See A.D. Deyermond, *Lazarillo de Tormes*, 2nd ed. (London: Grant and Cutler and Tamesis, 1993), 24-25.

2. The discussion may be traced in A.D. Deyermond, "Lazarus and Lazarillo," *Studies in Short Fiction* 2 (1964-65): 351-57, and *Lazarillo de Tormes*, 27-32; Mará Rosa Lida de Malkiel, "Función del cuento popular en el *Lazarillo de Tormes*," *Actas del Primer Congreso Internacional de Hispanistas* (Oxford: Dolphin, 1964), 350; *Lazarillo de Tormes and El Abencerraje*, ed. Claudio Guillén (New York: Dell, 1966), 28 and 136-37; B. W. Wardropper, "The strange case of Lázaro Gonzales Pérez," *Modern Language Notes* 92 (1977): 202-12; Terence O'Reilly, "The Erasmianism of *Lazarillo de Tormes*," in *Essays in Honour of Robert Brian Tate from his Colleagues and Pupils*, ed. Richard A. Cardwell (Nottingham: Department of Spanish, University of Nottingham, 1984), 91-100.

3. *La vida de Lazarillo de Tormes y de sus fortunas y adversidades*, ed. R. O. Jones (Manchester: University Press, 1963), 62-85.

4. *Lazarillo de Tormes and El Abencerraje*, 135-72.

5. *La vida de Lazarillo de Tormes y de sus fortunas y adversidades*, ed. Alberto Blecua (Madrid: Castalia, 1972).

6. *La vida de Lazarillo de Tormes y de sus fortunas y adversidades*, ed. Francisco Rico (Madrid: Cátedra, 1987). See the subsequent editions of the text by Félix Carrasco (New York: Peter Lang, 1997), Robert L. Fiore (Asheville, North Carolina: Pegasus, 2000), and Aldo Ruffinatto (Madrid: Castalia, 2001), as well as Alfonso de Valdés, *La vida de Lazarillo de Tormes y de sus fortunas y adversidades*, ed. Milagros Rodríguez Cáceres, with an introduction by Rosa Navarro Durán (Barcelona: Octaedro, 2003).

7. Víctor García de la Concha, *Nueva lectura del Lazarillo. El deleite de la perspectiva* (Madrid: Castalia, 1981), 157.

8. References to the text of *Lazarillo* follow the edition of R. O. Jones (see note 3 above), in which the lines are numbered.

TRATADO PRIMERO

9. See Stephen Gilman, "Matthew V, 10, in Castilian jest and earnest," in *Studia Hispanica in Honorem Rafael Lapesa*, ed. Eugenio Bustos and others, vol. 1 (Madrid: Cátedra, Seminario Menéndez Pidal, and Gredos, 1972), 257-66.

10. Fernando de Rojas, *La Celestina. Tragicomedia de Calisto y Melibea*, ed. Francisco J. Lobera and others (Barcelona: Crítica, 2000), 171-72 (Auto VII); on this and other reminiscences of the *Celestina* in the work see 647-48, 726-27. See too the general discussion in Alberto Martino, *Il "Lazarillo de Tormes" e la sua ricezione in Europa (1554-1753)*, 2 vols. (Pisa and Rome: Istituti Editoriali e Poligrafici Internazionale, 1999), 1:295-98, and the studies of Lida de Malkiel, "Función del cuento popular en el *Lazarillo de Tormes*," 351, Marcel Bataillon, *Novedad y fecundidad del Lazarillo de Tormes*, trans. Luis Cortés Vázquez (Salamanca: Anaya, 1973), 64-65, Rico in his 1987 edition of *Lazarillo*, xlix, n.13, and Navarro Durán in Alfonso de Valdés, *La vida de Lazarillo de Tormes y de sus fortunas y adversidades*, 75-99.

11. "Se aprovecha el valor polisémico de *por* (causal y agente) y *justicia* ('virtud' y 'poder judicial') para hacer un chiste sobre un célebre pasaje de San Mateo." Rico in *Lazarillo de Tormes*, 14, n.8.

12. See Guillén in *Lazarillo de Tormes and El Abencerraje*, 137.
13. Quoted from Rico's note in *Lazarillo de Tormes*, 14 n.6.
14. Fernando Lázaro Carreter, *Lazarillo de Tormes y la picaresca* (Barcelona: Ariel, 1972), 107-8.
15. Jeremy N.H. Lawrance, "Black africans in Renaissance Spanish literature," in T. F. Earle, and K. J. P. Lowe, eds., *Black Africans in Renaissance Europe* (Cambridge: Cambridge University Press, 2005), 79.
16. See Jones in *Lazarillo de Tormes*, xxx.
17. The allusion to Proverbs 8:10-11 is noted by Guillén in *Lazarillo de Tormes and El Abencerraje*, 140.
18. "No cabe duda de que el autor utilizó conscientemente la frase pronunciada por San Pedro al curar al paralítico, pues en seguida hace decir a Lázaro que, después de Dios, es el ciego quien le ha dado la vida y le ha alumbrado y adestrado 'en la carrera de vivir.'" Albert A. Sicroff, "Sobre el estilo del *Lazarillo de Tormes*," *Nueva Revista de Filología Hispánica* 11 (1957): 161.
19. The allusion to Psalm 118 is noted by R. W. Truman, "Parody and irony in the self-portrayal of Lázaro de Tormes," *Modern Language Review* 63 (1968): 604.
20. See Lázaro Carreter, *Lazarillo de Tormes y la picaresca*, 112-13, and Rico in *Lazarillo de Tormes*, 99, n.35.
21. *Persiles y Sigismunda*, Book 2, Chapter 15, cited by Rico in *Lazarillo de Tormes*, 25 n.49.
22. Epistle xiv, in Seneca, *Ad Lucilium epistulae morales*, ed. and trans. Richard M. Gummere, 3 vols. (Cambridge, Massachusetts: Harvard University Press, 1989), 1: 288-89. Further references may be found in Rico, *Lazarillo de Tormes*, 24-25. On this tradition, and its connection with *homo novus* writings of the Renaissance, see in particular the articles of R. W. Truman, "Parody and irony in the self-portrayal of Lázaro de Tormes," and "*Lazarillo de Tormes*, Petrarch's *De remediis adversae fortunae*, and Erasmus's *Praise of Folly*," *Bulletin of Hispanic Studies* 52 (1975): 33-53; also the discussion in Martino, *Il "Lazarillo de Tormes" e la sua ricezione in Europa*, 1: 278-87.
23. Parallel passages in the Old Testament include 1 Kings 2:7-8; Job 22:29; Psalm 74:8, 112:7-8; Proverbs 29:23; Ecclesiasticus 20:30; Isaiah 40:4; Ezekiel 17:24. In the New Testament, the theme recurs in Luke 14:11, 18:14; 1 Peter 5:5-6; James 4:10.
24. Jaume Pérez de Valencia, *Expositio [...] in cantica novi veterisque testamenti* (Paris: apud Franciscum Reynault, 1533), fol. 302v. On the life and writings of this influential Spanish exegete, see Nigel Griffin, "Spanish incunabula in the John Rylands University Library of Manchester," *Bulletin of the John Rylands University Library of Manchester*, 70 (1988): 48-52.
25. T. Anthony Perry, "Biblical symbolism in the *Lazarillo de Tormes*," *Studies in Philology* 67 (1970): 142. Less convincing is Perry's suggestion (143-44) that *Tratado* 1:106-7 contains an allusion to John 14:6; but see Deyermond, *Lazarillo de Tormes*, 24.
26. "The relatively high number of references to the devil in the first *tratado* suggests that the presence of the blind man is naturally associated with the demonic." Perry, "Biblical symbolism in the *Lazarillo de Tormes*," 143.
27. The devil is referred to as "enemigo de natura humana" in the Spanish translation of the *Legenda Sanctorum* of Iacopo da Varazze published in Seville by Juan de Varela in 1520: *Leyenda de los Santos*, ed. Félix Juan Cabasés, S.J., Monumenta Historica Societatis Iesu, Nova Series vol. 3 (Madrid: Universidad de Comillas and Institutum Historicum Societatis Iesu, 2007), 715. The phrase occurs in the life of St Onuphrius (San Onofre), folio 231r. See Leturia, *El gentilhombre Iñigo López de Loyola en su patria y en su siglo*, 169. In the *Spiritual Exercises* of Ignatius Loyola the devil is referred to repeatedly as "el enemigo de natura humana" (e.g. 7:2, 135:5, 326:4, 334:1), and on one occasion as "mortal enemigo de nuestra humana natura" (136:1). In the *Constitutions* of the Society of Jesus, he is said to be "el enemigo de la natura humana" (553:3). Detailed references may be found in Echarte, *Concordancia ignaciana*, under *enemigo*.
28. On these parallels and other sources, see Paul R. Olson, "An Ovidian conceit in Petrarch and Rojas," *Modern Language Notes* 81 (1966): 217-21, and the references provided by Rico in *Lazarillo de Tormes*, 33, n.88. Further biblical passages in which the theme may be found include 1 Kings 2:6; Tobias 11:17, 13:2; Wisdom 16:13.
29. See his comments in *Lazarillo de Tormes*, 50-51, n.96.

TRATADO SEGUNDO

30. *Lazarillo de Tormes*, 56-57, n.50. See too García de la Concha, *Nueva lectura del Lazarillo*, 171.

31. *Lazarillo de Tormes*, 50-51, n.24.

32. Gonzalo Correas, *Vocabulario de refranes y frases proverbiales*, ed. Louis Combet (Bordeaux: Institut d'Études Ibériques et Ibéro-Américaines de l'Université de Bordeaux, 1967), 430.

33. Francisco Rodríguez Marín, *Más de 21.000 refranes castellanos, no contenidos en la copiosa colección del Maestro Gonzalo Correas* (Madrid: Revista de Archivos, Bibliotecas y Museos, 1926), 76.

34. García de la Concha, *Nueva lectura del Lazarillo*, 170. See too Isaiah 22:13, cited in 1 Corinthians 15:32; Luke 15:23.

35. Ferdinand Cabrol, O.S.B., ed., *The Roman Missal in Latin and English*, 8th edition (London: Herder, 1931), 36-37.

36. García de la Concha, *Nueva lectura del Lazarillo*, 170, who notes that the allusion to the Last Supper was first suggested by J. Cejador in his edition of *Lazarillo* published in 1914. On this question, also see A. C. Piper, "The 'breadly paradise' of Lazarillo de Tormes," *Hispania* 44 (1961): 269-71; Perry, "Biblical symbolism in the *Lazarillo de Tormes*," 144; O'Reilly, "The Erasmianism of *Lazarillo de Tormes*," 94-95.

37. On the Secret in the Mass see Cabrol, ed., *The Roman Missal in Latin and English*, 62, 176. A different interpretation of the phrase in *Lazarillo* is defended by García de la Concha, *Nueva lectura del Lazarillo*, 164, and by Rico in *Lazarillo de Tormes*, 57-58, n.52.

38. See O'Reilly, "The Erasmianism of *Lazarillo de Tormes*," 95, and Stanislav Zimic, *Apuntes sobre la estructura paródica y satírica del Lazarillo de Tormes* (Madrid: Iberoamericana, 2000), 43-49.

39. *Lazarillo de Tormes*, 69, n.104.

TRATADO TERCERO

40. *Libro de la vida*, 2:9, 13:21, 19:11, in Santa Teresa de Jesús, *Obras completas*, ed. Efrén de la Madre de Dios, O.C.D., and Otger Steggink, O. Carm. (Madrid: Biblioteca de Autores Cristianos, 1972). See too Tomás Alvarez, *Diccionario de Santa Teresa de Jesús* (Burgos: Monte Carmelo, 2000), 169-70.

41. See also 1 Kings 25:32; Psalm 27:6, 30:22, 65:20, 123:6, 134:21, 143:1; Daniel 3:26.

42. The reference to Job 5:8-9 was noted by Guillén in *Lazarillo de Tormes and El Abencerraje*, 158, and by Blecua in his edition of the *Lazarillo*, 137. See also Job 9:10, 37:5; 1 Chronicles 16:2; Psalm 135:4.

43. On Ecclesiasticus 10:19-11: 6, "a splendid poem in five symmetrical stanzas," see Raymond E. Brown, Joseph A. Fitzmyer, and Roland E. Murphy, ed., *The New Jerome Biblical Commentary* (London: Chapman, 1990), 500-501, and John Barton and John Muddiman, eds., *The Oxford Bible Commentary* (Oxford: Oxford University Press, 2001), 676.

44. Denis the Carthusian, *Enarrationes [...] in quinque libros sapientiales* (Cologne: expensis Iohannis Solteris et Melchioris Novesiani, 1533), 239v-239r. On the biblical exegesis of Denis, and its widespread influence in the early sixteenth century, see Denis the Carthusian, *Spiritual Writings*, trans. Íde M. Ní Riain, RSCJ, with an introduction by Terence O'Reilly (Dublin: Four Courts, 2005), ix-xiv.

45. "Un problema de influencia de Erasmo en España. El *Elogio de la locura*," in Marcel Bataillon, *Erasmo y el erasmismo*, trans. Carlos Pujol, with an introduction by Francisco Rico (Barcelona: Crítica, 1977), 332. See also O'Reilly, "The Erasmianism of *Lazarillo de Tormes*," 96, and the comments of Francisco Rico, *La novela picaresca y el punto de vista. Nueva edición, corregida y aumentada* (Barcelona: Seix Barral, 2000), 57-58, n.70.

46. See also Deuteronomy 4: 26-27, 28:64; Leviticus 26:33; Job 40:6; Psalm 43:12, 105: 26-27; Jeremiah 9:16; Ezekiel 36:19.

47. "Nuestro personaje debe su condición un poco fantasmal a su situación de desarraigado; forastero, sin vínculo alguno en Toledo." Bataillon, *Novedad y fecundidad del Lazarillo de Tormes*, 42. On the "misterio" surrounding the squire and his origins see Francisco Rico, "Problemas del *Lazarillo*,"

Boletín de la Real Academia Española 46 (1966): 292; Lázaro Carreter, *Lazarillo de Tormes y la picaresca*, 139; Zimic, *Apuntes sobre la estructura paródica y satírica del Lazarillo de Tormes*, 91-107.

TRATADO QUINTO

48. See Terence O'Reilly, "Discontinuity in *Lazarillo de Tormes*: the problem of *Tratado* Five," *Journal of Hispanic Philology* 10 (1986): 141-49, and the discussion of the artistic unity of the text in Martino, *Il "Lazarillo de Tormes" e la sua ricezione in Europa*, 1: 366-78.

49. Anthony Ward, S.M., and Cuthbert Johnson, O.S.B., eds., *Missalis Romani editio princeps, Mediolani anno 1474 prelis mandata* (Rome: Centro Liturgico Vincenziano–Edizioni Liturgiche, 1996), 31. The history of the Collect is discussed in J. A. Jungmann, *El sacrificio de la Misa. Tratado histórico-litúrgico*, 4th ed. (Madrid: Biblioteca de Autores Cristianos, 1963), 310-12. On its influence on the Anglican *Book of Common Prayer*, see John Henry Blunt, *The Annotated Book of Common Prayer; being an historical, ritual and theological commentary on the devotional system of the Church of England* (London: Rivingtons, 1866), 165-66.

50. *Lazarillo de Tormes and El Abencerraje*, 167.

51. *Lazarillo de Tormes*, 121, n.34.

52. See too Ezekiel 18:32, 33:11; 2 Peter 3:9.

53. Cabrol, ed., *The Mass of the Western Rites*, 451. See too Ward and Johnson, *Missalis Romani editio princeps*, 145.

54. *Lazarillo de Tormes and El Abencerraje*, 168.

TRATADO SÉPTIMO

55. "En la superficie, el autor ha pretendido hacer buena la pretensión final de Lázaro: frente a su padre y a su madre, él ha triunfado [...]. Pero no es preciso ahondar mucho para percibir que el pregonero, al acabar la obra, *no contrasta* con sus padres: sigue sin superar a Tomé González, aunque ocupe otro lugar en el cortejo penitenciario; y, moralmente, está al mismo nivel—más bajo aún—que Antona Pérez." Lázaro Carreter, *Lazarillo de Tormes y la picaresca*, 92.

56. On this parallel, see the comments of Guillén, *Lazarillo de Tormes and El Abencerraje*, 11 and 172, Lázaro Carreter, *Lazarillo de Tormes y la picaresca*, 170, and Aldo Ruffinatto, "Revisión del 'caso' de Lázaro de Tormes (puntos de vista y *trompes-l'oeil* en el *Lazarillo*)," *Edad de Oro* 20 (2001): 169.

57. "He [the author] makes Lázaro a person who is capable of seeing his own career as a kind of practical burlesque of more generally conceived attitudes of a moral, and sometimes religious, kind." Truman, "*Lazarillo de Tormes*, Petrarch's *De remediis adversae fortunae*, and Erasmus's *Praise of Folly*," 49. On the narrator's mock-serious tone, see also the comments of Guillén in *Lazarillo de Tormes and El Abencerraje*, 10, and Truman, "Parody and irony in the self-portrayal of Lázaro de Tormes," 605; on the treatment of *honra* in the work, see in particular Martino, *Il 'Lazarillo de Tormes' e la sua ricezione in Europa*, 1:429-35, Lázaro Carreter, *Lazarillo de Tormes y la picaresca*, 178-79, as well as the texts assembled in Claude Chauchadis, *Honneur, morale et société dans l'Espagne de Philippe II* (Paris: Centre National de la Recherche Scientifique, 1984), 72, n.101; 73, n.108 and n.109; 148, n.39; 156, n.115.

58. "They [the theorists of nobility] are concerned with it being praiseworthy to rise in society by the exercise of virtue; Lázaro is concerned with its being a virtue simply to rise. He echoes the formula to state a principle opposite to the one normally expressed by it." R.W. Truman, "Lázaro de Tormes and the *Homo novus* tradition," *Modern Language Review* 64 (1965).

CONCLUSION

59. See Guillén, *Lazarillo de Tormes and El Abencerraje*, 22, and *La vida de Lazarillo de Tormes y de sus fortunas y adversidades*, ed. Francisco Rico (Barcelona: Planeta, 1980), lxvii-lxxi. The combination in the work of popular and learned traditions is considered in Truman, "*Lazarillo de Tormes*, Petrarch's *De remediis adversae fortunae*, and Erasmus's *Praise of Folly*," 41.

60. "Al escoger la fórmula autobiográfica, [el autor] se ve obligado a seguir el punto de vista del personaje para no faltar al decoro; pero como este personaje expresa una ideología opuesta a la del autor, éste sólo cuenta, para indicar cuál es su auténtico pensamiento, con un medio: la ironía." Blecua in his edition of *Lazarillo de Tormes*, 39.

61. On the sixteenth-century movements with which the author has been associated, including Spanish Erasmianism, see Martino, *Il "Lazarillo de Tormes" e la sua ricezione in Europa*, 1:315 onwards. The notion of the "implied author" is applied fruitfully to *Lazarillo* in E. H. Friedman, *The Antiheroine's Voice: Narrative Discourse and Transformations of the Picaresque* (Columbia: University of Missouri Press, 1987), 16, 18, and in Rodrigo Cacho Casal, "Hide-and-seek: *Lazarillo de Tormes* and the art of deception," *Forum for Modern Language Studies* 44 (2008), 332-34.

62. The various writers to whom *Lazarillo* has been attributed are discussed in Martino, *Il "Lazarillo de Tormes" e la sua ricezione in Europa*, 1: 183-242, and contributions to the debate by Rosa Navarro Durán and José Luis Madrigal are considered in the review article by Anne J. Cruz, "The *Lazarillo*'s author, *redivivus*: on recent studies by Rosa Navarro Durán and José Luis Madrigal," *Bulletin of Spanish Studies* 83 (2006): 855-61, who concludes (861): "until more proof—both intratextual and extratextual—is adduced, the identity of our most famous anonymous author remains tantalizingly out of reach." On the indeterminacy of the text, see, in particular, Friedman, *The Antiheroine's Voice*, 20-21, 31; Paul Julian Smith, "The rhetoric of representation in writers and critics of picaresque narrative: *Lazarillo de Tormes, Guzmán de Alfarache, El Buscón*," *Modern Language Review* 82 (1987): 88-108; and Peter N. Dunn, "Reading the text of *Lazarillo de Tormes*," in *Studies in Honour of Bruce W. Wardropper*, ed. Dian Fox, Harry Sieber, Robert TerHorst (Newark, Delaware: Juan de la Cuesta, 1989).

CHAPTER FOUR
POETRY: LUIS DE LEÓN AND THE ASCENSION OF CHRIST

1. See Colin P. Thompson, *The Strife of Tongues. Fray Luis de León and the Golden Age of Spain* (Cambridge: Cambridge University Press, 1988), esp. 33 onwards. The trial documents may be seen in Ángel Alcalá, ed., *Proceso inquisitorial de fray Luis de León. Edición paleográfica, anotada y crítica* (Salamanca: Junta de Castilla y León, 1991).

2. Bataillon, *Erasmo y España. Estudios sobre la historia espiritual del siglo xvi*, 761.

3. Santos Sabugal, "Exégesis y hermenéutica bíblica de Fray Luis de León," in *Fray Luis de León. IV centenario (1591-1991). Congreso interdisciplinar. Madrid, 16-19 de octubre de 1991. Actas*, ed. Teófilo Viñas Román (Madrid: Ediciones Escurialenses, 1992), 119, 122. The phrase *el mysterio de Christo* occurs in the *Dedicatoria* of the *Nombres de Christo*: Luis de León, *De los nombres de Cristo*, ed. Cristóbal Cuevas (Madrid: Cátedra, 1997), 147. Its roots are Pauline: see Ephesians 3:4, Colossians 1:26, Romans 16:25-26.

4. Ciriaco Morón Arroyo, "Fray Luis de León: sistema y drama," in *Fray Luis de León. Aproximaciones a su vida y obra*, ed. Ciriaco Morón Arroyo and Manuel Revuelta Sañudo (Santander: Sociedad Menéndez Pelayo, 1989), 316.

5. Cited in Saturnino Alvarez Turienzo, "Clave epistemológica para leer a Fray Luis de León," in *Fray Luis de León*, ed. Víctor García de la Concha (Salamanca: Universidad de Salamanca, 1981), 41.

6. Cited in Jesús María Nieto Ibáñez, *Espiritualidad y patrística en "De los nombres de Cristo" de Fray Luis de León* (El Escorial: Ediciones Escurialenses y Universidad de León, 2001), 11.

7. Luis de León, *De los nombres de Cristo*, 142-43.

8. These are considered individually and in detail in Thompson, *The Strife of Tongues*.

9. Both versions are edited in Luis de León, *Poesías completas. Obras propias en castellano y latín y traducciones e imitaciones latinas, griegas, bíblico-hebreas y romances*, ed. Cristóbal Cuevas (Madrid: Castalia, 1998), 156-57, to which all subsequent references refer. On the issue of authenticity Margherita Morreale has observed: "La cuestión depende de la ecdótica a la que habría que someter toda la trasmisión de los poemas luisianos." See the detailed analysis of the language of the shorter version in her study, *Homenaje a Fray Luis de León* (Salamanca:

Universidad de Salamanca/Zaragoza: Prensas Universitarias, 2007), 649-59 (p. 187 n. 1873).

10. Ricardo Senabre, "La oda de Fray Luis a la Ascensión," in *Tres estudios sobre Fray Luis de León* (Salamanca: Universidad de Salamanca, 1978), 79-80.

THE DISTRESS OF THE DISCIPLES

11. Colin P. Thompson, "*En la Ascensión*: artistic tradition and poetic imagination in Luis de León," in *Medaieval and Renaissance Studies on Spain and Portugal in Honour of P. E. Russell*, ed. F. W. Hodcroft and others (Oxford: Society for the Study of Mediaeval Languages and Literature, 1981), 111.

12. *Tractatus* 94:4 in Augustine, *In Iohannis Evangelium Tractatus CXXIV*, ed. Radbodus Willems, O.S.B., Corpus Christianorum Series Latina, vol. 36 (Turnhout: Brepols, 1954), 563.

13. *De Trinitate* 1:9, in Augustine, *De Trinitate libri xv*, ed. W.J. Mountain and Fr. Glorie, Corpus Christianorum Series Latina, vol. 50A (Turnhout: Brepols, 1968), 53-54. See William Marrevee, S.C.J., *The Ascension of Christ in the Works of St. Augustine* (Ottawa: Ottawa University Press, 1967), 63-64, 94-99.

14. *Sermo* 6:12 on the Ascension, in St. Bernard, *Sermones litúrgicos*, 2 vols. (Madrid: Biblioteca de Autores Cristianos, 1985-86), 2:188. On St. Bernard's approach to the Ascension, see Jean Leclercq, O.S.B., "The Mystery of the Ascension in the Sermons of St. Bernard," *Cistercian Studies* 25 (1990): 4-16.

15. *Summa Theologica* 3 q.57. a.1.

16. *Ibid.* The words of Augustine quoted by St. Thomas here are from *In Iohannis evangelium tractatus*, 94:4, 5.

17. Juan de Valdés, *Diálogo de doctrina christiana y El Salterio traducido del hebreo en romance castellano*, ed. Domingo Ricart (Mexico: Universidad Nacional Autónoma de México, 1964), 28-29; San Pedro de Alcántara, *Tratado de la oración y meditación*, in *Vida y escritos de San Pedro de Alcántara*, ed. Rafael Sanz Valdivielso, O.F.M. (Madrid: Biblioteca de Autores Cristianos, 1996), 311-12; San Alonso de Orozco, *Tratado de la suavidad de Dios*, ed. Teófilo Aparicio, 423, and *Catechismo provechoso*, ed. Luis Resines, 763-64, both in *Obras completas, 1: obras castellanas (1)*, ed. Rafael Lazcano (Madrid: Biblioteca de Áutores Cristianos, 2001).

18. San Juan de Ávila, *Obras completas*, ed. Luis Sala Balust and Francisco Martín Hernández, 6 vols. (Madrid: Biblioteca de Autores Cristianos, 1970-71), 2:382.

19. Bartolomé Carranza de Miranda, *Comentarios sobre el catechismo christiano*, ed. José Ignacio Tellechea Idígoras, 3 vols. (Madrid: Biblioteca de Autores Cristianos, 1972-99), 1:306-7.

20. Francisco de Osuna, *Tercer abecedario espiritual*, ed. Melquíades Andrés (Madrid: Biblioteca de Autores Cristianos, 1972), 126-27. See Luis de León, *Poesía*, ed. Antonio Ramajo Caño, with a preliminary study by Alberto Blecua and Francisco Rico (Barcelona: Galaxia Gutenberg/Círculo de Lectores, 2006), 116, 619. The reference to St. Cyprian is to a treatise by the Benedictine Arnaud Debonneval, a friend of St. Bernard, which was ascribed, mistakenly, to the early Church Father: *Liber de cardinalibus operibus Christi*, in *Patrologia Latina*, 189:1667-68. See J. Canivez, "Arnaud Debonneval," in *Dictionnaire de spiritualité*, 1: 888-90.

21. See Colin P. Thompson, "*Una elegancia desafeitada*: Fray Luis de León and Santa Teresa," in *San Juan de la Cruz and Fray Luis de León. A Commemorative International Symposium*, ed. Mary Malcolm Gaylord and Francisco Márquez Villanueva (Newark, Del.: Juan de la Cuesta, 1996), 289-98, and N. D. O'Donoghue, "The human form divine. St. Teresa and the humanity of Christ," in *Teresa de Jesús and Her World*, ed. Margaret A. Rees (Leeds: Trinity and All Saints' College, 1981), 75-88.

THE SHORTER VERSION

22. Elias L. Rivers, *Fray Luis de León. The Original Poems* (London: Grant and Cutler and Tamesis, 1983), 26-27. See too Thompson "*En la Ascensión*: artistic tradition and poetic imagination in Luis de León," 113: "it is an interim statement, not a final word: the mood of the disciples caught between Asension and Pentecost."

23. Thompson, "*En la Ascensión*: artistic tradition and poetic imagination in Luis de León," 114-15.

24. *Sermo* 72 (*De resurrectione Domini II*), in *Patrologia Latina*, 54: 391-92, translated in St. Leo the Great, *The Letters and Sermons*, trans. with an introduction and notes by Charles Lett Feltoe (Edinburgh: T. and T. Clark, 1989), 185.

25. Psalm 22:4 in the Hebrew Psalter reads: *sed et si ambulavero in valle mortis non timebo malum quoniam tu mecum es.* Cristóbal Cuevas in Luis de León, *Poesías completas*, 156, cites Psalm 83:7: *in valle lachrimarum.* See too the remarks of Antonio Ramajo Caño in his edition of Luis de León, *Poesía*, 620.

26. San Juan de Ávila, *Obras completas*, 2:393, following *Summa Theologica* 3 q.57.a.1: "licet praesentia corporalis Christi fuerit subtracta fidelibus per ascensionem, praesentia tamen divinitatis ipsius semper adest fidelibus." See also Luis de Granada, *Adiciones, 2: Meditaciones de la vida de Cristo*, ed. Alvaro Huerga (Madrid: Fundación Universitaria Española y Dominicos de Andalucía, 1995), 238: "cuando subió de la tierra al cielo, de tal manera subió al cielo, que no desamparó la tierra. Porque, aunque subió según la humanidad, no subió según la divinidad, porque ésta en todo lugar está presente."

27. Thompson, "*En la Ascensión*: artistic tradition and poetic imagination in Luis de León," 115.

28. Juan Maldonado, S.J., *Commentarii in quatuor evangelistas*, ed. J. M. Raich, 2 vols. (Mainz: Kirchheim, 1874), 1:198.

29. Thompson, "*En la Ascensión*: artistic tradition and poetic imagination in Luis de León," 115.

30. Joseph F. Chorpenning, "Christ the nursing mother in Fray Luis de León's *En la Ascensión*," *Journal of Hispanic Philology* 11 (1987): 199-204.

31. Augustine, *In Ioannis evangelium tractatus*, 94:4.

32. *Ibid.*, 98:6.

33. San Juan de Ávila, *Obras completas*, 2: 434.

34. *Sermo* 210:4, in *Patrologia Latina*, 38:1049.

35. St. Bernard *Sermones litúrgicos*, 2 vols. (Madrid: Biblioteca de Autores Cristianos, 1985-86), 2:140-42.

36. Senabre, "La oda de Fray Luis a la Ascensión," 90-91, citing *Sermo* X:4 in St. Bernard, *Sermones varios*, trans. with an introduction by Mariano Ballano (Madrid: Biblioteca de Autores Cristianos, 1988), 116.

37. *Sermo* 210:4, in *Patrologia Latina*, 38: 1049-50.

38. Bernard, *Sermones litúrgicos*, 2:188. See too Luis de Granada: "en esta vida ya no podremos contemplar aquel rostro lleno de todas las gracias, ni oir más aquella trompeta repitiendo como un eco los misterios divinos." *Sermón 124: La Ascensión del Señor*, in *Sermones de tiempo III/3*, trans. Ricardo Alarcón Buendía and ed. Alvaro Huerga (Madrid: Fundación Universitaria Española y Dominicos de Andalucía, 2002), 31.

39. Luis de León, O.S.A., *The Original Poems*, ed. with an introduction and notes by Edward Sarmiento (Manchester: Manchester University Press, 1972), 87-88.

40. Augustine, *In Ioannis evangelium tractatus*, 25:2.

41. *Ibid.*, 25:7.

42. Saint Thomas Aquinas, *In evangelia S. Matthaei et S. Joannis commentaria*, 2 vols. (Turin: ex officina Petri Marietti, 1919), 1:208. On the Matthew commentary of St. Thomas, first published in 1527, see Jean-Pierre Torrell, O.P., *St. Thomas Aquinas*, trans. Robert Royal, 2 vols. (Washington, D.C.: Catholic University of America, 1996), 1: 56-57. The patristic sources of the images of the sea of life and the ship of the Church are discussed in Hugo Rahner, *Greek Myths and Christian Mystery*, 341-53.

43. Rivers, *Fray Luis de León. The Original Poems*, 27.

44. Thompson, "*En la Ascensión*: artistic tradition and poetic imagination in Luis de León," 120.

45. See the comment of Cristóbal Cuevas in his edition of *Poesías completas*, 156.

46. "The collective nature of the poem's complaint must be taken seriously: *nos dexas*. It is not about Christ abandoning an individual, but his flock." Thompson, "*En la Ascensión*: artistic tradition and poetic imagination in Luis de León," 113.

47. San Juan de Ávila, *Obras completas*, 2:378.

48. Leo the Great, *Sermo* 73:1 (*De Ascensione Domini 1*), in *Patrologia Latina*, 54: 395, translated in St. Leo the Great, *The Letters and Sermons*, 186-87.

WITNESSES OF THE ASCENSION

49. Senabre, "La oda de Fray Luis a la Ascensión," 78-79. See too the comments of Antonio Ramajo Caño in Luis de León, *Poesía*, 116, 619.
50. *The Hours of the Divine Office in English and Latin. A Bilingual Edition of the Roman Breviary Text*, 3 vols. (Collegeville: The Liturgical Press, 1964), 2:1340. The passage cited is from the first sermon on the Ascension of St. Leo the Great. On the theology of the Ascension implicit in the liturgy, and its biblical context, see Jean Daniélou, S.J., *The Bible and the Liturgy* (Notre Dame, Indiana: University Press, 1966), 303-18.
51. Compare, for instance, the portrayal of their distress in his second Ascension sermon, in Bernard, *Sermones litúrgicos*, 2:140, with the evocation of their joy in *Sermo 101, De quattuor modis dilectionis*, in Bernard, *Sermones varios*, 478.
52. Bonaventure [Pseudo], *Meditationes vitae Christi*, in *S. Bonaventurae opera omnia*, ed. A.C. Peltier, vol. 12 (Paris: Vives, 1868), 623-24; Ludolph of Saxony, *Vita Jesu Christi* (Paris, 1502), part 2, chapters 81-82.
53. Thompson, "*En la Ascensión*: artistic tradition and poetic imagination in Luis de León," 109-10.
54. T. Ernest DeWald, "The iconography of the Ascension," *American Journal of Archaeology* 19 (1915): 315-18; Meyer Schapiro, "The image of the Disappearing Christ. The Ascension in English Art around the year 1000," *Gazette des Beaux-Arts*, ser.6, 23 (1943): 133-52, reprinted in *Selected Papers, vol.3: Late Antique, Early Christian and Mediaeval Art* (New York: Braziller, 1979); Victor I. Stoichita, *Visionary Experience in the Golden Age of Spanish Art* (London: Reaktion, 1995), 32-37.
55. Robert Deshman, "Another look at the Disappearing Christ: corporeal and spiritual vision in early medieval images," *Art Bulletin* 79 (1997): 518-46.
56. Noted by Edward Sarmiento in his edition of *The Original Poems*, 87.
57. See Eligius Dekkers, *Clavis patrum latinorum* (Bruges: Beyaert, 1951), 67-68; Iohannis Machielsen, *Clavis patristica pseudoepigraphorum Medii Aevii*, 2 vols. (Brepols: Turnhoult, 1990), 1a: 119, 121-22, 185-86.
58. Pseudo-Augustine, *Sermo* 179:1, in *Patrologia Latina*, 39: 2084.
59. Pseudo-Augustine, *Sermo* 130:2, in *Patrologia Latina*, 39: 2086. See too Pseudo-Augustine, *Liber meditationum*, in *Patrologia Latina*, 40: 942: "recessisti consolator vitae meae, nec vale dixisti mihi [...]. Quid dicam? quid faciam? quo vadam? ubi enim quaeram? ubi vel quando inveniam? Quem rogabo? Quis nuntiabit dilecto, quia amore langueo?"
60. Hilary Dansey Smith, *Preaching in the Spanish Golden Age. A Study of Some Preachers of the Reign of Philip III* (Oxford: Oxford University Press, 1978), 67.
61. Ibid., 67-68. On the classical background, see Heinrich Lausberg, *Manual de retórica literaria. Fundamentos de una ciencia de la literatura*, trans. José Pérez Riesco, 3 vols. (Madrid: Gredos, 1966), 1:339-49.
62. Luis de Granada, *Retórica Eclesiástica*, ed. Alvaro Huerga, 2 vols. (Madrid: Fundación universitaria española y Dominicos de Andalucía, 1999), 1:312-13. This edition reproduces, in revised form, the Spanish version of the Latin original by José Climent (Barcelona, 1775), from which the passages quoted here are taken.
63. Ibid., 343-49; Lausberg, *Manual de retórica literaria*, 2:235-41, 425-27.
64. *Retórica Eclesiástica*, 2:19.
65. Ibid., 1:386-93; 2:224-27.

SANTO TOMÁS DE VILLANUEVA

66. Luis de Granada, *Meditaciones de la vida de Cristo*, 232-33.
67. The pertinence of the sermon to the poem of Fray Luis was noted by Félix González Olmedo, "Musa Leonina. Notas y glosas" (reelaboración de A. Díez Escanciano), *Perficit* (Salamanca), 4

(1973): 173. On the sermon itself, see Argimiro Turrado, "Thomas de Villeneuve," *Dictionnaire de spiritualité* 15: cols. 874-90, and the same author's introduction to John E. Rotelle, O.S.A., ed., *St. Thomas of Villanueva. Sermons. Part 4: Easter Triduum, Easter Season*, trans. Michael S. Woodward (Villanova, Pa.: Augustinian Press, 1995), 11-46.

68. *In Ascensione Domini. Concio Tertia*, in Santo Tomás de Villanueva, *Opera omnia* (Augsburg, 1757: sumptibus Ignatii Adami et Francisci Antonii bibliopolarum), 344-46, translated in Rotelle, ed., *St Thomas of Villanueva. Sermons. Part 4: Easter Triduum, Easter Season*, 208-9.

69. Ibid.

70. Ibid.

71. Ibid. Here, and in the quotation that follows, I have adjusted the translation in Rotelle to bring it more closely in line with the Latin original.

72. Ibid.

73. Ibid.

74. Ibid.

75. Santo Tomás de Villanueva, *Conciones sacrae [...] Nunc primum in lucem editae* (Alcalá de Henares: Ioannes a Lequerica excudebat, 1572). On Uceda, see M. González Velasco, "Los agustinos en el proceso de fray Luis de León," in *Fray Luis de León. El fraile, el humanista, el teólogo*, ed. S. Alvarez Turienzo (Madrid: Ediciones Escurialenses, 1991), 681-82, and Luis de León, *Epistolario, cartas, licencias, poderes, dictámenes*, ed. José Barrientos García (Madrid: Revista Agustiniana, 2001), 119. The sermons are discussed in Jesús Martínez de Bujanda, *Diego de Estella (1524-1578). Estudio de sus obras castellanas* (Rome: Iglesia Nacional Española, 1970), 42ff.

THE LONGER VERSION

76. On the manuscript tradition, see Luis de León, *Poesía completa*, ed. José Manuel Blecua (Madrid: Gredos, 1990), 81-82, and *Poesías completas*, ed. Cristóbal Cuevas, 27-33.

77. *The Original Poems*, 87.

78. "Parece un remedio a las perplejidades expresadas por un teólogo, a quien dejaba estupefacto que la Ascensión infundiese en el hombre cristiano tales impulsos de dolor, tanta desesperación y añoranza inconsolada." Luis de León, *Poesías. Estudio, texto crítico, bibliografía y comentario*, ed. Oresti Macrí (Barcelona: Crítica, 1982), 78. Senabre, "La oda de Fray Luis a la Ascensión," 75.

79. "Los continuos cambios de destinatorio [...] introducen una movilidad meramente externa, basada en los cambios de enfoque y no, como en las estrofas de la versión auténtica, en la progresión de ideas y imágenes." Senabre, "La oda de Fray Luis a la Ascensión," 95. For the views of Sarmiento, see *The Original Poems*, 87.

80. "monet Apostolus, ut quaeramus quae sursum sunt, ubi Christus est in dextera Dei sedens (Colossians 3:1), quia illic profecto thesaurus noster est Iesus Christus, *in quo sunt omnes thesauri sapientiae et scientiae absconditi* (Colossians 2:2-3), in quo habitat omnis plenitudo divinitatis corporaliter (Colossians 2:9)." Bernard, *Sermones litúrgicos*, 2:140.

81. *Summa Theologica* 3 q.57.a.1.

82. Carranza, *Comentarios sobre el catechismo christiano*, 1: 306. See too Granada, *Meditaciones de la vida de Cristo*, 239-40: "si todo nuestro tesoro es Cristo, ¿dónde es razón que esté todo nuestro corazón, sino con él? [...] pues todas las cosas tenemos en él, claro está que, poniéndonos Dios este tesoro en el cielo, nos obligó a tener allá nuestro corazón."

83. *Patrologia Latina*, 39: 2084.

84. *Homelia 15: In Ascensione Domini*, in St. Bede, *Opera homiletica*, ed. D. Hurst, Corpus Christianorum Series Latina, vol. 122 (Turnhoult: Brepols, 1955), 287; translated in St. Bede, *Homilies on the Gospels. Book Two: Lent to the Dedication of the Church*, trans. Lawrence T. Martin and David Hurst, O.S.B. (Kalamazoo: Cistercian Publications, 1991), 144.

85. *Sermo 4:7*, in Bernard, *Sermones litúrgicos*, 2:167 (the version of Matthew 17:2 cited here by St. Bernard differs slightly from the standard Vulgate, which reads: *resplenduit facies eius ut sol*). On Bernard's use of sun imagery in this connection, see Leclercq, "The Mystery of the Ascension in the Sermons of St. Bernard," 13, and on ways in which the Transfiguration account

prefigures the Ascension narrative see Thompson, "*En la Ascensión*: artistic tradition and poetic imagination in Luis de León," 117. In one of his Ascension sermons, Fray Luis de Granada affirmed: "¿qué es para nosotros Cristo sino el sol de justicia? Pues dice él mismo, *soy la luz del mundo*. Si se apaga esta luz y desaparece el sol de justicia, ¿no es propio que quienes quedamos en las tinieblas del mundo sintamos la ausencia de este sol? Por eso, hermanos, en esta solemnidad la separación del Señor es la causa de nuestra tristeza." *Sermón 124: La Ascensión del Señor*, in Luis de Granada, *Sermones de tiempo III/3*, 31.

86. "Dominus noster Iesus Christus ascendit in coelum: ascendat cum illo et cor nostrum." Augustine, *Sermo* 263:2, in *Patrologia Latina*, 38:1210.

87. Augustine, *Sermo* 263:2, in *Patrologia Latina*, 38:1211: "Facile corpus levabitur in alta coelorum, si non premat spiritum sarcina peccatorum."

88. "Hay fórmulas que [...] aparecen elementos claramente desconectados del conjunto—así, el 'lazo de diamante', motivado sin duda por exigencias de la rima." Senabre, "La oda de Fray Luis a la Ascensión," 95.

89. St. Jerome, *Comentarios a los profetas menores. Edición bilingüe*, ed. Avelino Domínguez García (Madrid: Biblioteca de Autores Cristianos, 2003), 552.

90. Pseudo-Augustine, *Sermo* 177:1, in *Patrologia Latina*, 39: 2083.

91. *The Original Poems*, 88.

92. Gregory the Great, *Homilia* 32:2, in *Homiliae in evangelia*, ed. Raymond Étaix, Corpus Christianorum Series Latina, vol. 141 (Turnhout: Brepols, 1999), 279.

93. Cabrol, ed., *The Roman Missal in Latin and English*, 563; Ward and Johnson, *Missalis Romani editio princeps*, 199-200. The collect is echoed too in Luis de Granada, *Meditaciones de la vida de Cristo*, 241: "el que desea conformar la vida que vive con la fe que profesa, y responder como debe a la grandeza de este misterio, conviene que todo su corazón, sus gustos y todos sus sentidos tenga en el cielo, pues en él está todo su bien, y aunque aquí more con el cuerpo, allí esté con el espíritu y con el deseo."

94. Senabre, "La oda de Fray Luis a la Ascensión," 95-96.

Meditation

95. See José Ramón Alcántara Mejía, *La escondida senda: poética y hermenéutica en la obra castellana de fray Luis de León* (Salamanca: Universidad de Salamanca, 2002), 251-66 (esp. 261 n.4, on the longer version); Edward M. Wilson, "La estructura simétrica de la *Oda a Francisco Salinas*," in *Entre las jarchas y Cernuda. Constantes y variables en la poesía española* (Barcelona: Ariel, 1977), 195-201; Terence O'Reilly, "The image of the garden in *La vida retirada*," in *Belief and Unbelief in Hispanic Literature*, ed. Helen Wing and John Jones (Warminster: Aris and Phillips, 1995), 9-18.

96. "el tono y el vocabulario resultan familiares a cualquier lector de Fray Luis." Senabre, "La oda de Fray Luis a la Ascensión," 94.

97. *The Original Poems*, 87.

98. Ibid. On meditation manuals of the period, see Armando Pego Puigbó, *El Renacimiento espiritual. Introducción literaria a los tratados de oración españoles 1520-1566* (Madrid: Consejo Superior de Investigaciones Científicas, 2004).

99. *Ejercicios espirituales* [312], in Loyola, *Obras*, 293.

100. San Pedro de Alcántara, *Tratado de la oración y meditación* (Madrid: Rialp, 1991), 104. The text of the *Tratado* edited in *Vida y escritos de San Pedro de Alcántara*, 311, appears to be defective at this point.

101. *Vida y escritos de San Pedro de Alcántara*, 312.

102. See the description of *lectio* in Terence O'Reilly, "St. John of the Cross and the traditions of monastic exegesis," in *Leeds Papers on Saint John of the Cross*, ed. Margaret A. Rees (Leeds: Trinity and All Saints' College, 1991), 105-26.

103. The shortcomings of the longer version are analysed in detail by Senabre in "La oda de Fray Luis a la Ascensión," 94-96.

104. "Esta Oda tuvo dos redacciones [...] La definitiva es la corta." Luis de León, *Poesías originales*, ed. Angel Custodio Vega O.S.A. (Barcelona: Planeta, 1980), 57 n.4. On the process of revision to which Fray Luis appears to have subjected his poems, see the comments by José Manuel Blecua in his edition of Luis de León, *Poesía completa*, 27.

CHAPTER FIVE
DRAMA: EL CONDENADO POR DESCONFIADO

1. On the connection between the play and the *de auxiliis* controversy, see, in particular, R. J. Oakley, *Tirso de Molina. El condenado por desconfiado* (London: Grant and Cutler, 1994), 73-93; Miguel Angel Ferreyra Liendo, "*El condenado por desconfiado* de Tirso: análisis teológico y literario del drama," *Revista de la Universidad Nacional de Córdoba* 10 (1969): 925-46; Henry W. Sullivan, *Tirso de Molina and the Drama of the Counter-Reformation* (Amsterdam: Rodopi, 1981), 28-40; Mario F. Trubiano, *Libertad, gracia y destino en el teatro de Tirso de Molina* (Madrid: Ediciones Alcalá, 1985); Gabriel González, *Drama y teología en el Siglo de Oro* (Salamanca: Universidad de Salamanca, 1987); and the introduction to Tirso de Molina, *El condenado por desconfiado*, ed. Ciriaco Morón Arroyo (Madrid: Cátedra, 1992). References to the text are to the following edition: *El condenado por desconfiado. A play attributed to Tirso de Molina (Fray Gabriel Téllez)*, ed. with an introduction and notes by Daniel Rogers (Oxford: Pergamon, 1974).
2. T. E. May, "*El condenado por desconfiado*," *Bulletin of Hispanic Studies* 35 (1958): 138-56, reprinted in T.E May, *The Wit of the Golden Age. Articles on Spanish Literature* (Kassel: Reichenberger, 1986), 134-53 (143). Page references are to the reprinted version.
3. May, "*El condenado por desconfiado*," 145.
4. Jonathan Thacker, *A Companion to Golden Age Theatre* (London: Tamesis, 2007), 68-69. On the sermon literature of the time, see Miguel Ángel Núñez Beltrán, *La oratoria sagrada de la época del Barroco: doctrina, cultura y actitud ante la vida desde los sermones sevillanos del siglo XVII* (Seville: Universidad de Sevilla/Fundación Focus-Abengoa, 2000).

THE FEAR OF GOD

5. Alexander A. Parker, "Santos y bandoleros en el teatro español del Siglo de Oro," *Arbor* 13 (1949): 411.
6. San Francisco de Borja, *Tratados espirituales*, ed. Cándido de Dalmases (Barcelona: Juan Flors, 1964), 287.
7. See Chapter Two above.
8. Oakley notes that Paulo becomes a criminal, "because he thinks it is in his interests, just as he became a hermit for his own benefit." Oakley, *Tirso de Molina. El condenado por desconfiado*, 33.
9. *Catechismus ex decreto Concilii Tridentini*, (Rome: Ex typographia polyglotta S. Congregationis de Propaganda Fide, 1886), 454-55 [Part 4, Chapter 9:1]. The English version cited here and in subsequent quotations is *Catechism of the Council of Trent*, trans. J. Donovan (Dublin: James Duffy, c. 1880), 432. The *Catechism of the Council of Trent* (Rome, 1566) was not translated into Spanish during the Golden Age. The Spanish Inquisition, it seems, viewed it with hostility, because of its debt to the catechism of Bartolomé Carranza. It was available in Latin, however, to educated members of the laity, clergy, and religious orders, among whom may be included the author of the play, and it left its mark on catechisms in the vernacular, including the *Catecismo* of St. Alonso de Orozco (Zaragoza, 1568), in which it is cited. In 1584, the episcopal synod of Zamora urged clergy to make use of it. See *Catecismos de Astete y Ripalda*, ed. Luis Resines (Madrid: Biblioteca de Autores Cristianos, 1987), 21-23; San Alonso de Orozco, *Obras completas,1:obras castellanas (1)*, 704-5, 710; Diarmaid MacCulloch, *Reformation: Europe's House Divided, 1490-1700* (London: Allen Lane, 2003), 301. As Luis Resines has observed, "la influencia directa [del *Catecismo*] no se dejó sentir demasiado, a expensas de poder aportar nuevos datos. Sin embargo, otra cosa muy diversa es la influencia indirecta [...] no hay más remedio que afirmar que el *Catecismo* romano ejerció una notable influencia sobre la

catequesis española, aunque no sea fácilmente detectable." *La catequesis en España. Historia y textos* (Madrid: Biblioteca de Autores Cristianos, 2007), 187.

10. *Decrees of the Ecumenical Councils*, ed. Norman P. Tanner, S.J., 2 vols. (London: Sheed and Ward/Washington: Georgetown University Press,1990), 2:679 [Canon 8].

11. *Decrees of the Ecumenical Councils*, 2:674 [Chapter 9].

12. *Decrees of the Ecumenical Councils*, 2:672-73 [Chapter 6].

13. *Decrees of the Ecumenical Councils*, 2:677-78 [Chapter 16].

14. In the period after Trent, the image was used in this sense by St. Alonso de Orozco, who invoked it to urge perseverance in his *Tratado de la suavidad de Dios* (Salamanca, 1576): "Así lo dijo nuestro soberano maestro Jesucristo: 'El que persevera hasta el fin, ése se salvará' (Matthew 24:13). No dijo el que comenzare a vivir bien, que muchos hay principiantes que no perseveran, desmayando como flacos en el camino de la virtud [...]. Conforma con esto lo que san Pablo dijo: 'No será coronado sino el que peleare fielmente.' Lealmente pelea el que hasta el fin de la batalla persevera. Y como la vida sea continua guerra, hasta la muerte ha de pelear." Orozco, *Obras completas,1:obras castellanas (1)*, 495. On the image of the *corona*, see Leslie Levin, *Metaphors of Conversion in Seventeenth-Century Spanish Drama* (London: Tamesis, 1999), 58.

15. See Chapter Two above.

16. Pablo de León, O.P., *Guía del Cielo*, ed. Vicente Beltrán de Heredia, O.P. (Barcelona: Juan Flors, 1963), 479. On the sources on which Pablo de León drew, see 36-42.

17. *Traité de l'Amour de Dieu* (Lyon, 1616), Livre 11, Chapitre 18, in St. François de Sales, *Oeuvres*, ed. André Ravier and Roger Devos (Paris: Gallimard, 1969), 932.

18. *Camino espiritual* (Alcalá de Henares, 1626), Libro 1, Capítulo 18, in Luis de la Palma, S.J., *Obras*, ed. Francisco X. Rodríguez Molero, S.J. (Madrid: Biblioteca de Autores Cristianos, 1967), 470.

19. Nicholas Round, in his introduction to Tirso de Molina, *Damned for Despair (El condenado por desconfiado)*, ed. and trans. with an introduction and commentary by Nicholas G. Round (Warminster: Aris and Phillips, 1986), lxix.

20. *Catechismus ex decreto Concilii Tridentini*, 369, 370, 372 [Part 3, Chapter 5].

Despair

21. Pablo de León, *Guía del cielo*, 478.

22. Luis de la Palma, *Obras*, 486.

23. See the comments of Daniel Rogers in his edition of *El condenado por desconfiado*, 23-24; Teresa S. Soufas, "Religious melancholy and Tirso's despairing monk in *El condenado por desconfiado*," *Romance Quarterly* 34 (1987): 179-88; Susan Snyder, "The left hand of God: despair in Medieval and Renaissance tradition," *Studies in the Renaissance* 12 (1965): 45.

24. *El condenado por desconfiado*, 150.

25. Snyder, "The left hand of God: despair in Medieval and Renaissance tradition," 32. On the legend concerning Cain's death at the hands of Lamech, see Cornelius à Lapide on Genesis 4:23, in *Commentaria in Scripturam Sacram*, 1:121. See too Pablo de León, *Guía del cielo*, 152: "Los que desesperan son como Caín, que tienen la cabeza que les tiembla. Éste es como hombre vago y prófugo salido de la tierra de Dios."

26. "Nota hic in Caino effectus et poenas peccati. Primus est, tremor corporis; secundus est, exilium et fuga; tertius est, timor et consternatio mentis." Lapide, *Commentaria in Scripturam Sacram*, 1:120.

27. Pablo de León, *Guía del cielo*, 152.

28. Snyder, "The left hand of God: despair in Medieval and Renaissance tradition," 59.

29. *Catechismus ex decreto Concilii Tridentini*, 506 [Part 4, Chapter 14:11].

30. Orozco, *Obras completas,1:obras castellanas (1)*, 855.

31. Jaime Montañés, *Espejo de bien vivir y para ayudar a bien morir*, ed. Pablo María Garrido, O.C. (Salamanca: Universidad Pontificia/Madrid: Fundación Universitaria Española, 1976), 318. On the *ars moriendi* tradition, see Francisco Gago Jover, ed., *Arte de bien morir. Y Breve confesionario (Zaragoza, Pablo Hurus: c. 1479-1484)* (Palma de Mallorca: Olañera, 1999), and Carlos

M. N. Eire, *From Madrid to Purgatory. The Art and Craft of Dying in Sixteenth-Century Spain* (Cambridge: Cambridge University Press, 1995), 24-34.

32. Snyder, "The left hand of God: despair in Medieval and Renaissance tradition," 33.

33. San Juan de Ávila, *Obras completas*, 1: 605-6. On the image of *las suertes trocadas*, see Carlos A. Pérez, "Verosimilitud psicológica de *El condenado por desconfiado*," *Hispanófila* 27 (1966): 19, and the comments of Nicholas Round in *Damned for Despair (El condenado por desconfiado)*, 72.

34. *El condenado por desconfiado*, 14.

35. *Decrees of the Ecumenical Councils*, 2:681 [Canon 29].

36. See the detailed exegesis by Cornelius à Lapide in *Commentaria in Scripturam Sacram*, 9:178-81.

37. Pablo de León, *Guía del cielo*, 155.

38. Luis de Granada, *Obras castellanas*, ed. Cristóbal Cuevas, 2 vols. (Madrid: Turner, 1994-97), 1: 839.

39. Pablo de León, *Guía del cielo*, 155. On the patristic and medieval background to the distinction between presumption and despair, see Snyder, "The left hand of God: despair in Medieval and Renaissance tradition," 35-36. As Ciriaco Morón Arroyo notes in his edition of *El condenado por desconfiado*, 44: "la doctrina útil para entender *El condenado* es la relacionada con la esperanza, no las disputas sobre la predestinación."

40. *Summa Theologiae*, 2-2 q.21.a.2. See Snyder, "The left hand of God: despair in Medieval and Renaissance tradition," 50.

WISDOM

41. See the comments of Rogers in his edition of *El condenado por desconfiado*, 8-9.

42. May, "*El condenado por desconfiado*," 146-52.

43. Ibid., 149-50.

44. Cornelius à Lapide in *Commentaria in Scripturam Sacram*, 20:250, commenting on 1 Peter 1:6-7. Other passages in which the image occurs include: Psalm 65:10; Proverbs 17:3, 27:21; Ecclesiasticus 2:3-5; Wisdom 3:46; Isaiah 1:25, 48:9-10; Zacharias 13:9; Malachias 3:2-3.

45. *Tratado de la suavidad*, chapter 25, in Orozco, *Obras completas, 1: obras castellanas (1)*, 417. St. Teresa of Ávila uses the image of the *crisol* on two occasions in the *Libro de la vida* (20:16 and 30:14), as well as in the *Conceptos* (6:10) and *Las moradas* (4:2,8). See Tomás Alvarez, *Diccionario de Santa Teresa de Jesús*, 1254.

46. The first two pieces of advice [1186-89; 1191-94] are quoted from *El remedio en la desdicha* by Lope de Vega: see Rogers, *El condenado por desconfiado*, 155, and the pertinent remarks of I. L. McClelland: "The advice comes quite attractively into Lope's context but fits more naturally into Tirso's where it acquires a much more serious meaning and loses the Lopean air of casualness." *Tirso de Molina. Studies in Dramatic Realism* (Liverpool: Institute of Hispanic Studies, 1948), 148 n.1.

47. Rogers, *El condenado por desconfiado*, 155.

48. Edward M. Wilson and Duncan Moir, *The Golden Age: Drama 1492-1700* (London: Ernest Benn/New York: Barnes and Noble, 1971), 93. See too McClelland *Tirso de Molina. Studies in Dramatic Realism*, 150.

49. On the scholarly discussion provoked by these lines, see Oakley, *Tirso de Molina. El condenado por desconfiado*, 89-90, and Levin, *Metaphors of Conversion in Sixteenth-Century Spanish Drama*, 65-67.

50. Pablo de León, *Guía del cielo*, 156.

51. Luis de Granada, *Obras castellanas*, 1:800.

52. *Damned for Despair (El condenado por desconfiado)*, lxvi. See too Sullivan, *Tirso de Molina and the Drama of the Counter-Reformation*, 37, and Trubiano, *Libertad, gracia y destino en el teatro de Tirso de Molina*, 191-92, 197.

53. *Catechismus ex decreto Concilii Tridentini*, 312 [Part 2, Chapter 8:15]. On the biblical image of marriage and its metaphorical use, see Leland Ryken, James C. Wilhoit, Tremper Longman III, eds., *A Dictionary of Biblical Imagery* (Downers Grove, Illinois / Leicester, England: InterVarsity Press, 1998), 537-39.

54. Oakley, *Tirso de Molina. El condenado por desconfiado*, 30, 102. See too Alan Soons, "*El*

condenado por desconfiado y *El castigo sin venganza*," in his collection of essays, *Ficción y comedia en el Siglo de Oro* (Madrid: Estudios de la literatura española, 1966), 84, 86, and Levin, *Metaphors of Conversion in Seventeenth-Century Spanish Drama*, 56, 62.

55. The Vulgate text reads: "Qui maledixerit patri suo aut matri morte moriatur [...] sanguis eius sit super eum." Ronald Knox, whose version is cited here, comments: "Literally, 'his blood must be upon his own head,' that is, to kill him is execution, not murder." Parallel passages include: Exodus 21:17; Leviticus 20:9; Deuteronomy 27:16; Proverbs 20:30; 30:11, 17; Matthew 15:4; Mark 7:10.

56. May, "*El condenado por desconfiado*," 145.

57. "No se preocupa de explicar cómo obra la gracia para que siga existiendo la libertad humana, ni cómo debe entenderse la libertad humana para no anular la eficacia de la gracia." Ferreyra Liendo, "*El condenado por desconfiado* de Tirso: análisis teológico y literario del drama," 930.

58. Book 29:77, in Gregory the Great, *Moralia in Iob, libri xxiii-xxxv*, ed. M. Adriaen, Corpus Christianorum Series Latina, vol. 143B (Turnhout: Brepols, 1985), 1489. I have followed the translation in St. Gregory the Great, *Morals on the Book of Job*, 4 vols. (Oxford: John Henry Parker, 1844-1850), 3:358-59.

59. Ibid.

60. Ibid, 1490.

61. McClelland, *Tirso de Molina. Studies in Dramatic Realism*, 134.

CHAPTER SIX
PAINTING: THE BIBLICAL *BODEGONES* OF VELÁZQUEZ

1. "La búsqueda del verdadero Velázquez ha de hacerse desde un conocimiento profundo de su propio ambiente, del pensamiento de sus contemporáneos, que eran quienes habían de enfrentarse con sus obras, aún vírgenes; con una aproximación, lo más rigurosa posible, a sus fuentes formales y conceptuales, en un ejercicio de humildad ante los enigmas – pues tales son en realidad muchas de sus obras – que sus lienzos proponen, y que se corresponden, con perfecta adecuación, al mundo del conceptismo, su estricto contemporáneo." Alfonso E. Pérez Sánchez, "Enigmas," *Boletín Cultural* 194 (1999): 51. On *conceptismo*, see Arthur Terry, *Seventeenth-Century Spanish Poetry. The Power of Artifice* (Cambridge: Cambridge University Press, 1993), 56-64, and Mary Malcolm Gaylord, "The making of Baroque poetry," in Gies, *The Cambridge History of Spanish Literature*, 222-37.

2. Rosemarie Mulcahy, *Spanish Paintings in the National Gallery of Ireland* (Dublin: National Gallery of Ireland, 1988), 81.

3. See Allan Braham, "A second dated *bodegón* by Velázquez," *Burlington Magazine* 107 (1965): 362-63; Bonaventura Bassegoda, "Pacheco y Velázquez," in *Velázquez y Sevilla*, 2 vols. (Seville: Consejería Cultural de la Junta de Andalucía, 1999), 2:134.

4. Enriqueta Harris, "Velázquez, Sevillian painter of sacred subjects," in David Davies and Enriqueta Harris, *Velázquez in Seville*, ed. Michael Clarke (Edinburgh: National Gallery of Scotland, 1996), 48.

5. A parallel approach to the literary context of the painting has been developed by Leslie Anne Nelson, who relates the background inset to the use of discovery scenes in plays by Lope and Calderón: see Leslie Anne Nelson, *Velázquez's "Bodegones a lo divino" and the Spanish Theatre of the Golden Age* (Ann Arbor: UMI Dissertation Services, 1998).

CHRIST IN THE HOUSE OF MARTHA AND MARY

6. William B. Jordan, *Spanish Still Life in the Golden Age, 1600-1650* (Fort Worth: Kimbell Art Museum, 1985), 83.

7. See the remarks by Aidan Weston-Lewis, "Jacob Mathan, 1571-1631: four engravings after paintings by Pieter Aertsen," in Davies and Harris, *Velázquez in Seville*, 103.

8. José Ortega y Gasset, "Introducción a Velázquez," in *Obras completas*, vol. 8 (Madrid: Revista de Occidente, 1962), 482.

9. Lawrence Gowing, "Images of human separateness," *Times Literary Supplement*, 1 August, 1986, 831. See too A. Bustamante and F. Marías, "Entre práctica y teoría: la formación de Velázquez en Sevilla," in *Velázquez y Sevilla*, 2: 154: "lo sacro retrocede—incluso para desaparecer—ante el problema artístico."

10. Kenneth M. Craig, "*Pars ergo Marthae transit*: Pieter Aertsen's 'inverted' paintings of *Christ in the House of Martha and Mary*," *Oud Holland* 97 (1983): 25-39. The painting, now in the Boijmans Van Beuningen Museum in Rotterdam, is discussed on 30-35. The literary sources on which Aertsen drew are considered, with illustrations of his three versions, in Margaret A. Sullivan, "Aertsen's kitchen and market scenes: audience and innovation in Northern Art," *Art Bulletin* 81(1999): 236-66. On the innovative nature of Aertsen's "inverted" paintings and their significance, see Victor I. Stoichita, *L'instauration du tableau. Métapeinture à l'aube des temps modernes*, 2nd ed. (Geneva: Droz, 1999), 17-26.

11. Keith P. F. Moxey, *Pieter Aertsen, Joachim Beuckelaer, and the Rise of Secular Painting in the Context of the Reformation* (New York: Garland, 1977), 98.

12. David Davies, "Velázquez's *bodegones*," in *Velázquez in Seville*, 52-53.

13. Harris, "Velázquez, Sevillian painter of sacred subjects," 48; Weston-Lewis, "Jacob Mathan, 1571-1631: four engravings after paintings by Pieter Aertsen," 130.

14. Bassegoda, "Pacheco y Velázquez," 135-36.

15. Virginia Reinburg, "Prayer and the Book of Hours," in Roger S. Wieck, *The Book of Hours in Medieval Art and Life* (London: Sothebys, 1988), 44.

16. Ludolph of Saxony, *Vita Christi Cartuxano*, trans. Fray Ambrosio Montesino (Seville: J. Cromberger, 1530), fol.vii r. [from the *Prohemio del auctor*]. The *Vita Christi*, which was written in the second half of the fourteenth century, circulated in manuscript before becoming a bestseller with the advent of printing, and it continued to be published in Velázquez's time.

17. On the practice of meditation in sixteenth-century Spain, see Terence O'Reilly, "Meditation and contemplation: monastic spirituality in early sixteenth-century Spain," and on its connection with religious works of art, Juan Luis González García, "La sombra de Dios: *imitatio Christi* y contrición en la piedad privada de Felipe II," in *Felipe II: un monarca y su época. Un príncipe del Renacimiento* (Madrid: Museo del Prado, 1998), 185-201.

18. Ivens, *Understanding the Spiritual Exercises. Text and Commentary. A Handbook for Retreat Directors*, 90. As Ivens observes (3), prayer in the Ignatian *Exercises* is "a particular form of the process traditionally described as [...] *lectio, meditatio, oratio, contemplatio*." Ignatius, it may be said, modified the role of *lectio*, requiring his exercitant not to read the Gospel text directly, but, instead, to receive from the director a brief summary of the matter to be meditated (Ivens, 86-87), a provision that helped to make meditation accessible to people for whom reading was not easy, or even possible. On Ignatius and the traditions associated with *lectio*, see Simon Tugwell, O.P., *Ways of Imperfection. An Exploration of Christian Spirituality* (London: Darton, Longman and Todd, 1984), 110. The influence on Velázquez's painting of the *Adnotationes et meditationes in Evangelia* (1599) by the Jesuit Jerónimo Nadal is discussed in John Moffit, "Francisco Pacheco and Jerome Nadal: new light on the Flemish sources of the Spanish 'picture-within-the-picture,'" *Art Bulletin* 72 (1990): 631-38, and in Tanya J. Tiffany, "Visualizing devotion in early modern Seville: Velázquez's *Christ in the House of Martha and Mary*," *Sixteenth Century Journal* 36.2 (2005): 445-51.

19. Luis de Granada, *Libro de la oración y meditación*, ed. Alvaro Huerga (Madrid: Fundación Universitaria Española y Dominicos de Andalucía, 1994), 247.

20. *Introduction à la vie dévote*, Seconde partie, Chapitre 4, in François de Sales, *Oeuvres*, ed. André Ravier and Roger Devos (Paris: Gallimard, 1969), 85-86. The first translation of the *Introduction* into Spanish, by Sebastián Fernández Eyzaguirre, was published in Brussels in 1618. The later translation by Quevedo was published in Madrid in 1634; it has been reprinted in Francisco de Quevedo, *Obras completas*, ed. Felicidad Buendía (Madrid: Aguilar, 1988), 1740-1906. On the various methods of "composition of place," see Louis L. Martz, *The Poetry of Meditation. A Study in English Religious Literature of the Seventeenth Century* (New Haven: Yale University Press, 1962), 27-32.

21. "En el aposento no aparece ni Cristo, ni Marta ni María, pero allá, en lo alto del muro, hay colgado un cuadro y es en este cuadro interior donde la figura de Jesús y las dos santas mujeres logran una irreal persencia." Ortega y Gasset, "Introducción a Velázquez," 482.

22. The fresco, which is in the seventh cell in the dormitory of San Marco in Florence, is considered in William Hood, *Fra Angelico at San Marco* (New Haven: Yale University Press, 1993), 6 (illustration 10), 211, 213, 216, 217, 222, 244.

23. Gabriele Finaldi, *The Image of Christ* (London: National Gallery, 2000), 86-89.

24. The miniature occurs in an illustrated manuscript of Boethius, *De consolatione philosophiae* (Bourges, 1476). This manuscript (Harley Mss. 4335-4339) is discussed by Janet Backhouse, "French Manuscript Illumination, 1450-1530," in *Renaissance Painting in Manuscripts. Treasures from the British Library*, ed. Thomas Kren (New York: Hudson Hills, 1983), 158-62.

25. The painting, which is in the Metropolitan Museum of Art, New York, is reproduced and discussed in Peter Humfrey, *Lorenzo Lotto* (New Haven: Yale University Press, 1997), 156 (and plate 155).

26. Victor Stoichita, *Visionary Experience in the Golden Age of Spanish Art*, 11-14. The painting is in the Museo del Prado in Madrid.

27. Pacheco's own description of the painting, which was destroyed in 1936, may be seen in Francisco Pacheco, *Arte de la pintura*, ed. F. J. Sánchez Catón (Madrid: Instituto de Valencia de Don Juan, 1956), 2: 327-30. On the painting itself, and its relation to Velázquez's *bodegón*, see in particular: José López Rey, *Velázquez. The Artist as a Maker, with a Catalogue Raisonné of his Extant Works* (Lausanne: Bibliothèque des Arts, 1979), 17; Enriqueta Harris, *Velázquez* (Oxford: Phaidon, 1982), 44-45; Antonio Domínguez Ortiz, A. E. Pérez Sánchez, J. Gállego, *Velázquez* (Madrid: Museo del Prado, 1990), 66; Moffit, "Francisco Pacheco and Jerome Nadal: new light on the Flemish sources of the Spanish "picture-within-the-picture,'" 631-38; Odile Delenda, *Velázquez, peintre religieux* (Geneva: Tricorne, 1993), 29-30; Bustamante and Marías, "Entre práctica y teoría: la formación de Velázquez en Sevilla," 154; Tiffany, "Visualizing devotion in early modern Seville: Velázquez's *Christ in the House of Martha and Mary*," 445-50. On other instances of Spanish paintings of the period in which "there is a direct iconographical relationship between foreground and background, but no unity of time and space," see Marta Cacho Casal, "The old woman in Velázquez's *Kitchen Scene with Christ's Visit to Martha and Mary*," *Journal of the Warburg and Courtald Institutes* 63 (2000), 298.

28. Leo Steinberg, reviewing José López Rey, *Velázquez. A Catalogue Raisonné of his Oeuvre and an Introductory Study* (London: Faber, 1963), *Art Bulletin* 47 (1965): 282.

29. Granada, *Libro de la oración y meditación*, 261.

THE FOREGROUND FIGURES

30. The Vulgate text reads: "Factum est autem, dum irent, et ipse intravit in quoddam castellum: et mulier quaedam Martha nomine, excepit illum in domum suam, et huic erat soror nomine Maria, quae etiam sedens secus pedes Domini, audiebat verbum illius. Martha autem satagebat circa frequens ministerium: quae stetit, et ait: Domine non est tibi curae quod soror mea reliquit me solam ministrare? dic ergo illi, ut me adiuvet. Et respondens dixit illi Dominus: Martha, Martha, sollicita es, et turbaris erga plurima. Porro unum est necessarium. Maria optimam partem elegit, quae non auferetur ab ea." On the patristic exegesis of this story, particularly the approaches of Augustine and Gregory the Great, see F. J. Steele, *Towards a Spirituality for Lay-Folk: The Active Life in Middle English Religious Literature from the Thirteenth Century to the Fifteenth* (Lewiston: Mellen, 1995), 1-34.

31. Giles Constable, *Three Studies in Medieval Religious and Social Thought. The Interpretation of Mary and Martha, the Ideal of the Imitation of Christ, the Orders of Society* (Cambridge: Cambridge University Press, 1995), 141.

32. See Francisco J. Rodríguez-Molero, "Maldonado (Maldonat, Jean de)," *Dictionnaire de spiritualité* 10.1: 163-65.

33. See P. Suñer, "Toledo, Francisco de, S.I.," *Diccionario de la historia eclesiástica de España* 4: 2572-74.

34. On Spanish Jesuit exegesis of the period, see Terence O'Reilly, "The scriptural scholarship of the early Spanish Jesuits—a survey," *Journal of the Institute of Romance Studies* 4 (1996): 135-43; and on the impact of the Society of Jesus in early seventeenth-century Seville and its painters, see Julián Gállego, *Diego Velázquez* (Barcelona: Anthropos, 1983), 26. Both subjects are discussed in Guy Lazure, "Perceptions of the Temple, projections of the Divine. Patronage, biblical scholarship and Jesuit imagery in Spain, 1580-1620," *Calamus Renascens* 1 (2000): 155-88. The connection between exegesis and art in Velázquez and his contemporaries is considered in Delenda, *Velázquez, peintre religieux*, 135-36.

35. The many critics who have considered her to be Martha include Harris, *Velázquez*, 48, and Davies and Harris, *Velázquez in Seville*, 132. See also Elizabeth Du Gué Trapier, *Velázquez* (New York: Hispanic Society of America, 1948), 73. Dissenting views have been expressed by Domínguez Ortiz, Pérez Sánchez, and Gállego, *Velázquez*, 62, 64, and by López Rey, *Velázquez. The Artist as a Maker, with a Catalogue Raisonné of his Extant Works*, 16.

36. Juan Maldonado, S.J., *Commentarii in quatuor evangelistas*, ed. J.M. Raich, 2: 194.

37. Ibid., 195.

38. Ibid.,196; Francisco de Toledo, S.J., *Commentarii in [...] Evangelium secundum Lucam* (Cologne: sumptibus A. Boëtzeri, 1611), 643. The significance of the left-handed gesture is considered by Steinberg, 289. On the specific moment that the inset depicts see Thomas L. Glen, "Velázquez's *Kitchen Scene with Christ in the House of Martha and Mary*: an image both 'reflected' and to be reflected upon," *Gazette des Beaux-Arts* 136 (2000): 27.

39. Toledo, *Commentarii in Evangelium secundum Lucam*, 642; Maldonado, *Commentarii in quatuor evangelistas*, 196-98. The passage Toledo quotes is from the commentary on 1 Kings traditionally attributed to Gregory, but no longer accepted as certainly his: see R. A. Markus, *Gregory the Great and His World* (Cambridge: Cambridge University Press, 1997), xiv, 25-26.

40. Granada, *Libro de la oración y meditación*, 351-52; Francis de Sales, *Introduction à la vie dévote*, Troisième partie, Chapitre 10, 159. On Santa Teresa's reading of the Bethany story, and its influence on Philip II's desire to integrate the two lives, see González García, "La sombra de Dios: *imitatio Christi* y contrición en la piedad privada de Felipe II," 189-91. See too Glen, "Velázquez's *Kitchen Scene with Christ in the House of Martha and Mary*," 28, who argues that the painting "responds to Jesuit thinking" on the two lives, but mistakenly refers to Francis de Sales as "a great Jesuit scholar." Tiffany, "Visualizing devotion in early modern Seville," 439-42, relates it to the "mixed life" of contemplation and action as understood by Pedro de Valderrama and Antonio Cordeses, both of whom lived in Seville.

41. The tag, whose origins lie in the *Satires* of Horace (Book 1, 1:68-70), is discussed in connection with the moral function of literature in Deyermond, *Lazarillo de Tormes*, 9. Pertinent also is the Renaissance convention of including in paintings a figure whose pointing gesture draws the viewer's eye towards a significant part of the scene portrayed, a convention defined in the celebrated treatise *On Painting* by Leon Battista Alberti: see Leon Battista Alberti, *On Painting*, trans. Cecil Grayson, with an introduction and notes by Martin Kemp (London: Penguin, 1991), 77-78. Velázquez probably owned a copy of Alberti's treatise: see *Velázquez. Homenaje en el tercer centenario de su muerte*, (Madrid: Instituto Diego Velázquez, 1960), 314b (number 508). On the *post mortem* inventory of Velázquez's books see F. J. Sánchez Cantón, "La librería de Velázquez," in *Homenaje ofrecido a Menéndez Pidal*, 3 vols. (Madrid: Hernando, 1925), 3: 379-406; Pedro Ruiz Pérez, *De la pintura y las letras. La biblioteca de Velázquez* (Seville: Consejería Cultural de la Junta de Andalucía, 1999); and Tiffany, "Visualizing devotion in early modern Seville," 451.

42. Ruth Fainlight's poem, "Velázquez's *Christ in the House of Martha and Mary*," is cited in Harris, "Velázquez, Sevillian painter of sacred subjects," 48. The identity of the old woman has been examined in the light of apocryphal accounts of Martha's life by Cacho Casal, who argues that she may represent Marcella, the housekeeper or servant of Martha in the *Legenda aurea* of Jacobus of Voragine: see "The old woman in Velázquez's *Kitchen Scene with Christ's Visit to Martha and Mary*," 299-302.

The Still-Life

43. John Moffit, "*Terebat in mortario:* symbolism in Velázquez's *Christ in the House of Martha and Mary,*" *Arte Cristiana* 72 (1984): 13-24.

44. Jonathan Brown, *Velázquez: Painter and Courtier* (New Haven: Yale University Press, 1986), 285, n.43. See too the comments of Cacho Casal, 296. Critics who have detected symbolism in the still-life include Delenda, *Velázquez, peintre religieux,* 30-31; Ronald Cueto, "The Great Babylon of Spain and the devout: politics, religion and piety in the Seville of Velázquez," in Davies and Harris, *Velázquez in Seville,* 33; Yves Bottineau, *Velasquez* (Paris: Citadelles et Mazenod, 1998), 53.

45. Peter Cherry, "Los *bodegones* de Velázquez y la verdadera imitación del natural," in *Velázquez y Sevilla,* 2: 87. See too Thomas S. Acker, *The Baroque Vortex. Velázquez, Calderón and Gracián under Philip IV* (New York: Peter Lang, 2000), 85: "the key to the intended message lies in the relationship between the biblical scene and the emblematic significance of the elements in the painting's foreground."

46. Maldonado, *Commentarii in quatuor evangelistas,* 194.

47. Toledo, *Commentarii in Evangelium secundum Lucam,* 644: "praestat spirituale corporali, et cibus mentis cibo corporis."

48. "Velázquez has [...] encouraged the viewer to relate the ostensibly secular kitchen scene to the religious episode by placing the fish, a familiar symbol of Christ, directly beneath the figure of the Lord." Tiffany, "Visualizing devotion in early modern Seville," 438.

49. Harris, *Velázquez,* 46; Davies and Harris, *Velázquez in Seville,* 132.

50. Toledo, *Commentarii in Evangelium secundum Lucam,* 643-44.

51. In some manuscript traditions of the Lucan text, the mention of bread here is omitted: see Burton H. Jr. Throckmorton, *Gospel Parallels. A Synopsis of the First Three Gospels with Alternative Readings from the Manuscripts and Noncanonical Parallels* (Nashville: Nelson, 1979), 29, 106.

52. "Christus enim exempla posuit eorum quae ad victum moderatum spectant." Toledo, *Commentarii in Evangelium secundum Lucam,* 662.

53. Davies, "Velázquez's *bodegones,*" 63.

The Frame

54. Ortega y Gasset, "Introducción a Velázquez," 482; José Antonio Maravall, *Velázquez y el espíritu de la modernidad* (Madrid: Alianza, 1987), 110.

55. López Rey advanced this view in *Velázquez. A Catalogue Raisonné of his Oeuvre and an Introductory Study,* and he reaffirmed it, in the face of criticism, in *Velázquez. The Artist as a Maker,* 16, 17, n.35, and *Velázquez. Painter of Painters,* 1: 38, 231 n.35.

56. They include Braham, "A second dated *bodegón* by Velázquez," 363-64; Jordan, *Spanish Still Life in the Golden Age, 1600-1650,* 85; Brown, *Velázquez: Painter and Courtier,* 16; Harris, *Velázquez,* 162; Cherry, "Los *bodegones* de Velázquez y la verdadera imitación del natural," 88; Manuela B. Mena Marqués, "Cristo en casa de Marta y María," in *Velázquez y Sevilla,* 1:180; John Drury, *Painting the Word. Christian Pictures and their Meanings* (New Haven: Yale University Press, 1999), 156.

57. Braham, "A second dated *bodegón* by Velázquez," 363; Brown, *Velázquez: Painter and Courtier,* 16. On the controversial nature of the approach to restoration accepted in the National Gallery at the time, see Sarah Walden, "Amber for ever. E.H. Gombrich vindicated as an advocate of restraint in the restoration of Old Masters," *Times Literary Supplement,* October 29, 2004, 13-14.

58. Davies and Harris, *Velázquez in Seville,* 132.

59. Delenda, *Velázquez, peintre religieux,* 27. Art historians in Spain have generally taken an agnostic or non-committal view: see, for instance, José Gudiol Ricart, *Velázquez, 1599-1660. Historia de su vida, catálogo de su obra, estudio de la evolución de su técnica* (Barcelona: Polígrafa, 1973), 21; Gállego, *Diego Velázquez,* 42; Domínguez Ortiz, Pérez Sánchez and Gállego, *Velázquez,* 62. See too Cacho Casal, "The old woman in Velázquez's *Kitchen Scene with Christ's*

Visit to Martha and Mary," 298 n.13, and Tiffany, "Visualizing devotion in early modern Seville," 452-53. Cf. Jane Boyd and Philip F. Esler, *Visuality and Biblical Text: Interpreting Velázquez' "Christ with Martha and Mary" as a Test Case* (Florence: Olschi, 2004), 61: "It is not a window, mirror or painting: it is a vision."

60. See Braham, "A second dated *bodegón* by Velázquez," 362-63; López Rey, *Velázquez. The Artist as a Maker, with a Catalogue Raisonné of his Extant Works,* 16.

61. Davies and Harris, *Velázquez in Seville,* 132, 152-53.

62. "La perspectiva de esta apertura no concuerda con la de la mesa, lo cual sugiere que existen dos puntos de vista diferentes para los dos espacios del cuadro." Cherry, "Los *bodegones* de Velázquez y la verdadera imitación del natural," 88. Tiffany observes in turn: "If the picture-within-a-picture were read as a window and the lines in its corners as orthogonals, the foreground and background scenes would appear to have vanishing points on opposite sides of the composition." "Visualizing devotion in early modern Seville," 452.

63. *The Musical Trio* is discussed in Davies and Harris, *Velázquez in Seville,* 132 and 140.

64. See Domínguez Ortiz, Pérez Sánchez, and Gállego, *Velázquez,* 423. John Moffit comments: "were this [...] a painting hanging on a wall, it would be at least (if not more so) as dark as the wall behind it." "*Terebat in mortario:* symbolism in Velázquez's *Christ in the House of Martha and Mary,*" 24 n.38.

65. See López Rey, *Velázquez. The Artist as a Maker, with a Catalogue Raisonné of his Extant Works,* 17; and Glen, "Velázquez's *Kitchen Scene with Christ in the House of Martha and Mary:* an image both 'reflected' and to be reflected upon," 24. It has been suggested that Velázquez based the whole painting on a mirror-reflection: see Boyd and Esler, *Visuality and Biblical Text: Interpreting Velázquez' "Christ with Martha and Mary" as a Test Case.*

66. See Domínguez Ortiz, Pérez Sánchez and Gállego, *Velázquez,* 428 (*Las Meninas*), 368-73 (*Rokeby Venus*).

67. On the significance of this gesture of Christ in Aertsen's painting and in that of Velázquez, see Stoichita, *L'instauration du tableau,* 22 and 31. See too Craig, "*Pars ergo Marthae transit:* Pieter Aertsen's 'inverted' paintings of *Christ in the House of Martha and Mary,*" 26; Sullivan, "Aertsen's kitchen and market scenes: audience and innovation in Northern Art," 257.

68. Steinberg, 289; Brown, *Velázquez: Painter and Courtier,* 21. See Giulia Bartrum, ed., *Albrecht Dürer and His Legacy. The Graphic Work of a Renaissance Artist* (London: British Museum, 2002), 188. Other arguments against the mirror hypothesis are brought forward by Davies and Harris, *Velázquez in Seville,* 132.

69. "The picture-within-a-picture is not a mirror reflection, for the illumination emerges from opposite sides in the foreground and biblical scenes." Tiffany, "Visualizing devotion in early modern Seville," 452.

70. See Domínguez Ortiz, Pérez Sánchez, and Gállego, *Velázquez,* 30. The painting is in the Metropolitan Museum of Art, New York.

71. See Renato Guttuso and Angela Ottino della Chiesa, eds, *L'opera completa del Caravaggio* (Milan: Rizzoli, 1967), 92 (plate 19). The painting is in the National Gallery, London.

72. *Zurbarán,* exhibition catalogue (Madrid: Ministerio de Cultura, 1988), 394-96 (*El Salvador bendiciendo*). Christ has the cloak over His left arm also in Zurbarán's *La cena de Emaús* (392-94).

73. Alfonso E. Pérez Sánchez and Nicola Spinosa, eds, *La obra pitórica de Ribera* (Barcelona: Noguer, 1979), 101 (*Cristo Salvador*). Christ's mantle is on His left side in Ribera's *Bautismo de Cristo* (120, plate 48), and *Sagrada Familia con San Bruno y otros santos* (105, plate 15). The covered left hand occurs also in several of Ribera's portraits of saints: see *Museo del Prado. Catálogo de las pinturas* (Madrid: Ministerio de Educación y Cultura, 1996), catalogue numbers 1082 (*Santiago el Mayor*), 1091 (*San Simón*), 1098 (*San Jerónimo penitente*).

74. *Zurbarán,* 25 (*San Jerónimo flagelado por ángeles*). The depiction of a covered right arm also has parallels in religious works by Velázquez and his contemporaries. It is, however, less common than a covered left arm, and it is not customary in portraits of Christ. It occurs, for instance, in Velázquez's portrait of St. Paul (Museu Nacional d'Art de Catalunya, Barcelona); in some of

the portraits of saints by Ribera: *Museo del Prado. Catálogo de las pinturas* Museo del Prado, catalogue numbers 1071, 1072 (*San Pedro*); 1096 (*San Jerónimo*); and in two of Ribera's depictions of *Ecce Homo*: Pérez Sánchez and Spinosa, *La obra pitórica de Ribera*, 95 (catalogue number 27); 105 (catalogue number 86).

75. "Velázquez no nos dice si hay una ventana, un espejo o un cuadro; menos explícito que Pacheco, que en su San Sebastián citado nos habla de una ventana, Velázquez ya se complace en las ambigüedades de la óptica." Gállego, *Diego Velázquez*, 42. See too Stoichita, *L'instauration du tableau*, 30: "L'image du second plan peut être envisagée soit comme une fenêtre, soit comme un tableau. C'est dans son indécision même qu'elle révèle sa structure et son rôle figuratif dans l'ensemble du tableau"; and Tiffany, "Visualizing devotion in early modern Seville," 452: "he used his studies of linear perspective and optics to heighten the indeterminate nature of the framed scene."

COHERENCE

76. N. MacLaren and A. Braham, *National Gallery Catalogues. The Spanish School* (London: National Gallery, 1988), 122; Brown, *Velázquez: Painter and Courtier*, 16. See also Braham, "A second dated *bodegón* by Velázquez," 365; Drury, *Painting the Word. Christian Pictures and their Meanings*, 168.

77. Alexander A. Parker, *Polyphemus and Galatea. A Study in the Interpretation of a Baroque Poem, with a Verse Translation by Gilbert F. Cunningham* (Edinburgh: Edinburgh University Press, 1977), 92 n.19. Gracián defines the word thus: "quien dice misterio, dice preñez, verdad escondida y recóndita, y toda noticia que cuesta, es más estimada y gustada." Baltasar Gracián, *Agudeza y arte de ingenio*, ed. Evaristo Correa Calderón, 2 vols. (Madrid: Castalia, 1969), 1: 88. On the pertinence of this definition to the meaning of "misterio" in the prologue to Cervantes's *Novelas Ejemplares* (1613), see Alban K. Forcione, *Cervantes and the Humanist Vision. A Study of Four Exemplary Novels* (Princeton: Princeton University Press, 1982), 9.

78. Real Academia Española, *Diccionario de Autoridades*, edición facsímile, 3 vols. (Madrid: Gredos, 1963), 2: 639.

79. These and further quotations from the Fathers are cited in the entry under *misterium* in the *Thesaurus Linguae Latinae* (Leipzig: Teubner, 1900-), 8: 1755-56.

80. Augustine, *De Doctrina Christiana*, ed. and trans. R. P. H. Green (Oxford: Clarendon, 1995), 2:14: "qui enim prorsus non inveniunt quod quaerunt, fame laborant; qui autem non quaerunt, quia in promptu habent, fastidio saepe marescunt;" 2:13: "nemo ambigit et per similitudinis libentius quaeque cognosci et cum aliqua difficultate quaesita multo gratius inveniri."

81. On the cultivation of difficulty associated with *conceptismo* see Fernando Lázaro Carreter, "Sobre la dificultad conceptista," in *Estilo barroco y personalidad creadora* (Madrid: Cátedra, 1974), 13-43.

82. Ángel Manrique, *Laurea Evangélica, hechos de varios discursos predicables* (Salamanca: Antonia Ramírez, 1614), 27, quoted in Sagalés Cisquella, O.Cist., "Espirituales cistercienses en las congregaciones de Castilla y Aragón," *Cistercium* 50 (1999): 286. The *Catálogo Colectivo del Patrimonio Bibliográfico Español* records three earlier editions of this work (1605, 1609, and 1610), all of them published in Salamanca. Manrique appears to have been influenced by his fellow Cistercian, Cipriano de la Huerga, whose views on obscurity and enigma, and their sources, are considered in the study by Gaspar Morocho Gayo et al., "Cipriano de la Huerga, maestro de humanistas," in *Fray Luis de León. Historia, humanismo y letras*, ed. Víctor García de la Concha and Javier San José Lera (Salamanca: Universidad de Salamanca, 1996), 184. Golden Age views on the desirability of reconciling "agudeza" with "la verdadera sabiduría" are considered in Aurora Egido, "El águila de San Juan de la Cruz: mística y poesía en las coplas *Entréme donde no supe* y *Tras de un amoroso lance*," in *San Juan de la Cruz and Fray Luis de León*, ed. Mary Malcolm Gaylord and Francisco Márquez Villanueva (Newark, Del.: Juan de la Cuesta), 77-78.

83. "Velázquez has further related the contemporary and biblical scenes by creating visual analogues between the foreground and background figures." Tiffany, "Visualizing devotion in

early modern Seville," 438-39. See too Stoichita, *L'instauration du tableau*, 31; Braham, "A second dated *bodegón* by Velázquez," 365; Gudiol Ricart, *Velázquez, 1599-1660. Historia de su vida, catálogo de su obra, estudio de la evolución de su técnica*, 22; Domínguez Ortiz, Pérez Sánchez, and Gállego, *Velázquez*, 62.

84. Parker, *Polyphemus and Galatea. A Study in the Interpretation of a Baroque Poem*, 13. On the nature of wit, and the terms used in connection with it, see M. J. Woods, *Gracián Meets Góngora. The Theory and Practice of Wit* (Warminster: Aris and Phillips, 1995). Cf. Stoichita, *L'instauration du tableau*, 34, who notes that in both the biblical *bodegones* of Velázquez, "le travail du spectateur est escompté. C'est lui qui doit opérer le jeu combinatoire—jeu fait de similitude et différences."

85. See Terry, *Seventeenth-Century Spanish Poetry. The Power of Artifice*, 56-64.

86. Woods, *Gracián Meets Góngora. The Theory and Practice of Wit*, 4.

THE SUPPER AT EMMAUS

87. The possible influence on the *bodegón* of Jacob Matham's engraving *Kitchen Scene with the Supper at Emmaus* is considered in Weston-Lewis, "Jacob Mathan, 1571-1631: four engravings after paintings by Pieter Aertsen."

88. The Chicago painting is considered in detail in Alfonso E. Pérez Sánchez and Benito Navarrete Prieto, *De Herrera a Velázquez. El primer naturalismo en Sevilla* (Bilbao: Museo de Bellas Artes, 2006). The two versions are compared in Xavier Bray, "Kitchen Scene with Christ in the House of Martha and Mary," in *Velázquez*, ed. Dawson W. Carr (London: National Gallery, 2006), 122-25.

EMMAUS

89. See Mulcahy, *Spanish Paintings in the National Gallery of Ireland*, 79.

90. The Vulgate text reads: "Et factum est, dum recumberet cum eis, accepit panem et benedixit ac fregit et porrigebat illis. Et aperti sunt oculi eorum, et cognoverunt eum; et ipse evanuit ex oculis eorum."

91. See Filippo Pedrocco, *Titian: The Complete Paintings* (London: Thames and Hudson, 2001), 157. The two versions of the scene attributed without question to Titian (one now in the Louvre, the other in the Walker Art Gallery in Liverpool), and the iconographic and literary traditions on which they draw, are discussed in the section entitled "Emmaus i precedenti" in Giovanni Morale, ed., *La Cena di Tiziano: Immagini del Risorto tra Louvre e Ambrosiana* (Milan: Skira, 2006), 59-89.

92. Timothy Wilson-Smith, *Caravaggio* (London: Phaidon, 1998), 98. See too *Caravaggio e l'Europa. Il movimento caravaggesco internazionale da Caravaggio a Mattia Preti*, exh. cat. (Milan: Skira, 2005), 158, and 71 (on the influence of the Caravaggio tradition on Velázquez's *bodegón*).

93. See Wilson-Smith, *Caravaggio*, 70. On the iconographic context of the London painting, see Lorenzo Pericolo, "Visualising appearance and disappearence: on Caravaggio's London *Supper at Emmaus*," *Art Bulletin* 89 (2007), 519-39.

94. "Les mains dans la ceinture, l'aubergiste demeure étranger à la bouleversante révélation [...]. Il le regarde [Jésus] sans le reconnaître." Dominique Ponnau, *Caravage: une lecture* (Paris: Editions du Cerf, 1993), 66-67. See too Wilson-Smith, *Caravaggio*, 70: "Both react with violent, clumsy gestures, while the host, oblivious of any spiritual happening, stays calm."

95. See Karl-Adolf Knappe, *Dürer: The Complete Engravings, Etchings and Woodcuts* (London: Thames and Hudson, 1965), figure 286.

96. The liturgy of the Mass may be seen in Cabrol, ed., *The Roman Missal in Latin and English*, 515-20, and the Office of Matins in *Breviarivm Romanvm ex decreto sacrosancti Concilij Tridentini restitutum* (Salamanca: Mathias Gastius, 1575), 412-13.

97. *Homilia* 23:1, in Gregory the Great, *Homiliae in evangelia*, ed. Raymond Étaix (Turnhoult: Brepols, 1999), 193. In this and subsequent quotations from the homily, I follow (with

occasional amendments) the translation in Gregory the Great, *Forty Gospel Homilies*, ed. Dom David Hurst (Kalanazoo, Michigan: Cistercian Publications, 1990), 175-78.

98. Gregory the Great, *Homilia* 23:1-2, in *Homiliae in evangelia*, 194.

99. "*Quid ergo significat quod se ire longius Dominus finxit*, cum comitaretur discipulis exponens eis sanctas scripturas, utrum ipse esset ignorantibus? Quid putamus nisi quia hospitalitatis officio ad suam cognitionem peruenire posse homines intimauit?" Augustine, *Quaestiones evangeliorvm*, 51:2, ed. Almut Mutzenbecher, Corpus Christianorum Series Latina, vol. 44B (Turnhout: Brepols, 1980), 117. On this and cognate passages in Augustine's writings, see Finbarr G. Clancy, S.J., "St. Augustine's commentary on the Emmaus scene in Luke's Gospel," *Studia Patristica. Papers Presented at the Fourteenth International Conference on Patristic Studies held in Oxford 2003*, ed. F. Young, M. Edwards and P. Parvis (Louvain: Peeters, 2006), 51-58.

100. Gregory the Great, *Homilia* 23:2, in *Homiliae in evangelia*, 194-95. The exegesis developed by Gregory was a theme in the sermon literature of the Golden Age: see Luis de Granada, *Sermones de tiempo III /I*, ed. Alvaro Huerga (Madrid: Fundación Universitaria Española y Dominicos de Andalucía, 2001), 136-37; and Alonso de Cabrera, O.P., "Consideraciones del lunes después del domingo de la Resurrección," in *Sermones*, ed. Miguel Mir, Nueva Biblioteca de Autores Españoles, vol. 3 (Madrid: Bailly-Baillière, 1906), 460: "en el partir y bendecir el pan le conocieron; y luego se les quitó delante de los ojos. ¡Bienaventurados ojos que tal merecieron ver, y dichosa misericordia que hospeda al peregrino y después halla ser Dios! Regalámosle en sus pobres, partiendo con ellos el pan que tenéis, pues paga tan bien el escote, aquí con gracia y después con gloria."

The Paterfamilias

101. Gregory the Great, *Homilia* 23:2, in *Homiliae in evangelia*, 195. This story did not form part of the reading in the Office of Matins on Easter Monday. However, it was available to Velázquez's contemporaries in the famous edition of Gregory's *Opera omnia* prepared by P. Tossianensis and published in Rome between 1588 and 1603. A second edition followed in 1613: see Gregory the Great, *Opera*, second edition, 4 vols. (Rome: ex typographia Camerae Apostolicae), 3: 463-65. Luis de Granada cites the story *verbatim* in the sermon mentioned in the previous note above.

102. Iacopo da Varazze, *Legenda aurea*, ed. Giovanni Paulo Maggioni, second edition, 2 vols. (Florence: Sismel, 1998), 1:293.

103. Pedro de Ribadeneira, *Flos sanctorum, o libro de las vidas de los santos* (Madrid: Luis Sánchez, 1616), 250.

Exegesis

104. Bray, "Kitchen Scene with Christ in the House of Martha and Mary," 126.

105. Desiderius Erasmus, *In evangelium Lucae paraphrasis* (Basle: Froben, 1524), 258-59.

106. Maldonado, *Commentarii in quatuor evangelistas*, 2:354.

107. "Benedictio haec non videtur fuisse initio coenae [...]. Fuit ergo in medio, vel potius in fine coenae: fuit igitur benedictio haec non communis, quae praemittitur mensae, sed sacra et Eucharistica." Lapide, *Commentaria in Scripturam Sacram*, 16: 278.

Conclusion

108. Helen Gardner, ed., *The Metaphysical Poets*, revised edition (Harmondsworth: Penguin, 1966), 19.

109. Gregory the Great, *Homilia* 23:2, in *Homiliae in evangelia*, 194.

110. Bray, "Kitchen Scene with Christ in the House of Martha and Mary," 126.

111. The contrast between the two teachings occurs in the Bible itself, for instance in Psalm 118, where verse 73 reads, "Give me understanding and I will learn [to carry out] thy commandments," while verse 104 proclaims, "By thy commandments [i.e. by performing them] I have understanding." On these verses and their Patristic interpretation, see Jennifer O'Reilly, "The

wisdom of the scribe and the fear of the Lord in the *Life of Columba*," in *Spes Scotorum, Hope of Scots: Saint Columba, Iona and Scotland*, ed. Dauvit Brown and Thomas Owen Clancy (Edinburgh: Clark, 1999), 192.

112. Harris, *Velázquez*, 44, and "Velázquez, Sevillian painter of sacred subjects," 48; Mulcahy, *Spanish Paintings in the National Gallery of Ireland*, 81, and *Philip II of Spain, Patron of the Arts* (Dublin: Four Courts, 2004), 161-62.

113. Tanya J. Tiffany, "Light, darkness, and African salvation: Velázquez's *Supper at Emmaus*," *Art History* 31.1 (2008): 33-56. See also Antonio Domínguez Ortiz, *Historia de Sevilla: la Sevilla del siglo xvii* (Seville: University of Seville, 1986), 181. The skincolour of the maid in the picture suggests that if Velázquez used a model she was probably a mulatta (i.e. of mixed African and European descent) rather than a *negra*. Either way it is significant that in the Spain of the time, "the dominating ideology made black and slave synonymous": Aurelia Martín Casares, "Free and freed black africans in Granada in the time of the Spanish Renaissance," in T. F. Earle and K. J. P. Lowe, eds, *Black Africans in Renaissance Europe* (Cambridge: Cambridge University Press, 2005), 252. On slavery in the Spanish Golden Age, see also Glyn Redworth, "Mythology with attitude? A black Christian's defence of negritude in early modern Europe," *Social History* 28 (2003): 49-66; Kate Lowe, "The black african presence in Renaissance Europe," in Earle and Lowe, *Black Africans in Renaissance Europe*, 11; Jeremy N. H. Lawrance, "Black africans in Renaissance Spanish literature," in Earle and Lowe, *Black Africans in Renaissance Europe*, 70-71. Velázquez's portrait of Juan de Pareja, the slave of Moorish descent whom he freed in 1654, is discussed in Dawson W. Carr, "Painting and reality: the art and life of Velázquez," in *Velázquez*, ed. Carr, 45-46.

114. Alfonso E. Pérez Sánchez, "Velázquez y su arte," in Domínguez Ortiz, Pérez Sánchez, and Gállego, *Velázquez*, 29. More recently, it has been speculated that the London painting was intended, "for the domestic setting of a wealthy and educated art patron and connoisseur": see Peter Cherry and Xanthe Brooke, *Murillo: Scenes of Childhood*, exh. cat. (London: Merrell, 2001), 80-81.

EPILOGUE

1. See Jan den Boeft, "Erasmus and the Church Fathers," in Irena Backus, ed., *The Reception of the Church Fathers in the West from the Carolingians to the Maurists*, 2 vols. (Boston and Leiden: Brill, 2001), 2: 537-72.

2. The best recent discussion of the subject is John W. O'Malley, *The First Jesuits* (Cambridge, Mass./London: Harvard University Press, 1993), 256-59, who also surveys the general theological culture of the young Society. See too C. Pozo, "Compagnia di Gesù: Teologia," *Dizionario degli istituti di perfezione*, 2:1300-1304; Melquíades Andrés, *La teología española en el siglo xvi*, 2 vols. (Madrid: Editorial Católica, 1976-77), 1:174-95; Evangelista Vilanova, *Historia de la teología cristiana*, 3 vols. (Barcelona: Herder, 1987-92), 2:188-95, 619-25.

3. Passages in the *Exercises* where non-scriptural elements occur include the descriptions of the creation of Adam (51), the birth of Jesus (111-14), and His appearance, after the Resurrection, to His mother (219-20).

4. Jaroslav Pelikan, *Whose Bible Is It? A History of the Scriptures through the Ages* (London: Penguin, 2006), 164.

5. The decree may be seen in Tanner, ed., *Decrees of the Ecumenical Councils*, 2: 663-64.

6. See Jean-Louis Quantin, "The Fathers in seventeenth century Roman Catholic theology," in Backus, ed., *The Reception of the Church Fathers in the West from the Carolingians to the Maurists*, 2:953.

Works Cited

Primary Sources

Acosta, José de. *Historia natural y moral de las Indias*. Seville: Juan de León, 1590.

Alberti, Leon Battista. *On Painting*. Translated by Cecil Grayson, with an introduction and notes by Martin Kemp. London: Penguin, 1991.

Alcalá, Ángel, ed. *Proceso inquisitorial de fray Luis de León. Edición paleográfica, anotada y crítica*. Salamanca: Junta de Castilla y León, 1991.

Alcántara, San Pedro de. *Tratado de la oración y meditación*. Madrid: Rialp, 1991.

—. *Tratado de la oración y meditación*. In *Vida y escritos de San Pedro de Alcántara*. Edited by Rafael Sanz Valdivielso, O.F.M. Madrid: Biblioteca de Autores Cristianos, 1996.

Aldana, Francisco de. *Poesías castellanas completas*. Edited by José Lara Garrido. Madrid: Cátedra, 1985.

Alonso de la Madre de Dios, O.C.D. *Vida, virtudes y milagros del santo padre Fray Juan de la Cruz*. Edited by Fortunato Antolín, O.C.D. Madrid: Editorial de Espiritualidad, 1989.

Antolínez, Fray Agustín, O.S.A. *Amores de Dios y el alma*. Edited by A. Custodio Vega. Madrid: El Escorial, 1956.

Aquinas, St. Thomas. *In evangelia S. Matthaei et S. Joannis commentaria*. 2 vols. Turin: ex officina Petri Marietti, 1919.

—. *Summa Theologiae, cura fratrum eiusdem Ordinis*. 5 vols. Madrid: Biblioteca de Autores Cristianos, 1961-65.

—. *Summa Theologiae, vol 33: Hope (2a-2ae. 17-22)*. Edited and translated by W. J. Hill, O.P. London: Blackfriars and Eyre and Spottiswoode, 1966.

Arias Montano, Benito. *Biblia Sacra*. 8 vols. Antwerp: Plantin, 1569-73.

Augustine, St. *Letters, vol.4 (165-203)*. Translated by Sister Wilfrid Parsons, S.N.D. New York: Fathers of the Church, 1955.

—. *Enarrationes in psalmos ci-cl*. Edited by Eligivs Dekkers, O.S.B., and Iohannes Fraipont. Corpus Christianorum Series Latina, vol. 40. Turnhout: Brepols, 1956.

—. *In Iohannis Evangelium Tractatus CXXIV*. Edited by Radbodus Willems, O.S.B. Corpus Christianorum Series Latina, vol. 36. Turnhout: Brepols, 1954.

—. *De Trinitate libri xv*. Edited by W.J. Mountain and Fr. Glorie. Corpus Christianorum Series Latina, vol. 50A. Turnhout: Brepols, 1968.

—. *Quaestiones evangeliorvm*. Edited by Almut Mutzenbecher. Corpus Christianorum Series Latina, vol. 44B. Turnhout: Brepols, 1980.

—. *De Doctrina Christiana*. Edited and translated by R. P. H. Green. Oxford: Clarendon, 1995.

Ávila, San Juan de. *Obras completas*. Edited by Luis Sala Balust and Francisco Martín Hernández. 6 vols. Madrid: Biblioteca de Autores Cristianos, 1970-71.

Balbuena, Bernardo de. *El Bernardo*. In *Poemas épicos I*, edited by Cayetano Rosell. Biblioteca de Autores Españoles, vol. 17. Madrid: Real Academia Española, 1945.

Basil, St. *Les Règles monastiques*. Edited by Léon Lèbe, O.S.B. Maredsous: Editions de Maredsous, 1969.

Bede, St. *Opera homiletica*. Edited by D. Hurst. Corpus Christianorum Series Latina, vol. 122. Turnhoult: Brepols, 1955.

———. *In Lucae evangelium expositio*. Edited by D. Hurst, O.S.B. Corpus Christianorum Series Latina, vol. 120. Turnhout: Brepols, 1960.

———. *In Cantica Canticorum*. Edited by D. Hurst, O.S.B. Corpus Christianorum Series Latina, vol. 119B. Turnhout: Brepols, 1983.

———. *Homilies on the Gospels. Book Two: Lent to the Dedication of the Church*. Translated by Lawrence T. Martin and David Hurst, O.S.B. Kalamazoo: Cistercian Publications, 1991.

Benavente, Toribio de. *Memoriales o libro de las cosas de la Nueva España y de los naturales de ella*. Edited by E. O'Gorman. Mexico: U.N.A.M., 1971.

Benedict, St. *La Règle de Saint Benoît*, vol.1. Edited by Adalbert de Vogüé and Jean Neufville. Paris: Editions du Cerf, 1972.

———. *The Rule of St Benedict: A Guide to Christian Living*. Edited with a commentary by George Holzherr. Dublin: Four Courts, 1994.

Bernard, St. *Sermones litúrgicos*. 2 vols. Madrid: Biblioteca de Autores Cristianos, 1985-86.

———. *Sermones sobre el Cantar de los Cantares*. Translated by Iñaki Aranguren with an introduction by Juan María de la Torre. Madrid: Biblioteca de Autores Cristianos, 1987.

———. *Sermones varios*. Translated with an introduction by Mariano Ballano. Madrid: Biblioteca de Autores Cristianos, 1988.

Biblia sacra Vulgatae editionis Sixti V Pontificis Maximi iussu recognita et Clementis V111 auctoritate edita. Milan: Edizioni San Paolo, 2003.

Bonaventure, Pseudo. *Meditationes vitae Christi*. In *S. Bonaventurae opera omnia*, edited by A.C. Peltier, 12: 510-630. Paris: Vives, 1868.

Bonaventure, St. *De triplici via*. In *Obras de San Buenaventura*, vol.4. Edited by Bernardo Aperribay, O.F.M. and Miguel Oromi, O.F.M. Madrid: Biblioteca de Autores Cristianos, 1963.

Borja, San Francisco de. *Tratados espirituales*. Edited by Cándido de Dalmases. Barcelona: Juan Flors, 1964.

Breviarivm Romanvm ex decreto sacrosancti Concilij Tridentini restitutum. Salamanca: Mathias Gastius, 1575.

Bujanda, J.M. de. *Index de livres interdits: Index de l'Inquisition espagnole, 1551, 1554, 1559*. Sherbrooke: Université de Sherbrooke, 1984.

Cabrera, Alonso de, O.P. "Consideraciones del lunes después del domingo de la Resurrección." In *Sermones*, edited by Miguel Mir. Nueva Biblioteca de Autores Españoles, 3: 452-60. Madrid: Bailly-Baillière, 1906. First published in *Consideraciones sobre los Evangelios de la Cuaresma desde el Domingo cuarto y Ferias hasta la Resurrección*. 2 vols. Córdoba: Andrés Barrera, 1601.

Cabrol, Ferdinand, O.S.B., ed. *The Roman Missal in Latin and English*. 8th ed. London: Herder, 1931.

Calveras, J., S.J., and Dalmases, C., S.J., ed. *Exercitia spiritualia. Textuum antiquissimorum nova editio*. Rome: Institutum Historicum Societatis Iesu, 1969.

Carranza de Miranda, Bartolomé. *Comentarios sobre el catechismo christiano*. Edited by José Ignacio Tellechea Idígoras. 3 vols. Madrid: Biblioteca de Autores Cristianos, 1972-99.

Caso González, José, ed. *La vida de Lazarillo de Tormes y de sus fortunas y adversidades*. Boletín de la Real Academia Española, anejo XVII. Madrid: Real Academia Española, 1967.

Cassian, John. *Conférences vii-xvii*. Edited and translated by E. Pichery. Paris: Editions du Cerf, 1958.

Catechism of the Council of Trent. Translated by J. Donovan. Dublin: James Duffy, c. 1880.

Catechismus ex decreto Concilii Tridentini. Rome: ex typographia polyglotta S. Congregationis de Propaganda Fide, 1886.

Catecismos de Astete y Ripalda. Edited by Luis Resines. Madrid: Biblioteca de Autores Cristianos, 1987.

Catherine of Siena, St. *The Dialogue of the Seraphic Virgin, Catherine of Siena*. Translated by Algar Thorold. London: Kegan Paul, Trench, Trübner, 1896.

Cervantes, Miguel de. *Los trabajos de Persiles y Sigismunda*. Edited by Carlos Romero Muñoz. Madrid: Cátedra, 2002.

Clement of Alexandria, St. *Miscellanies: Book VII*. Edited and translated by Fenton John Anthony Hort and Joseph B. Mayor. London: MacMillan, 1902.

Columbus, Christopher. *Cristóbal Colón: textos y documentos completos. Relaciones de viajes, cartas y memoriales*. Edited by Consuelo Varela. Madrid: Alianza, 1982.

——————. *Journal of the First Voyage (Diario del primer viaje) 1492*. Edited and translated by B. W. Ife, with an essay on Columbus's language by R. J. Penny. Warminster: Aris and Phillips, 1990.

——————. *The Book of Prophecies*. Edited by Roberto Rusconi and translated by Blair Sullivan. Berkeley: University of California Press, 1997.

Compendio breve de ejercicios espirituales, compuesto por un monje de Montserrat entre 1510-1555. Edited by Javier Melloni, S.J. Madrid: Biblioteca de Autores Cristianos, 2006.

Correas, Gonzalo. *Vocabulario de refranes y frases proverbiales*. Edited by Louis Combet. Bordeaux: Institut d'Études Ibériques et Ibéro-Américaines de l'Université de Bordeaux, 1967.

Cortés, Hernán. *Letters from Mexico*. Translated and edited by A. R. Pagden with an introduction by J. H. Elliott. New Haven: Yale University Press, 1986.

Covarrubias Orozco, Sebastián de. *Tesoro de la lengua castellana o española*. Edited by Felipe C. R. Maldonado and revised by Manuel Camarero. Madrid: Castalia, 1995.

Cunningham, Gilbert F., trans. *The Solitudes of Luis de Góngora*. With a Preface by A. A. Parker and an Introduction by Elias L. Rivers. Baltimore: Johns Hopkins Press, 1969.

Decrees of the Ecumenical Councils. Edited by Norman P. Tanner, S.J. 2 vols. London: Sheed and Ward/Washington: Georgetown University Press, 1990.

Denis the Carthusian. *Enarrationes [...] in quinque libros sapientiales*. Cologne: expensis Iohannis Solteris et Melchioris Novesiani, 1533.

——————. *In sancta quatuor D.N. Iesu Christi evangelia praeclarae admodum enarrationes*. Venice: ex officina Bartholomaei Rubina, 1569.

——————. *Opera omnia*. 42 vols. Montreuil, Tournai and Parkminster, 1896-1935.

——————. *Spiritual Writings*. Edited by Íde M. NíRiain, with an introduction by Terence O'Reilly. Dublin: Four Courts, 2005.

Díaz del Castillo, Bernal. *Historia verdadera de la conquista de la Nueva España*. Edited by Carmelo Sáenz de Santa María, with an introduction and notes by Luis Sáinz de Medrano. Barcelona: Planeta, 1992.

Dio Chrysostom. "The Euboean Discourse, or The Hunter." In *Dio Chrysostom*, translated by J. W. Cohoon, 1: 286-373. London: Heinemann/New York: Putnam, 1932.

Donne, John. *Selected Prose*. Edited by Neil Rhodes. Harmondsworth: Penguin, 1987.

Erasmus, Desiderius. *In evangelium Lucae paraphrasis*. Basle: Froben, 1524.

Ercilla, Alonso de. *La Araucana*. Edited by Isaías Lerner. Madrid: Cátedra, 1993.

Fernández de Oviedo, Gonzalo. *Historia general y natural de las Indias*. Edited by Juan Pérez de Tudela Bueso. 5 vols. Biblioteca de Autores Españoles, vols 117-21. Madrid: Real Academia Española, 1959.

François de Sales, St. *Oeuvres*. Edited by André Ravier and Roger Devos. Paris: Gallimard, 1969.

Genebrard, Gilbert. *Canticum Canticorum Salomonis Regis*. Paris: apud M. Iuuenum, 1570.

Góngora, Luis de. *Poems*. Edited by R. O. Jones. Cambridge: Cambridge University Press, 1966.

—————. *Soledades*. Edited by John Beverley. Madrid: Cátedra, 1980.

—————. *Soledades*. Edited by Robert Jammes. Madrid: Castalia, 1994.

Gracián, Baltasar. *El Criticón*. Edited by M. Romera-Navarro. 3 vols. Philadelphia: University of Pennsylvania Press, 1938-40.

—————. *Agudeza y arte de ingenio*. Edited by Evaristo Correa Calderón. 2 vols. Madrid: Castalia, 1969.

—————. *Oráculo manual y arte de prudencia*. Edited by Emilio Blanco. Madrid: Cátedra, 1997.

Granada, Luis de. *Obras castellanas*. Edited by Cristóbal Cuevas. 2 vols. Madrid: Turner, 1994-97.

—————. *Libro de la oración y meditación*. Edited by Álvaro Huerga. Madrid: Fundación universitaria española/Dominicos de Andalucía, 1994.

—————. *Guía de pecadores (texto definitivo)*. Edited by Herminio de Paz Castaño. Madrid: Fundación universitaria española/Dominicos de Andalucía, 1995.

—————. *Adiciones, 2: Meditaciones de la vida de Cristo*. Edited by Álvaro Huerga. Madrid: Fundación universitaria española/Dominicos de Andalucía, 1995.

—————. *Retórica Eclesiástica*. Edited by Álvaro Huerga. 2 vols. Madrid: Fundación universitaria española/Dominicos de Andalucía, 1999.

—————. *Sermones de tiempo III /I*. Edited by Álvaro Huerga. Madrid: Fundación universitaria española/Dominicos de Andalucía, 2001.

—————. *Sermones de tiempo III/3*. Edited by Álvaro Huerga and translated by Ricardo Alarcón Buendía. Madrid: Fundación universitaria española/Dominicos de Andalucía, 2002.

Gregory the Great, St. *Opera*. 2nd edition. 4 vols. Rome: ex typographia Camerae Apostolicae, 1613.

—————. *Moralia in Iob, libri xxiii-xxxv*. Edited by M. Adriaen. Corpus Christianorum Series Latina, vol. 143B. Turnhout: Brepols, 1985.

—————. *Morals on the Book of Job*. 4 vols. Oxford: John Henry Parker, 1844-50.

—————. *Forty Gospel Homilies*. Edited by Dom David Hurst. Kalanazoo, Mich.: Cistercian Publications, 1990.

—————. *Homiliae in evangelia*. Edited by Raymond Étaix. Corpus Christianorum Series Latina, vol. 141. Turnhout: Brepols, 1999.

Gregory of Nazianzus, St. *Discours 38-41*. Edited by Claudio Moreschini and translated by Paul Gallay. Paris: Editions du Cerf, 1990.

Huerga, Cipriano de la. *Comentario al Cantar de los Cantares (1582)*. Edited by Avelino Domínguez García. 2 vols. In *Obras completas*, vols. 5 and 6. León: Universidad de León, 1991.

Isidore of Seville, St. *Etimologías*. Edited by José Oroz Reta and Manuel C. Diaz y Diaz. 2 vols. Madrid: Biblioteca de Autores Cristianos, 1982.

Jerome, St. *Comentarios a los profetas menores. Edición bilingüe*. Edited by Avelino Domínguez García. Madrid: Biblioteca de Autores Cristianos, 2003.

Jiménez de Cisneros, García. *Obras completas*. Edited by C. Baraut, O.S.B. 2 vols. Montserrat: Abadía de Montserrat, 1965.

Juan de la Cruz, San. *Poesía*. Edited by Domingo Ynduráin. Madrid: Cátedra, 1984.

—————. *Obras completas*. Edited by Eulogio Pacho. Burgos: Monte Carmelo, 1997.

—————. *Cántico espiritual y poesía completa*. Edited by Paola Elia and María Jesús Mancho. Barcelona: Crítica, 2002.

Keats, John. *The Complete Poems*. Edited by John Barnard, with an introduction by Andrew Motion and engravings by Simon Brett. London: Folio Society, 2001.

Knox, Ronald. *The Old Testament, newly translated from the Latin Vulgate*. 2 vols. London: Burns Oates and Washbourne, 1949.

Lapide, Cornelius à. *Commentaria in Scripturam Sacram*. 21 vols. Paris: Vivès, 1868-76.

Las Casas, Bartolomé de. *Historia de las Indias*. Edited by J. Pérez de Tudela and E. López Oto. Biblioteca de Autores Españoles, vol. 95. Madrid: Real Academia Española, 1957.

—————. *A Short Account of the Destruction of the Indies*. Edited and translated by Nigel Griffin with an introduction by Anthony Pagden. London: Penguin, 1992.

La vida de Lazarillo de Tormes y de sus fortunas y adversidades. Edited by R. O. Jones. Manchester: University Press, 1963.

—————. Edited by Alberto Blecua. Madrid: Castalia, 1975.

—————. Edited by Francisco Rico. Barcelona: Planeta, 1980.

—————. Edited by Francisco Rico. Madrid: Cátedra, 1987.

—————. Edited by Félix Carrasco. New York: Peter Lang, 1997.

—————. Edited by Robert L. Fiore. Asheville, N.C.: Pegasus, 2000.

—————. Edited by Aldo Ruffinatto. Madrid: Castalia, 2001.

Lazarillo de Tormes and El Abencerraje. Edited by Claudio Guillén. New York: Dell, 1966.

Leo the Great, St. *The Letters and Sermons*. Translated with an introduction and notes by Charles Lett Feltoe. Nicene and Post-Nicene Fathers, vol.12. Edinburgh: T. and T. Clark, 1989.

León, Luis de, O.S.A. *The Original Poems*. Edited by Edward Sarmiento. Manchester: Manchester University Press, 1972.

—————. *Poesías originales*. Edited by Angel Custodio Vega, O.S.A. Barcelona: Planeta, 1980.

—————. *Poesías. Estudio, texto crítico, bibliografía y comentario*. Edited by Oresti Macrí. Barcelona: Crítica, 1982.

—————. *Poesía completa*. Edited by José Manuel Blecua. Madrid: Gredos, 1990.

—————. *Cantar de los Cantares. Interpretaciones: literal, espiritual, profética*. Edited by José María Becerra Hiraldo. Real Monasterio del Escorial: Ediciones Escurialenses, 1992.

—————. *De los nombres de Cristo*. Edited by Cristóbal Cuevas. Madrid: Cátedra, 1997.

—————. *Poesías completas. Obras propias en castellano y latín y traducciones e imitaciones latinas, griegas, bíblico-hebreas y romances*. Edited by Cristóbal Cuevas. Madrid: Castalia, 1998.

—————. *Poesías completas: propias, imitaciones y traducciones*. Edited by Cristóbal Cuevas. Madrid: Castalia, 2001.

—————. *Epistolario, cartas, licencias, poderes, dictámenes*. Edited by José Barrientos García. Madrid: Revista Agustiniana, 2001.

—————. *Poesía*. Edited by Antonio Ramajo Caño, with a preliminary study by Alberto Blecua and Francisco Rico. Barcelona: Galaxia Gutenberg/Círculo de Lectores, 2006.

León, Pablo de, O.P. *Guía del cielo*. Edited by Vicente Beltrán de Heredia, O.P. Barcelona: Juan Flors, 1963.

López de Gómara, Francisco. *Historia general de las Indias*. Edited by Pilar Guibelaide with an introduction by Emiliano M. Aguilera. 2 vols. Barcelona: Iberia, 1954.

Loyola, Ignatius, St. *Obras. Edición manual*. Edited by Ignacio Iparraguirre, S.J., Cándido de Dalmases, S.J., Manuel Ruiz Jurado S.J. 5th edition. Madrid: Biblioteca de Autores Cristianos, 1991.

—————. *Saint Ignatius of Loyola: Personal Writings*. Translated by Joseph A. Munitiz and Philip Endean. London: Penguin, 1996.

Ludolph of Saxony. *Vita Jesu Christi*. Paris, 1502.

—————. *Vita Cristi Cartuxano*. Translated by Fray Ambrosio Montesino. 4 vols. Alcalá de Henares: Stanislao de Polonia, 1502-03.

—————. *Vita Christi Cartuxano*. Translated by Fray Ambrosio Montesino. Seville: J. Cromberger, 1530.

Maldonado, Juan, S.J. *Commentarii in quatuor evangelistas*. Edited by J.M. Raich. 2 vols. Mainz: Kirchheim, 1874.

Manrique, Ángel. *Laurea Evangélica, hechos de varios discursos predicables*. Salamanca: Antonia Ramírez, 1614.

Mártir de Anglería, Pedro. *Décadas del Nuevo Mundo*. Translated by Joaquín Torres Asensio. Buenos Aires: Bajel, 1944.

—————. *De orbe novo decades. A facsimile reprint of the edition of 1516*. Alicante: Rembrandt, 1986.

—————. *Cartas sobre el Nuevo Mundo*. Translated by Julio Bauzano, with an introduction by Ramón Alba. Madrid: Polifemo, 1990.

Migne, Jacques-Paul, ed. *Patrologiae cursus completus. Series Latina*. 221 vols. Paris: Garnier, 1844-64.

Montañés, Jaime. *Espejo de bien vivir y para ayudar a bien morir*. Edited by Pablo María Garrido, O.C. Salamanca: Universidad Pontificia/Madrid: Fundación universitaria española, 1976.

Montemayor, Jorge de. *Omelías sobre Miserere mei Deus*. Edited by Terence O'Reilly. Durham: University of Durham, 2000.

Nadal, J. *Epistolae IV*. Madrid: Monumenta Historica Societatis Iesu, 1905.

Orozco, San Alonso de. *Obras completas, 1: obras castellanas (1)*. Edited by Rafael Lazcano. Madrid: Biblioteca de Autores Cristianos, 2001.

—————. *Tratado de la suavidad de Dios*. Edited by Teófilo Aparicio. In Orozco, *Obras completas, 1: obras castellanas (1)*, 333-517.

—————. *Catechismo provechoso*. Edited by Luis Resines. In Orozco, *Obras completas, 1: obras castellanas (1)*, 695-843.

Osuna, Francisco de. *Tercer abecedario espiritual*. Edited by Melquíades Andrés. Madrid: Biblioteca de Autores Cristianos, 1972.

Ovid. *Metamorphoses*. Edited and translated by Frank Justus Miller, and revised by G.P. Goold. 2 vols. Cambridge, Mass.: Harvard University Press/London: Heinemann, 1977.

Pacheco, Francisco. *Arte de la pintura*. Edited by F. J. Sánchez Catón. Madrid: Instituto de Valencia de Don Juan, 1956.

Palma, Luis de la, S.J. *Obras*. Edited by Francisco X. Rodríguez Molero, S.J. Madrid: Biblioteca de Autores Cristianos, 1967.

Pérez de Oliva, Hernán. *Historia de la invención de las Yndias*. Edited by José Juan Arrom. Bogotá: Instituto Caro y Cuervo, 1965.

Pérez de Valencia, Jaume. *Expositio [...] in cantica novi veterisque testamenti.* Paris: apud Franciscum Reynault, 1533.

Puente, Luis de la, S.J. *Expositio moralis et mystica in Canticum Canticorum.* Cologne: I. Kinckium, 1622.

Quevedo, Francisco de. *Obras completas.* Edited by Felicidad Buendía. Madrid: Aguilar, 1988.

Real Academia Española. *Diccionario de Autoridades. Edición facsímile.* 3 vols. Madrid: Gredos, 1963.

Ribadeneira, Pedro de. *Flos sanctorum, o libro de las vidas de los santos.* Madrid: Luis Sánchez, 1616.

Rodríguez de Montalvo, Garci. *Amadís de Gaula.* Edited by Edwin B. Plaice. 4 vols. Madrid: Consejo superior de investigaciones científicas, 1959-69.

———. *Amadís de Gaula.* Edited by Juan Manual Cacho Blecua. 2 vols. Madrid: Cátedra, 1987.

———. *Amadís de Gaula.* Edited by Juan Bautista Avalle-Arce. 2 vols. Madrid: Espasa Calpe, 1991.

———. *Sergas de Esplandián.* Edited by Carlos Sainz de la Maza. Madrid: Castalia, 2003.

Rojas, Fernando de. *La Celestina. Tragicomedia de Calisto y Melibea.* Edited by Francisco J. Lobera and others. Barcelona: Crítica, 2000.

Rotelle, John E., O.S.A., ed. *St Thomas of Villanueva. Sermons. Part 4: Easter Triduum, Easter Season.* Translated by Michael S. Woodward. Villanova, Pa.: Augustinian Press, 1995.

Seneca. *Ad Lucilium epistulae morales.* Edited and translated by Richard M. Gummere. 3 vols. Cambridge, Mass.: Harvard University Press, 1989.

Sotomayor, Luis de, O.P. *Cantici Canticorum Salomonis interpretatio.* Paris: apud M. Sonnium, 1605.

Tanner, Norman P., S.J., ed. *Decrees of the Ecumenical Councils.* 2 vols. London: Sheed and Ward/Washington: Georgetown University Press, 1990.

Teresa de Jesús, Santa. *Obras completas.* Edited by Efrén de la Madre de Dios, O.C.D., and Otger Steggink, O. Carm. Madrid: Biblioteca de Autores Cristianos, 1972.

The Holy Bible Translated from the Latin Vulgate and Diligently Compared with Other Editions in Divers Languages (Douay, A.D. 1609; Rheims, A.D. 1582). London: Burns Oates and Washbourne, 1914.

The Hours of the Divine Office in English and Latin. A Bilingual Edition of the Roman Breviary Text. 3 vols. Collegeville: The Liturgical Press, 1963.

Thesaurus Linguae Latinae. Leipzig: Teubner, 1900-.

Tirso de Molina. *El condenado por desconfiado. A play attributed to Tirso de Molina (Fray Gabriel Téllez).* Edited with an introduction and notes by Daniel Rogers. Oxford: Pergamon, 1974.

———. *Damned for Despair (El condenado por desconfiado).* Edited and translated with an introduction and commentary by Nicholas G. Round. Warminster: Aris and Phillips, 1986.

———. *El condenado por desconfiado.* Edited by Ciriaco Morón Arroyo. Madrid: Cátedra, 1992.

Toledo, Francisco de, S.J. *Commentarii in [...] Evangelium secundum Lucam.* Cologne: sumptibus A. Boëtzeri, 1611.

Tomás de Villanueva, Santo. *Conciones sacrae [...] Nunc primum in lucem editae.* Alcalá de Henares: Ioannes a Lequerica excudebat, 1572.

———. *Opera omnia.* Augsburg: sumptibus Ignatii Adami et Francisci Antonii bibliopolarum, 1757.

Valdés, Alfonso de. *La vida de Lazarillo de Tormes y de sus fortunas y adversidades.* Edited by Milagros Rodríguez Cáceres, with an introduction by Rosa Navarro Durán. Barcelona: Octaedro, 2003.

Valdés, Juan de. *Diálogo de doctrina christiana y El Salterio traducido del hebreo en romance castellano.* Edited by Domingo Ricart. Mexico: Universidad Nacional Autónoma de México, 1964.

Varazze, Iacopo da. *Legenda aurea*. Edited by Giovanni Paulo Maggioni. 2nd ed. 2 vols. Florence: Sismel, 1998.

──────. *Leyenda de los Santos*. Edited by Félix Juan Cabasés, S.J. Monumenta Historica Societatis Iesu, Nova Series, vol. 3. Madrid: Universidad de Comillas and Institutum Historicum Societatis Iesu, 2007.

Vatable, François. *Biblia*. Paris: Robert Estienne, 1545

──────. *Biblia sacra*. 2 vols. Salamanca: apud Gaspard de Portonariis suis et Rouillii, Benedictus Boierii expensis, 1584-85.

Ward, Anthony, S.M., and Cuthbert Johnson, O.S.B. eds. *Missalis Romani editio princeps, Mediolani anno 1474 prelis mandata*. Rome: Centro Liturgico Vincenziano - Edizioni Liturgiche, 1996.

Weber, Robert, ed. *Biblia sacra iuxta vulgatam versionem*. 4th ed. Prepared by Roger Gryson. Stuttgart: Deutsche Bibelgesellschaft, 1994.

SECONDARY SOURCES

Acker, Thomas S. *The Baroque Vortex. Velázquez, Calderón and Gracián under Philip IV*. New York: Peter Lang, 2000.

Alcántara Mejía, José Ramón. *La escondida senda: poética y hermenéutica en la obra castellana de fray Luis de León*. Salamanca: Universidad de Salamanca, 2002.

Alonso, Dámaso. "Góngora y América." In *Estudios y ensayos gongorinos*. Madrid: Gredos, 1955.

Alphonso, Herbert. "La vida diaria como oración." In García Lomas, ed., *Ejercicios Espirituales y mundo de hoy*, 265-78.

Alvarez, Tomás. *Diccionario de Santa Teresa de Jesús*. Burgos: Monte Carmelo, 2000.

Alvarez Turienzo, Saturnino. "Clave epistemológica para leer a Fray Luis de León." In *Fray Luis de León*, edited by Víctor García de la Concha, 23-45. Salamanca: Universidad de Salamanca, 1981.

Archer, Robert. "The overreaching imagination: the structure and meaning of Aldana's *Carta para Arias Montano*." *Bulletin of Hispanic Studies* 65 (1988): 237-49.

Arellano, Ignacio, ed. *Las Indias (América) en la literatura del Siglo de Oro. Homenaje a Jesús Cañedo*. Kassel: Reichenberger, 1992.

──────. "La imagen de las Indias y los puntos de vista de la escritura." In Arellano, ed., *Las Indias (América) en la literatura del Siglo de Oro*, 301-12.

Armas Wilson, Diana de. *Cervantes, the Novel and the New World*. Oxford: Oxford University Press, 2000.

──────. "Cervantes and the New World." In *The Cambridge Companion to Cervantes*, ed. Anthony J. Cascardi, 206-25. Cambridge: Cambridge Unioversity Press, 2002.

Arzubialde, Santiago, S.J. *Ejercicios Espirituales de San Ignacio. Historia y análisis*. Bilbao: Mensajero/Santander: Sal Terrae, 1991.

──────. "Casiano e Ignacio. Continuidad y ruptura. Una original aportación de Ignacio a la historia de la tradición espiritual." In Plazaola, ed., *Las fuentes de los Ejercicios Espirituales de San Ignacio*, 123-86.

──────. "El llamamiento del Rey Temporal en la *Escala celeste* de San Juan Clímaco." In Plazaola, ed., *Las fuentes de los Ejercicios Espirituales de San Ignacio*, 537-42.

Aurigemma, Marcello. "Purgatorio." In *Enciclopedia Dantesca*, 4: 745-50.

Avalle-Arce, Juan Bautista. *Amadís de Gaula: el primitivo y el de Montalvo*. Mexico: Fondo de cultura económica, 1990.

Backhouse, Janet. "French Manuscript Illumination, 1450-1530." In *Renaissance Painting in Manuscripts. Treasures from the British Library*, edited by Thomas Kren, 145-86. New York: Hudson Hills, 1983.

Backus, Irena, ed. *The Reception of the Church Fathers in the West from the Carolingians to the Maurists.* 2 vols. Boston and Leiden: Brill, 2001.

Ballesteros, M., ed. *La Découverte de l'Amérique*. Paris: Vrin, 1968.

Barand, Nieves. "El espejismo del Preste Juan de las Indias en su reflejo literario en España." In *Actas del X Congreso de la Asociación Internacional de Hispanistas*. Edited by Antonio Vilanova. 4 vols. 1: 359-64. Barcelona: Promociones y publicaciones universitarias, 1992.

Barnard, John. *John Keats*. Cambridge: Cambridge University Press, 1987.

Barton, John, and John Muddiman, eds. *The Oxford Bible Commentary*. Oxford: Oxford University Press, 2001.

Bartrum, Giulia, ed. *Albrecht Dürer and His Legacy. The Graphic Work of a Renaissance Artist.* London: British Museum, 2002.

Bassegoda, Bonaventura. "Pacheco y Velázquez." In *Velázquez y Sevilla*, 2: 124-39.

Bataillon, Marcel. "Sobre la génesis poética del *Cántico Espiritual* desde la estética de su recepción." In *Varia lección de clásicos españoles*, 167-82. Madrid: Gredos, 1964.

———. *Erasmo y España. Estudios sobre la historia espiritual del siglo xvi.* Translated by Antonio Alatorre. Mexico: Fondo de cultura económica, 1966.

———. "Les Indes occidentales, découverte d'un monde humain." In Ballesteros, ed., *La Découverte de l'Amérique*, 7-10.

———. *Novedad y fecundidad del Lazarillo de Tormes*. Translated by Luis Cortés Vázquez. Salamanca: Anaya, 1973.

———. *Erasmo y el erasmismo*. Translated by Carlos Pujol, with an introduction by Francisco Rico. Barcelona: Crítica, 1977.

Bedouelle, Guy, and Bernard Roussel, eds. *Le Temps des Réformes et la Bible*. Paris: Beauchesne, 1989.

Bergamín, José. "*Hombre adentro y las Indias de Dios*." In *Beltenebros y otros ensayos sobre literatura española*, 151-64. Barcelona: Noguer, 1973.

Bernard-Maitre, Henri, S.J., "Saint Ignace de Loyola mystique et les anciennes traductions espagnoles de l'*Imitation de Jésus-Christ*." *Ons Geestelijk Erf* 30 (1956): 25-42.

Blanco, Mercedes. "*Homo homini lupus*. Estado de naturaleza y hombre artificial en Baltasar Gracián y Thomas Hobbes." *Insula* 655-56 (2001): 13-16.

Blunt, John Henry. *The Annotated Book of Common Prayer; being an historical, ritual and theological commentary on the devotional system of the Church of England.* London: Rivingtons, 1866.

Boeft, Jan den. "Erasmus and the Church Fathers." In Backus, ed., *The Reception of the Church Fathers in the West from the Carolingians to the Maurists*, 2: 537-72.

Bolaños, Álvaro Félix. "The historian and the Hesperides: Fernández de Oviedo and the limitations of imitation." *Bulletin of Hispanic Studies (Liverpool)* 72 (1995): 273-88.

Bottineau, Yves. *Velasquez*. Paris: Citadelles et Mazenod, 1998.

Boyce, James, O. Carm. "From Rule to Rubric: the impact of Carmelite liturgical legislation upon the order's Office tradition." *Ephemerides Liturgicae* 108 (1994): 262-98. Reprinted in Boyce, *Praising God in Carmel. Studies in Carmelite Liturgy*, 180-230.

———. *Praising God in Carmel. Studies in Carmelite Liturgy*. Washington, D.C.: Carmelite Institute, 1999.

—————. "The Carmelite feast of the Presentation of the Virgin: a study in musical adaptation." In *The Divine Office in the Latin Middle Ages*, edited by Margot E. Fassier and Rebecca A. Baltzer, 485-518. Oxford: Oxford University Press, 2000.

Boyd, Jane, and Philip F. Esler. *Visuality and Biblical Text: Interpreting Velázquez' "Christ with Martha and Mary" as a Test Case*. Florence: Olschi, 2004.

Braham, Allan. "A second dated *bodegón* by Velázquez." *Burlington Magazine* 107 (1965): 362-65.

Bray, Xavier. "Kitchen Scene with Christ in the House of Martha and Mary." In Carr, ed., *Velázquez*, 122-25.

—————. "Kitchen Scene with Christ at Emmaus." In Carr, ed., *Velázquez*, 126-27.

Brioso Santos, Héctor. *Cervantes y América*. Madrid: Fundación Carolina/Marcial Pons, 2006.

Brotton, Jerry. "Terrestrial globalism: mapping the globe in Early Modern Europe." In Cosgrove, ed., *Mappings*, 71-89.

Brown, Jonathan. *Velázquez: Painter and Courtier*. New Haven: Yale University Press, 1986.

Brown, Raymond E., S.S., Joseph A. Fitzmyer, S.J., and Roland E. Murphy, O. Carm., eds. *The New Jerome Biblical Commentary*. London: Chapman, 1990.

Buckley, Michael, S.J. "The Contemplation to Attain Love." *The Way Supplement* 24 (1975): 92-104.

—————. "Misticismo eclesial en los *Ejercicios Espirituales*: dos notas sobre Ignacio, la Iglesia y la vida en el Espíritu." In García Lomas, ed., *Ejercicios Espirituales y mundo de hoy*, 175-95.

—————. "Ecclesial Mysticism in the *Spiritual Exercises* of Ignatius." *Theological Studies* 56 (1995): 441-63.

Bustamente, A., and F. Marías, "Entre práctica y teoría: la formación de Velázquez en Sevilla." In *Velázquez y Sevilla*, 2: 140-57.

Cabrol, Fernand. *The Mass of the Western Rites*. Translated by C. M. Antony. London: Sands, 1934.

Cacho Blecua, Juan Manuel. *Amadís: heroísmo mítico cortesano*. Madrid: Cupsa, 1979.

Cacho Casal, Marta. "The old woman in Velázquez's *Kitchen Scene with Christ's Visit to Martha and Mary*." *Journal of the Warburg and Courtald Institutes* 63 (2000): 295-302.

Cacho Casal, Rodrigo. "Hide-and-seek: *Lazarillo de Tormes* and the art of deception." *Forum for Modern Language Studies* 44 (2008): 322-39.

Caldera, Ermanno. "El manierismo en San Juan de la Cruz." In *En torno a San Juan de la Cruz*, edited by J. Servera Baño, 57-88. Madrid: Júcar, 1986.

Canivez, J. "Arnaud Debonneval." In *Dictionnaire de spiritualité*, 1: 888-90.

Caravaggio e l'Europa. Il movimento caravaggesco internazionale da Caravaggio a Mattia Preti. Exh. cat. Milan: Skira, 2005.

Carr, Dawson W. "Painting and reality: the art and life of Velázquez." In Carr, ed., *Velázquez*, 26-53.

—————., ed. *Velázquez*. London: National Gallery, 2006.

Casalduero, Joaquín. *Sentido y forma de "Los trabajos de Persiles y Sigismunda."* Buenos Aires: Sudamericana, 1947.

Certeau, Michel de. *La Fable mystique. XVI-XVII siècle*. Paris: Gallimard, 1982.

—————. *Heterologies: Discourse on the Other*. Translated by Brian Massumi, with a foreword by Wlad Godzich. Minneapolis: University of Minnesota, 1986.

Chauchadis, Claude. *Honneur, morale et société dans l'Espagne de Philippe II*. Paris: Centre National de la Recherche Scientifique, 1984.

Checa, Jorge. "Didactic prose, history, politics, life writing, convent writing, *Crónicas de Indias*." In Gies, ed., *The Cambridge History of Spanish Literature*, 283-90.

Cherry, Peter. "Los *bodegones* de Velázquez y la verdadera imitación del natural." In *Velázquez y Sevilla*, 2: 77-91.

————— and Xanthe Brooke. *Murillo: Scenes of Childhood*. Exh. cat. London: Merrell, 2001.

Chorpenning, Joseph F. "Christ the nursing mother in Fray Luis de León's *En la Ascensión*." *Journal of Hispanic Philology* 11 (1987): 199-204.

Cisquella, Sagalés, O.Cist. "Espirituales cistercienses en las congregaciones de Castilla y Aragón." *Cistercium* 50 (1999): 277-96.

Clancy, S.J., Finbarr G. "St. Augustine's commentary on the Emmaus scene in Luke's Gospel." *Studia Patristica. Papers Presented at the Fourteenth International Conference on Patristic Studies Held in Oxford 2003*, ed. F. Young, M. Edwards and P. Parvis, 51-58. Louvain: Peeters, 2006.

Close, Anthony. *Cervantes and the Comic Mind of His Age*. Oxford: Oxford University Press, 2000.

Close, Lorna. "The play of difference: a reading of Góngora's *Soledades*." In *Conflicts of Discourse: Spanish Literature of the Golden Age*, edited by Peter Evans, 184-98. Manchester: Manchester University Press, 1990.

Codina, Arturo, S.J. *Los orígenes de los Ejercicios Espirituales de San Ignacio de Loyola. Estudio histórico*. Barcelona: Balmes, 1926.

Constable, Giles. *Three Studies in Medieval Religious and Social Thought. The Interpretation of Mary and Martha, the Ideal of the Imitation of Christ, the Orders of Society*. Cambridge: Cambridge University Press, 1995.

Corella, Jesús, S.J. *Sentir la Iglesia. Comentario a las reglas ignacianas para el sentido verdadero de la Iglesia*. Bilbao: Mensajero/Santander: Sal Terrae, 1995.

Coroleu, Alejandro. "Anti-Erasmianism in Spain." In Erika Rummel, ed., *Biblical Humanism and Scholasticism in the Age of Erasmus*, 73-92. Leiden and Boston: Brill, 2008.

Cosgrove, Denis, ed. *Mappings*. London: Reaktion, 1999.

Cossío, José María de. "Rasgos renacentistas y populares en el *Cántico Espiritual* de San Juan de la Cruz." *Escorial* 25 (1942): 205-28.

Craig, Kenneth M. "*Pars ergo Marthae transit*: Pieter Aertsen's 'inverted' paintings of *Christ in the House of Martha and Mary*." *Oud Holland* 97 (1983): 25-39.

Crehan, F. J., S.J. "The Bible in the Roman Catholic Church from Trent to the Present Day." In *The Cambridge History of the Bible*, vol. 3, edited by S. L. Greenslade, 199-237. Cambridge: Cambridge University Press, 1963.

Cro, Stelio. *Realidad y utopía en el descubrimiento y conquista de la América Hispana, 1492-1682*. Madrid: Fundación universitaria española, 1983.

Cruz, Anne J. *Imitación y transformación. El petrarquismo en la poesía de Boscán y Garcilaso de la Vega*. Amsterdam and Philadelphia: John Benjamins, 1988.

—————. "The *Lazarillo*'s author, *redivivus*: on recent studies by Rosa Navarro Durán and José Luis Madrigal." *Bulletin of Spanish Studies* 83 (2006): 855-61.

Cuevas, Cristóbal. "Estudio literario." In *Introducción a la lectura de San Juan de la Cruz*, edited by Salvador Ros and others, 125-201. Salamanca: Junta de Castilla y León, 1991.

Cueto, Ronald. "The Great Babylon of Spain and the devout: politics, religion and piety in the Seville of Velázquez." In Davies and Harris, *Velázquez in Seville*, 29-33.

Cummins, J. S. "Christopher Columbus: crusader, visionary and *servus Dei*." In *Medieval Hispanic Studies presented to Rita Hamilton*, edited by A.D. Deyermond, 45-55. London: Tamesis, 1976. Reprinted in Cummins, *Jesuit and Friar in the Spanish Expansion to the East*.

—————. *Jesuit and Friar in the Spanish Expansion to the East* (London: Variorum, 1986).

Cusson, Gilles, S.J. "Breve historia de la interpretación de los *Ejercicios*. Escuelas y tendencias." *Manresa* 66 (1994): 87-103. Originally published in French as "Petite histoire de l'interprétation des *Exercices*. 'Écoles' et 'tendances.'" *Supplément de Cahiers de Spiritualité Ignatienne* 34 (1993): 15-34.

Dadson, Trevor. *Libros, lectores y lecturas. Estudios sobre bibliotecas particulares españolas del Siglo de Oro*. Madrid: Arco/Libros, 1998.

Daniélou, Jean, S.J. *The Bible and the Liturgy*. Notre Dame, Indiana: University Press, 1966.

Davies, David. "Velázquez's *bodegones*." In Davies and Harris, *Velázquez in Seville*, 51-65.

————— and Enriqueta Harris. *Velázquez in Seville*. Edited by Michael Clarke. Edinburgh: National Gallery of Scotland, 1996.

Dekkers, Eligius. *Clavis patrum latinorum*. Bruges: Beyaert, 1951.

Delenda, Odile. *Velázquez, peintre religieux*. Geneva: Tricorne, 1993.

—————. "Velázquez, peintre religieux." *Dossier de l'art* 63 (1999-2000): 82-97.

Deshman, Robert. "Another look at the Disappearing Christ: corporeal and spiritual vision in early medieval images." *Art Bulletin* 79 (1997): 518-46.

DeWald, Ernest T. "The iconography of the Ascension." *American Journal of Archaeology* 19 (1915): 277-319.

Deyermond, A.D. "Lazarus and Lazarillo." *Studies in Short Fiction* 2 (1964-65): 351-57.

—————. *Lazarillo de Tormes*. 2nd ed. London: Grant and Cutler and Tamesis, 1993.

Domínguez Ortiz, Antonio. *The Golden Age of Spain, 1516-1659*. London: Weidenfeld and Nicolson, 1971.

—————. *Historia de Sevilla: la Sevilla del siglo xvii*. Seville: University of Seville, 1986.

—————, A.E. Pérez Sánchez, J. Gállego. *Velázquez*. Madrid: Museo del Prado, 1990.

Drury, John. *Painting the Word. Christian Pictures and their Meanings*. New Haven: Yale University Press, 1999.

Dunn, Peter N. "Reading the text of *Lazarillo de Tormes*." In *Studies in Honour of Bruce W. Wardropper*, edited by Dian Fox, Harry Sieber, Robert TerHorst, 91-104. Newark, Del.: Juan de la Cuesta, 1989.

Earle, T. F. and K. J. P. Lowe, eds. *Black Africans in Renaissance Europe*. Cambridge: Cambridge University Press, 2005.

Echarte, Ignacio, ed. *Concordancia ignaciana. An Ignatian Concordance*. Bilbao: Mensajero/Maliaño: Sal Terrae, 1996.

Egido, Aurora. *La rosa del silencio. Estudios sobre Gracián*. Madrid: Alianza, 1996.

—————. "El águila de San Juan de la Cruz: mística y poesía en las coplas *Entréme donde no supe y Tras de un amoroso lance*." In *San Juan de la Cruz and Fray Luis de León*, edited by Mary Malcolm Gaylord and Francisco Márquez Villanueva, 69-96. Newark, Del.: Juan de la Cuesta, 1996.

—————. *Las caras de la prudencia y Baltasar Gracián*. Madrid: Castalia, 2000.

—————. *Humanidades y dignidad del hombre en Baltasar Gracián*. Salamanca: Universidad de Salamanca, 2001.

Eire, Carlos M. N. *From Madrid to Purgatory. The Art and Craft of Dying in Sixteenth-Century Spain*. Cambridge: Cambridge University Press, 1995.

Eisenberg, Daniel. *Romances of Chivalry in the Spanish Golden Age*. Newark, Del.: Juan de la Cuesta, 1982.

————. Review of Armas Wilson, *Cervantes, the Novel and the New World. Bulletin of Hispanic Studies* 80 (2003): 130-31.

Elliott, J. H. *The Old World and the New: 1492-1650*. Cambridge: Cambridge University Press, 1970.

————. *Empires of the Atlantic World. Britain and Spain in America, 1492-1830*. New Haven and London: Yale University Press, 2006.

Evennett, H. Outram. *The Spirit of the Counter-Reformation*. Edited with a postscript by John Bossy. Cambridge: Cambridge University Press, 1968.

Farges, Jacques, and Marcel Viller. "La charité chez les Pères." *Dictionnaire de spiritualité*, 2: 523-69.

Fernández-Armesto, Felipe. *Before Columbus. Exploration and Colonisation from the Mediterranean to the Atlantic, 1229-1492*. London: Macmillan, 1987.

Fernández López, Sergio. *Lectura y prohibición de la Biblia en lengua vulgar: defensores y detractores*. León: Universidad de León, 2003.

Ferreyra Liendo, Miguel Angel. "*El condenado por desconfiado* de Tirso: análisis teológico y literario del drama." *Revista de la Universidad Nacional de Córdoba* 10 (1969): 925-46.

Fessard, Gaston, S.J. *La dialectique des Exercices Spirituels de Saint Ignace de Loyola*. 2 vols. Paris: Aubier, 1956 and 1966.

Finaldi, Gabriele. *The Image of Christ*. London: National Gallery, 2000.

Flint, Valerie. *The Imaginative Landscape of Christopher Columbus*. Princeton: Princeton University Press, 1992.

Forcione, Alban K. *Cervantes' Christian Romance. A Study of "Persiles y Sigismunda."* Princeton: Princeton University Press, 1972.

————. *Cervantes and the Humanist Vision. A Study of Four Exemplary Novels*. Princeton: Princeton University Press, 1982.

Friedman, E. H. *The Antiheroine's Voice: Narrative Discourse and Transformations of the Picaresque*. Columbia: University of Missouri Press, 1987.

Gago Jover, Francisco, ed. *Arte de bien morir. Y Breve confesionario (Zaragoza, Pablo Hurus: c. 1479-1484)*. Palma de Mallorca: Olañera, 1999.

Gállego, Julián. *Velázquez en Sevilla*. Seville: Diputación Provincial, 1974.

————. *Diego Velázquez*. Barcelona: Anthropos, 1983.

————. *El cuadro dentro del cuadro*. Madrid: Cátedra, 1984.

————. "La mulata." In Domínguez Ortiz, Pérez Sanchez and Gállego, *Velázquez*, 58-61.

García de Castro, José, and others, eds. *Diccionario de Espiritualidad Ignaciana*. Bilbao: Mensajero/Santander: Sal Terrae, 2007.

García de la Concha, Víctor. *Nueva lectura del Lazarillo. El deleite de la perspectiva*. Madrid: Castalia, 1981.

García Domínguez, Luis María, S.J. "Orden/desorden." In García de Castro, ed., *Diccionario de Espiritualidad Ignaciana*, 1378-87.

García Lomas, Juan M., ed. *Ejercicios Espirituales y mundo de hoy. Congreso Internacional de Ejercicios, Loyola, 20-26 setiembre de 1991*. Bilbao: Mensajero/Santander: Sal Terrae, 1992.

García Mateo, Rogelio, S.J. "Amadís de Gaula." In García de Castro, ed., *Diccionario de Espiritualidad Ignaciana*, 132-36.

————. "Imitación de Cristo." In García de Castro, ed., *Diccionario de Espiritualidad Ignaciana*, 994-1001.

Gardner, Helen, ed. *The Metaphysical Poets*. Revised ed. Harmondsworth: Penguin, 1966.

Gaylord, Mary Malcolm. "The making of Baroque poetry." In Gies, ed., *The Cambridge History of Spanish Literature*, 222-37.

Gerbi, Antonello. *Nature in the New World. From Christopher Columbus to Gonzalo Fernández de Oviedo*. Translated by Jeremy Moyle. Pittsburgh: University of Pittsburgh Press, 1985.

Gerli, E. Michael. "The antecedents of the novel in sixteenth-century Spain." In Gies, ed., *The Cambridge History of Spanish Literature*, 178-200.

Giamatti, A. Bartlett. *The Earthly Paradise and the Renaissance Epic*. Princeton: Princeton University Press, 1966.

Giard, Luce. "Epilogue: Michel de Certeau's heterology and the New World." In Greenblatt, ed., *New World Encounters* 313-22.

Gies, David T., ed. *The Cambridge History of Spanish Literature*. Cambridge: Cambridge University Press, 2004.

Gil, J. *Mitos y utopías del Descubrimiento. Vol. 1: Colón y su tiempo*. Madrid: Alianza, 1989.

Gil-Albarellos, Susana. *"Amadís de Gaula" y el género caballeresco en España*. Vallalolid: Universidad de Valladolid, 1999.

Gil Fernández, Luis. *Estudios de humanismo y tradición clásica*. Madrid: Universidad Complutense, 1984.

Gillet, Joseph E. *Torres Naharro and the Drama of the Renaissance*. Edited by Otis H. Green. Philadelphia: University of Pennsylvania Press, 1961.

Gilman, Stephen. "Matthew V, 10, in Castilian jest and earnest." In *Studia Hispanica in Honorem Rafael Lapesa*, edited by Eugenio Bustos and others, 1: 257-66. Madrid: Cátedra, Seminario Menéndez Pidal and Gredos, 1972.

Glen, Thomas L. "Velázquez's *Kitchen Scene with Christ in the House of Martha and Mary*: an image both 'reflected' and to be reflected upon." *Gazette des Beaux-Arts* 136 (2000): 21-30.

Gómez Canseco, Luis and Valentín Núñez Rivera. *Arias Montano y el "Cantar de los cantares." Estudio y edición de la "Paráfrasis en modo pastoril."* Kassel: Reichenberger, 2001.

González, Gabriel. *Drama y teología en el Siglo de Oro*. Salamanca: Universidad de Salamanca, 1987.

González García, Juan Luis. "La sombra de Dios: *imitatio Christi* y contrición en la piedad privada de Felipe II." In *Felipe II: un monarca y su época. Un príncipe del Renacimiento*, 185-201. Madrid: Museo del Prado, 1998.

González Olmedo, Félix. "Musa Leonina. Notas y glosas." [Reelaboración de A. Díez Escanciano]. *Perficit* (Salamanca) 4 (1973): 121-226.

González Velasco, M. "Los agustinos en el proceso de fray Luis de León." In *Fray Luis de León. El fraile, el humanista, el teólogo*, edited by S. Alvarez Turienzo, 631-99. Madrid: Ediciones Escurialenses, 1991.

Gowing, Lawrence. "Images of human separateness." *Times Literary Supplement*, 1 August, 1986, 831.

Green, Otis H. *Spain and the Western Tradition. The Castilian Mind in Literature from El Cid to Calderón*. 4 vols. Madison and Milwaukee: University of Wisconsin Press, 1963-65.

Greenblatt, Stephen. *Marvellous Possessions. The Wonder of the New World*. Oxford: Clarendon, 1991.

————, ed. *New World Encounters*. Berkeley: University of California Press, 1993.

Griffin, Nigel. "Spanish incunabula in the John Rylands University Library of Manchester." *Bulletin of the John Rylands University Library of Manchester* 70 (1988): 6-141.

Gudiol Ricart, José. *Velázquez, 1599-1660. Historia de su vida, catálogo de su obra, estudio de la evolución de su técnica.* Barcelona: Polígrafa, 1973.

Guibert, J. de, S.J. *The Jesuits: Their Spiritual Doctrine and Practice.* St. Louis: Institute of Jesuit Sources, 1972.

Guttuso, Renato, and Angela Ottino della Chiesa, eds. *L'opera completa del Caravaggio.* Milan: Rizzoli, 1967.

Haase, Wolfgang, and Meyer Reinhold, eds. *The Classical Tradition and the Americas. Vol.1: European Images of the Americas and the Classical Tradition.* Berlin and New York: Walter de Gruyter, 1994.

Hammond, N. G. L., and H. H. Scullard. *The Oxford Classical Dictionary.* Oxford: Clarendon, 1970.

Harley, J. B., and David Woodward, eds. *Cartography in Prehistoric, Ancient and Medieval Europe and the Mediterranean.* Chicago: University of Chicago Press, 1987.

Harris, Enriqueta. *Velázquez.* Oxford: Phaidon, 1982.

———. "Velázquez, Sevillian painter of sacred subjects." In Davies and Harris, *Velázquez in Seville,* 45-49. First published in *Symbol and Image in the Iberian Arts,* edited by Margaret A. Rees. Leeds: Trinity and All Saints, 1994.

Henríquez Ureña, P. "El descubrimiento del Nuevo Mundo en la imaginación europea." In *Las corrientes literarias en la América hispánica,* 9-34. Mexico: Fondo de cultura económica, 1969.

Hitchcock, Richard. "Góngora and the Hyrcanian tigress." In *What's Past is Prologue. A collection of Essays in Honour of L.J. Woodward,* edited by Salvador Bacarisse, Bernard Bentley, Mercedes Clarasó and Douglas Gifford, 82-87. Edinburgh: Scottish Academic Press, 1984.

Hood, William. *Fra Angelico at San Marco.* New Haven: Yale University Press, 1993.

Hornedo, Rafael María de, S.J. "El humanismo de San Juan de la Cruz." *Razón y Fe* 129 (1944): 133-50.

Hügel, Friedrich von. *The Mystical Element of Religion as Studied in Saint Catherine of Genoa and her Friends.* 2 vols. London: Dent and Clarke, 1961.

Humfrey, Peter. *Lorenzo Lotto.* New Haven: Yale University Press, 1997.

Ife, Barry W. "Las dos cartas de Colón de 1493: transmisión y público." *Edad de Oro* 12 (1993): 131-39.

———. "The literary impact of the New World: Columbus to Carrizales." *Journal of the Institute of Romance Studies* 3 (1994-95): 65-85.

———. Review of Armas Wilson, *Cervantes, the Novel and the New World.* In *The Times Literary Supplement,* June 1, 2001: 6.

——— and John W. Butt. "The literary heritage." In *The Hispanic World,* edited by J.H. Elliott, 203-16. London: Thames and Hudson, 1991.

Iparraguirre, Ignacio, S.J. *Práctica de los Ejercicios de San Ignacio de Loyola en vida de su autor (1522-1556).* Bilbao: Mensajero/Rome: Institutum Historicum Societatis Iesu, 1946.

———, ed. *Directorium Exercitiorum Spiritualium (1540-1599).* Rome: Monumenta Historica Societatis Iesu, 1955.

Ivens, Michael, S.J. *Understanding the Spiritual Exercises. Text and Commentary. A Handbook for Retreat Directors.* Leominster: Gracewing, 1998.

Jammes, Robert. *Études sur l'oeuvre poétique de Don Luis de Góngora y Argote.* Bordeaux: Féret, 1967.

Jordan, William B. *Spanish Still Life in the Golden Age, 1600-1650*. Fort Worth: Kimbell Art Museum, 1985.

Jungmann, J.A. *El sacrificio de la Misa. Tratado histórico-litúrgico*. 4th ed. Madrid: Biblioteca de Autores Cristianos, 1963.

Kadir, Djelal. *Columbus and the Ends of the Earth. Europe's Prophetic Rhetoric as Conquering Ideology*. Berkeley: University of California Press, 1992.

Kamen, Henry. *Spain 1469-1714. A Society of Conflict*. London: Longman, 1991.

—————. *Spain's Road to Empire. The Making of a World Power 1492-1763*. London: Penguin, 2003.

Kaplis-Hohwald, Laurie. *Translation of the Biblical Psalms in Golden Age Spain*. Lewiston: Mellen, 2003.

Kassier, Theodore L. *The Truth Disguised. Allegorical Structure and Technique in Gracián's "Criticón."* London: Tamesis, 1976.

Kinder, A. Gordon. *Casiodoro de Reina, Spanish Reformer of the Sixteenth Century*. London: Tamesis, 1975.

Knappe, Karl-Adolf. *Dürer: The Complete Engravings, Etchings and Woodcuts*. London: Thames and Hudson, 1965.

Lara Garrido, José. "Las ínsulas extrañas de San Juan de la Cruz." In *Estudios románicos dedicados al Profesor Andrés Soria Ortega*, edited by Jesús Montoya Martínez and Juan Paredes Núñez, 2 vols, 2: 287-302. Granada: Universidad de Granada, 1985.

—————. *Los mejores plectros. Teoría y práctica de la épica culta en el Siglo de Oro*. Málaga: Universidad de Málaga, 1999.

Lausberg, Heinrich. *Manual de retórica literaria. Fundamentos de una ciencia de la literatura*. Translated by José Pérez Riesco. 3 vols. Madrid: Gredos, 1966.

Lawrance, Jeremy N.H. "Humanism in the Iberian Peninsula." In *The Impact of Humanism on Western Europe*, edited by Anthony Goodman and Angus MacKay, 220-58. London: Longman, 1990.

—————. "Black africans in Renaissance Spanish literature." In Earle and Lowe, eds., *Black Africans in Renaissance Europe*, 70-93.

Lázaro Carreter, Fernando. *Lazarillo de Tormes y la picaresca*. Barcelona: Ariel, 1972.

—————. "Sobre la dificultad conceptista." In *Estilo barroco y personalidad creadora*, 13-43. Madrid: Cátedra, 1974.

—————. "El género literario de *El Criticón*." In *Clásicos españoles. Desde Garcilaso a los niños pícaros*, 359-82. Madrid: Alianza, 2003.

Lazure, Guy. "Perceptions of the Temple, projections of the Divine. Patronage, biblical scholarship and Jesuit imagery in Spain, 1580-1620." *Calamus Renascens* 1 (2000): 155-88.

Leclercq, Jean, O.S.B. "The Mystery of the Ascension in the Sermons of St. Bernard." *Cistercian Studies* 25 (1990): 4-16.

Leonard, Irving A. *Books of the Brave*. With a new Introduction by Rolena Adorno. Berkeley: University of California Press, 1992. First published in 1949 by Harvard University Press.

Lera, José María, S.J. "Influjos patrísticos en la *Contemplación para alcanzar amor* en los *Ejercicios* de San Ignacio." In Plazaola, ed., *Las fuentes de los Ejercicios Espirituales de San Ignacio*, 207-22.

Lerner, Isaías. "América en la poesía épica áurea: la versión de Ercilla." *Edad de Oro* 10 (1991): 125-40.

—————. "La visión humanística de América: Gonzalo Fernández de Oviedo." In Arellano, ed., *Las Indias (América) en la literatura del Siglo de Oro*, 3-22.

Leturia, Pedro de, S.J. *El gentilhombre Iñigo López de Loyola en su patria y en su siglo*. 2nd ed. Barcelona: Labor, 1949.

————. *Estudios ignacianos*, edited by I. Iparraguirre, S.J. 2 vols. Rome: Institutum Historicum Societatis Iesu, 1957.

Levin, H. *The Myth of the Golden Age in the Renaissance*. London: Faber, 1970.

Levin, Leslie. *Metaphors of Conversion in Seventeenth-Century Spanish Drama*. London: Tamesis, 1999.

Levinson, Marjorie. *Keats's Life of Allegory. The Origins of a Style*. Oxford: Blackwell, 1988.

Lewis, Charlton T., and Charles Short. *A Latin Dictionary*. Oxford: Clarendon, 1879.

Lida de Malkiel, María Rosa. Review of Dámaso Alonso, *La poesía de San Juan de la Cruz (desde esta ladera)*. Madrid, 1942. *Revista de filología hispánica* 5 (1943): 377-95.

————. "La visión del trasmundo en las literaturas hispánicas." An appendix in Patch, *El otro mundo en la literatura medieval*.

————. "Función del cuento popular en el *Lazarillo de Tormes*." *Actas del Primer Congreso Internacional de Hispanistas*, edited by Frank Pierce and Cyril A. Jones, 349-59. Oxford: Dolphin, 1964.

————. "El hilo narrativo de las *Soledades*." In *La tradición clásica en España*, 243-51. Barcelona: Ariel, 1975.

Lies, Lothar, S.J. "La doctrina de la discreción de espíritus en Ignacio de Loyola y Orígenes de Alejandría." In Plazaola, ed., *Las fuentes de los Ejercicios Espirituales de San Ignacio*, 101-21.

Lipking, Lawrence. *The Life of the Poet. Beginning and Ending Poetic Careers*. Chicago: University of Chicago Press, 1981.

Lop Sebastià, Miguel, S.J. *Los Directorios de Ejercicios 1540-1599*. Bilbao: Mensajero/Santander: Sal Terrae, 2000.

López García, María de los Ángeles. "El léxico de la maravilla en la obra de San Juan de la Cruz." In *Estado actual de los estudios sobre el Siglo de Oro*, edited by M. García Martín, 2: 569-77. Salamanca: Universidad de Salamanca, 1993.

López Rey, José. *Velázquez. A Catalogue Raisonné of his Oeuvre and an Introductory Study*. London: Faber, 1963.

————. *Velázquez. The Artist as a Maker, with a Catalogue Raisonné of his Extant Works*. Lausanne: Bibliothèque des Arts, 1979.

————. *Velázquez. Painter of Painters*. 2 vols. Cologne: Taschen, 1996.

Lowe, Kate. "The black african presence in Renaissance Europe." In Earle and Lowe, eds., *Black Africans in Renaissance Europe*, 1-14.

Lupher, David A. *Romans in the New World. Classical Models in Sixteenth-Century Spanish America*. Ann Arbor: University of Michigan Press, 2003.

MacCulloch, Diarmaid. *Reformation: Europe's House Divided, 1490-1700*. London: Allen Lane, 2003.

McGinn, Bernard. "Ocean and desert as symbols of mystical absorption in the Christian tradition." *Journal of Religion* 74 (1994): 155-81.

Machielsen, Iohannis. *Clavis patristica pseudoepigraphorum Medii Aevii*. 2 vols. Brepols: Turnhout, 1990.

McKendrick, Melveena. *Theatre in Spain, 1490-1700*. Cambridge: Cambridge University Press, 1989.

Mckim-Smith, Gridley. "La técnica sevillana de Velázquez." In *Velázquez y Sevilla*, 109-203.

MacLaren, N., and A. Braham, *National Gallery Catalogues. The Spanish School*. London: National Gallery, 1988.

McClelland, I. L. *Tirso de Molina. Studies in Dramatic Realism*. Liverpool: Institute of Hispanic Studies, 1948.

McNally, Paul. "Keats and the rhetoric of association. On looking into the Chapman's Homer sonnet." *Journal of English and Germanic Philology* 79 (1980): 530-40.

Mancho Duque, María Jesús. *Palabras y símbolos en San Juan de la Cruz*. Madrid: Fundación universitaria española/Universidad Pontificia de Salamanca, 1993.

Marasso, Arturo. "Aspectos del lirismo de San Juan de la Cruz." *Boletín de la Academia Argentina de Letras* 14 (1945): 579-607.

Maravall, José Antonio. *Velázquez y el espíritu de la modernidad*. Madrid: Alianza, 1987.

March, K., and K. Passman. "The Amazon myth and Latin America." In Haase and Reinhold, eds., *The Classical Tradition and the Americas. Vol.1: European Images of the Americas and the Classical Tradition*, 285-338.

Markus, R.A. *Gregory the Great and His World*. Cambridge: Cambridge University Press, 1997.

Marrevee, William, S.C.J. *The Ascension of Christ in the Works of St Augustine*. Ottawa: University Press, 1967.

Martín Casares, Aurelia. "Free and freed black africans in Granada in the time of the Spanish Renaissance." In Earle and Lowe, eds., *Black Africans in Renaissance Europe*, 247-60.

Martinengo, Alessandro. "Gracián, las Indias y la interpretación de un pasaje de *El Criticón* (II,3)." In Arellano, ed., *Las Indias (América) en la literatura del Siglo de Oro*, 23-35.

Martínez de Bujanda, Jesús. *Diego de Estella (1524-1578). Estudio de sus obras castellanas*. Rome: Iglesia Nacional Española, 1970.

Martino, Alberto. *Il 'Lazarillo de Tormes' e la sua ricezione in Europa (1554-1753)*. 2 vols. Pisa and Rome: Istituti Editoriali e Poligrafici Internazionale, 1999.

Martz, Louis L. *The Poetry of Meditation. A Study in English Religious Literature of the Seventeenth Century*. New Haven: Yale University Press, 1962.

Mason, P. "Classical ethnography and its influence on the European perception of the peoples of the New World." In Haase and Reinhold, eds., *The Classical Tradition and the Americas. Vol.1: European Images of the Americas and the Classical Tradition*, 135-72.

Maurel, Serge. *L'univers dramatique de Tirso de Molina*. Poitiers: University of Poitiers, 1971.

May, T. E. "*El condenado por desconfiado*." *Bulletin of Hispanic Studies* 35 (1958): 138-56. Reprinted in *The Wit of the Golden Age. Articles on Spanish Literature*, 134-53. Kassel: Reichenberger, 1986.

Melloni, Javier, S.J. "Las influencias cisnerianas en los *Ejercicios*." In Plazaola, ed., *Las fuentes de los Ejercicios Espirituales de San Ignacio*, 353-77.

———. *The Exercises of St Ignatius Loyola in the Western Tradition*. Translated by Michael Ivens, S.J. Leominster: Gracewing, 2000.

———. *La mistagogía de los Ejercicios*. Bilbao: Mensajero/Santander: Sal Terrae, 2001.

———. "Ejercicios espirituales: génesis del texto." In García de Castro, ed., *Diccionario de Espiritualidad Ignaciana*, 685-89.

Mena Marqués, Manuela B. "Cristo en casa de Marta y María." In *Velázquez y Sevilla*, 1: 180.

Middleton Murry, John. *Keats*. London: Cape, 1955.

Midgley, Mary. *The Myths We Live By*. London: Routledge, 2004.

Moffit, John. "*Terebat in mortario:* symbolism in Velázquez's *Christ in the House of Martha and Mary.*" *Arte Cristiana* 72 (1984): 13-24.

————. "Francisco Pacheco and Jerome Nadal: new light on the Flemish sources of the Spanish 'picture-within-the-picture.'" *Art Bulletin* 72 (1990): 631-38.

————. "Medieval *mappaemundi* and Ptolomey's *Chorographia.*" *Gesta* 32/1 (1993): 59-68.

Moffit Watts, Pauline. "Prophecy and discovery." *American Historical Review* 90 (1985): 73-102.

Montero Delgado, Juan. "Sobre imprenta y poesía a mediados del xvi (con nuevos datos sobre el *princeps* de *Las obras* de Jorge de Montemayor)." *Bulletin Hispanique* 106 (2004): 81-102.

Morale, Giovanni, ed. *La Cena di Tiziano: Immagini del Risorto tra Louvre e Ambrosiana.* Milan: Skira, 2006.

Morales, José L. *El Cántico Espiritual de San Juan de la Cruz: su relación con el Cantar de los Cantares y otras fuentes escriturísticas y literarias.* Madrid: Editorial de Espiritualidad, 1971.

Morales Padrón, F. "L'Amérique dans la littérature espagnole." In Ballesteros, ed., *La Découverte de l'Amérique,* 279-98.

Moreno Mengíbar, A., and J. Martos Fernández. "Mesianismo y Nuevo Mundo en fray Luis de León: *In Abdiam Prophetam Expositio.*" *Bulletin Hispanique* 98: (1996) 261-89.

Morocho Gayo, Gaspar, and others. "Cipriano de la Huerga, maestro de humanistas." In *Fray Luis de León. Historia, humanismo y letras,* edited by Víctor García de la Concha and Javier San José Lera, 173-93. Salamanca: Universidad de Salamanca, 1996.

Morón Arroyo, Ciriaco. "Fray Luis de León: sistema y drama." In *Fray Luis de León. Aproximaciones a su vida y obra,* edited by Ciriaco Morón Arroyo and Manuel Revuelta Sañudo, 311-35. Santander: Sociedad Menéndez Pelayo, 1989.

Morreale, Margherita. "Sobre algunas acepciones de 'extraño' y su valor ponderativo." *Revista de filología española* 36 (1952): 310-17.

————. *Homenaje a Fray Luis de León.* Salamanca: Universidad de Salamanca/Zaragoza: Prensas Universitarias, 2007.

Morros, Bienvenido. "Amadís y Don Quijote." *Criticón* 91 (2004): 41-65.

Moxey, Keith P. F. *Pieter Aertsen, Joachim Beuckelaer, and the Rise of Secular Painting in the Context of the Reformation.* New York: Garland, 1977.

Mulcahy, Rosemarie. *Spanish Paintings in the National Gallery of Ireland.* Dublin: National Gallery of Ireland, 1988.

————. *Philip II of Spain, Patron of the Arts.* Dublin: Four Courts, 2004.

Museo del Prado. Catálogo de las pinturas. Madrid: Ministerio de Educación y Cultura, 1996.

Navarro Durán, Rosa. *Alfonso de Valdés, autor del Lazarillo de Tormes.* Madrid: Gredos, 2003.

Nelson, Leslie Anne. *Velázquez's "Bodegones a lo divino" and the Spanish Theatre of the Golden Age.* Ann Arbor: UMI Dissertation Services, 1998.

Nieto, José Constantino. *Místico, poeta, rebelde, santo.* Mexico: Fondo de Cultura Económica, 1982.

Nieto Ibáñez, Jesús María. *Espiritualidad y patrística en "De los nombres de Cristo" de Fray Luis de León.* El Escorial: Ediciones Escurialenses y Universidad de León, 2001.

Norton, F. J. *A Descriptive Catalogue of Printing in Spain and Portugal 1501-1520.* Cambridge: Cambridge University Press, 1978.

Núñez Beltrán, Miguel Ángel. *La oratoria sagrada de la época del Barroco: doctrina, cultura y actitud ante la vida desde los sermones sevillanos del siglo XVII.* Seville: Universidad de Sevilla/Fundación Focus-Abengoa, 2000.

Oakley, R.J. *Tirso de Molina. El condenado por desconfiado*. London: Grant and Cutler, 1994.

O'Donoghue, N.D. "The human form divine. St Teresa and the humanity of Christ." In *Teresa de Jesús and Her World*, edited by Margaret A. Rees, 75-88. Leeds: Trinity and All Saints' College, 1981.

O'Gorman, E. *La invención de América*. Mexico: Fondo de Cultura Económica, 1958.

O'Leary, Brian, S.J. "Third and Fourth Weeks. what the Directories say." *The Way Supplement* 58 (1987): 3-20.

——. "Foundational values in the *Spiritual Exercises* of St Ignatius." *Milltown Studies* 33 (1994): 5-21.

Olschi, Leonardo. *Storia letteraria delle scoperte geografiche*. Florence: Olschi, 1937.

Olson, Paul R. "An Ovidian conceit in Petrarch and Rojas." *Modern Language Notes* 81 (1966): 217-21.

O'Malley, John W., S.J., *The First Jesuits*. Cambridge, Mass. and London: Harvard University Press, 1993.

O'Neill, Michael, ed. *Keats: Bicentenary Readings*. Edinburgh: Edinburgh University Press, 1997.

O'Reilly, Jennifer. "The wisdom of the scribe and the fear of the Lord in the *Life of Columba*." In *Spes Scotorum, Hope of Scots: Saint Columba, Iona and Scotland*, edited by Dauvit Brown and Thomas Owen Clancy, 159-211. Edinburgh: Clark, 1999.

——. "The art of authority." In *After Rome*, edited by Thomas Charles-Edwards, 140-89. Oxford: Oxford University Press, 2003.

——. "Islands and idols at the ends of the earth: exegesis and conversion in Bede's *Historia Ecclesiastica*." In *Bède le Vénérable entre tradition et postérité*, edited by Stéphane Lebecq, Michel Perrin and Olivier Szerwiniack, 119-45. Lille: University of Lille, 2005.

O'Reilly, Terence. "The structural unity of the *Exercitatorio de la vida spiritual*." *Studia Monastica* 15 (1973): 287-324. Reprinted in O'Reilly, *From Ignatius Loyola to John of the Cross*.

——. "The *Exercises* of St. Ignatius Loyola and the *Exercitatorio de la vida spiritual*." *Studia Monastica* 16 (1974): 301-23. Reprinted in O'Reilly, *From Ignatius Loyola to John of the Cross*.

——. "The Erasmianism of *Lazarillo de Tormes*." In *Essays in Honour of Robert Brian Tate from his Colleagues and Pupils*, edited by Richard A. Cardwell, 91-100. Nottingham: Department of Spanish, University of Nottingham, 1984. Reprinted in O'Reilly, *From Ignatius Loyola to John of the Cross*.

——. "Discontinuity in *Lazarillo de Tormes*: the problem of *Tratado* Five." *Journal of Hispanic Philology* 10 (1986): 141-49.

——. "St. John of the Cross and the traditions of monastic exegesis." In *Leeds Papers on Saint John of the Cross*, edited by Margaret A. Rees, 105-26. Leeds: Trinity and All Saints' College, 1991. Reprinted in O'Reilly, *From Ignatius Loyola to John of the Cross*.

——. *From Ignatius Loyola to John of the Cross. Spirituality and Literature in Sixteenth-Century Spain*. London: Variorum, 1995.

——. "The image of the garden in *La vida retirada*." In *Belief and Unbelief in Hispanic Literature*, edited by Helen Wing and John Jones, 9-18. Warminster: Aris and Phillips, 1995.

——. "The scriptural scholarship of the early Spanish Jesuits—a survey." *Journal of the Institute of Romance Studies* 4 (1996): 135-43.

——. "Meditation and contemplation: monastic spirituality in early sixteenth-century Spain." In *Faith and Fanaticism: Religious Fervour in Early Modern Spain*, edited by Lesley K. Twomey, 37-57. Aldershot: Ashgate, 1997.

——. "El tránsito del temor servil al temor filial en los 'Ejercicios Espirituales' de san Ignacio."

In Plazaola, ed., *Las fuentes de los Ejercicios Espirituales de San Ignacio*, 223-40.

—————. "Temor." In García de Castro, ed., *Diccionario de Espiritualidad Ignaciana*, 1676-80.

—————. "Golden Age Studies: Spain and Spanish America in the sixteenth and seventeenth centuries." In *The Companion to Hispanic Studies*, edited by Catherine Davies, 50-67. London: Arnold, 2002.

—————. "Friendship and contemplation in the *Carta para Arias Montano*." *Calíope* 14 (2008): 47-60.

Ortega y Gasset, José. "Introducción a Velázquez." In *Obras completas*, 8: 457-87. Madrid: Revista de Occidente, 1962.

Pacho, Eulogio. *San Juan de la Cruz. Historia de sus escritos*. Burgos: Monte Carmelo, 1998.

—————, ed. *Diccionario de San Juan de la Cruz*. Burgos: Monte Carmelo, 2000.

—————. "Agustín Antolínez, O.S.A. (1554-1626)." In *Diccionario de San Juan de la Cruz*, 119-20.

—————. "Méjico." In *Diccionario de San Juan de la Cruz*, 945-47.

Padrón, Ricardo. *The Spacious Word. Cartography, Literature and Empire in Early Modern Spain*. Chicago: University of Chicago, 2004.

Pagden, Anthony. *The Fall of Natural Man. The American Indian and the Origins of Comparative Ethnology*. Cambridge: Cambridge University Press, 1982.

—————. *European Encounters with the New World. From Renaissance to Romanticism*. New Haven and London: Yale University Press, 1993.

Palenzuela, Nilo. "*El Criticón*: entre viejo y nuevo mundo." *Insula* 655-56 (2001): 39-42.

Parker, Alexander A. "Santos y bandoleros en el teatro español del Siglo de Oro." *Arbor* 13 (1949): 395-416.

—————. *Polyphemus and Galatea. A Study in the Interpretation of a Baroque Poem, with a Verse Translation by Gilbert F. Cunningham*. Edinburgh: Edinburgh University Press, 1977.

—————. *The Philosophy of Love in Spanish Literature 1480-1680*. Edited by Terence O'Reilly. Edinburgh: Edinburgh University Press, 1985.

Parry, J.H. *The Spanish Seaborne Empire*. Berkeley: University of California Press, 1990. The first edition was published in London in 1966.

Patch, Howard Rollin. *El otro mundo en la literatura medieval*. Mexico: Fondo de cultura económica, 1956.

Pedro, Valentín de. *América en las letras españolas del Siglo de Oro*. Buenos Aires: Editorial Sudamericana, 1954.

Pedrocco, Filippo. *Titian: The Complete Paintings*. London: Thames and Hudson, 2001.

Pego Puigbó, Armando. *El Renacimiento espiritual. Introducción literaria a los tratados de oración españoles 1520-1566*. Madrid: Consejo Superior de Investigaciones Científicas, 2004.

Pelikan, Jaroslav. *Whose Bible Is It? A History of the Scriptures through the Ages*. London: Penguin, 2006.

Pellicer, Rosa. "La 'maravilla' de las Indias." *Edad de Oro* 10 (1991): 141-54.

Peña, Margarita. "Epic Poetry." In Robert González Echaverría and Enrique Pulpo-Walker, eds., *The Cambridge History of Latin America*, 1: 231-59. Cambridge: Cambridge University Press, 1996.

Pérez, Carlos A. "Verosimilitud psicológica de *El condenado por desconfiado*." *Hispanófila* 27 (1966): 1-21.

Pérez, Joseph. *The Spanish Inquisition: A History*. Translated by Janet Lloyd. London: Profile Books, 2004.

Pérez de Tudela y Bueso, Juan. *"Mirabilis in altis." Estudio crítico sobre el origen y significado del proyecto descubridor de Cristóbal Colón.* Madrid: Consejo Superior de Investigaciones Científicas, 1983.

Pérez Sánchez, Alfonso E. "Velázquez y su arte." In Domínguez Ortiz, Pérez Sánchez and Gállego, *Velázquez,* 21-56.

————. "Enigmas." *Boletín Cultural* 194 (1999): 50-52.

———— and Benito Navarrete Prieto. *De Herrera a Velázquez. El primer naturalismo en Sevilla.* Bilbao: Museo de Bellas Artes, 2006.

———— and Nicola Spinosa, eds. *La obra pitórica de Ribera.* Barcelona: Noguer, 1979.

Pericolo, Lorenzo. "Visualising appearance and disappearence: on Caravaggio's London *Supper at Emmaus.*" *Art Bulletin* 89 (2007), 519-39.

Perry, T. Anthony. "Biblical symbolism in the *Lazarillo de Tormes.*" *Studies in Philology* 67 (1970): 139-46.

Peters, William A. M., S.J. *The Spiritual Exercises of St Ignatius. Exposition and Interpretation.* Jersey City: Program to Adapt the Spiritual Exercises, 1968.

Pierce, Frank. *The Heroic Poem of the Spanish Golden Age. Selections.* Oxford: Dolphin, 1947.

————. *La poesía épica del Siglo de Oro.* Madrid: Gredos, 1968.

————. *Amadís de Gaula.* Boston: Twayne, 1976.

————. *Alonso de Ercilla y Zúñiga.* Amsterdam: Rodopi, 1984.

Piper, A. C. "The 'breadly paradise' of Lazarillo de Tormes." *Hispania* 44 (1961): 269-71.

Plazaola, Juan, S.J., ed. *Las fuentes de los Ejercicios Espirituales de San Ignacio.* Bilbao: Mensajero, 1998.

Poggi, Vincenzo, S.J. "El Oriente en las fuentes de los *Ejercicios* a través de la *Vita Christi* de Ludolfo." In Plazaola, ed., *Las fuentes de los Ejercicios Espirituales de San Ignacio,* 187-205.

Ponnau, Dominique. *Caravage: une lecture.* Paris: Editions du Cerf, 1993.

Pourrat, Pierre. "Commençants." *Dictionnaire de spiritualité,* 2.i: 1143-56.

Pozo, C. "Compagnia di Gesú: Teologia." *Dizionario degli istituti di perfezione,* 2: 1300-1304.

Prest, J. *The Garden of Eden.* New Haven: Yale University Press, 1981.

Pring-Mill, Robert. "Some techniques of representation in the *Sueños* and *Criticón.*" *Bulletin of Hispanic Studies* 45 (1968): 270-84.

Pupo-Walker, Enrique. *La vocación literaria del pensamiento histórico en América. Desarrollo de la prosa de ficción: siglos XVI, XVII, XVIII y XIX.* Madrid: Gredos, 1982.

Quantin, Jean-Louis. "The Fathers in seventeenth century Roman Catholic theology." In Backus, ed., *The Reception of the Church Fathers in the West from the Carolingians to the Maurists,* 2: 951-86.

Quint, David. *Epic and Empire: Politics and Generic Form from Virgil to Milton.* Princeton: Princeton University Press, 1993.

Rahner, Hugo. *Greek Myths and Christian Mystery.* London: Burns and Oates, 1963.

Rahner, Karl. "Reflections on the problem of the gradual ascent to Christian perfection." In *Theological Investigations,* 3: 3-23. London: Darton, Longman and Todd, 1967.

Randles, W. G. L. "Classical models of world geography and their transformation following the discovery of America." In Haase and Reinhold, eds., *The Classical Tradition and the Americas. Vol.1: European Images of the Americas and the Classical Tradition,* 5-76.

Redworth, Glyn. "Mythology with attitude? A black Christian's defence of negritude in early modern Europe." *Social History* 28 (2003): 49-66.

Reinburg, Virginia. "Prayer and the Book of Hours." In Roger S. Wieck, *The Book of Hours in Medieval Art and Life*, 39-44. London: Sothebys, 1988.

Resines, Luis. *La catequesis en España. Historia y textos*. Madrid: Biblioteca de Autores Cristianos, 2007.

Rico, Francisco. "Problemas del *Lazarillo*." *Boletín de la Real Academia Española*, 46 (1966): 277-96.

————. "El nuevo mundo de Nebrija y Colón." In *Nebrija y la introducción del Renacimiento en España*, edited by Victor García de la Concha, 157-85. Salamanca: Universidad de Salamanca, 1983.

————. *El sueño del humanismo (De Petrarca a Erasmo)*. Madrid: Alianza, 1993.

————. *La novela picaresca y el punto de vista*. Nueva edición, corregida y aumentada. Barcelona: Seix Barral, 2000.

Riley, E. C. *Don Quixote*. London: Allen and Unwin, 1986.

Riquer, Martín de. "California." In *Homenaje al profesor Antonio Vilanova*, edited by A. Sotelo Vázquez and M.C. Carbonell, 1: 581-99. Barcelona: Universidad de Barcelona, 1989.

Rivers, Elias L. *Fray Luis de León. The Original Poems*. London: Grant and Cutler and Tamesis, 1983.

————. "Góngora y el Nuevo Mundo." *Hispania* 75 (1992): 856-61.

Robbins, Jeremy, *The Challenges of Uncertainty. An Introduction to Seventeenth-Century Spanish Literature*. London: Duckworth, 1998.

————. "Baltasar Gracián (1601-2001)." *Bulletin of Hispanic Studies* 80 (2003): 41-55.

————. "Renaissance and Baroque: continuity and transformation in early modern Spain." In Gies, ed., *The Cambridge History of Spanish Literature*, 137-48.

————. *Arts of Perception: The Epistemological Mentality of the Spanish Baroque, 1580-1720*. A special issue of *Bulletin of Spanish Studies* 82, number 8 (2005).

Robertson, Fiona. "Keats' New World: on emigrant poetry." In O'Neill, ed., *Keats: Bicentenary Readings*, 27-47.

Rodríguez Marín, Francisco. *Más de 21.000 refranes castellanos, no contenidos en la copiosa colección del Maestro Gonzalo Correas*. Madrid: Revista de archivos, bibliotecas y museos, 1926.

Rodríguez-Molero, Francisco J. "Maldonado (Maldonat, Jean de)." *Dictionnaire de spiritualité*, 10.1: 163-65.

Romanos, Melchora. "El discurso contra las navegaciones en Góngora y sus comentaristas." In Arellano, ed., *Las Indias (América) en la literatura del Siglo de Oro*, 37-49.

Romm, James S. *The Edges of the Earth in Ancient Thought. Geography, Exploration and Fiction*. Princeton: Princeton University Press, 1992.

Rosenblat, Ángel. *La primera visión de América y otros estudios*. Caracas: Ministerio de Educación, 1969.

Ross, Kathleen. "Historians of the conquest and colonisation of the New World: 1550-1620." In Robert González Echaverría and Enrique Pulpo-Walker, eds., *The Cambridge History of Latin America*, 1: 101-42. Cambridge: Cambridge University Press, 1996.

Ruffinatto, Aldo. "Revisión del 'caso' de Lázaro de Tormes (puntos de vista y *trompes-l'oeil* en el *Lazarillo*)." *Edad de Oro* 20 (2001): 163-79.

Ruiz Jurado, Manuel, S.J. "¿Influyó en S. Ignacio el *Exercitatorio* de Cisneros?" *Manresa* 51 (1979): 65-75.

————. "Fuentes de las Elecciones." In Plazaola, ed., *Las fuentes de los Ejercicios Espirituales de San Ignacio*, 339-51.

Ruiz Pérez, Pedro. *De la pintura y las letras. La biblioteca de Velázquez*. Seville: Consejería Cultural de la Junta de Andalucía, 1999.

Ruiz Ramón, Francisco. *América en el teatro clásico español. Estudios y textos*. Pamplona: Universidad de Navarra, 1993.

Ruiz Salvador, Federico. *Introducción a San Juan de la Cruz*. Madrid: Biblioteca de Autores Cristianos, 1968.

Rupnik, Marko Ivan. "Paralelismos entre el discernimiento según San Ignacio y el discernimiento según algunos autores de la *Filocalia*." In Plazaola, ed., *Las fuentes de los Ejercicios Espirituales de San Ignacio*, 241-80.

Ryken, Leland, James C. Wilhoit, Tremper Longman III, eds. *A Dictionary of Biblical Imagery*. Downers Grove, Ill./Leicester, England: InterVarsity Press, 1998.

Sabat-Rivers, Georgina. "Interpretación americana de tópicos clásicos en Domínguez Camargo: la navegación y la codicia." *Edad de Oro* 10 (1991): 187-98.

Sabugal, Santos. "Exégesis y hermenéutica bíblica de Fray Luis de León." In *Fray Luis de León. IV centenario (1591-1991). Congreso interdisciplinar. Madrid, 16-19 de octubre de 1991. Actas*, edited by Teófilo Viñas Román, 117-28. Madrid: Ediciones Escurialenses, 1992.

Sampaio Costa, Alfredo, S.J. "Elección." In García de Castro, ed., *Diccionario de Espiritualidad Ignaciana*, 726-34.

Sánchez, Jean-Pierre. "Myths and legends in the Old World and European expansionism on the American continent." In Haase and Reinhold, eds., *The Classical Tradition and the Americas. Vol.1: European Images of the Americas and the Classical Tradition*, 189-240.

Sánchez-Albornoz, Claudio. *La Edad Media española y la empresa de América*. Madrid: Ediciones Cultura Hispánica de Cooperación Iberoamericana, 1983.

Sánchez Cantón, F.J. "La librería de Velázquez." In *Homenaje ofrecido a Menéndez Pidal*, 3: 379-406. Madrid: Hernando, 1925.

Sayers, Dorothy L. "The physical aspect of the Mountain." In *The Comedy of Dante Alighieri the Florentine, Cantica II : Purgatory*, 69-71. Harmondsworth: Penguin, 1955.

Scafi, Alessandro. "Mapping Eden: cartographies of the Earthly Paradise." In Cosgrove, ed., *Mappings*, 50-70.

————. *Mapping Paradise. A History of Heaven on Earth*. London: British Library, 2006.

Schapiro, Meyer. "The image of the Disappearing Christ. The Ascension in English Art around the year 1000." *Gazette des Beaux-Arts*, ser. 6, 23 (1943): 133-52. Reprinted in *Selected Papers, vol.3: Late Antique, Early Christian and Mediaeval Art*. New York: Braziller, 1979.

Schwartz Lerner, Lía. "Quevedo junto a Góngora: recepción de un motivo clásico." In *Homenaje a Ana María Barrenechea*, edited by Lía Schwartz Lerner and Isaías Lerner, 313-25. Madrid: Castalia, 1984.

————. "El motivo de la *auri sacra fames* en la sátira y en la literatura moral del siglo xvii." In Arellano, ed., *Las Indias (América) en la literatura del Siglo de Oro*, 51-72.

Senabre, Ricardo. "La oda de Fray Luis a la Ascensión." In *Tres estudios sobre Fray Luis de León*, 75-96. Salamanca: Universidad de Salamanca, 1978.

————. *Gracián y "El Criticón."* Salamanca: Universidad de Salamanca, 1979.

Shalev, Zur. "Sacred geography, antiquarianism and visual erudition: Benito Arias Montano and the maps in the Antwerp Polyglot Bible." *Imago Mundi* 55 (2003), 56-80.

Shore, Paul. "Ludolfo de Sajonia." In García de Castro, ed., *Diccionario de Espiritualidad Ignaciana*, 1149-53.

Sicroff, Albert A. "Sobre el estilo del *Lazarillo de Tormes*." *Nueva revista de filología hispánica* 11 (1957): 157-70.

Simson, Ingrid. *Amerika in der spanischen Literatur des Siglo de Oro: Bericht, Inszenierung, Kritik.* Frankfurt am Main: Vervuert, 2003.

————, ed. *América en España: influencias, intereses, imágenes.* Madrid: Iberoamericana/Frankfurt: Vervuert, 2007.

Smith, Hilary Dansey. *Preaching in the Spanish Golden Age. A Study of Some Preachers of the Reign of Philip III.* Oxford: Oxford University Press, 1978.

Smith, Paul Julian. "The rhetoric of representation in writers and critics of picaresque narrative: *Lazarillo de Tormes, Guzmán de Alfarache, El Buscón.*" *Modern Language Review* 82 (1987): 88-108.

————. *Representing the Other. "Race," Text and Gender in Spanish and Spanish American Narrative.* Oxford: Clarendon, 1992.

Snyder, Susan. "The left hand of God: despair in Medieval and Renaissance tradition." *Studies in the Renaissance* 12 (1965): 18-59.

Solignac, Aimé, S.J. "Voies (purificative, illuminative, unitive)." *Dictionnaire de spiritualité*, 16: 1200-1215.

————. "Le *Compendio Breve* de l'*Exercitatorio* de Cisneros et les *Exercices Spirituels.*" *Archivum Historicum Societatis Iesu* 63 (1994): 141-59.

Soons, Alan. "*El condenado por desconfiado y El castigo sin venganza.*" In *Ficción y comedia en el Siglo de Oro*, 83-97. Madrid: Estudios de la literatura española, 1966.

Soufas, Teresa S. "Religious melancholy and Tirso's despairing monk in *El condenado por desconfiado.*" *Romance Quarterly* 34 (1987): 179-88.

Špidlík, Tomáš. *Ignazio di Loyola e la spiritualità orientale. Guida alla lettura degli Esercizi.* Rome: Studium, 1994.

Steele, F.J. *Towards a Spirituality for Lay-Folk: the Active Life in Middle English Religious Literature from the Thirteenth Century to the Fifteenth.* Lewiston: Mellen, 1995.

Steggink, Otger. "Iñigo López de Loyola, el peregrino vasco de Montserrat, y la *devotio moderna.*" In *Fuentes neerlandesas de la mística española*, edited by Miguel Norbert Ubarri and Lieve Behiels, 71-79. Madrid: Trotta, 2005.

Steinberg, Leo. Review of López Rey, *Velázquez. A Catalogue Raisonné of his Oeuvre and an Introductory Study. Art Bulletin* 47 (1965): 274-94.

Stoichita, Victor I. *Visionary Experience in the Golden Age of Spanish Art.* London: Reaktion, 1995.

————. *L'instauration du tableau. Métapeinture à l'aube des temps modernes.* 2nd ed. Geneva: Droz, 1999.

Sullivan, Henry W. *Tirso de Molina and the Drama of the Counter-Reformation.* Amsterdam: Rodopi, 1981.

Sullivan, Margaret A. "Aertsen's kitchen and market scenes: audience and innovation in Northern Art." *Art Bulletin* 81 (1999): 236-66.

Suñer, P. "Toledo, Francisco de, S.I." *Diccionario de la historia eclesiástica de España*, 4: 2572-74.

Teinon, Seppo A. *Concordancia de los Ejercicios Espirituales de San Ignacio de Loyola.* Helsinki: Academia Scientiarum Fennica, 1981.

Teixidor, L. "Algo sobre la regla 18." *Manresa* 8 (1932): 312-26.

Tellechea José Ignacio. "Bible et théologie en 'langue vulgaire,' discussion à propos du *Catéchisme* de Carranza." In *L'Humanisme dans les lettres espagnoles*, edited by A. Redondo, 219-32. Paris: Urin, 1979.

Terry, Arthur. *Seventeenth-Century Spanish Poetry. The Power of Artifice.* Cambridge: Cambridge University Press, 1993.

Thacker, Jonathan. *A Companion to Golden Age Theatre*. London: Tamesis, 2007.

Thomas, Hugh. *Rivers of Gold. The Rise of the Spanish Empire*. London: Weidenfeld and Nicholson, 2003.

Thompson, Colin P. *The Poet and the Mystic. A Study of the "Cántico Espiritual" of San Juan de la Cruz*. Oxford: Oxford University Press, 1977.

—————. "*En la Ascensión*: artistic tradition and poetic imagination in Luis de León." In *Mediaeval and Renaissance Studies on Spain and Portugal in Honour of P.E. Russell*, edited by F.W. Hodcroft and others, 109-20. Oxford: Society for the Study of Mediaeval Languages and Literature, 1981.

—————. *The Strife of Tongues. Fray Luis de León and the Golden Age of Spain*. Cambridge: Cambridge University Press, 1988.

—————. "*Una elegancia desafeitada*: Fray Luis de León and Santa Teresa." In *San Juan de la Cruz and Fray Luis de León. A Commemorative International Symposium*, edited by Mary Malcolm Gaylord and Francisco Márquez Villanueva, 289-98. Newark, Del.: Juan de la Cuesta, 1996.

—————. *St. John of the Cross. Songs in the Night*. London: S.P.C.K., 2002.

Throckmorton, Burton H., Jr. *Gospel Parallels. A Synopsis of the First Three Gospels with Alternative Readings from the Manuscripts and Noncanonical Parallels*. Nashville: Nelson, 1979.

Tiffany, Tanya J. "Visualizing devotion in early modern Seville: Velázquez's *Christ in the House of Martha and Mary*." *Sixteenth Century Journal* 36.2 (2005): 433-53.

—————. "Light, darkness, and African salvation: Velázquez's *Supper at Emmaus*." *Art History* 31.1 (2008): 33-56.

Tolias, George. "*Isolarii*, Fifteenth to Seventeeth Century." In Woodward, ed., *Cartography in the Renaissance*, 263-84.

Torrell, Jean-Pierre, O.P. *St Thomas Aquinas*. Translated by Robert Royal. 2 vols. Washington, D.C.: Catholic University of America, 1996.

Trapier, Elizabeth Du Gué. *Velázquez*. New York: Hispanic Society of America, 1948.

Trubiano, Mario F. *Libertad, gracia y destino en el teatro de Tirso de Molina*. Madrid: Ediciones Alcalá, 1985.

Truman, R.W. "Lázaro de Tormes and the *Homo novus* tradition." *Modern Language Review* 60 (1965): 62-67.

—————. "Parody and irony in the self-portrayal of Lázaro de Tormes." *Modern Language Review* 63 (1968): 600-605.

—————. "*Lazarillo de Tormes*, Petrarch's *De remediis adversae fortunae*, and Erasmus's *Praise of Folly*." *Bulletin of Hispanic Studies* 52 (1975): 33-53.

—————. "Lazarillo de Tormes." In *The Continental Renaissance, 1500-1600*, edited by A. J. Krailsheimer, 334-36. Hassocks: Harvester Press, 1978. Originally published in Middlesex by Penguin Books in 1971.

—————. *Spanish Treatises on Government, Society and Religion in the Time of Philip II. The "De regimine principum" and Associated Traditions*. Leiden: Brill, 1999.

Tugwell, Simon, O.P. *Ways of Imperfection. An Exploration of Christian Spirituality*. London: Darton, Longman and Todd, 1984.

Turrado, Argimiro. "Thomas de Villeneuve." *Dictionnaire de spiritualité*, 15: 874-90.

Uriz Echaleco, E. "Santa Elena, isla de." In *Gran Enciclopedia Rialp*, 20: 820.

Veale, Joseph, S.J. "Dominant orthodoxies." *Milltown Park Studies* 30 (1992): 43-65. Reprinted in *Manifold Gifts*, 127-49. Oxford: Way Books, 2006.

Velázquez. Homenaje en el tercer centenario de su muerte. Madrid: Instituto Diego Velázquez, 1960.

Velázquez y Sevilla. 2 vols. Seville: Consejería Cultural de la Junta de Andalucía, 1999.

Venard, Marc. "La Bible et les Nouveaux Mondes." In Bedouelle and Roussel, eds., *Le Temps des Réformes et la Bible,* 489-514.

Vendler, Helen. *Coming of Age as a Poet. Milton: Keats, Eliot, Plath.* Cambridge, Mass.: Harvard University Press, 2003.

Vigneras, Louis-André. *The Discovery of South America and the Andalusian Voyages.* Chicago: University of Chicago Press, 1976.

Vilanova, Evangelista. *Historia de la teología cristiana.* 3 vols. Barcelona: Herder, 1987-92.

Vivar, Francisco. "Representación y símbolo de la frontera en *El Criticón.*" *Bulletin of Hispanic Studies* 75 (1998): 425-34.

Vogüé, Adalbert de. *La Règle de Saint Benoît: Commentaire historique et critique.* 3 vols. Paris: Editions du Cerf, 1971.

————. *La Règle de Saint Benoît: Commentaire doctrinal et spirituel.* Paris: Editions du Cerf, 1977.

Walden, Sarah. "Amber for ever. E. H. Gombrich vindicated as an advocate of restraint in the restoration of Old Masters." *Times Literary Supplement,* October 29, 2004: 13-14.

Waldoff, Leon. *Keats and the Silent Work of Imagination.* Urbana: University of Illinois Press, 1985.

Wardropper, B. W. "The strange case of Lázaro Gonzales Pérez." *Modern Language Notes* 92 (1977): 202-12.

Watrigant, Henri, S.J. "La genèse des *Exercices* de saint Ignace." *Études* 71 (1897): 506-29; 72 (1897):195-216; 73 (1897): 199-228.

Watson, J.R. "Keats and silence." In O'Neill, ed., *Keats: Bicentenary Readings,* 71-87.

Weber, Alison P. "Religious literature in early modern Spain." In Gies, ed., *The Cambridge History of Spanish Literature,* 149-58.

Weston-Lewis, Aidan. "Jacob Mathan, 1571-1631: four engravings after paintings by Pieter Aertsen." In Davies and Harris, *Velázquez in Seville,* 130-31.

Williamson, Edwin. *The Halfway House of Fiction. Don Quixote and Arthurian Romance.* Oxford: Clarendon, 1984.

Wilson, Edward M. "Continental versions to c.1600: Spanish versions." In *The Cambridge History of the Bible,* vol. 3, edited by S.L. Greenslade, 125-29. Cambridge: Cambridge University Press, 1963.

————. "Continental versions from c.1600 to the present day." In *The Cambridge History of the Bible,* vol. 3, edited by S.L. Greenslade, 354-55. Cambridge: Cambridge University Press, 1963.

————. "La estructura simétrica de la *Oda a Francisco Salinas.*" In *Entre las jarchas y Cernuda. Constantes y variables en la poesía española,* 195-201. Barcelona: Ariel, 1977.

———— and Duncan Moir. *The Golden Age: Drama 1492-1700.* London: Ernest Benn/New York: Barnes and Noble, 1971.

Wilson-Smith, Timothy. *Caravaggio.* London: Phaidon, 1998.

Woodring, Carl. "On looking into Keats's Voyagers." *Keats-Shelley Journal* 14 (1965): 14-22.

Woods, M. J. *Gracián Meets Góngora. The Theory and Practice of Wit.* Warminster: Aris and Phillips, 1995.

Woodward, David, ed. *Cartography in the Renaissance.* Chicago: University of Chicago Press, 2007.

Woodward, L.J. Review of Cristoforo Colombo, *Libro delle Profezie,* translated by William Melczer (Palermo, 1992). *Bulletin of Hispanic Studies* (Liverpool) 71 (1994): 503-5.

Zamora, Margarita. *Reading Columbus*. Berkeley: University of California Press, 1993.

Zimic, Stanislav. *Apuntes sobre la estructura paródica y satírica del Lazarillo de Tormes*. Madrid: Iberoamericana, 2000.

Zurbarán. Exh. cat. Madrid: Ministerio de Cultura, 1988.

Biblical Index

OLD TESTAMENT

Genesis
3:1	97, 112
4:13	159-60
4:15	159
4:23	251n
11:4	105, 112
11:8	105
18:14	106, 112

Exodus
| 21:17 | 253n |

Leviticus
| 20:9 | 173, 253n |
| 26:33 | 242n |

Numbers
| 16:30 | 107, 112 |

Deuteronomy
4:26-27	242n
28:64	242n
32:39	91, 94, 98, 103, 112
33:3	192

1 Kings
2:6	94
2:7-8	241n
2:10	40
25:32	242n

3 Kings
| 9:26-28 | 22 |

1 Chronicles (1 Paralipomenon)
| 16:2 | 242n |

Tobit
| 11:17 | 241n |
| 13:2 | 241n |

Judith
| 8:27 | 169 |

Job
3:21	102, 112
5:8-9	104, 242n
5:17-18	91, 98, 103, 112
9:10	242n
22:29	241n
23:10	169
28:15	94, 112
37:5	242n
38:33	174
40:6	242n

Psalms
2	142
4	170
15	94
18	65, 74
22	122
27	242n
30	242n
31	91, 94, 112
44	91
49	232n
50	7
64	34, 40
65	242n
71	18, 40
74	241n
84	192
94	40
96	18, 40
100	74
110	65, 167
112	232n, 241n
115	142
118	x, 34, 94, 103, 112, 241n
123	242n
127	65, 237n
134	242n

143	242n
146	96

Proverbs

1·7	167
3:14	94
6:23	94
8:10-11	94, 241n
9:10	167
10:17	94, 112
13:24	91, 98, 112, 169
16:16	94
17:3	252n
19:18	98
20:22	107, 112
20:30	253n
22:15	169
23:13	98
27:21	252n
29:17	98, 169
29:23	241n
30:11	253n
31:11-12	170

Ecclesiastes

8:15	99, 112

Song of Songs

8:8	19

Wisdom

3:46	252n
5:16-17	154
7:9	94
16:13	94, 241n

Ecclesiasticus (Sirach)

1:16	167
2:3-5	169, 252n
2:9	159
3:12-15	173
3:27	163
5:6-9	166
9:1-2	170
10:17	96, 112
10:19	242n
11:2	104
11:4-6	104, 112, 242n
15:5	xi, 114
17:11	125
17:13	106, 112
20:30	241n
25:28-29	170
30:1	98, 112

Isaiah

39:24	106
47:17	18
1:25	252n
6:9-10	125
7:14	122
11:11	18
22:13	242n
24:15	18
28:9	123-24
40:4	241n
41:1, 5	18, 231n
42:3-4	18
45:6	232n
48:9-10	252n
48:17	94
49:1	18
49:15-16	18, 136
51:5	18
59:19	232n
60:9	18
64:4	125
66:19	18, 231n

Jeremiah

2:10	18
9:16	242n
16:17	106
21:8	94
25:17-18	18
31:10	18, 40
32:17	106

Ezekiel

17:24	241n
18	162
18:21	163
18:23	107, 112, 162
18:32	91, 243n
22:15	105, 112
33:11	91, 243n
36:19	242n

Daniel

3:26	242n

Hosea

6:2	91, 98, 103

Jonah

2:1	91, 102, 112

Micah

2:13	136

Zephaniah

2:11	16

Zechariah

7:12	141
8:6	106

11:16-17	121
13:9	252n

Malachi

1:11	232n
3:2-3	252n
4:2	141

New Testament

Matthew

1:23	122
5:1-12	122
5:10	90-91, 109, 112
6:14	106, 112
6:21	140
7:3-5	93, 112
7:15	101, 112
8:23-27	126
9:15	123-24
10:22	154
10:39	101, 112
10:42	122-23
11:25	122-23
12:31	166
12:40	91, 102, 112
13:16-17	125
13:33	85
13:44-46	38
14:22-36	126
14:25	126
15:4	253
15:14	91, 94
17:2	141, 248n
23:12	96, 112
24:13	251n
25:35	213
25:40	213
26:26	100, 112, 215
28:20	121

Mark

4:36-41	126
6:45-52	126
6:48	126
7:10	253
9:48	65
10:27	106
11:25	91, 107, 112

Luke

1:37	106
1:51	105, 112
1:52	96, 112
1:68	104, 112
6:39	94, 112
6:41-42	93
7:47	160
8:22-25	126
10:38-41	192
11:11-13	196
12:19	100, 112
14:11	241n
15:23	242n
18:14	241n
23:34	106, 112
23:43	160
24:30-31	206

John

1:20	90-91, 112
6:16-21	126-27
8:12	141
10:12	121
10:14	121
12:40	125
14:6	x, 34, 241
14:18	123
14:27-29	117-18
15:15	73
16:7	119
16:20	122
21:15-17	160

Acts

1:9	116
2:28	94
3:6	91, 94, 112
20:29	101

Romans
8:15	72
11:33	91, 104, 112
12:12	35
12:17	107, 112
16:25-26	244n

1 Corinthians
2:10	125
3:1-2	123
11:24	91
15:28	138
15:32	242n

2 Corinthians
1:8-9	102, 112
4:11-12	102, 112
5:16	118
6:9	102, 112

Galatians
2:20	143

Ephesians
3:27	244n
4:19	163

Philippians
1:2	118
1:23	81
2:7	118

Colossians
1:26	244n
2:2-3	248n
2:9	248n
3:1	248n

1 Thessalonians
5:15	107, 112

1 Timothy
6:13	94

2 Timothy
4:8	154-55

Hebrews
5:12	123
13:1-2	213

James
1:12	154
4:10	241n

1 Peter
1:6-7	252n
1:18-19	94
2:2	123
3:9	107, 112
3:14	90
4:9	213
5:4	154
5:5-6	241n

2 Peter
3:9	243n

1 John
4:18	65, 74

Apocalypse
2:10	154
9:6	102, 112

Index

A

acedia, 159

Achilles, 29, 43

Acosta, José de, S.J. (1539-1600. Theologian, missionary, naturalist), 23, 39, 227n, 231n

Acteon, 46-47

Adam, 48, 262n

admiratio, 149

Adnotationes et meditationes in Evangelia, see Nadal

Adorno, Rolena, 228n

Aertsen, Pieter (1507/8-75. Dutch historical painter), xii-xiii, 178-79, 198-99, 253-54n, 258n

Africa, 42; Africans, 51, 205, 216, 262n

agudeza, 9, 47, 205; see *conceptismo*; Wit

Agudeza y arte de ingenio, see Gracián

Ailath, 22

Alcalá de Guadaira, Spain, xiii, 191

Alcántara, Pedro de, St. (1499-1562. Spiritual writer), 119, 144-45, 245n

Alcaraz, Pedro Ruiz de, 108

Aldana, Francisco de (1537-78. Soldier and poet), 36, 230n

Alexander VI, Pope (Rodrigo de Borja, 1431-1503, elected 1492), 22

Alexander VII, Pope (Fabio Chigi, 1599-1667, elected 1655), xi, 137

allegory, 5, 47, 167, 195

Allen, John J., xi, 148

Alonso, Dámaso, 231-32n

Amadís, ix, 23-33, 92, 109

Amadís de Gaula, see Rodríguez de Montalvo; romance; *Palmerín de Inglaterra*

Amazons, 29-30, 229n

Ambrose, St. (339-97. Bishop of Milan, theologian), 203

America, 6, 11-12, 25, 43, 223n; Americas, 5, 30; Native Americans, 226n; Spanish America, 11, 217, 227n

amplificatio, 132

Anareto (character in *El condenado por descon-fiado*), 151, 155-56, 158, 165, 167, 169-73

Andalusia, Spain, 13

Andrade, Jerónimo, xii, 168

Andrenio (character in *El Criticón*), 47-48, 50-51, 54-55, 234n

angels, 173, 234n

Anglería, Peter Martyr de (1457-1526. Historian), 22, 226-37n

Anselm of Canterbury, St. (c.1033-1109. Monk, theologian, archbishop of Canterbury), 238n

Antarctic, 43

Antilla, islands of, 22, 227

Antipodes, 52

Antolínez, Agustín, O.S.A. (1554-1626. Theologian and biblical exegete), 35, 230n

Antwerp, Belgium, ix-xi, 3, 8, 15, 79, 88, 227n

Apolidón, 25-27

Apollo, 58

apostles, 119-21, 128-30, 178, 219

Aragon, Spain, 5, 7, 55

Archer, Robert, 230n

archipelagos, ix, 12, 15

Argensola, Lupercio Leonardo de (1559-1613. Poet), 233n

Ariosto, Ludovico (1474-1533), 30, 229n

Armas Wilson, Diana, 12, 222n, 224n, 228-29n

ars moriendi, 162, 251n

Arteaga, Matías de, x, 34

Arthurian tales, 23

Arzubialde, Santiago, S.J., 76, 236n, 239n

Ascension of Christ, 8, 115-18, 128-30, 132, 144-45, 245-46n; Aquinas on, 119, 127, 140; Augustine on, 123-24, 127, 129, 140-42; Bernard on, 124, 129, 245n; Leo the Great on, 128; Tomás de Villanueva on, 134-39; see Jesus Christ

Asensio, Eugenio, 98

Asia, 6, 18, 22, 29; see The East, Far East

Asion-Gaber, 22

Atlantic Ocean, 5, 12, 22, 42-43, 50, 58

Audi, Filia, see Ávila, Juan de

Augustine of Hippo, St. (354-430), 16-18, 33, 65-66, 72-73, 116-19, 123-27, 129-30, 141, 144-46, 203, 212, 217, 226n, 237n, 245n, 255n, 259n, 261n; pseudo-Augustine, 35, 130, 140, 142, 247n

Augustinians (Ordo Sancti Augustini, estab. 1256), xi, 134, 137, 139

autos sacramentales, 203
Avalle-Arce, Juan Bautista, 229n
Ávila, Juan de, St. (c.1500-1569. Preacher and
    spiritual writer), xii, 119, 122, 124, 128, 163-
    64, 218, 246n; *Audi,Filia*, xii, 163-64
Azores Islands, 12, 22
Aztecs, 23, 59

B

Babel, 105
Backhouse, Janet, 255n
Backus, Irena, 105, 222n, 226n, 240n, 242n, 262n
Balboa, Vasco Núñez de (1475-1519.
    Conquistador and explorer), 30, 42-43, 59
Balbuena, Bernardo de (1568-1627. Bishop of
    Puerto Rico, Poet), 30
ballads, 11
bandits, 150, 159
barbarians, 17, 234n
Barbe, Jean-Baptiste, x, 67
Barcelona, Spain, ix, 15
Basil the Great, St. (330-79), 66, 72
Basle, Switzerland, ix, x, 15, 57, 221n
Bataillon, Marcel, 220n
Beatitudes, 122
Bede the Venerable, St. (c. 672-735), 19, 73, 140,
    226n, 248n
Beltrán, Miguel Ángel Núñez, 250n
Benavente, Toribio de, O.F.M. (1482-1568.
    Missionary to Mexico and writer), 22, 227n
Benedict of Nursia, St. (480-547), 66
Benedictines, 245n
Benedictus (Canticle of Zachariah), 104
Bernard of Clairvaux, St. (1090-1153), 118, 124-
    25, 129, 140-41, 245n
Bethany, Israel, 178, 184, 192, 195-97, 256n
Bethulia, Israel, 169-70
Beuckelaer, Joachim (c.1533-76. Flemish painter),
    xii, 178, 180
Bible, *passim*; authority, ix, 2, 111; commentaries,
    4-5, 8-9, 18, 65-66, 104, 116-17, 123, 126-27,
    141, 193, 197, 215, 217, 219, 246n; Douay-
    Rheims, xiv; epistles, 3, 66, 72, 123, 154;
    exegesis, xvi, 4, 6, 9, 86, 115-16, 146, 159,
    169, 196, 203, 215, 217-19, 242n, 252n, 255-
    56n, 261n; gospels, x, 3, 16, 8, 79, 126, 193;
    Greek Septuagint, 3, 16, 217-18, 222n; Latin
    Vulgate, 3-4, 40, 115, 123, 217-18, 221-22n,
    226n, 231n, 248n, 253n, 255n, 260n; New
    Testament, xiv, 89, 96, 99, 105, 107, 117, 121-
    22,154, 184, 205-6, 241; Old Testament, xiv,
    3, 5, 17, 19, 23, 94, 96, 99, 103, 105, 107,
    121, 123, 141, 167, 169, 195, 217, 241n;
    polyglot, 3, 8, 227n; Spanish Protestant, 3;
    scholarship, xv, 4, 6, 217, 256n; translations,
    xiv, 3, 6, 217, 221n, 227n; Vatable Bible,

227n; vernacular, 3, 217; see *Biblical Index*
Blanco, Mercedes, 48, 238n
Blecua, Alberto, 89, 242n, 244-45n
Blecua, José Manuel, 248n, 250n
Blecua, Juan Manuel Cacho, 228n
Blessed Virgin Mary, 122, 156, 161, 182
Blunt, John Henry, 243n
bodegones, 9, 177-216, 218, 253n, 260n
Boeft, Jan den, 262n
Boethius, (c.480-524), 185, 255
Bolaños, Álvaro Félix, 227n
Bonaventure, St. (c.1217-74), 81
Book of Hours, xii, 6, 61, 182-83, 185
Borja, Francisco de, S.J., St. (1510-72), 150
Boscán de Almogáver, Juan (c. 1474-1542. Poet), 7
Boyce, James, O. Carm., 231n
Braham, Allan, 203, 253n, 257-59n
Bray, Xavier, 260n
breviary, 40, 129, 231n, 260n
Brooke, Xanthe, 262n
Brown, Jonathan, 196, 203, 257-58n
Brown, Raymond, S.S., 242n
Brussels, Belgium, 254n
Buckley, Michael, S.J., 238n
Bujanda, Jesús Martínez de, 221n, 248n
Burgos, Spain, xi, 88

C

Cabrera, Alonso de, O.P. (1548-98. Preacher and
    writer), 261n
Cain, 159-60, 163, 165, 251n
Calafia, 29
Calderón de la Barca, Pedro (1600-1681), 203, 253n
California, x, 27, 29-31, 229n
Calveras, J., S.J., 61, 236n
Camões, Luis Vaz de (c. 1524-80), 30, 229n
Campi, Vincenzo (1536-91. Lombard artist), xii,
    178, 181
Canary Islands, 12
Caño, Antonio Ramaj, 245-47n
Canseco, Luis Gómez, 223n
Cape Horn, Chile, 43
Cape Verde Islands, 12
Cappadocian Fathers (Sts. Basil, Gregory of Nyssa,
    Gregory Nazianzus), 66
Caravaggio, Michelangelo Merisi da (c.1571-
    1610), xiii, 198, 206, 208, 210, 212, 260n
Carmelites (Ordo Fratrum Beatae Virginis Mariae
    de Monte Carmelo, estab. c. 1155), 36, 40,
    231n; Ordinal of Sibert de Beka (promulgated
    c.1312), 231n
Carmelites, Discalced (estab. 1593), 231n
Carranza, Bartolomé, O.P. (1503-76. Theologian,
    writer, archbishop of Toledo), 120, 140, 250n
Casal, Marta Cacho, 255-56n
Casal, Rodrigo Cacho, 244n

Casalduero, Joaquín, 230n
Casares, Aurelia Martín, 262n
Cassian, John, St. (c. 360-435), 66, 73
Castile, Spain, 4-5, 7-8, 11-12, 16, 45, 50, 59, 68, 223n
Catalayud, Spain, x, 49
catechesis, 8, 149; catechetical writings, xiii, 3, 153
catechism, xii, 120, 140, 150, 153, 158, 160, 172, 222n, 245n, 250n; of Astete and Ripalda, 250n; of Carranza, 120; of Council of Trent, xii, 150, 153, 158, 160, 172, 250n;
Catherine of Siena, St. (1347-80), 73
Celestina, 90, 240n
Certeau, Michel de, S.J., 230n, 235n
Cervantes Saavedra, Miguel de (1547-1616), 12, 23, 32, 96, 99, 228n, 230n; *Don Quixote*, 12, 23, 32, 228; *Novelas Ejemplares*, 259n; *Persiles y Sigismunda*, 32, 230n
Challoner, Richard, xiv
Charlemagne, 30
Charles of Ghent, 7; see Charles V
Charles V, Holy Roman Emperor (1500-1558), 30, 55, 109, 218
Checa, Jorge, 222
Cherry, Peter, 198, 257-58n, 262n
Chicago, Illinois, 205, 260n
chivalry, 5, 23, 25, 30, 40, 42, 76, 92, 228n, 238n; see romance, chivalric
Chorpenning, Joseph, O.S.F.S., xv, 123
Christ, see Jesus Christ
Christianity & Christians, 29, 80-82, 84, 124-25, 128, 144-46, 154, 162, 175, 192; see Church
Christus, Petrus (c.1420-75/6. Flemish painter), xii, 185, 187
Church, Catholic, 7, 9, 17-19, 64, 66, 72, 78, 80, 84, 108, 126-28, 160, 162, 172, 217-19, 246n; Church Militant, 63; see Christianity
Cisneros, García Jiménez de, O.S.B. (1455-1510. Abbot of Montserrat), 64, 68, 74, 81, 218, 237n, 239n
Cistercians (Ordo Cisterciensis, estab. 1098), 8, 80, 204, 259n
Clancy, Finbarr G., S.J., 261n
Clark, Charles Cowden, 58
Clement of Rome, St., Pope (d. c. 97/101), 73
Codina, Arturo, S.J., 237n
Cologne, Germany, 193
Colombe, Jean (c. 1430-c. 1493. Miniature painter and illuminator), xii, 185, 188
Colón, Hernando, 227n
colonization and colonies, 5-6, 50, 217
Columbus, Christopher (c. 1451-1506), ix, xv, 5, 10, 12- 19, 22, 25, 27, 29, 38-39, 42-44, 54, 56, 58, 217, 225-26n
Columnis, Guido de (c.1215-c.1290), 29, 229n
comedia, 8, 149-75, 203, 218; see *corral*, theatres
conceptismo, 9, 177, 216, 253n, 259n; see Wit

conquistadors, 5, 25, 55, 59
Constable, Giles, 192
Constantinople, Turkey, 29
Conte, Jacopino del (1510-98), x, 60
contemplation, 9, 72, 82, 83, 84, 120, 130, 194, 204, 216, 236n, 254n, 256n; see meditation
conversos, 110
Copernicus, Nicolaus (1473-1543), 50, 233n
Cordeses, Antonio, S.J. (1518-1601. Theologian and spiritual writer), 256
Cordoba, Spain, 193
Corella, Jesús, S.J., 64, 236n
Coroleu, Alejandro, xvi, 222n
corral, 149; Corral del Príncipe, Madrid, xi, 148
Correas, Gonzalo de, 99
Cortés, Hernán (1485-1547. Conquistador), 23, 30, 59
Critilo (character in *El Criticón*), 47, 50-52, 54
Cuba, 30
Cuevas, Cristóbal, 232-33n, 244-46n
Cunningham, Gilbert F., 232n, 259n
Cyprian, St. (d. 258), 120, 245n
Cyprus, 18-19

D

Dadson, Trevor, 222-23
Dalmases, Cándido de, S.J., 61, 236n
Daniélou, Jean, S.J., 247n
Dante Alighieri (c. 1265-1321), 26, 228n
Dati, Giuliano, ix, 14
David, King, 170n
Davies, Catherine, xv, 221n
Davies, David, xv, 197, 253n, 256-58n
De Auxiliis Controversy, 8, 250n
Debonneval, Arnaud, O.S.B. (d. 1225), 245n
Delenda, Odile, 197, 255-57n
Denis the Carthusian (c.1402-71), 18, 104, 242n
Deshman, Robert, 130
Devil, 66, 81, 94, 97, 107, 150-51, 172-73, 175, 241n.
Diana, 46-47
Díaz del Castillo, Bernal (c.1495-1584. Conquistador and historian), 23, 228n
Dio Chrysostom (c.40-120), 42, 232n
Dionysius the Pseudo-Areopagite (fl. c.500), 81
discernment, 81, 84, 86
disciples, 6, 100, 116-19, 121-30, 134, 140-41, 143-45, 205-6, 212-13, 216, 245n
Dominicans (Ordo Praedicatorum, estab. 1216), 8, 156
Don Quixote, see Cervantes
Donne, John (1572-1631), 3, 56, 235n
Dorremochea, Carlos, ix, 148
Douay-Rheims Bible, see Bible
drama, see *comedia*
Duque, María Jesús Mancho, 231n

Durán, Rosa Navarro, 240n, 244n
Dürer, Albrecht (1471-1528), xi, xiii, 133, 198, 200, 206, 211-12, 260n

E

The East, ix, 14, 23, 26, 30, 43-44, 46, 50, 66, 72, 80-81; see Asia; Far East
Easter, 206, 248n, 261n
Ecclesiasticae Rhetoricae, see Granada, Luis de
Eden, 26, 225n, 228m
Edom, 22
Egido, Aurora, 234-35, 259
Eisenberg, Daniel, 224, 228
El condenado por desconfiado, see Molina, Tirso de
El Criticón, see Gracián
El Greco (1541-1614) (Doménikos Theotokópulos), ix, 2
emblems, ii, 55, 197, 257n
Emmaus, Israel, 198, 205-6, 212-13, 215
enigmas, 9, 19, 174, 177, 203-4, 218, 253n, 259n
epics, 11, 30, 42, 47, 223n, 229n
Erasmus, Desiderius (c. 1466-1536), 7, 105, 215, 217-18, 222n; Erasmianism, 110
Ercilla y Zúñiga, Alonso de (1533-94), 11, 223n
Esplandían (character in Amadís de Gaula), 27, 29
Eucharist, 101, 195, 215, 261n; see Mass
Europa, 50
Eurotas, 46-47
Evagrius Ponticus the Solitary (345-99. Monk, ascetic), 81
exclamatio, 132
exploration, 43, 45, 59; explorers, 12, 18, 23, 30, 42, 46, 58-59; Iberian, 55
Extremadura, Spain, 193
Eyzaguirre, Sebastián Fernández, 254n

F

Fainlight, Ruth, 195, 256n
faith, 17, 19, 23, 73, 117, 119, 122-24, 127-29, 141, 143, 151, 165, 175, 206, 212
Far East, ix, 12, 20; see Asia; The East
Fathers of the Church, 6, 17, 33, 63, 65, 115
fear, 52, 65-66, 68, 71-74, 80-81, 93, 105, 122, 127-28, 142, 159, 234n, 237n; of God, 9, 64-66, 149, 150-58, 159-60, 167; filial, 63-64, 66, 68-69, 72-73, 76, 82-86; servile, 6, 66, 68-69, 72-73, 76, 78, 82-86, 150-51, 158
Felisinda (character in *El Criticón*), 50
Ferdinand II, King of Aragon (1452-1516), ix, 4, 12, 14, 218
Fernández-Armesto, Felipe, 224n
Fernandina Island, 13
Flandes, Juan de (d. 1519. Netherlandish painter, active in Spain), xi, 131

Flint, Valerie, 225n
Florence, Italy, ix, xii, 21, 186, 255n
Forcione, Alban K., 230n, 259n
Fortunate Isles, 26, 228n
Fortune, 42, 92, 96, 109
Fra Angelico (c.1387-1455), xii, 184, 186, 255n
France, xi, xiii, 85, 152, 209
Franciscans (Ordo Fratrum Minorum, estab. 1209), 22
free will, 8, 149, 174
Freux, André des, S.J. (d.1556), x, 62
Friedman, E. H., 244n

G

Gállego, Julián, 203, 256-59, 262
Gama, Vasco da (c. 1460-1524), 42, 44
Garcilaso de la Vega (c. 1501-36. Poet and courtier), 7
Gayo, Gaspar Morocho, 259n
Génébrard, Gilbert, O.S.B. (1535-97. Biblical exegete), 19
Gerbi, Antonello, 225n
Giamatti, A. Bartlett, 228n
Gillet, Joseph E., 223n, 231n
Glen, Thomas L., 198, 256n, 258n
Goa, India, 50
God, of Israel, 17, 104; Father, 73, 100, 106-7, 118-19, 134, 150, 196; fear of, 9, 65-66, 149, 159, 167, 238n; love of, 65-66, 71-72, 84, 156, 238n; mercy, 50, 69,151,160; presence, 83; providence, 145; Word of, 5, 215, 218; see Jesus Christ; Holy Spirit
gods, pagan, 16-17, 55
Gómara, Francisco López de, see López de Gómara
Góngora y Argote, Luis de (1561-1627), x, 5, 41-47, 203, 232-33n
González, José Caso, 7, 222n
Cámara, Luis Gonçalves da, S.J. (c.1519-75), 236n
Gowing, Lawrence, 178, 254n
grace, 8, 69, 71-72, 83, 130, 141, 145, 149, 151, 154, 158, 171-72, 174
Gracián, Baltasar y Morales, S.J. (1601-58), x, 5, 47- 56, 203, 233-35n; *Agudeza y arte de ingenio*, 203; *El Criticón*, x, 47-48, 53, 56, 234n; *Oráculo manual y arte de prudencia*, 234n
Granada, Luis de, O.P. (1504-88. Writer, theologian, preacher), xii, 35, 132, 134, 166, 168, 171, 184-85, 195, 218, 246n, 248n, 261n; *Ecclesiasticae Rhetoricae*, 132; *Guía de pecadores*, 166; *Libro de la oración y meditación*, 184
Greeks, 29, 42, 45
Gregory, William H., Sir, 176
Gregory the Great, St., Pope (c. 540-604, elected 590), 80, 143, 174, 194, 206, 212-15, 253n, 255-56n, 260-61n

Gregory of Nazianzus, St. (c. 330-89), 73
Guía del Cielo, see León, Pablo de
Guía de pecadores, see Granada, Luis de
Guibert, J. de, S.J., 239n
Guigo II (d. 1193. Prior of Grande Chartreuse), 80
Guillén, Claudio, 89, 107-8, 241-43n

H

Hades, 45, 232n
Hapsburg Empire, 7
Heaven, 35, 37, 54-55, 90, 100, 105-7, 117, 119-20, 122, 126-27, 129, 136, 138, 140-43, 145, 150, 155, 160, 166, 171, 174, 196
Hell, 66, 68-69, 107, 150-51, 155, 159, 163, 166-67, 174
Hesperides, 23
Hesychius of Jerusalem,17
Hiram I (king of Tyre), 22
Hitchcock, Richard, 233n
Holy Spirit, x, 23, 34, 106, 117, 119-20, 124, 167
Homer, 42, 44, 55, 58-59, 235n
honra, 7, 103, 105, 156, 243n; *deshonra*, 92, 109
Hood, William, 255n
Huerga, Cipriano de la, O.Cist. (c.1514-60. Theologian and biblical exegete), 8, 19, 226n, 259n
Hugh of Balma, O.F.M. (d. 1439), 81
humanism, 6, 222n; humanists, 7, 22, 30, 39, 110, 177, 216-17, 235n

I

Ibáñez, Jesús María Nieto, 244n
idolatry and idols, 17, 105, 108, 226n
Ignatius of Loyola, St., see Loyola, Ignatius
illuminism, 110
Imitation of Christ, 6, 61, 82, 85
India, 22
indiano, 11, 223n
Indians, 16, 54
Indices of Prohibited Books, xii, 4, 164, 218, 221n
Indies, 5, 11, 22-23, 29, 32-33, 35-37, 39
indulgence, plenary, 108, 185
Inquisition, xiii, 3-4, 108, 164, 221n, 250n
interrogatio, 132
Introduction à la vie devote, see Sales, Francis de
Iparraguirre, Ignacio, S.J., 236n, 238n, 240n
Irene, St., xiii, 185, 191
Isabella I, Queen of Castile (1451-1504), 4, 12, 218
Isidore of Seville, St. (c. 560-636), 43, 232n
islands, ix-x, 5, 11-59, 224n, 228-29n, 231-34n
isolarii, 224n
Israel, 17, 104, 116
Italy, xii-xiii, 7, 85, 181, 186, 210

J

Jacobus of Voragine, Bd. (c. 1230-98), 61, 214, 256n
James the Less, St., 154
Jammes, Robert, 232n
Jeremiah, Prophet, 3, 94
Jerome, St. (c. 341-420), ix, xiv, 2, 4, 123, 141, 198, 217
Jesuits, see Society of Jesus
Jesus Christ, 78, 83, 94, 102, 105, 108, 116-17, 119-29, 134, 136, 138, 142-45, 154, 162, 178, 185, 193, 194, 196-98, 204, 206; see Ascension; God; Holy Spirit; Resurrection; Transfiguration
John the Baptist, 90
John the Deacon, 214
Jonah, 102
Jones, R. O., 89, 91, 233n, 240n
Juan de la Cruz, St. (1542-91. Discalced Carmelite, poet, theologian, mystic), 5, 33-42, 61
Juan de Santa Ana, 37
Juanes, Juan de (c. 1523-79. Renaissance painter), xi, xiii, 135, 185, 190
Judith, 169-70
Jungmann, J.A., S.J., 243n
justification, 8, 103, 151, 154, 165, 174; see Trent, Council of

K

Kadir, Djelal, 225n
Kamen, Henry, 222-24n
Kaplis-Hohwald, Laurie, 221n
Keats, John (1795-1821), *On First Looking Into Chapman's Homer* (1816), 58 sqq.
Kempis, Thomas à (c.1380-1471), see *Imitation of Christ*
Kinder, Gordon, 221n
Knappe, Karl-Adolf, 260n
Knox, Ronald Arbuthnott, 226n, 253n
Korah, 107

L

La Española, 22-23, 226n
La lozana andaluza , 99
Lamech, 251n
Lapide, Cornelius à, S.J. (1567-1637. Biblical exegete), 159, 169, 215, 226n, 251-52n, 261n
Las Casas, Bartolomé de, O.P. (1474-1566. Missionary and historian), 11, 223n, 227, 234n
Latin language, ix, x, xiv, 3-4, 6, 15-16, 33, 39, 42, 61-62, 115-16, 123, 195, 203, 217-19, 222n, 225n

Lausberg, Heinrich, 247n

Lawrance, Jeremy, 93, 222n, 262n

Lazarillo de Tomes, xi, 88-112, 218, 222n, 240n, 243n

Lázaro, xi, 89-90, 92-95, 97-98, 100-105, 108-10, 241n, 243n

Lazure, Guy, 256n

Leclercq, Jean, O.S.B., 245n, 248n

lectio divina, 146, 184

Leefdael, Francisco, x, 34

Legenda aurea, see Jacobus of Voragine

Leo the Great, St. Pope (d.461, elected 440), 121, 128, 246-47n

León, Luis de, O.S.A. (1527-91. Biblical exegete, writer and poet), xi, 8, 19, 46, 114-46, 245-46n, 251n

León, Pablo de, O.P., xii, 157

Leonard, Irving A., 228n

Lerner, Lía Schwartz, 233n

letrados, 4, 224n

Leturia, Pedro de, S.J., 78, 238n

Levin, H., 224n

Levin, Leslie, 251-53n

Levinson, Marjorie, 236

liberals and liberalism, 3, 76

Libro de la oración y meditación, see Granada, Luis de

Lipking, Lawrence, 235n

liturgy, 9, 99-100, 106, 110, 129, 146, 206, 247n, 260n; liturgical year, xi, 3, 79

Lombard, Peter (c. 1100-1160. Theologian and biblical exegete), 73

Lombards, 178

London, England, ix, xii-xiii, 2, 9, 176-77, 187, 206, 208, 260n, 262n

López de Gómara, Francisco (1510- c.1555. Historian), 234n

Lotto, Lorenzo (c. 1480-1556. Venetian painter), xii, 185, 189

Low Countries, 7

Loyola, Ignatius, St. (1491-1556), x, 6, 40, 60-86, 184, 218, 236-37n, 241n, 254n; *Spiritual Exercises*, x, xv, 6, 61-86, 184, 218, 236n

Luciani, Sebastiano, see Piombo, Sebastiano del

Ludolph of Saxony (c. 1300-1378. Devotional writer and biblical exegete), 6, 61, 64, 68, 74, 129, 182, 218, 254n

Lupher, David A., 224n, 227n

M

MacCulloch, Diarmaid, 250n

MacLaren, N., 203

Macrí, Oresti, 139, 248n

Madeira Island, 12

Madrid, Spain, xi-xiii, 9

Madrigal, José Luis, 244n

Magdalene, Mary, St., 160, 162

Magellan, Ferdinand (c. 1480-1521), 42-44, 232n

Magnificat (Marian Canticle), 96, 105

Maldonado, Juan, S.J. (1533-83. Theologian and biblical exegete), 55, 123, 193-94, 196, 215, 217

Manresa, Spain, x, 6, 61, 67, 85, 218

Manrique, Angel, 204, 259n

mappaemundi (medieval maps of world), ix, 12, 20, 225n

maps, x, 12, 20-22, 27, 31, 42-43, 48, 224-25n

Marín, Francisco Rodríguez, 99

Mark the Hermit, 80

Marrevee, William, S.C.J., 245n

Martellus, Henricus, ix, 21

Martha (Sister of Lazarus), 177-181, 192-95, 197-98, 255-56n

Martinengo, Alessandro, Count, 234n

Martz, Louis L., 254n

Mary, see Blessed Virgin Mary

Mary of Burgundy, Duchess (1457-82) , xii, 182-83

Mass, 6, 100, 102, 206, 242n, 260n; of Holy Spirit, 106; see Eucharist

Matham, Jacob (1571-1631. Dutch engraver), 178, 260n

Matins, 206, 260-61n

Matthew, St., 127, 162, 246n

May, Terence, 8, 149, 16

Maza, Carlos Sainz de la, 228-29n

McKendrick, Melveena, 223n

Medina del Campo, xi, 88

meditation, x, 6-7, 9, 68-69, 71, 74-77, 79, 81, 120, 139, 144-46, 159, 182, 185, 254n; manuals, 9, 184, 195, 249n; see contemplation

Mediterranean Sea, ix, 11, 18, 58

Melloni, Javier, S.J., 64, 236-37n, 240n

Mexico, 25, 30, 36

Middle Ages, 33, 43, 73-74, 80, 124, 129-30, 217

Midgley, Mary, 5

Milan, Italy, xiii, 206, 210

Milton, John, 3

missionaries, ii, 5, 17, 22

misterio, 9, 174, 184-85, 203-4, 216, 242n, 246n, 249n, 259n

Modena, Italy, xii, 181

Moffit, John, 195, 254-55n, 258n

Molina, Tirso de (Fray Gabriel Téllez) (c. 1584-1648. Mercedarian friar, dramatist, poet), 8, 250-52n; *El condenado por desconfiado*, xv, 8, 149-75, 218, 250-53n

Moluccas, 232n

Montañés, Jaime, 162

Montalvo, Garci Rodríguez de, see Rodríguez de Montalvo

Montano, Benito Arias (1527-1598. Biblical scholar and exegete), 7-8, 23, 30, 36, 223n, 227n

Montemayor, Jorge de (c. 1520-61. Poet and novelist), 7, 222-23n
Montesino, Ambrosio, O.F.M. (c.1448-1512. Poet and translator), 182
Montserrat, 61, 64, 218, 237n
Morales, José L., 231n
More, Thomas, Sir, St. (1478-1535), x, 56-57
Moses, 107
Mulcahy, Rosemarie, 216, 260n
myths, 5, 12, 26, 48, 56; classical, 32, 47; medieval, 29, 32

N

Nadal, Jerónimo, S.J. (1507-80. Assistant to Ignatius Loyola) 83; *Adnotationes et meditationes in Evangelia*, x, 79, 254n
Naharro, Bartolomé de Torres (c.1484-c.1525. Playwright), 39
narratio, 132
Nazareth, Israel, 94
Nelson, Leslie Anne, 253n
Netherlands, 178
New World, xii, 5, 11-12, 19, 22-23, 27, 30, 32-33, 35-36, 39, 42, 45, 48, 50, 54-56, 59, 152, 222-24n, 229n, 234-35n; see America; Old World
Nicholas of Lyra (c. 1270-1349. Biblical exegete), 22
Novelas Ejemplares, see Cervantes
Novels of chivalry, see romance, chivalric
Nucio, Martín, xi, 95
nymphs, 47

O

Oakley, Robert J., xv, 173, 250, 252
O'Gorman, E., 224n, 227n
Old World, 11, 16, 23, 38, 42, 47, 50, 54, 56, 227n
Olmedo, Félix González, 247
O'Malley, John W., S.J., 262n
Onuphrius, St. (San Onofre), 241n
Ophir, 22-23, 226-27n
Oráculo manual y arte de prudencia, 234n; see Gracián
Ordinal of Sibert de Beka, see Carmelites
O'Reilly, Jennifer, 226n, 261n
Origen (c. 185-254), 217
Orozco, Alonso de, O.S.A., St. (1500-1591. Spiritual writer and Biblical exegete), xii, 119, 160-61, 169, 218, 245n, 250-52n
Ortelius, Abraham (1527-98. Flemish cartographer), x, 31, 227n
Ortiz, Antonio Domínguez, 222n, 255-58n, 262n
Osuna, Francisco de, O.F.M. (c.1492-c.1540. Spiritual writer), 120-21, 145, 245n
Ovid, Publius Ovidius Naso, 46-47, 233n

Oviedo y Váldes, Gonzalo Fernández de (1478-1557. Historian), 23, 224n, 227n

P

Pacheco, Francisco de (1564-1644. Painter and scholar), xi, xiii, 114, 177, 185, 191, 216, 255n
Pacific Ocean, x, 23, 30-31, 42-43, 46-47, 58-59, 229n
Padrón, Ricardo, 223-24n
pagans, 17, 29, 108
Pagden, Anthony, 223-24n, 234n, 236n
Palestine, 162, 184
Palma, Luis de la, S.J. (1560-1641. Spiritual writer), 84, 156, 159, 239n, 251n
Palmerín de Inglaterra, 92
Panama, 30, 42-43
parables, 38, 77, 93, 99-100, 197
paradise, 5, 12, 26, 29, 48, 225n; see Eden, Heaven
Pareja, Juan de, 262n
Paris, France, ix, xi, xiii, 15, 152, 193, 209, 218
Parker, Alexander, 150, 203, 230n, 232n
Pármeno (character in *Celestina*), 90
parody, 7, 23
Parsons, Wilfrid, Sr., 226n
Patch, Howard Rollin, 228n
Paul of Tarsus, St., 72, 102, 140, 143, 154, 162, 165, 213, 258n
Paul III, Pope (Alessandro Farnese, 1468-1549, elected 1534), xi, 152
Paulo (character in *El condenado por desconfiado*), 150-51, 154-56, 159-60, 163, 165, 167, 173-75, 250n
Pedro, Valentín de, 223n
Pedrocco, Filippo, 260n
peninsula, Iberian, 4, 6-7; Mexico, 30
Pentecost, 117, 121, 145, 245n
Penthesilea (Queen of Amazons), 29
Peraldus, William, O.P. (c. 1190-1271. Theologian), 156
Pérez, Joseph, 221n
Pérez de Valencia, Jaume, O.S.A (c.1408-90. Theologian and biblical exegete), 96, 241n
Pericolo, Lorenzo, 260n
Perry, T. Anthony, 97, 241-42n
Persians, 29
Persiles y Sigismunda, see Cervantes
Peru, x, 11, 23, 30-31, 227n
Peter, St., 94, 154, 160, 162, 213
Philip II, King of Spain (1527-98), 50, 256n
Philip IV, King of Spain (1605-65), 4, 50
Piombo, Sebastiano del (c. 1485-1547. Painter), ix, 10
Plato, 96, 99
Plazaola, Juan, S.J., xv, 221n, 236-38n

Pliny the Younger, 23
Polo, Marco (c.1254-1324), 13, 22, 29
polyglot bibles; see Bible
Portugal, 47, 50, 232n
preaching, 18-19, 108, 149, 193, 218
Prest, J., 225n
printers and printing, xi-xiii, 3-4, 6, 133, 168, 200,
    206, 211, 218, 224n, 254n
prophecy, 19, 23, 124, 151, 225n
prophets, 17, 124-25, 136, 140-41, 192; false, 101
Protestantism and Protestants, 3, 110, 215, 217-18
pseudo-Augustine, see Augustine
Puente, Luis de la , S.J., Ven. (1554-1624.
    Spiritual writer and biblical exegete), 226n
Puigbó, Armando Pego, 249n
Purgatory, 228n
Pyrenees Mountains, 4
Pyrrhus, 29

Q

Quevedo y Villegas, Francisco Gómez de (1580-
    1645), 8, 254n
Quint, David, 223n

R

Rahner, Hugo, S.J., 230n, 246n
Ramón, Francisco Ruiz, 11
Red Sea, 22
Redworth, Glyn, 262n
Reformation, ii, 3; see Protestantism
Reina, Casiodoro de (1520-94. Protestant reformer
    and Bible translator), 3, 221n
Reinburg, Virginia, 182, 254n
Religious Orders, 4-5, 8, 116, 250n
Renaissance, 6-7, 42, 129, 234n, 241n, 256n
Resurrection of Christ, 71, 101, 134, 136, 195,
    262n; see Jesus Christ
Rey, José López, 197-98, 255-58n
rhetoric, 56, 134, 139, 177, 225n
Ribadeneira, Pedro de, S.J. (1527-1611. Historian
    and spiritual writer), 214
Ribera, Jusepe de (1591-1652), 198, 258-59n
Ricart, José Gudiol, 257n, 260n
Rico, Francisco, 89, 91, 98-99, 102, 107, 224n,
    240-42n, 245n
Rivera, Valentín Núñez, 223n
Rivers, Elias, 121, 232n
Robbins, Jeremy, 222n, 233-34n
Robertson, William, 58
Rodríguez de Montalvo, Garci (d. 1504), 23, 27,
    29-30, 56, 228-29n; Amadís de Gaula, ix, 23-33,
    76, 228n; Sergas de Esplandián, 27, 228- 29n
Rogers, Daniel, xv, 159, 165, 170, 250-52n
Rojas, Fernando de, 241n
romance, 23, 109; Cervantine, 5; chivalric, 23, 30,
    40, 76, 92; see Amadís de Gaula; chivalry

Rome, Italy, x, 6, 17, 60, 193; Romans, 17, 19, 42,
    72, 224n
Romera-Navarro, Miguel, 54, 233-34n
Romm, James S., 226n, 232n
rosary, 102
Rosenblat, Ángel, 12, 227n
Rossi, Elena, xv-xvi
Round, Nicholas, 172, 251-52n
Rubens, Peter Paul (1577-1640), x, 67, 70
Rusconi, Roberto, 16, 18, 225n, 227n

S

Sabbath, 100
Sabia, Juan Antonio de, ix, 28
Sabugal, Santos, 244n
sacraments, 165, 203
Saint Helena (Atlantic island), 47-48, 50, 52,
    234n
Salamanca, Spain, xi, 8, 92-93, 95, 227n
Sales, Francis de, St. (1567-1622), 156, 184, 195,
    251n, 254n, 256n; Introduction à la vie devote,
    184, 254n, 256n
Salve Regina (Marian antiphon), 122
Sánchez-Albornoz, Claudio, 224n
Sánchez, Alfonso Pérez, 177, 216, 253n, 255-58n
Sanhedrin, 185
Santángel, Luis de (d. 1498), ix, 14-15
Santos, Héctor Brioso, 223n, 230n
Sarmiento, Edward, 139, 143-44, 246-48n
Satan, see Devil
Scaliger, Joseph (1540-1609), 227n
Scío de San Miguel, Felipe (1738-96. Bible trans-
    lator), 3, 221n
Sebastian, St., xiii, 185, 191, 259n
Senabre, Ricardo, 116, 125, 129, 139, 141, 235n,
    248-49n
Seneca, 96, 241n
Septuagint, see Bible
Sergas de Esplandián, see Rodríguez de Montalvo
sermocinatio, 132
sermons, 3, 8, 77, 107, 117, 132, 247n, 250n;
    Augustine, 118; Bernard, 129, 140, 245-48n;
    Donne, 56, 235n; Gregory the Great, 261n;
    Juan de Ávila, 119; Leo the Great, 121, 128,
    247n; Luis de Granada, 249n, 261n; pseudo-
    Augustine, 130, 140, 142; Tomás de Villaneuva,
    134, 136, 138-39, 248n; see preaching
Seville, Spain, x, 9, 22, 34, 177, 193, 205, 216,
    227n, 241n, 256-57n
Sicily, 18-19
Simson, Ingrid, 223n
scepticism, 25, 100, 110, 227n
slaves, 72, 74, 77-78, 92, 96, 118, 150, 216, 262n
Smith, Paul Julian, 51, 235n, 244n
Sobrino, Hipólito Escolar, 227n
Society of Jesus (Societas Iesu, estab. 1540), x, 4,
    8, 60, 62, 193, 218, 254n, 256n, 262n;

colleges, x, 49; *Constitutions*, 241n; foundation, 218; seminarians, xi, 79; see Loyola, Ignatius
Soledades, see Góngora
Solomon, King, 22-23, 30
Soto, Luis Barahona de (1548-95), 229n
Sotomayor, Luis de, O.P. (1526-1610. Biblical exegete) 226n
soul, 33, 35-36, 38, 40, 80, 83, 85-86, 99, 122, 136, 141-44, 155-56, 158, 160, 162, 169, 194
Spain, ix, xii, xv-xvi, 2-4, 8, 42, 46, 110, 119, 130, 224n, 257n, 262n; and Council of Trent, 153, 218; Jesuits, 6, 8, 65, 193; modern, 3, 219; territories, 5, 47, 50; union w/ Portugal,47; Spaniards, 4, 5, 19, 22, 54, 58-59, 193, 217; Spanish, x, xv, 3, 5, 6-7, 29-30, 33, 51, 62, 203, 218
Spanish America, see America
Spice Islands, 43-45, 59
Špidlík, Tomáš, S.J., 236n
Spiritual Exercises, see Loyola, Ignatius, St
Steele, F. J., 255n
Stoichita, Victor I., 247n, 254n, 258-60n
Stoics, 96, 110
Stopp, Elisabeth, xv
Strabo (c.63 b.c. – c.24 a.d), 43

T

Tarshish, 22
Tate, Nahum, 3
Te Deum, 234n
Tennyson, Alfred, 59
Tenochtitlán, Mexico, 228n
Teresa of Avila, St. (1515-82), 40, 103, 252n, 256n
Terry, Arthur, 45, 229n, 253n
Thacker, Jonathan, 149, 250n
theatres, 8, 48, 149, 218; see *comedia*; *corral*
Thomas, Hugh Swynnerton, 228n, 233n
Thompson, Colin, xv, 123, 129, 230-31n, 236n, 244-46n
Throckmorton, Burton H., Jr., 257n
Tiffany, Tanya, 198, 216, 254-58n
Titian, Tiziano Vecellio or Vecelli (c.1488-1576), xiii, 209, 260
Toledo, Spain, 40, 109, 227n, 242n
Toledo, Francisco de, S.J., Cardinal (1532-96. Philosopher, theologian, biblical exegete), 193-94, 196-97, 217, 256n
Tomás de Villanueva, O.S.A., St. (1486-1555. Preacher, theologian, biblical exegete), xi, 134-37, 248n
Transfiguration of Christ, 71, 141, 248-49n; see Jesus Christ
Trent, Council of (1545-1563), ix, 152; decree on justification (1547), 8, 151, 154, 174
Triana, Rodrigo de, 54, 234n

Troy, 29
Truman, R. W., 7, 110, 222n, 241n, 243n
Tugwell, Simon, O.P., 254n

U

Uceda y Guerrero, Luis, Fray, 139
universities, 4, 7, 218, 222n; Alcalá de Henares, 8; Louvain, 221n; Salamanca, 8

V

Valderrama, Pedro de, 256n
Valdés, Juan de (c. 1490-1541. Religious reformer and humanist), 119, 240n
Valencia, Spain, 221n
Valencia, Jaume Pérez de, see Pérez de Valencia
Vatable, François (d. 1547. Humanist and biblical exegete), 23, 227n; Vatable Bible, see Bible
Velázquez, Diego Rodríguez de Silva (1599-1660), x, xii-xiii, xv, 9, 41, 176-79, 181-85, 193, 196-98, 201, 203-7, 212-15, 218, 253-56n
Vendler, Helen, 59, 236n
Venice, Italy, ix, 16, 28, 40, 193
Veronica, St., 185
Vespers, 129
viceroys, 11-12, 58, 235n
Vigneras, Louis-André, 227n
Virgin Mary, see Blessed Virgin Mary
Von Hügel, Friedrich, 238n
Voragine, Jacobus de, see Jacobus de Voragine
Vulgate Bible, see Bible, Latin

W

Walden, Sarah, 257n
Weber, Alison P., 222n
Weber, Robert, 221n
Weston-Lewis, Aidan, 182, 253-54n, 260n
William of St. Thierry, O.S.B. (c.1085-1148. Theologian), 80
Wilson, Diana de Armas, 12, 222n, 224n, 228-29n, 235n
Wilson, Edward M., 221n, 249n
Wit, 9, 42, 47, 203, 205, 216-17, 260n; see *agudeza*; *conceptismo*
Woods, Michael, 205, 260n

Z

Zaide (character in *Lazarillo*), 92
Zamora, Episcopal Synod (1584), 250n
Zaragoza, Spain, x, 49, 53, 228n, 234n, 250n
Zimic, Stanislav, 242-43n
Zurbarán, Francisco de (1598-1664), xiii, 198, 202, 258n